D0909302

Martin Van Buren

Martin Van Buren

LAW, POLITICS, AND THE SHAPING OF
REPUBLICAN IDEOLOGY

Jerome Mushkat and Joseph G. Rayback

Northern Illinois University Press   DeKalb 1997

KF368
.V35
M87
1997

© 1997 by Northern Illinois University Press

Published by the Northern Illinois University Press,

DeKalb, Illinois   60115

Manufactured in the United States using acid-free paper

All Rights Reserved

Design by Julia Fauci

Engraving courtesy of the Library of Congress

Library of Congress Cataloging-in-Publication Data
Mushkat, Jerome.
Martin Van Buren : law, politics, and the
shaping of Republican ideology /
Jerome Mushkat and Joseph G. Rayback.
p.   cm.
Includes bibliographical references and index.
ISBN 0-87580-229-X (alk. paper)
1. Van Buren, Martin 1782–1862. 2. Lawyers—
New York (State)—Biography. 3. Presidents—
United States—Biography. 4. Republicanism—
United States—History. I. Rayback, Joseph G. II. Title.
KF368.V35M87   1997
973.5'7'092—dc21   97-8710
[B]   CIP

Contents

APR 1 6 1998

Preface

This study analyzes how the relationship between ideology, law, and politics shaped Martin Van Buren's career in law and politics and laid the basis for much of Jacksonianism. Integral to this argument is the contention that Van Buren's political success cannot be understood without a detailed analysis of the nature, scope, and significance of his legal practice, nor without a thorough consideration of the implications of republicanism in his dual career. Unlike other studies, this work is not a standard biography of Van Buren, nor is it intended as a traditional treatment of his political life. It begins by investigating Van Buren's Dutch-American background and ends in 1828, when he discontinued his profession as a lawyer to become a full-time politician.

There has been much scholarly discussion about the multiple and conflicting definitions of republicanism. Yet Van Buren's dual career revealed that this ideology was an evolving, malleable body of thought, not a static set of immutable values and imperatives. While a teenager, Van Buren absorbed Thomas Jefferson's and James Madison's eighteenth-century classical republicanism, and he used many of their principles as guides during his first years as a practicing lawyer. As Van Buren's legal practice and political career developed, he adapted his classical republican ideas to new conditions by accepting several key components of liberal republicanism. Thus his ideological approach developed over time as conditions changed. His dual career revolved around republicanism while, at the same time, illustrating the complexities of republicanism itself—as a dynamic, evolving ideology that meant different things to different people over the course of time.

The late Joseph G. Rayback, a specialist in the history of American labor and antebellum politics, originated this investigation. During the preparation of his book *Free Soil: The Election of 1848* (1970), Rayback was struck by the absence of a scholarly biography of Martin Van Buren. Although Robert V. Remini inaugurated the modern appreciation of Van Buren as an innovative political organizer and tactician with two pioneering monographs, *Martin Van Buren and the Making of the Democratic Party* (1959) and *The Election of Andrew Jackson* (1963), both concentrated chiefly on the period from 1821 to 1828. Determined to give Van Buren his proper due, Rayback spent more than a decade gathering voluminous research notes and writing a meticulous first volume of a proposed two-volume life and times study. But he died in 1983 with his task incomplete.

Other historians were equally hard at work filling the void. John Niven's *Martin Van Buren: The Romantic Age of American Politics* (1983) and Donald B. Cole's *Martin Van Buren and the American Political System* (1984) were both full-scale biographies. Major L. Wilson's *The Presidency of Martin Van Buren* (1984) added fresh insights to augment James C. Curtis's 1970 monograph, *The Fox at Bay: Martin Van Buren and the Presidency.* As a result, Remini, who had completed a dissertation about Van Buren in 1951 at Columbia University, "The Early Political Career of Martin Van Buren, 1782-1828," which he intended to turn into a complete biography, concluded in his preface to *Henry Clay: Statesman for the Union* (1991) that a fifth work on Van Buren was unnecessary.

During that period, James M. Rayback, Joseph Rayback's son and literary trustee, sought a historian to complete his father's efforts. After assessing the manuscript, I decided that the historical profession could indeed profit from another Van Buren inquiry. Every previous work, starting with William M. Holland's impressionistic hagiography of 1835, *The Life and Political Opinions of Martin Van Buren, Vice President of the United States,* had assumed a single truism: Van Buren's profession as a lawyer made him a success in politics. But no previous investigator had demonstrated the exact nature of this process, nor the precise interplay that existed between Van Buren's republican principles, his legal practice, and his political activities.

Using these unexamined points to organize this study, I rearranged and condensed Joseph Rayback's manuscript around a series of questions. What role did Van Buren's Dutch-American inheritance play in his dual career? Why did he select the law as a profession? What was the nature of his legal training and practice? Why did he become a politician? For which reasons did he find republicanism congenial? How did the shifting nature of republicanism shape that dual career? In what ways did his practice illuminate social, political, racial, ethnic, gender, and economic conditions in New York's Upper Hudson Valley, especially its peculiar system of landownership? How did these ingredients affect the texture of his dual career? What judicial and ideological principles determined his thinking about jurisprudence, economic policies, government operations, and political organization? To what extent did these factors contribute to the Jacksonian Movement?

To answer these questions, I expanded Joseph Rayback's examination of Van Buren's appellate cases in New York's highest courts, the Supreme Court of Judicature and the Court for the Trial of Impeachments and Corrections of Errors, the venues in which Van Buren established his lasting reputation as the state's leading lawyer of last resort. I also explored Van Buren's legal education, the range of his practice, the character and salience of the appellate cases he handled, his work before the Court of Chancery, the judicial system in which he functioned, the public offices he held (particularly as state senator and New York's attorney general), and the evolving role republicanism played in shaping his life in the law and politics.

I also sought to make legalistic concepts understandable to nonspecialists by avoiding legal terminology. Where legal terms had to be used, I provided definitions in the text, augmented by a glossary. Moreover, I consciously avoided replicating a detailed description of the political events worked over by other historians. I consolidated their material but added new information to document my thesis that Van Buren's professional work, bolstered by his republican principles, shaped his approach to the political process and Jacksonianism.

Van Buren's dual career evolved through four distinct phases: the rising lawyer and political apprentice; the lawyer-politician; the politician-lawyer; and the full-time politician. This thematic structure is not entirely novel. Historical studies abound with the correct assumption that the law made Van Buren a public man. Other practicing attorneys of Van Buren's era—most notably, Andrew Jackson, Henry Clay, Daniel Webster, John C. Calhoun, Thomas Hart Benton, Millard Fillmore, and Abraham Lincoln—duplicated Van Buren's experience by using the law as an irreplaceable avenue to political advancement.

But Van Buren was an exception among his contemporaries. For thirty-two years, including his training, Van Buren practiced as an attorney. For much of that time, his work as a lawyer dominated his efforts as a politician. Van Buren's practice was also important in itself. His cases touched myriad issues that dealt with most aspects of human interaction and demonstrated legal developments in the nation's most important state during the early years of the nineteenth-century. Yet, in the largest sense, Van Buren was more than a mere case lawyer or all-purpose attorney, an advocate who represented clients as they walked in the door. Van Buren's evolving republicanism set him apart from his contemporaries, both in the law and in politics. As an advocate, his principled republican methodology influenced new departures in the implementation of jurisprudence. Even Van Buren's most prominent contribution to his era, the formation and justification of political parties, stemmed from his profession. In short, Van Buren did not draw a dichotomy between the law and politics. Each served the same end: the creation of a just and equitable republican society.

Many of Van Buren's political peers followed the same trajectory as they moved from striving young attorneys to positions of national prominence. To put this career pattern into perspective, twenty-four of the forty-one men who have served as president of the United States to date were lawyers. But while the political literature about these men is extensive, their professional careers appear as passing interludes, briefly discussed, rarely analyzed, and secondary to politics.

Van Buren deserves better. Besides being the most successful practicing attorney of his generation to become president, he was the only lawyer-politician among his peers who fashioned republicanism into a practical ideology in both law and politics. This study of the linkage between ideology, law, and politics in Van Buren's career unlocks the least appreciated part of his dual career. The story needs attention.

In the course of writing this study, I have accumulated a number of scholarly debts that I wish to acknowledge. James M. Rayback generously shared both the material his father had gathered and a first draft of this manuscript. A grant from The University of Akron allowed me to investigate documents at the New York State Archives in Albany, where James D. Folts and his staff were most helpful, as well as other information stored at the Columbia County Historical Society. I am also indebted to my colleagues, Professors David E. Kyvig and James F. Richardson, for their thoughtful criticism. Above all, I wish to thank my wife, Attorney Barbara S. Mushkat, for her encouragement and guidance in working my way through many of Van Buren's complex cases. Special thanks are also due to Louis, my silent friend, for our long and thoughtful walks.

I wish to dedicate this study to the memory of two brothers and fellow historians, Joseph G. Rayback and Robert J. Rayback.

Martin Van Buren

The Making of a Republican Dual Career

The three-story brick Georgian house at 92 State Street in Albany, a few blocks from the capitol, bustled with life in December 1828. At the center of all the activity stood Martin Van Buren—a short, stout man of forty-six, impeccably dressed in the latest style, carefully selected to highlight his blue eyes, thinning reddish-blond hair, and ruddy features—the newly elected governor of New York and the chief architect of Andrew Jackson's triumphant victory in the recent presidential election.[1]

Van Buren had much on his mind. Supporters clamored for patronage. A draft of his unfinished inaugural address waited on his desk. Correspondence and discussions with other Democrats gave him few clues about Jackson's coming presidential policies. Yet Van Buren had reached one decision. As he noted years later in his *Autobiography,* he had decided to terminate his more than a quarter-century-long "practice of law." What Van Buren failed to mention was how his "professional capacity" as a republican attorney had shaped his dual life up to that point in law and politics—and would eventually make him the eighth president of the United States of America.[2]

Several factors molded that two-fold career, starting with Van Buren's large nuclear and extended Dutch-American family, bound by ties of blood, kinship, and religion, and augmented by neighbors and African-American slaves.

The two sides of his immediate family had much in common. Most of them numbered among the New Netherlands' first settlers. Almost all had started as tenants or hired laborers on the vast proprietary estates that dotted the Upper Hudson Valley, and almost all became freeholders, settling in or around the village of Kinderhook in what would become Columbia County. Van Buren inherited a number of enduring traits from this legacy. Traditionally stable, ethical, self-sufficient, and thrifty, as well as homogenous, disciplined, and religious, Dutch-Americans were devoted to improving their family's communal fortunes, forming cohesive communities, and cherishing children. Women were especially important, for they maintained a demanding schedule of domestic tasks while also assuming responsibility for their husband's affairs. Equally significant, women enjoyed essential individual rights, notably the custom of communal property, mutual wills, and a partible division of communal property, which allowed widows an equal share of assets.[3]

But there was little in young Martin Van Buren's Dutch-American background to indicate that he would select the law and politics as an adult. His father, Abraham Van Buren, an easy-going, unambitious man, was content with his station in life. He had continued his family's farming tradition and supplemented his income by running a small wayside tavern that he had inherited from his father. In 1776, Abraham Van Buren married Maria Hoes Van Alen, the widow of Johannes Van Alen and the mother of three adolescent children, one daughter and two sons. Before the end of the War of Independence, the couple had two daughters, Dirckie and Jannetje. Their first son, Martin, was born on December 5, 1782. Three siblings followed, Lawrence, Abraham, and Maria.[4]

Although few records exist about Martin Van Buren's mother Maria Van Buren, beyond his vague description of her as an idealized eighteenth-century woman, she was far more influential than his father in molding his future. Her family background differed from that of the Van Burens. The Hoeses had prospered as substantial property holders, owned thirty-six African-American slaves by 1790, and operated a variety of small enterprises. Maria Van Buren also had personal qualities that set her apart from the typical woman of her generation. She was a commanding person, fond of politics and strong-willed. Breaking with the farming tradition that had guided the Van Burens for over six generations in America, she encouraged her sons by her first marriage, James J. and John I. Van Alen, to become attorneys. She was no less ambitious for her favorite child, Martin Van Buren, whom she believed had far more talent for books than the life of a farmer or tavern keeper.[5]

Anglicanization, especially of the law, was equally vital in the development of Van Buren's career as a lawyer and politician. This policy, begun two years after the abortive Leisler Rebellion of 1689, carried out the British imperial intent to impose its authority on a "fractious" colony and bring an end to Dutch institutions. In particular, the Judiciary Act of 1691 established a Supreme Court of Judicature and created a hierarchy of inferior courts. The result eliminated Dutch law, a predominantly abstract set of rules for ethical justice based on the version of Roman law first codified by the Emperor Justinian in the sixth century. Instead, Anglicanization emphasized the common law, with its elaborate and confusing formalism in proceedings, terminology, pleadings, precedents, judges' opinions, and the unwritten British constitution.[6]

Anglicanization variously affected Dutch-Americans. In commercial centers, chiefly New York City and Albany, Dutch merchants, with all their urban and bourgeois values, readily adopted the British system, particularly as the expanding export trade involved them in numerous litigations over questions of civil and commercial law. On the western frontier and in the settlements of the Upper Hudson Valley such as Kinderhook, the Dutch were often more "conservative and obstinate," usually making "selective adaptations" within regional subcultures.[7]

The need for a trained class of lawyers to cope with the implications of Anglicanization was of key importance to Van Buren's future. The Dutch of New Netherland had not utilized professional attorneys. Rather, they relied upon a system of untrained arbitrators and magistrates to settle legal disputes. Nor were juries involved. Litigants, without lawyers, appeared before magistrates who acted as advocates, prosecutors, juries, and judges. The common law forced Dutch-Americans to move in new directions. Trained attorneys were now indispensable to deal with the complexities of the new law. Specialization also became the norm with the growth of a monied economy, exports, conflicts between creditors and debtors, and expanding internal markets. As New Yorkers, including Dutch-Americans, pursued remedies in civil, commercial, and property law, the legal system matured into a profession—and a lucrative one for some elitist practitioners. Increasingly, this new profession became a means for underprivileged, lower-class men, such as Van Buren, to gain wealth and prominence.[8]

After the American Revolution, far-reaching developments in commercial capitalism and politics also played a role in forging Van Buren's dual life. Soon after independence, a great surge of New Englanders, the "Yankees," shifted from sparsely settled and unproductive lands in western Massachusetts and Connecticut into the adjoining area of eastern New York and the vast Albany County region, including the more established areas of Kinderhook and Claverack. This influx of new residents touched the Van Burens in 1783, when two promoters, Seth and Thomas Jenkins, formed the settlement of Hudson, near the southwestern corner of Kinderhook. By 1792, Hudson had nearly 1,500 inhabitants; numerous businesses, whaling companies, agricultural enterprises, and home manufacturers had been formed; a burgeoning shipping trade had developed between Boston, Albany, and New York City; and boosters had secured a charter for the Bank of Columbia, which provided local residents with a supply of ready investment capital. In response, the New York Legislature made Hudson an incorporated city, reorganized this thriving region into Columbia County, subdivided it into townships, and designated Claverack as the county seat.[9]

Such developments affected the Van Burens and the small village of Kinderhook in unexpected ways. A fresh spirit of acquisitiveness pervaded the achievement-orientated Dutch-Americans. Many started to reorder their lives around these new enterprises. The traditional bonds of kinship, communal life, and agrarian habits—the fabric of families in a preindustrial society— were now secondary to fresh market values geared to private choices. Among those effected by the change were the youthful Martin Van Buren and his mother.[10]

Property-ownership and land development, the earliest and chief forms of wealth, commercial farming, and entrepreneurship in Kinderhook and its environs, were the next factors that fashioned Van Buren's two careers. His home region was unique on the eastern side of the Upper Hudson Valley. It was unique because it had never been part of the colonial manors or patents that various British governors had awarded New York's most influential landed families, particularly the Van Rensselaers and Livingstons, in what became Columbia County.

Colonial land awards took two forms, manor grants and letters of patent. A governor, acting with the advice of his council and following complicated procedures often linked to graft and political favoritism, authorized manor grants to a "nascent gentry." Theoretically, landlords enjoyed semi-feudal rights and ran estates as self-perpetuating judicial, economic, and political domains farmed by tenants. Governors, through a somewhat similar process, also awarded letters of patent to individuals or groups of individuals. But these men lacked manorial privileges and usually sold the land in fee simple, which gave the purchaser and heirs absolute title to the property.[11]

In Van Buren's home region, one Dutch-American family, the Van Rensselaers, owned nearly 750,000 acres, roughly encompassing modern Albany and Rensselaer counties to the north, and about 250,000 acres in Columbia County to Claverack in the south. The second great family, the Scottish-English Livingstons, claimed more than 250,000 acres in Columbia, circling the Manor with ill-defined boundaries on the borders of modern Dutchess County to the south, between the Manor and Claverack in the center. These two great manorial landlords and their descendants sought to confirm their feudalistic aims by strategic marriages, political pay-offs, and land grabs—and bent the law to suit their purposes. Both families shared another trait: they did not usually sell their property to tenants in fee simple. Instead, these landlords formed long-term leases and sought to control tenants through an arbitrary system of hereditary feudal tenures and privileges based on British aristocratic customs.[12]

The colonial lease structure fell into several patterns under the common law doctrine of free and common socage. Under this doctrine, land was held in perpetuity and continual occupancy, and subject to a quitrent, which required tenants to pay a fee or perform services to quit themselves from responsibilities to the landlord. Leases in fee simple, in theory giving the holder an absolute title, generally allowed the landlord to retain a perpetual rent, usually a quitrent. Under durable leases, made for the lifetime of the holder or for a specified number of years to heirs and assigns, landlords could still extract certain privileges in quitrent, paid either in cash or in-kind. Three-lives leases, an extension of durable leases, gave landlords the right to let land over three generations, also liable to quitrent. Tenancy from year to year allowed either party to terminate their relationship with proper notice, normally a half-year. Tenancy at sufferance meant that a lease had expired, but lessees remained by implicit agreement until the landlord ejected them. Tenants at will acknowledged the transfer of a lease to a second party, but the original lessor had the right to revoke the lease.

Still more restrictions existed. Landlords often appointed clergymen, tithed tenants for their support, and ordered tenants to build roads and fences. Through escheat, a common law form of descent, the land reverted to the original grantor when the tenant died or was convicted of a felony. In practice, some landlords were flexible enough to moderate leases in order to attract tenants. Yet a gnawing gap remained in comparative wealth and power between landed families and their tenants.[13]

Independence brought some reforms. The state constitution and various legislative statutes essentially ended quitrents and abolished primogeniture and entail. New York confiscated some Loyalist manorial estates under attainders and decreed that the land office sell this property in fee simple. Moreover, new statutes attempted to limit the common law of tenures and estates, the system that defined the legal connection between landlords and tenants and allowed landlords an unlimited time to hold property. The legislature also stripped Livingston Manor's right to elect its assembly seat; raised property taxes; passed wartime *ad valorem* taxes on unimproved land, price ceilings, and trade regulations; and stipulated that popularly-elected assessors would determine future taxation values. But the constitution was defective in one salient feature. It left in place the existing property titles, leases, and franchises of Patriotic landlords in the Upper Hudson Valley. Even worse, the state court system negated legislative statutes that sought to end feudal tenures and privileges while enforcing the old landlord system.[14]

As a consequence, the Livingstons and Van Rensselaers retained an unequal balance of power under real property law that protected and perpetuated their positions. Once landlords established a lease, even though terms might vary from tenant to tenant, their control over the property continued, due to the legal principle that tenants had an absolute liability for the duration of the lease, unless modified in the original contract. Personal property of tenants was forfeit if landlords recovered unpaid back rent. Using the common law doctrine of waste, landlords held that tenants were responsible for any damage to the property, even if their actions improved that property, such as cutting trees, erecting fences, or clearing underbrush. Landlords also denied tenants the privilege of estovers, which allowed them a reasonable right to secure wood from the demised property for fuel, fences, and other agrarian functions. Tenants were liable for maintaining the property, while the landlord had no such obligation. Landlords' rights included equally imbalanced covenants that further restricted the use of the land, prohibited sub-leasing, and set substantial fines for nonperformance.[15]

Tenants resented not only this lease structure but a system that prevented them from buying, in fee simple, what amounted to over a million acres of land. During the colonial period, their anger had flared into periodic outbursts of violence. The most serious occurred in 1766, when a number of Livingston and Van Rensselaer tenants demanded changes in leases. But they met with defeat at the hands of the British military and the unsympathetic local courts that sustained the landlords. Restlessness increased after the American Revolution. Tenants, imbued with the spirit of republicanism and buoyed up by free market expectations, continued to press for changes in property law and land usage.[16]

That spirit reached Columbia County during Martin Van Buren's impressionable youth. In 1791, a "revolt" erupted when the Van Rensselaers and their agents attempted to oust tenants who refused to pay a year's rent. An armed band of seventeen men, disguised as American Indians, shot and killed Van Buren's distant relative, Sheriff Cornelius Hogeboom, when he attempted to auction off some of the seized property. Four years later, over 200 manorial leaseholders fruitlessly petitioned the legislature to abolish Governor Thomas Dongan's 1686 patent, which had purportedly legitimatized the Livingstons' claim.[17]

Colonial letters of patent were less autocratic, but posed equally acrimonious conflicts in Columbia that engendered thorny legal problems of land ownership. Richard Nicolls, governor from 1664 to 1667, confirmed an ambiguous patent that Evert Luycus and John Hendrickse DeBruyn had purportedly purchased from American Indians along upper Kinderhook Creek, as well as the equivocal Powell Patent, stretching about one mile along the Hudson River and extending slightly southeast for about three miles. Nicolls also allowed Abraham Staats' patent for "ground rent," a perpetual fee simple reserved to him, his assigns, and heirs, covering some of the area along the Hudson River between Staats and Powell. In addition, Nicolls allotted an undefined patent of "bushland" of indeterminate acreage to John Baker and Jacob Jansen Flodden. In short, Nicolls created a monumental problem for Van Buren. Because of inexact surveys and uncertain boundaries, many of these patents overlapped.[18]

Subsequent governors instigated even more confusion by layering other patents over existing ones. Seeking clarification in 1686, thirty-one residents of Kinderhook, including Van Buren's forbears on both sides, petitioned Governor Dongan for a confirmation of their rights to these holdings. Dongan responded with the "Great Kinderhook Patent." He combined all the previous patents, except those of Staats, De Bruyn, Powell, and Baker-Flodden, on the north side of the earlier ones. Dongan then formed the area into the Town of Kinderhook, liable to an annual quitrent of twelve bushels of winter wheat, and endorsed the petitioners' property titles, including houses and buildings. These provisions meant that the petitioners, including their heirs and assigns, held the property in common and were not bound by previous manorial grants or patents.[19]

But problems were hardly solved. Still other governors issued more patents before the Revolution, substantially increasing the number of overlaps. In October 1715, the whole question of property-holding reached new levels of complexity. Governor Robert Hunter confirmed Robert Livingston's title for the Manor of Livingston and accepted his demand for near feudal privileges. More critical for the future, the Manor's bounds were unclear and subject to differing judicial interpretations.[20]

Additional difficulties surfaced. During the decade before the Revolution, several Livingstons and Van Rensselaers claimed ownership of parcels in the Great Kinderhook Patent. They failed. Special legislative commissioners divided the land among the heirs and assigns of the thirty-one original patentees into six "allotments," ranging from about 1,000 to 8,500 acres, with each further subdivided into thirty-one "lots" of 30 to 300 acres. The commissioner then conveyed the lots to the original petitioners' heirs and assigns, including the Van Burens and Hoeses, by free lottery. Finally, they adjusted the parcels among themselves. The upshot was that ownership in severalty—land held as freehold personal property, not jointly as under Dutch law—had replaced ownership in common.[21]

By the 1780s, all these twists and turns in ownership meant that Columbia County was a region where genuine grievances existed between leaseholders and landlords, especially over the continuance of the traditional landlord-tenant system and the inability of tenants to purchase farmsteads that often had been in their families for generations. Kinderhook was only immune to this endemic restlessness in that it consisted of individually owned tracts largely held by self-governing freeholders. However, since many residents of Kinderhook, such as the Van Burens, had friends and relatives on those patent estates, they could not avoid either the conflicts or their legal ramifications. To make matters worse, the issue of property ownership in patent lands was still unclear, due to overlays, and laid the foundation for continual litigation.[22]

This mosaic of manors, patents, tenants, and freeholders created a legal quagmire in Columbia County that lasted well into the nineteenth-century, especially as the area flourished and land values escalated. For the ambitious Martin Van Buren, these conditions would determine his professional career. Equally important, questions about the use and allocation of land ownership induced Van Buren to enter politics. Although property-owning requirements inhibited mass democracy, the state Constitution of 1777 expanded the older colonial electorate and encouraged aspiring politicians to campaign among eligible voters. Partisan affiliations in Columbia County varied from election to election during the 1780s, especially among Kinderhook voters who had no fixed allegiances and commonly supported a man, not a party. The Van Buren and Hoes families reflected this fluidity; they became both Antifederalists and Federalists. But Van Buren's parents supported George Clinton, the state's five-time governor and the leader of the Antifederalists. Overall, Columbia voters, splintered by the ethnic, social, economic, and religious divisions between Dutch-Americans, landlords and tenants, and their Yankee invaders, made the county one of New York's great political battlegrounds. Many of the state's most vigorous and effective politicians first tested their skills in this area—notably, the adolescent Martin Van Buren.[23]

By the late 1790s, a more institutionalized political party system emerged. Federalists, led by Alexander Hamilton and John Jay, established the state's first organized party. Clintonians, with Aaron Burr's followers known as the "Little Band" and most of the followers of Chancellor Robert R. Livingston, fused with Thomas Jefferson and James Madison of Virginia in the Democratic-Republican party, commonly called Republicans.[24]

Van Buren, while still a juvenile, affiliated with the Republicans, although he was never explicit about his reasons. Some biographers have assumed that he inherited this allegiance from his father and mother, both "zealous" Clintonians and Republicans. But both his half-brothers were Federalists, as were a number of Hoeses.[25]

A more credible explanation exists. During Van Buren's lifetime, critics contended that he lacked a consistent political philosophy and sacrificed the few principles he did have for political gain. Yet Van Buren's posthumous *Inquiry into the Origins and Course of Political Parties in the United States* together with his *Autobiography,* reveal a deep sense of classical republican ideology, which Van Buren himself identified as the "Principles of '98."[26]

Van Buren partially deduced this credo from the classical republican concepts that Jefferson and Madison enunciated in their 1798 Virginia and Kentucky Resolutions. Van Buren found their ideas congenial, for they served preexisting needs in Columbia County that were linked to his agrarian background, the realities of a growing marketplace economy, tenants' rights, and landholding issues. Liberty, which Jefferson and Madison defined as characterized by negative government, states' rights, and the ability of citizens to govern themselves, fit Van Buren's belief in limiting the powers that the landed elite held over tenants, freehold farmers, and small entrepreneurs. Liberty, Van Buren also believed, emphasized privatism. Neither the government nor the courts had a right to intervene in private matters. As a result, tenants, freeholders, and upwardly mobile businessmen could form economic agreements in which the parties to such agreements had the right to weigh risks and allocate benefits in direct proportion to their own interests. Furthermore, such principles reinforced two other classical republican values that Van Buren cherished: equality, or the idea that all persons—namely, white men—were equal; and individualism, or the autonomous ability of citizens to protect their social, political, and economic rights from any type of coercion, for the most part from the landlord class. Moreover, Van Buren associated these concepts with the classical republican value of property-ownership as the lack of dependency on others. The totality of these principles, Van Buren maintained, would widen economic opportunities for the underprivileged and restrict feudalism. He also accepted the classical republican notion of virtue as the disinterested belief in civic betterment, which he believed affirmed his Dutch-American moral commitment to communal obligations. Above all, classical republicanism rested on popular sovereignty. As Van Buren later explained, the best public policies derived from the "good sense and good feeling of the people."[27]

Other reasons also explained Van Buren's devotion to classical republicanism. His New Netherland forbears had adhered to their liberal European tendencies by seeking to establish local governments that permitted ordinary white people to participate in self-rule and to protect their liberties. While not all New York Dutch-Americans became Republicans, many, including Van Buren, did—by aligning their allegiance to local sovereignty with Jeffersonian ideals.[28]

Van Buren's classical republicanism, however, was not a fixed doctrine. While he continued to emphasize its essential aspects throughout his legal and political career, Van Buren was equally influenced by the acquisitive Dutch enterprisers who had settled and prospered first in the New Netherlands and then in the state of New York. These businessmen anticipated nineteenth-century liberal republicanism, with its emphasis on individual gain, bourgeois values, and equality of opportunity in a free market economy. Van Buren had no quarrel with this spirit of self-advancement. Nor did he believe that these two interpretations of republicanism were mutually exclusive. Rather, Van Buren gradually accepted the point that classical republicanism must adapt to changing conditions, both in the law and politics. This adaptation was a process, an evolutionary development. His ultimate goal remained consistent: to create the groundwork for an egalitarian society of free and equal producers. But by melding and refashioning key elements of classical republicanism with those of liberal republicanism, Van Buren formed a coherent, functional ideology, one that adapted over time to meet the demands of his era. All that he needed now was a means to put his ideological beliefs into practical operation.[29]

Legal Training, the Dual Career, and Republicanism

In 1796, the fourteen-year-old Martin Van Buren resolved the first element in his dual career when he picked the law for his profession. But a pervasive antilawyer bias, which had existed before and after the Revolution, made his choice a calculated gamble. Attorneys had attempted to counter this prejudice by promoting their image as civic-spirited gentlemen, rather than as elitists or tools of the upper class, especially when they were instrumental in drafting new state and national constitutions. Yet, while citizens revered those documents for protecting them collectively, they resented how they restrained them individually.[1]

Unappeased public outrage over the harsh economic consequences of the Revolution further harmed the bar's repute. Debtors excoriated lawyers as the unremitting collectors of back taxes, which resulted in foreclosures, insolvencies, and recoveries of property; as the enforcers of unfair contracts, accountable for harassing harmless tenants and imprisoning them for debt; and as men who viewed justice as secondary to amassing ill-gotten wealth. Lawyers were also advocates within an adversarial system that made critics of those who could not comprehend the system, or those whom it negatively affected.[2] That lawyers were busy and even prosperous when hard-working artisans and farmers were in economic straits only added to this scorn. It came as no surprise, then, when some New Yorkers pressured the legislature to democratize the profession by allowing any man of sound character to practice law, by making judges elective, and by setting fee ceilings for legal services.[3]

Despite these stereotypes, Van Buren found much in the law that was attractive. In New York, it was an uncrowded field with room for growth, given that many lawyers had supported the British and left the country. It was also a field where some of its members were scantily prepared and poorly qualified, inviting men with superior education or superior native abilities to fill the vacuum.[4]

The need for lawyers in a republican society, especially Columbia County, also captivated Van Buren. The area was rich with litigants, landlords, tenants, entrepreneurs, and freeholders alike. Creditors and debtors, in prosperity or depression, needed legal services dealing with real estate, commerce, civil law, and criminal law. Lawyers also had an opportunity to make a comfortable living from the honest practice of law because of their continuous contact with the business community. The result produced a fresh entrepreneurial ethic that eroded the older image of the elitist attorney, and the law gradually evolved into a legitimate, money-making profession. An equally promising factor was that trials, heavily reported in newspapers in a highly politicized age, gave lawyers the public exposure necessary for political careers. In addition, attorneys were often a force for probity and civility in a fluid republican culture. Van Buren's Dutch-American background, despite lacking a heritage of attorneys, settled his decision. The law, whether it honored traditional Dutch codes of universal ethics and justice or accepted the common law, could ensure a just, ordered society in an era of flux by seeking to establish rules for moral behavior that protected basic human rights as an extension of communal obligation.[5]

In sum, the law and its opportunities gave Van Buren a unique outlet to adapt his talents with the new possibilities of a republican society and a marketplace economy. Whatever the bar's unsavory reputation, Van Buren recognized that some of Kinderhook's most respectable and affluent citizens were attorneys, chiefly the Federalists Peter Van Schaack and Peter Silvester. Their example was hard to ignore, as was that of his half-brothers who were both lawyers.[6]

Despite this decision, Van Buren still faced a problem: the means to gain a proper legal education. As a child, Van Buren had been a precocious student who excelled in the mediocre Kinderhook village school. Due to the ambitions of his mother, Van Buren then enrolled at eleven in the Kinderhook Academy, which prepared young men for college. The curriculum in this "literary institute" instructed students in history, English literature, and Latin. But while this schooling was a step above that of his peers in Kinderhook, what Van Buren actually learned during his three years at the academy was unclear. In 1835, William M. Holland, Van Buren's first biographer, relying on

impressionistic anecdotes, interviews, and oral traditions, claimed that the
academy taught Van Buren vital skills in critical analysis and argumentation.
Whatever Van Buren's promise, four facts about his general education were
certain. He never attended college; he envied more academically trained men
and experienced fits of self-doubt and insecurity; he later forged a systematic
program of independent study to counter these feelings; and his familiarity
with Latin helped his coming legal career.[7]

Other facts were also apparent. Van Buren's lower-class standing, his limited family finances, and his nation's bustling nationalism precluded customary legal preparation. Well-connected colonial attorneys had earned bac-
calaureate degrees and studied with a practicing lawyer or an eminent judge
for three years. A few finished at the Inns of Court in Great Britain.[8] Van Buren's sole option lay in finding a local attorney-at-law willing to accept him
as an apprentice or clerk, as the position was called, preferably in Kinderhook. In practical terms, this person needed to have the time to work with an
apprentice, particularly an impoverished one, and to think out legal problems
with him. He needed to teach him the nature and general rules of law, to
shepherd him to court to meet judges and study other lawyers in action, and
to introduce him to prospective clients. To complete his training and gain
added maturity, Van Buren hoped to cap this procedure with a New York
City attorney familiar with specialties foreign to local lawyers.[9]

New York's unfolding statutory laws and native jurisprudence would set
the framework for Van Buren's studies during his apprenticeship. The state
constitution's Article 35, which organized the judiciary, retained British common law and colonial statutes, subject to legislative "alterations and provisions." Since this hybrid system was so imprecise, the state designated two
teams of legal scholars, Samuel Jones and Richard Varick in 1786, and James
Kent and Jacob Radcliff in 1803, to codify the material in a logical, pre-
dictable, and unified format. As a result, Van Buren had to learn an evolving
system of jurisprudence in which many of its branches were unsettled.[10]

Article 28, which gave the state Supreme Court power to accredit attorneys, also set the terms for Van Buren's training and licensing. The court authorized an apprenticeship lasting seven years under "a practicing attorney of
the court," but deducted up to four years for a man who had pursued a "classical" education or studied under "a professor or a Counsellor at Law." Additionally, the candidate had to be at least twenty-one and submit proof of a
"skillful" and "honest disposition." As for the actual examination, three members of the bar, selected by the court, administered an oral test and approved
the applicant.[11]

The Supreme Court further continued a colonial distinction derived from
Great Britain between an "attorney at law" and a "counsellor at law" that affected Van Buren. An attorney was an advocate, the court's official agent in
preparing and managing but not pleading cases in court, nor practicing before the Supreme Court. A counsellor was a grade above: he advised attor-

neys, litigated causes in open court, and could practice in the Supreme Court. In 1783, the Supreme Court ruled that an attorney must have two years service before being eligible to take an examination for counsellor. Although the court amended its rules in 1804 by allowing all attorneys with three years experience to become counsellors without an examination, the change came too late for Van Buren. He trained, tested, and was licensed for the lesser rank of attorney.[12]

The Court of Chancery, another holdover from the colonial period with exclusive jurisdiction over equity, also shaped Van Buren's legal training. This court continued the traditional distinction between a "solicitor in chancery" and a "counsellor in chancery." A solicitor in chancery was an attorney who had practiced before the court for two years and had the same general functions as an attorney under the Supreme Court's definition. After that period, a solicitor could take an examination, given by three counsellors in chancery, before being licensed. A counsellor in chancery generally paralleled the functions of a counsellor under the Supreme Court's rules. Becoming a counsellor in chancery indicated that the person had reached the bar's highest level.[13]

Bound by these regulations and limitations, Van Buren faced a hard choice in finding an appropriate mentor among the few available in Kinderhook. Peter Van Schaack was the best known. He enjoyed a prominent reputation as a scholar of the common law and had established a successful "school" in Kinderhook for novice attorneys. Van Buren considered enrolling with Van Schaack, largely because he was a distant relative. But Van Schaack was suspect. He had supported the British, left New York as an exile, and returned home to become a dogged Federalist. Van Buren rejected him, mainly to avoid the taint of disloyalty that was so prevalent among Kinderhook residents, the "place of Tories." As he later rationalized, Van Schaack's "prejudices against me in early life were of the rankest kind."[14]

Peter Silvester, another distant relative, was a second possibility. He had served in New York's Provincial Congresses of 1775 and 1776, been a judge of common pleas, and was currently a congressman. Van Buren described him as "one of the purest men I ever knew." But Peter Silvester was more interested in politics than the law and had little desire to take on an apprentice. Yet he did have two sons, Francis, a lawyer, and Cornelius, a storekeeper. Both were friendly toward the teenage boy. Francis accepted him as an apprentice, and Cornelius supplied a bedroom above his store where Van Buren lived and sometimes helped as a combination general clerk and janitor.[15]

The program Van Buren entered was that of master and apprentice. Although documentation of the arrangement is not extant, his parents likely signed a written legal contract, presumably registered with the court, in which they paid Francis Silvester an unspecified sum for the training of their son, who bound himself to serve the grueling seven-year term. In return, Silvester acted as Van Buren's mentor, teaching him the principles, practices, and procedures of the law, and providing housing and board. A stickler for fashion,

Silvester also served as Van Buren's initial tutor in the proper dress for an advocate, substituting a more "sartorial" appearance for the homespun clothing his mother had made.[16]

No evidence exists of the relationship that developed between apprentice and master, beyond Van Buren's description of Silvester as "a just and honorable man." Nevertheless, Silvester probably carried out his obligations to his fullest abilities by providing Van Buren with a useful course of study and acting as a demanding teacher. How extensive or qualitative a library Silvester owned is also impossible to assess. Some scholars suggest that country lawyers, even those as reputable as Silvester, had less than a dozen books. Other shortcomings existed. Until 1801, when *Coleman's Cases* first appeared sporadically covering the period only as far back as 1794, lawyers and clerks had no printed reports of precedent-setting cases in the Supreme Court or Court of Chancery. *Caines' Reports,* the Supreme Court's first authorized compilations, issued in 1804, were more thorough in presenting r'sum's of arguments and decisions. Prior to 1814, the Court of Chancery did not publish decisions. As for local courts, no stenographic or official reports were available. Lawyers and clerks depended on their notes. Because of this paucity of information, Van Buren lacked sound training in *stare decisis,* the common law practice of relying on precedents that judges had laid down in previous cases.[17]

Under these conditions, Van Buren's curriculum probably consisted of unsystematic readings in theories of natural law; state statutes concerning contracts, property law, civil law, and criminal law, the bulk of Kinderhook's litigation; form books; rules of practice, pleading, and evidence; and standard English texts and commentaries. The emphasis upon British sources and their practical application was imperative. New York's legal system was still essentially English, steeped in the common law and its functions. Most critical for the future, Van Buren probably absorbed William Wyche's 1794 *Treatise on the Practice of the Supreme Court of Judicature of the State of New York in Civil Actions,* the appellate venue where he gained lasting prominence. As part of this training, Silvester had to instruct Van Buren in the unfamiliar legal phrases and terminology, as well as the confusing, obscure verbiage that filled these law books. Moreover, Silvester surely primed Van Buren in private law, which involved litigation between citizen and citizen, and public law, which concerned the functions of the state in its political and sovereign capacity. From all indications, Silvester was a thoroughgoing professional, a virtue Van Buren learned from him. When he prepared briefs in the future, Van Buren developed an action beginning with its historical background and established, step by step, points of law to sustain his advocacy.[18]

Becoming a professional demanded even more tutelage. Common law forms and usages were technical, tedious, and often intellectually sterile. Van Buren had to master them. A typical clerk drew declarations, bills in chancery, pleadings, answers, praecipes, and the administration and filing of wills—all procedures that took painstaking care. Again, Silvester laid a sturdy basis for his apprentice's growth as a lawyer. During Van Buren's subsequent legal career, he revealed a command of common law principles and a firm grounding in the fundamentals of his profession, accomplishments that the bar viewed as proof of a strong legal foundation. Van Buren had further duties as well. Like other apprentices, he copied wills, indentures, and other common law forms; served, entered, and filed court papers; and carried on the minutiae of Silvester's practice by keeping a schedule of litigations, collecting bills, and attending him in court.[19]

Van Buren left no hint of his progress as a student, nor did Silvester. The only first-hand recollections came from the observant Holland. According to his version of events, which may be unreliable, Van Buren was thoughtful, industrious, and mentally swift. Van Buren partially substantiated Holland in describing his youthful mind as "uncommonly active." Even more remarkable, considering his multiple duties, Van Buren was a glutton for work. While still a clerk, he tested his preparation in Columbia County's justices of the peace court.[20]

As with other parts of the law, New York had inherited the judicial format of the justices of the peace from Great Britain. In 1780, the legislature had defined the jurisdiction of justices of the peace court to cover all "causes, actions, and cases of debt, slander, trespass, replevin," a personal action to recover goods unlawfully taken, "or for damages where the amount demanded did not exceed the sum of £100 or under." Either side could ask for a jury trial, consisting of "six freeholders and freemen." Justices received salaries from user fees. Subsequent statutes redefined damages as $50, but did not alter the courts' authority. Since these courts were closest to the public, the majority of minor litigations in Columbia's rural areas originated and were completed in them.[21]

Justices frequently set trials in a tavern, scheduling them at night so that the parties and witnesses would not miss regular work. Legal forms and issues were generally simple, but the litigants were serious and often passionate about any infringements of their rights. This setting also meant that cases had an ample number of spectators in varying degrees of alcoholic hazes, who frequently took sides in the trial and made their views vocal. Success in this crude environment was no criterion of legal ability. But Silvester showed confidence in his budding clerk by allowing him some cases to gauge his progress. Silvester's trust was certainly fortunate for Van Buren. This tribunal gave him the opportunity to prepare a brief based on the often emotional and confused narration of clients, to examine witnesses, and to place the whole case favorably before a jury.[22]

Van Buren appeared before these courts "at a very early age," although the precise date is unclear. One early biographer suggested that Van Buren's clients, mainly local freehold farmers, much like his Dutch-American nuclear and extended family, hired him "incessantly." Although no verification exists for that assertion, these experiences, Van Buren recollected, "severely and usefully disciplined" his mind "for the examination and discussion of facts." The only negative, he admitted, was that it inhibited his grooming for the bar.[23]

As Van Buren rose to fame, folklore developed about his adolescent triumphs in these courts. He modestly cautioned admirers to avoid exaggerating, yet he was indeed quite successful. According to a secondhand report published some years later, which became the key source for ensuing biographers, Van Buren had not yet reached full stature when he presented his first case, and he needed to stand on a chair or table in order to speak. Opposing counsel was "the formidable [Aaron] Gardenier," a "pettifogger" who had "grown gray in the art and science of advocating small causes." The case, a conflicting land claim, drew "hordes" of onlookers, and the battle between them was "dire" and "terrible." While the jury deliberated, both sides hung "in suspense." When Van Buren won, supporters lifted him on their shoulders amid shouts of an "admiring audience."[24]

This report and other copies abounded with contradictions, historically dubious, but nonetheless illuminating. Later accounts suggested that he was about sixteen when the trial took place, making him a second-year apprentice and surely too inexperienced in Silvester's mind for such responsibility; they are even confused about his exact opponent. Yet these versions agreed on one point: as a student of the law, this neophyte was already exhibiting great legal flair.[25]

Such promise created unforeseen political and legal problems for Van Buren. Columbia County was Federalist, but partisan lines in Kinderhook remained blurred. As a result, the Silvesters and local Federalists, who recognized Van Buren's potential both as a budding attorney and as a promising political recruit with a large group of relatives, pressured him to join their organization.[26]

Van Buren never succumbed. Although already committed to Jeffersonian republicanism, Van Buren's experiences before the justices of the peace reinforced his ideological allegiance. If he had been crudely ambitious, Van Buren would have acquiesced with the Silvesters. After all, they represented the bulk of Kinderhook's educated, wealthy, and influential upper-class interests, a bumper crop of future clients. That was the problem as far as Van Buren was concerned. Since Francis Silvester was a notable politician and a leading attorney, his practice was typically Federalist. His clients were people of property; his function was to protect their property. Van Buren came from a different class. His was an agrarian with a freehold ancestry whose upward mobility rested on preserving and expanding liberty, equality, individualism, and property rights, and whose long memory included tenantry and resentment to the point of violence against manorial landlords. The Federalists, Van Buren believed, continued the feudal tradition of dependency, a condition contrary to the republican principle of property. As such, Jeffersonian republicanism fit his class biases against the landed elite and reinforced his political commitments.[27]

Van Buren's first campaign as an avowed member of the Republican party occurred in the congressional election of 1801. Kinderhook Republicans selected him, barely eighteen and ineligible to vote, as a delegate to their district caucus at Troy. But while he lobbied successfully for the nomination of Burrite John Peter Van Ness, a distant cousin, and worked for his eventual election, Van Buren forfeited his legal arrangement with the furious Francis Silvester. They mutually agreed that Van Buren should find "another place to complete [his] studies."[28]

Van Buren now faced a crisis. Nearly two years short of completing his studies, he needed another mentor. The Van Nesses came to his rescue. John Peter Van Ness, aware of Van Buren's "increasing embarrassment," urged him to enter one of New York City's prominent offices and promised to advance funds needed for living expenses while he searched for an appropriate firm. This offer fit Van Buren's plan to complete his training in the city, the site of the state's most successful attorneys.[29]

But Van Buren was chronically short of cash. He expected John Peter to advance finances for almost a full year and a half of study. Van Buren also intended to borrow the rest from James Van Alen, his half-brother, which John Peter would repay. Van Buren assumed as well that John Peter had contacts to locate the right tutor. Van Buren then enlisted the aid of John Peter's brother, William Peter Van Ness, who had just established a practice in New York City and whom he had aided in litigations in Columbia County.[30]

A pact soon developed. William Peter dispatched "a very friendly invitation to come down," assuring Van Buren that he would do all in his power to procure "an agreeable situation" and promising the use of his books and office in the interim. In November of 1802, Van Buren journeyed southward. Once in the city he decided, "upon the most mature consideration," to remain over the winter in William Peter's office at 4 Wall Street. In the spring, Van Buren intended to seek "some extensive practitioner" and "attend to practice exclusively." With matters settled, Van Buren found his first lodgings in a "retired place" on Catherine Street, some sixteen blocks from the office of William Peter Van Ness.[31]

Money remained Van Buren's major woe during the seven months he lived in New York City. He left Kinderhook with $130 borrowed from James Van Alen. Van Buren's "elegantly furnished" housing, including board and laundry, cost $4.00 a week. Firewood and candles ran another $1.50. He also had to buy a return fare, clothes, and books. By January, Van Buren received $25 more from his half-brother, plus another $20 from John Peter, who was attending Congress.[32]

Van Buren managed to cope until April of 1803 when he found himself owing $30 to William Peter. These "impervious circumstances" forced Van Buren to seek new housing. After "a diligent search," he located a less expensive spot in a "respectable house" run by a "proper" Republican. Yet cash remained short. He again appealed to James Van Alen, this time unsuccessfully.

The "hard pressed"Van Buren then braced John Peter, who forwarded $20. That amount was insufficient, and Van Buren asked for an additional $70 to last until November. John Peter never forwarded that sum, and Van Buren ultimately left the city in debt.[33]

Despite John Peter's broken promise, Van Buren's attachment to him never wavered. During the course of his stay in the city, Van Buren expressed embarrassment about his neediness and assured John Peter that he had no wish to "inconvenience" him. Throughout the letters they exchanged, Van Buren remained deferential, often obsequious. He asked for advice, relayed Kinderhook social and political gossip, reported the results of errands undertaken for John Peter, and expressed concerns for his brother Cornelius's growing personal "coolness" toward Van Buren and "flamming" attacks on "Mr. Burr & his friends." John Peter's replies were less frequent but no less friendly.[34]

Becoming an attorney remained Van Buren's first priority, and he had sufficient time for his studies. Few clients called at William Peters's office, and Van Buren had little paper filing or court duties to distract him. As summer continued, he discovered two neighboring law students. Sharing what they had learned, they exchanged ideas and tested each other. Van Buren flourished in this environment. By the end of 1802, he was satisfied that one month in New York City was worth a year in Kinderhook.[35]

Van Buren also found the time for other activities. He ran down a few tax assessments on property for Francis Silvester, an indication that they had parted amicably. On behalf of John C. Hogeboom, the leader of Columbia County's Republicans, Van Buren collected some interest due on notes. He even chased around in unsettled Brooklyn to deliver a summons for John Peter.[36]

Not all of Van Buren's interests involved the law. New York City had many ways to distract a young man on his own for the first time. Van Buren discovered the joys of the theater and became a frequent and enthusiastic playgoer. By January, he had attended five performances. But his indulgences made him feel guilty. He asked John Peter for "some advice and directions" for his future conduct, specifically, how much he should "attend the theater," for "I am determined to undergo anything which is necessary to obtain" true "eminence in the [legal] profession." John Peter replied quickly in a paternal fashion. Warning Van Buren to avoid "*vice*" and "Idleness," John Peter suggested that he mix with "good society." As for the theater, Van Buren could continue attending, but avoid making it a habit.[37]

Van Buren's reply was dutiful, if stilted. "With your advice as my Polar Star," he pledged to follow "a strict and assiduous attention to my business." As for the theater, he concluded in practical fashion. Since he had seen all the "principal actors perform & the best plays," he limited himself to only a few.[38]

The major stumbling block in Van Buren's apprenticeship was neither study nor frivolity, but politics. Buoyed by his yeoman's work in the 1801 congressional campaign, Van Buren scrutinized partisan maneuverings by reading the city's many newspapers. But he shelved active involvement, as he explained to John Peter, because "I have all my Life before me to make myself a politician and but one year to make myself a lawyer."[39]

Yet political temptations proved hard to resist. From upstate, Hogeboom sent news about legislative activities. Van Buren kept abreast of the Columbia 1803 spring assembly race in which James Van Alen, who had switched to the Republican party, received the second-highest vote in a losing effort. National events also interested Van Buren. He informed John Peter that President Jefferson's annual address to Congress was "very well" received in the city "by the friends of virtue & [of] good government."[40]

Amid these developments, comments about Vice-President Burr were oddly absent from Van Buren's letters. By 1802, Burr stood at the center of a raging internecine conflict among Republicans over his purported disloyalty to Jefferson in the tied presidential election of 1800. This battle divided local Republicans into two camps, the Clintonian-Livingstons and the Burrites.[41]

In late 1802, the Clintonian-Livingstons, led by De Witt Clinton, Governor George Clinton's brilliant and accomplished nephew, and Supreme Court Judge Ambrose Spencer, the state's leading lawyer-politician, gained the upper hand through the unique Council of Appointment. This Council was composed of the governor and four senators, elected by the assembly on an annual basis, and eventually named over 14,000 appointees for terms as short as one year. Clinton and Spencer turned the council into a vast patronage engine, hardly used by other politicians in such a manner. Within months, they centralized patronage, purged Federalists, handed Burrites a few token crumbs, and conditioned New Yorkers to consider politics a system of spoils where one earned or lost favors based on services, real or imaginary.[42]

Van Buren, an insignificant figure in this interparty brawl, was an unwitting hostage to Burr's fortunes because the Van Nesses were key leaders of the Little Band. But the Burrites were short of capital and defeated at nearly every turn. Just as Van Buren arrived in the city, the flow of events carried them downhill.[43]

Later, when Burr became dishonored and Van Buren a major national figure, malicious gossip held that both were cut from the same malign stripe. Some even suggested that Van Buren, who bore a striking physical likeness to the womanizing Burr, was his illegitimate son. John Quincy Adams for one, after his first meeting with Van Buren, noted that "there is much resemblance of character, manner, and even person, between the two men."[44]

Van Buren's initial relationship with Burr was unavoidable, considering the role of the brothers Van Ness in his life at this point. When Van Buren first met Burr is uncertain, but the date was probably after March 1803 when Burr returned from his duties in Washington. As Van Buren remembered, William Peter "carried me occasionally to visit" Burr at his home in Richmond Hill, "and I met him sometimes at Mr. Van Ness's house." The charming Burr, who consciously nurtured promising young men as potential allies, treated Van Buren with "much attention" and sparked his "sympathies."

Moreover, Burr, as slight as Van Buren, was quite conscious of his personal appearance and served as a second model for turning Van Buren into something of a dandy. From a political standpoint, however, Van Buren was impressed that Burr rose to prominence without family connections, important patrons, or wealth, the traditional means of advancement in New York politics. Burr had also built a thriving law practice at every level of the state's court system. In short, Burr represented what Van Buren wished to become: a successful attorney who combined law with politics.[45]

The Van Nesses came to the same conclusion and believed that Van Buren was a partisan Burrite. Yet Van Buren was habitually cautious; he sensed that a premature commitment to either side could destroy his legal and political dreams. To avoid taking a stand he might regret, Van Buren used his incomplete bar preparation as an excuse to leave the city, ostensibly to study in Albany with John Van Ness Yates, a respected Court of Chancery counsellor and another Van Ness relative.[46]

Back in Kinderhook, Van Buren retained his connections to the Little Band. He assured William Peter that local Republicans were not suspicious about Burr, did some legal errands for the Van Nesses, and provided local politicians, especially the Clintonian Hogeboom, with "impartial & general" political information. Even so, Van Buren created a dilemma for himself. By appearing as a Burrite, he risked alienating local Republicans who favored Clinton and Spencer.[47]

But for the moment, preparing for his upcoming examination was Van Buren's major goal. Instead of going to Albany, he read in James Van Alen's office and formed a study schedule for his test in New York City. Tangled money woes were still distracting. While he expected that James Van Alen, who had by now advanced $250, would pay for all expenses, Van Buren asked John Peter for the promised but delayed funds. John Peter was slow to reply, making Van Buren's suspense "very disagreeable." When the apologetic John Peter finally answered, he claimed a shortage of cash but commited the use of his credit for six months or a year.[48]

Van Buren also mulled over another matter: where to set up his practice. James Van Alen solved the problem by offering him a partnership in Kinderhook. After agreeing, Van Buren left for the city, accompanied by James. On November 23, Van Buren presented himself for an examination before Samuel Boyd, Samuel Jones, and William Johnson, all distinguished members of the bar. "They declared themselves perfectly and entirely" satisfied, a relieved Van Buren reported to John Peter, "and we were of course admitted to the Bar this day." Martin Van Buren was now a fully accredited "attorney at law," thirteen days short of his twenty-first birthday, still too young to begin an immediate practice.[49]

The Dual Career Begins

Van Buren began 1804 owing creditors some $300, a substantial debt that was almost equal to a year's income for a common laborer. Yet Van Buren could afford to think of the future in rosy terms, because his partnership with Van Alen generated immediate and considerable income. As Van Buren proudly reminisced, "I was not worth a shilling when I commenced my professional career," but "I have never since owned a debt that I could not pay on demand nor known what it was to want money."[1]

Wealth indeed flowed steadily into his coffers for a number of reasons. To begin with, the firm was well-established. Van Alen, a practicing lawyer for nearly ten years, had constructed a dependable clientele based on his record for effective advocacy, nine year's tenure as town clerk, and his current position as surrogate of Columbia County. In addition, Van Buren was less a junior partner than an equal who split fees down the middle; he brought to the firm a capacity for hard work and a keen legal mind, even though he was a tyro in the law. Early triumphs in justices of the peace courts attracted other clients, as did Van Buren's wide acquaintanceship with all types of people from his father's tavern, as well as his drove of Dutch-American relatives and neighbors.

Republican attorneys were also in short supply in Columbia County. While the area had as many as thirty practitioners, only eight besides Van Alen enjoyed wide-spread public recognition. Four of the most noticeable, Elisha Williams, Francis Silvester, William W. Van Ness, and Jacob R. Van Rensselaer, were Federalists and leaders of the Columbia Junto, a partisan group with close attachments to similar lawyers throughout the state who were intimately tied to the county's landowners and Hudson businessmen. Judges who presided over cases in Columbia County were also usually Federalists. When Republican clients lost, they generally appealed. In an era when litigants sought advocates according to their own political leanings, Van Buren was in an ideal position. Although his party's constituency in Columbia was smaller than the Federalists (by about ten percentage points) and less affluent, it was large enough, monied enough, and litigious enough to need talented legal services. In fact, the most trenchant reason for Van Buren's overnight prosperity was that his sobriety and judgment proved on a par with the best Federalist attorneys.[2]

On March 19, 1805, Van Buren recorded the extent of the firm's business and his own burgeoning prospects. In their first year, the partners had collected $821.17 from clients. Accounts receivable from forty-seven more amounted to $1,584.33. Other estimated receipts in thirty-four unfinished appellate cases before the Supreme Court, which Van Alen handled, totaled $524, plus $393 from thirty-six cases pending in Columbia's courts of common pleas and general sessions of the peace. Fees ranged from a low of $4 to a high of $60. On the debit side, Van Buren estimated costs from incomplete litigation at $253. All told, the year's net stood at $3,322.50. Van Buren's self-satisfaction bubbled over in another memorandum of the same date. He projected his present worth at $2,355, based on a half-share of the firm's income, a small legacy, and interest derived from money-lending, a habit he followed throughout his life. If he continued to accrue funds at the same rate, Van Buren jubilantly concluded, he should have $120,000 by the time he reached sixty-five. Even at this early date, then, Van Buren was not opposed either to making profits, increasing his wealth, or personal acquisitiveness, three hallmarks of liberal republicanism.[3]

Van Buren had every reason for optimism. According to his ledger, which cited 118 clients but left many unnamed, the firm had at least 200 actions by 1805. Some actions were in justices of the peace courts, while others were in Columbia's court of common pleas that met in May, September, and December, hearing "all actions, real, personal, and mixed, arising within" the county. Still others were in the court of general sessions of the peace, its criminal branch, surrogate court, Hudson's mayor's court, and the Columbia circuit court at Claverack, headed by a Supreme Court justice. The ledger documented the extent of Van Buren's practice, but did not fully indicate the scope of most cases, his briefs, or his working methods. Unfortunately, the answers to these questions remain elusive, because local court proceedings were either too fragmentary, lost, or unrecorded.[4]

Yet the little information that remains reveals that Van Buren's docket as a country attorney reflected his era and class standing. A few were criminal cases, but most were small civil litigations over real estate, related forms of agricultural property, and minor commercial transactions. Like other lawyers, he prepared cases using common form pleadings. Among these, he drew up writs and answers, took declarations, and addressed interrogatories. He also issued rejoinders, a defendant's second pleading to the plaintiff's answer, rebutters, the answer to a plaintiff's rejoinder, and surebutters, the plaintiff's response to a defendant's rebutter. While still ineligible to argue cases before the Supreme Court, since he lacked the necessary three-year's experience, Van Buren drafted many of Van Alen's appeals. This dreary and lengthy handwritten process recapitulated an action in all it details: the names of litigants and their attorneys; the form of action; the name of the court, its term, and presiding judge; summaries of testimony, supporting evidence, and arguments of counsels for both sides; extracts of court proceedings with judge's instructions, and jury verdict; and the grounds for review. As an all-purpose attorney outside the courtroom, Van Buren drew wills, administered probate, collected debts, interviewed clients, and wrote contracts, bills of sale, mortgages, and deeds. Busy as Van Buren was doing the law, he learned more law through professional self-improvement. In 1805, he and six other starting attorneys organized the nonpartisan "Kinderhook Law Society," dedicated to the "importance of *Elocution and Legal Knowledge.*"[5]

Actions reaching adjudication normally fell into six categories. Criminal cases involved assault and battery, a threat to commit bodily harm, and an actual commission of bodily harm. Civil work included trespass, the doing of an unlawful act or a lawful act in an unlawful manner to another's person or property. Replevin dealt with efforts to recover goods unlawfully taken. Trover sought compensation for property wrongfully converted. Ejectment concerned the removal of a person or persons wrongfully in possession of landed property. Debt recovered moneys due.[6]

On the whole, the majority of Van Buren's cases were ordinary and small paying. He generally took clients as they came. Most were poor tenants and small freeholders. Only seven of the forty-seven clients who owed the firm for services were in debt in excess of $50. Of the seventy-one pending, only two were worth more than $40. Even so, Van Buren paid scrupulous care to his clients, never forgetting that the law served human beings with all their complex concerns and needs.[7]

One action deviated from the pattern. In 1805, Van Buren began developing the "Great Possession" cause that concerned conflicting colonial patents between the descendants of John Baker and Jacob Jansen Flodden on one side, and those of John Hendrickse De Bruyn on the other. The Baker-Flodden Patent, which covered parts of Columbia County near Kinderhook, encroached on De Bruyn. The initial problem, which became more acute as the area attracted sizeable numbers of new settlers, lay in the patents' exact boundaries. Baker-Flodden was vague. De Bruyn was more precise, although the description varied in separate surveys. Until the end of the eighteenth century, both sets of heirs, assigns, and claimants had not questioned their titles. Those living on Baker-Flodden erected homes, barns, gristmills, and sawmills. The De Bruyn Patent passed into the possession of Lauren Van Alen's many descendants and assigns. These conveyances became so complex that in 1793 and again in 1799, the Columbia County Court of Common Pleas named commissioners to certify the partitions. The commissioners split undivided patent lands to satisfy the claims of five Van Alens, together with Peter M. Van Buren and Johannis Van Dusen. Rather than settling anything, these distributions created greater muddles. The divided lands sprawled across both patents. Heirs and claimants further subdivided them, while others transferred parts through deeds and wills. In the meantime, a small army of attorneys, among them Van Buren and Van Alen, shot off ejectment volleys.[8]

The Great Possession cause provided Van Buren with his first chance to use classical republicanism in a long crusade to redefine property law, modify the common law through fresh legal doctrines in tune with this ideology, and attack the nature of the state's entire system of inherited landownership. This case, along with similar ones in the future, would establish Van Buren's reputation as a champion of small claimants against the rich and well-born landlord class.

In this early stage of his practice, Van Buren was a lawyer who set a strenuous work pace, content in making a prosperous livelihood from the sheer bulk of his practice, as his ledger records. Although this volume might have appeared too heavy for two men and could have diminished their efficiency, it represented a practical mix of old and new actions, because clients normally delayed payments until a case was settled.

Clearly, Van Buren was not a dull, pettifogging, small town lawyer. By assessing his legal ability from the vantage point of subsequent published Supreme Court proceedings, inferences about his professionalism may be drawn to replace impressionistic suppositions and unavailable data. Neither a backslapping, flamboyant courtroom showman, nor a cheap trickster, Van Buren's briefs and addresses to judges reveal a sharp analytic mind honed by careful preparations, which stressed salient points while avoiding technical errors that might lose a case. Van Buren further trained himself to understand and anticipate the position of an opponent and to counter with a key judicial doctrine, based on pertinent precedent. Immersing himself in the law, Van Buren was forging his future reputation as an attorney of true distinction, constantly in demand for appellate work in the state's highest courts.[9]

Van Buren's legal accomplishments became the basis for decades of a reciprocal relationship that linked his republicanism to the law and politics. According to one contemporary, Van Buren was "a great lawyer" before becoming a great politician. His "legal training," the "sedulous and patient toil with which his intellectual powers, strong by nature, were tempered and polished in the slow process of his professional career," laid the "foundation" for the "rare supremacy in his political life."[10] In 1804, Van Buren could not divine that future. Instead, he carefully hammered out the first phase of his inter-twined legal and political career. At this point, however, the law predomi-nated for a practical reason. Van Buren's political prospects paled in compari-son to his meteoric legal rise.

Over the next three years, Van Buren remained a political apprentice, one who viewed politics through an unemotional ideological and legalistic lens. In particular, he studied two master politicians at work, Aaron Burr and De Witt Clinton. From them Van Buren learned the art of making and unmak-ing public men and of shaping events most advantageously. Of the two, Van Buren still seemed tied to Burr. But as any aspiring politician would, Van Bu-ren weighed the personal costs and benefits in his relationship to the Little Band. Although older leaders in Columbia County, such as the Van Nesses, were Burrites, all the newer men were patronage beneficiaries of the Clin-tonian system.[11]

The passionate gubernatorial race of 1804 tested Van Buren's ability to embark upon his dual career. He had to decide between Morgan Lewis, the Livingstonian chief justice of the Supreme Court, whom the Clintonian-dominated legislative caucus had nominated, and the insurgent Burr, who ran with Federalist backing, despite Alexander Hamilton's objections. In a wrenching decision, Van Buren informed William Peter Van Ness, the leading local Burrite, that after "the most mature and dispassionate reflection," his en-dorsement of Burr would not "be expedient."[12]

Compelling pragmatic rationales led Van Buren to back Lewis. Van Buren's foremost priorities were self-preservation and advancement. On that basis, the comparison between Burr and Clinton was all in Clinton's favor. Burr placed republicanism secondary to self-interest; Clinton was a dependable party ideo-logue. Burr was mercurial; Clinton was consistent. Burr had broken with Jef-ferson; Clinton was his agent in New York. Burr lacked patronage; Clinton controlled the Council of Appointment. Burr defied party discipline; Clinton adhered to the principle of party regularity. In short, Van Buren, despite his "strong personal prejudices" for Burr, understood that he represented the past and Clinton the future. Moreover, Van Buren had begun a political code that guided future New York and national politics: the need to back official candi-dates through the regular organization. Yet Van Buren had an even more pri-vate concern; he had to protect his legal career from politics. Some local Bur-rites and Federalists, he told William Peter, were uttering "illiberal & unmanly remarks" that hurt his partnership with Van Alen.[13]

Except for Burr's defeat, the election settled little about partisan politics and led to a major political reshuffling of state politics. After the campaign, Hamilton's death in his notorious duel with Burr, followed by Burr's arrest for alleged treason in the Southwest, plunged the Little Band into disgrace. At the same time, the Lewisite-Clintonian alliance unravelled as the governor and his Federalist allies used the council to purge Clintonians. In response, the Clintonians aligned themselves with New York City Republicans, or the

"Martling-Men," and exploited Vice-President George Clinton's influence with President Jefferson to dominate federal patronage. Political matters sorted themselves out in the 1807 gubernatorial race. To oppose Lewis, Clintonians nominated the "Farmer's Boy," the young and capable Daniel D. Tompkins of Staten Island, a one-time Burrite and an associate Supreme Court justice at the time.[14]

Later, many critics would castigate Van Buren for reacting to events rather than anticipating them. This accusation was not true during this three-year period. Instead, he took the initiative through calculation and elimination. After severing his link to the now infamous Little Band, Van Buren sought to repair his relationship with its members as individuals. As one example, he defended William Peter against the state's charge that he was an accessory to murder when he served as Burr's second in the duel. On principle, Van Buren scorned Governor Lewis as a covert Federalist. That left the Clintonians, but Van Buren had to convince them that he was worth cultivating.[15]

Against this backdrop, Van Buren made himself invaluable to Columbia County Clintonians as a partisan organizer and propagandist. Part of this effort came from his innate political talents. But beyond that, Van Buren's experience as a lawyer contributed two components to his political aspirations: the ability to think logically and to present ideas persuasively. Van Buren set these attributes in motion during the 1805 assembly race. He became secretary of several Kinderhook Clintonian rallies, a delegate to the county caucus that nominated Van Alen, and headed his own losing campaign in a rancorous contest against the Lewisite-Federalist William W. Van Ness.[16]

Van Buren's political profile thus grew larger. At a time when Americans celebrated the Fourth of July as a major patriotic and social holiday, Kinderhook Clintonians honored "Martin Van Buren esq." by choosing him to read the Declaration of Independence and offer a celebratory toast. This recognition was a sign that Van Buren's Clintonian neighbors recognized that his legal and political talents were destined for more material preferment.[17]

Van Buren's maturity and confidence flowered with increased responsibility. During the 1806 congressional contest, he again directed the county Clintonian campaign and infused it with his own energy. As Federalist Charles Foote complained, Van Buren's "exertions" were "almost incredible"; he turned "an assured election into a hard struggle." Foote was correct. Van Alen beat Robert LeRoy Livingston by a narrow four-vote margin, 1721 to 1717.[18]

Van Buren's stature was even more pronounced in the jockeying that preceded the gubernatorial race. At the December 1806 Columbia Circuit Court session, he organized a corresponding committee comprised of attorneys to cooperate with other Clintonians in the upcoming "violent" struggle for "state supremacy." By February of 1807, the committee integrated tactics with other Clintonians in the Upper Hudson Valley and issued a public address calling on voters to reject Lewis. The main paragraphs in this address, especially a section attacking the governor for his aristocratic pretensions and rejection of republicanism, bore unmistakable signs of Van Buren's style and indicated how much he had guided the local contest in Tompkins's winning campaign.[19]

Van Buren had absorbed four important lessons over the past three years: a party required organization and management for success; his legal experience was invaluable in politics; a politician had to think strategically, not merely in terms of tactics; and a strict adherence to republican ideology could solve interparty factionalism. On a personal level, Van Buren was fulfilling a dream he had formed during his teenage years. He was knowledgeable about men and events and was able to meet influential politicians on equal terms. He felt the heady rush of directing campaigns, probed the extent of his political talents, and swayed people who could help him. Even so, Van Buren had gained nothing tangible from the Council of Appointment, the driving force of the state's patronage engine.[20]

But his neighbors and clients appreciated his aptitude for politics. In April of 1806, a "town-meeting" of Kinderhook "freeholders and inhabitants" selected Van Buren to his first public office as a fence viewer. This appointment, though apparently insignificant, was far more remarkable than it seemed and was destined to play a key role in his future. A fence viewer's duties included checking the proper boundaries and fences between farms, "meadows," and "vacant land," appraising violations, ordering repairs, and assessing fines for neglect. He was also accountable for noting and ordering payments for "any distress" and "damages" caused by straying "beasts" to fences and property. Van Buren's duties were rarely time-consuming, except during the spring when "floods and high tides" frequently "destroyed" fences. In such instances, he ascertained the condition of "partition fences" and demanded immediate mending. Pay ran six cents per mile for travel and twenty-five cents per report.[21]

This office, far short of the council's bountiful cornucopia, reinforced Van Buren's republicanism and bolstered his emerging career in law and politics. In Kinderhook, landlords, tenants, and freeholders were primarily concerned with agrarian ownership, land speculation, wills leaving propertied estates or intestates having no wills, the exact boundaries of property, tenanted farms without clear titles, communal pasture rights, even the possession of wandering cattle and sheep. These concerns formed the basis of many economic undertakings, political differences, and legal disputes. As a fence viewer, Van Buren had the opportunity to see these problems first-hand, mediate conflicts over questions of contributory negligence, and enhance his practice by impressing potential clients. From a political standpoint, fence viewing kept him in close contact with the farm community, his basic constituency, and indicated that he was a young man of promise. The imprecise nature of so many colonial grants and patents provided Van Buren with a fertile background to assert his republican values in later litigations with the Livingstons and Van Rensselaers.

Just as Van Buren had intended, law and politics formed a reciprocal relationship in his life. He used only a small part of his days politicking, since
campaigns were usually confined to a few months in the late winter and early
spring. As a result, his growing political fame attracted new clients without
detracting from his professional obligations. Van Buren added to his legal
prestige even more in February 1806. After a test administered by Albany attorneys Philip S. Parker and Daniel Whiting, Van Buren secured a license as a
counsellor of the state Supreme Court. Before, only Van Alen had that distinction. Now Van Buren enjoyed the privilege of conducting legal work before the Supreme Court, a privilege that increased both the volume of his
practice and his professional status. Van Buren wasted no time. In the court's
November 1806 term in Albany, he argued and won two procedural cases,
harbingers of a process that would make him the foremost attorney to practice in the state Supreme Court for the next two decades.[22]

Van Buren's partnership with Van Alen ended in 1808 when Van Alen assumed his congressional seat. Direct evidence of the firm's practice and
growth over the past four years is spotty. Van Buren left a few letters showing
that he sought legal business through De Witt Clinton and became an associate in some trials with Peter Van Schaack, William Van Schaack's son, and
William Peter Van Ness. Otherwise, the evidence consists of varying kinds of
incomplete records: Columbia County's partial docket listing forty-six of the
firm's cases between 1806 and 1808; a Legal Record Book Van Buren started
in late 1807, with notations on ninety-nine actions begun before the partnership dissolved; and a "Statement of Van Buren's Notes," prepared on December 24, 1808, which listed accounts receivable.[23]

Important questions remain unresolved. Although Van Buren wrote the
names of clients in his Legal Record Book, only a few of the docket's actions
are traceable. Perhaps not all or even a majority of his actions ended in court,
but he should have listed those that did in the Legal Record. Similarly, most
of the clients Van Buren noted in his "Statement" were duplicated in the Legal Record, but some were not. Perhaps the answer was that some clients paid
bills promptly. But Van Buren omitted others who did. The surviving records,
then, are incomplete, probably because Van Buren was an indifferent office-
manager who failed to keep full records and did not, therefore, disclose to future generations the full range of his legal work.[24]

Nonetheless, the existing data reveals a great deal. Little if any differences
appeared in the nature of the firm's practice after its first year. But the partners added more lucrative clients, mainly Clintonian small freeholders, along
with some Hudson Clintonian businessmen. Opposing attorneys were either
Federalists or Lewisites. During this period, Van Buren's most notable antago-
nist was Elisha Williams, a brilliant attorney, equally competent in civil and
criminal cases. Van Buren certainly respected his talents and recalled that "it
seemed scarcely possible to exceed [Williams's] skill in the examination of

witnesses or his addresses to the jury." In time, their encounters took on the aura of legend, particularly when Van Buren wrote that they were "employed in almost every cause" in the county. The legend was never true. Two men, no matter how proficient, could not have handled such a caseload.[25]

Yet even if Van Buren's memory was defective, his practice did amass considerable reputation and increased business. One comparison sufficiently judged his continued success. In the first year of operation, the partnership had earned $3,222.50; accounts receivable ran $1,584.33. Although Van Buren left no statement about net earnings at the end of 1808, the firm held $6,326 in accounts receivable, of which $4,496 had accrued in 1808 alone. The result indicated that the partners just about tripled their revenue. As a further sign of their standing, they raised fees from those of 1804, when they rarely billed as much as $60, to $100 and even $500 in 1808. Besides, the partner in question charged 1 percent interest per month on unpaid balances, amounting to $720. All in all, Van Buren's lawyering revealed how much his practice was a business within a market economy where compensation directly flowed from how much his clients were willing to pay. To place these figures in the context of the contemporary judicial system, state Supreme Court justices and the Court of Chancery's chancellor each earned $3,000 a year.[26]

Van Buren's belief in the classical republican definition of property as the lack of dependency on others now started to evolve toward the liberal republican emphasis on property as materialism and capital accumulation. In the fall of 1806, he multiplied his legal income to begin a life-long interest in real estate ventures. Taking advantage of a forced sheriff's sale in October, he bought a farm and tenements, along with a share in a Kinderhook gristmill, for $7, a price far below its true value. Later that month, he paid $50 for nine acres on Valatie Creek in the town of Kinderhook, part of the De Bruyn Patent.[27]

Both transactions were connected to Van Buren's involvement in the litigation over the De Bruyn and Baker-Flodden patents. In July of 1808, Van Buren sued for relief on behalf of several plaintiffs who claimed property in the De Bruyn Patent. Van Buren's brief asserted that the defendants, Daniel Frier and Peter Copper, illegally claimed De Bruyn properties adjacent to Kinderhook. Elisha Williams represented the Baker-Flodden heirs and assigns. The case was adjudicated in Columbia County Circuit Court, under presiding Supreme Court Justice Tompkins.

The proceedings of the case were unreported except for some newspaper squibs, leaving little means to chronicle actual content. But later appellate records permit a reconstruction. In his charge to the jury, Judge Tompkins followed four key contentions that Van Buren developed, largely from his experiences as a fence viewer. The construction of a boundary was "a question of law," not a fact for the jury to decide. The De Bruyn Patent contained the area in dispute. But the Baker-Flodden Patent, which Williams could not describe precisely, was "void" because it was "incapable of location." The defendants, whose claim rested on Baker-Flodden, did not have lawful rights under the doctrine of adverse possession, since they had lived on the land in question for the required twenty-year period.[28]

The jury found for the plaintiffs, partially on the indistinct bounds of Baker-Flodden, but chiefly due to Van Buren's reading of adverse possession. Under this doctrine of prescription in real property, if persons occupied land openly, continuously, and without challenge for twenty years, they gained title from the original holder. The sticking point was that Williams differed with Van Buren over whether the claimants had sufficient continuous possession to establish adverse possession. As a result, Williams appealed to the Supreme Court through a bill of exceptions in which he alleged that Judge Tompkins had misinstructed the jury based on Van Buren's brief.[29]

When the Supreme Court upheld Judge Tompkins and Van Buren, Williams filed a writ of error in the Court for the Trial of Impeachments and Correction of Errors, New York's highest branch of last resort. His case rested on two main grounds: the exact boundaries of the competing patents, and whether Tompkins had wrongly instructed the jury concerning adverse possession.[30]

While the issues remained in abeyance until the Court of Errors ruled in 1811, Van Buren's stress on adverse possession, even if he denied its applicability in this instance, anticipated his future strategy in redefining property law. In coming cases, he would couple adverse possession to the contention that patent and manorial lands were commodities that private individuals, unhindered by colonial restrictions, could buy and sell in a republican free market economy. On a more immediate level, his twin triumphs in the circuit and Supreme Court marked his initial victories in a significant property cause, while confirming his status as one of the more prominent attorneys in the county. On February 21, 1807, the twenty-five-year-old Van Buren felt secure enough in the law and politics to marry Hannah Hoes, a first cousin once removed, at the home of Judge Moses I. Cantine, her brother-in-law. Little evidence exists about her, except oral traditions and Van Buren's cryptic remarks that she was "modest and unassuming" with a "mild" disposition. Yet some facts are apparent. Hannah Hoes Van Buren was a representative Dutch-American wife and mother who avoided intruding on her husband's legal and political affairs. In the Van Buren tradition, she also quickly became pregnant. Almost nine months to the day after their marriage, on November 27, 1807, Hannah bore her first child, Abraham, named for his paternal grandfather. Van Buren's happiness reached a new level three months later when the Clintonian Council of Appointment officially ended his political apprenticeship. Recognizing his manifest ability and promise, the council named Van Buren surrogate of Columbia County.[31]

CHAPTER FOUR

Republicanism
in Law and Politics

*I*n 1808, surrogate Martin Van Buren, the county official responsible for probate and related matters, assumed office. Being surrogate was vital to the development of Van Buren's dual career. A surrogate touched almost all Columbia residents at some point in their lives. At death, in particular, he interacted with heirs and assigns, since real and personal estates were the main forms of property in Columbia County's agricultural and business communities. As such, the office allowed Van Buren to oversee and protect individual property rights, including those of women, and brought him into closer and more intimate association with his basic constituency, further cementing his political strength and becoming another source for future clients.

To administer this office, rooted in colonial Dutch and British law, Van Buren had to review earlier probate methods and settlements and study relevant statutes.[1] The *Laws of the State of New York* was explicit about Van Buren's duties. His multiple tasks included taking proofs of wills dealing with real and personal estates, as well as settling those estates. He granted letters of administration, made inventories, directed settlements of accounts involving estates, supervised the payments of all outstanding debts, disbursed legacies, and distributed the estates of intestates. Van Buren also ordered the sale and dispersal of the real estate of decedents and, if a minor was involved, supervised the sale of a testator's or intestate's real and personal property. Van Buren also appointed or removed guardians and regulated their activities to protect the rights of minors. For other underage heirs Van Buren enforced curtesy, the right a widower held during his lifetime to any real property his wife had owned separately, provided they had a lawful issue who might inherit the estate. For women, Van Buren enforced dower, that portion of an estate a deceased husband allowed his widow. On a related matter, Van Buren arranged the admeasurement of dower, which allowed an heir, on reaching majority, to rectify an unfair assignment of dower made during minority in which a wife received more than her legal one-third share of her husband's estate.

Surrogates also performed a judicial function through a county surrogate court, which held jurisdiction over persons who owned property and died within that county. The Court of Probates, a holdover from British practices, had authority over county residents and intestates who died in other counties, and nonresidents who died within the county; it possessed appellate jurisdiction over surrogate court, subject to Court of Chancery review. As for politics, a surrogate had some patronage. He appointed commissioners to inventory an estate if a will or an intestate did not specify the nature of that estate. Van Buren transcribed these activities in six indexed books, open to public inspection for a fee, and filed them in Albany.[2]

The legislature regulated surrogates in order to assure heirs and assigns that estates were fairly apportioned and protected by statutes. Other statutes barred a surrogate from representing litigants in his own court, and set costs and fixed stipends for every function a surrogate undertook. These emoluments ran from a low of "twelve and an half cent" for administering an oath, to a high of "$2.50" for "hearing and determining" contested wills.[3]

While the legal documents a surrogate wrote were relatively simple, the procedures were technical. Van Buren had to gather facts surrounding each case, value assets, set a just distribution of those assets, determine ownership, and satisfy heirs, assigns, creditors, and debtors. If situations warranted, he consulted and researched earlier dispositions of wills to ensure conformity with settled regulations and previous dispositions.[4] By the middle of 1808, Van Buren was settling into a daily routine of conducting surrogate affairs, running a burgeoning legal practice, caring for his family, and plotting a political course.

But one new aspect of Van Buren's professional life, his growing docket before the Supreme Court of Judicature, placed him on an even larger stage than that of the Columbia hustings. The multifaceted Supreme Court, a modified carryover from the colonial era, had broad appellate jurisdiction to hear arguments, motions, and rulings on points of law raised in various inferior courts and in its own proceedings. These fell into two categories: the court placed "enumerated business," points of law that shaped the final outcome of a case, on its calendar and noted the action in records of declarations and pleadings; "nonenumerated business" sought procedural rulings that did not involve a case's merits, such as changes of venue, orders for out-of-state testimony, and a variety of motions to set aside or enforce various judgments or executions. Clerks recorded each category in the court's "Judgement Rolls," generally a report of the entire proceedings. In bailable civil cases, the court permitted a defendant special bail, secured by two sureties at double the plaintiff's debts or damages, or common bail, in which the defendant signed a promissory note.[5]

The majority of appeals in civil and criminal cases came from circuit courts. One of the parties filed a demurrer to evidence that admitted the facts in the case, but alleged that the jury or judge erred on those facts. An attorney could then file a number of motions. A special case accepted the jury verdict, but contended the evidence did not sustain the alleged facts and reserved a question of law for the Supreme Court to determine. A bill of exceptions challenged the trial judge's decisions, rulings, or instructions to the jury that contradicted either points of law or the facts themselves. A party could also make a motion for a new trial on two separate grounds: irregularity, defined as "improper notice of jury, improper jury, or misconduct by the winning party or jurors"; or on the case's merits, consisting of new evidence, a verdict that contradicted the evidence or law, "improper rulings on evidence," or incorrect damages. Other court functions included "real actions," dealing with titles or possessions of real property, and "mixed actions," dealing with recovery of real property or ejectment from real property. In all such instances, the court had extensive supervisory powers over inferior courts, public officials, and various litigants through sundry writs, usually executed by a county sheriff.[6]

The Supreme Court's chief original jurisdiction lay in certain cases under public law relating to public officials. These were mainly *quo warranto* actions entered by the state attorney general under common law forms, which alleged that individuals or corporations had violated some government functions, engaged in fraudulent public land transactions, or usurped a legislative charter. The attorney general could also seek a writ of *scire facias* over other violations of charters "obtained by mistake or fraud."[7]

The court had other duties as well. It was composed of one chief justice and four associates named by the Council of Appointment; they remained in office, unless impeached, until the age of sixty. Each presided over a separate circuit court that tried jury trials in county seats and heard major criminal cases in courts of oyer and terminer. The legislature mandated that the judges hold four regular terms a year, rotating between Albany and New York City and later Utica.[8]

The state constitution modeled the state's highest appellate court, the Court for the Trial of Impeachments and the Correction of Errors, on the British House of Lords. Combining judicial, administrative, and political roles, this court consisted of the senate president, the senators, the chancellor of the Court of Chancery, and the five Supreme Court judges. Appeals derived from writs of error in Supreme Court judgments and courts of probates, and final decrees in equity and discretional orders from chancery. A majority of the court's members formed a quorum, but a binding decision needed the concurrence of at least ten members. The senate president presided and cast the deciding vote in ties. To prevent conflicts of interest, the chancellor and Supreme Court justices could list reasons for their decrees and judgments, but not vote in such cases.[9]

Van Buren was a consummate lawyer within the bounds of this appellate system, scoring a record number of winning cases that few of his peers matched. His professional reputation soared so high that Elisha Williams and other Federalists sought his aid as co-counsel. As an early example of this effectiveness, Van Buren, in 1808 alone, the first year in which he argued cases without Van Alen, won twenty-three actions worth $13,545.27, plus $500.31 for damages and costs. Many were mundane, as the February 1808 case of *Peter Vosburgh v. Abraham Vosburgh,* a nonenumerated debt collection from the Columbia Circuit. Van Buren stood for the plaintiff against Abraham Vosburgh, both of whom were Kinderhook residents. He filed a simple brief with the facts outlined, as did Silvanus Miller, Abraham Vosburgh's attorney. Associate Judge John Woodworth ruled for Van Buren, scribbling an order for the defendant to pay the debt, costs, and damages, but he handed down no opinion to sustain the decision.[10]

In many ways, this case epitomized much of the court's operations. The Supreme Court lacked an official reporter until 1804 when a new statute authorized the chief justice to select such a person and empowered the court to print cases "deemed important" as "conveniently" as possible "after the expiration of each term." George Caines, the first reporter, published selective enumerated business. These reports set the state's case law authority, which judges and attorneys cited as precedents in subsequent judgments and briefs. James Kent, who succeeded Morgan Lewis as chief justice in 1804, replaced Caines with William Johnson. Johnson was far more thorough than Caines and set a demanding standard for future reporters. But the judges, outside of Kent, often did not treat their opinions in a professional manner. They generally allowed Kent to issue a *per curiam* in enumerated business for the entire court, which Johnson often reported. In cases of nonenumerated business, which were unreported, judges normally signed a judgment without citing relevant points of law. Politics and judicial philosophy also complicated the system. The appointive judges, divided between Federalists and Republicans, disagreed about how much their decisions should reflect or alter the common law.[11]

Although *Vosburgh v. Vosburgh* did not set case law because it was unreported, Van Buren won over two hundred similar actions. His reported cases in *Johnson's Report,* a number that grew every year from 1808 to 1828, did become guides for comparable cases and analogous legal questions through *stare decisis.* Here, Van Buren was at his best. In the largest professional sense, appellate cases demanded expert knowledge of the law; briefs were pared down to the core of relevant facts and presented in a succinct manner. A master of this process, Van Buren prepared briefs with painstaking care and exhibited a keen knowledge of the law on both sides of the issue.

Van Buren's methods had even more significant dimensions. The early decades of the nineteenth century were a time when American lawyers and judges were forging fresh and lasting legal doctrines that redefined common law and outlined innovative approaches in jurisprudence. As an attorney infused with classical republicanism, Van Buren helped shape new departures in New York's legal and political culture. These were most crucial during the formative years of the new nation, especially in cases involving the nature of changing social institutions, partisan commitments, and marketplace developments, chiefly in contract, property, and commercial law. In the process, Van Buren wove his ideology into a cohesive pattern that mixed judicial principles with political programs. This endeavor defined him as a lawyer-politician and anticipated his role in the Jacksonian Movement. Van Buren also formed close personal contacts with a number of other attorneys who practiced before the Supreme Court and the Court of Errors. Van Buren's appellate work thus became an inseparable ingredient in his political career.[12]

Van Buren's first reported action appeared in the third volume of *Johnson's Reports,* the May 1808 case of *Wilson and Gibbs v. Ephraim Reed,* out of the Greene County Circuit before Chief Justice Kent. The litigation was significant in two ways. In economic terms, the facts illustrated fresh marketplace transactions in the old Dutch-American river counties of the state's Middle District, a political division encompassing most of the Upper Hudson River Valley. From a legal standpoint, the case began Van Buren's long effort to redefine common law contracts in a free market system.[13]

A circuit court jury had found Reed liable to pay Wilson and Gibbs $80 for their share of a hogshead of rum, which a sheriff seized and sold to Reed to satisfy a debt against Gibbs, a co-owner of the rum with Wilson. Van Buren appealed for Reed on the grounds of trover, the remedy for wrongful interference with the goods of another. Reed, Van Buren asserted, was an innocent purchaser who had honestly made a contract; his intent was to "acquire a title to the whole property" through a sheriff's sale, an intent the sheriff accepted. Williams, representing Wilson and Gibbs, replied that the sale made Reed a "co-tenant" of the property, not the sole owner, and responsible for satisfying their stake in the property. Justice Ambrose Spencer, ruling for the court, upheld the jury. Reed was liable for what he had no right to sell.[14]

This loss meant that Van Buren failed in his initial attempt to establish the will theory of contracts as a new precedent. This legal doctrine sought to redefine contractual terms based on the private intent of the parties to that contract. The traditional elements in a contract were straightforward and featured three components: the contracting parties must have the capacity to make an agreement; the contracting parties must have mutually consented to the agreement; and the contracting parties must have arranged consideration, something fungible or an obligation of some sort, that the makers of the agreement exchanged.

Van Buren accepted these requirements. But he also tried to modernize older concepts of contracts, which judged such transactions on abstract principles of fairness, guided by the amorphous natural law of equity. Through the will theory of contracts, Van Buren maintained that individuals who made a contract, in this case Reed and the sheriff, had freely entered a legitimate bargain. This theory, which assumed that equality existed between the makers of the agreement, argued that intent was the ruling guide for legal contracts. Consequently, the three elements in a contract remained viable but were modified. These modifications specifically involved intent, the key to the agreement, and consideration, which judged the bargain not on fungible terms or obligations, but on whether the parties had actually concluded the agreement.

The will theory of contracts reflected classical republicanism in that it checked the power of the judiciary through limited government, for judges must honor the makers' intent. Likewise, judges and juries had no role in determining equity, since all economic arrangements were private and the contracting parties were equal. Van Buren's belief in legal instrumentalism, which visualized the law as a utilitarian instrument of policy, not a set of immutable principles, was another avenue through which will theory affected the common law. Domesticating the common law, implementing the will theory of contracts, utilizing legal instrumentalism, and altering equity, would all become key concepts in Van Buren's two-fold career.[15]

These devices also formed links to Van Buren's gradual acceptance of selected aspects of liberal republicanism. Such concepts did not necessarily contradict classical republicanism, but rather modified its principles in fresh directions. Intent and privatism redefined individualism and liberty as unfettered commercial development and the personal accumulation of wealth. Legal instrumentalism suggested that older patterns of human behavior, including deference, authority, elitism, and even civic virtue, were secondary to human progress, which was secured through popular sovereignty and determined public policy. As a result, legal instrumentalism vindicated the evolution of self-sacrifice into self-interest. Van Buren's goal that the common law should reflect American realities strengthened his argument that the law must adapt to new conditions, particularly in an emerging free market economy. By implication, Van Buren's adaptation of classical republicanism to liberal republicanism also allowed citizens the flexibility to adjust the law and politics through popular sovereignty in ways that would create the possibility of a free and independent nation liberated from past restrictions.[16]

In the midst of these developments, Van Buren remained an insignificant political figure. Contrary to his historical image as a man obsessed with politics, Van Buren's main interests between 1807 and 1811 lay in expanding his legal practice, earning a secure livelihood, performing surrogate duties, and solidifying his professional standing. Only then was politics important. His eventual political ascent, nevertheless, was a direct consequence of the growing stature he gained from the law.[17]

Nothing came easily, however. Over those four years, Van Buren kept a low political profile in an unpredictable partisan environment. De Witt Clinton, with some Federalist support, and Governor Daniel Tompkins, backed by the former Burrites, the Martling–Men, grappled for party leadership in a struggle that ruptured the state organization. Two major issues divided them. Tompkins favored President Jefferson's 1807 Embargo Act, which Clinton opposed because it virtually ended New York's export trade. Tompkins endorsed Madison for president, but George Clinton defied the party's official congressional caucus nomination of Madison and launched an insurgent bid for the office. Federalists were the chief beneficiaries of this internecine Republican warfare. Appropriating De Witt Clinton's arguments against the Embargo, Federalists gained public support as defenders of New York's farmers and exporters.[18]

These problems placed Van Buren in a personal crisis. As a lawyer, he knew that desperate local farmers, his core constituency, were flaunting the unpopular Embargo through a variety of stratagems in order to make a living through extensive but illegal smuggling with Canada. In addition, he could not choose between Tompkins and Clinton because conditions were in a state of flux. Consequently, Van Buren decided that the best decision was no decision at all. During the 1808 campaign he did not participate in Van Alen's failed bid for reelection, keeping lines open to Tompkins and Clinton and remaining passive on the presidential question.[19]

Instead, Van Buren's law practice occupied his time. In the Supreme Court's August term in 1808, he won for the plaintiff against Williams in *Jackson, ex. dem. Whitbeck and Gardiniere, v. Deyo*, a minor property case that concerned the validity of a will. The case of *Jackson, ex. dem. Vandeuzen and Others, v. Scissam* during the November term was more significant. Van Buren joined Williams against Abraham Van Vechten and Ebenezer Foote in a vital property case for freeholders in the Kinderhook Patent. Chief Justice Kent, in circuit court, had instructed the jury to sustain a squatter on the basis of adverse possession. In their appeal, Williams and Van Buren, using Van Buren's background as a fence viewer to buttress their brief, stressed that their clients, in erecting a "possession fence" and performing "repeated acts of cutting wood," had established that their property claims should "prevail" against a "mere intruder without any title." As for adverse possession, Williams and Van Buren argued that it did not apply since the squatter had not fulfilled the twenty-year standard required for a good title. Justice Smith Thompson, for the full court, supported Van Buren and Williams, ruled that Kent had "misdirected" the jury, and granted their motion for a new trial.[20]

By late summer of 1808, Van Buren had established his reputation as an effective lawyer and a promising, if stalled, politician. He also realized that his thriving practice had reached its optimum limits in Kinderhook. Although he had low social origins, minimal legal education, and an initial practice in a small firm—not normally elements for success in his profession—Van Buren, with his growing family, needed more clients, especially more lucrative ones. Hudson, some fifteen miles from Kinderhook, had both. Relocation had additional advantages. The bulk of his court work as surrogate was in Hudson. Hudson was also a river city, with convenient sailing packets and stage lines for his frequent trips to Albany and New York City for Supreme Court appearances.[21]

In January 1809, Van Buren inserted a notice in the *Hudson Bee* that announced, "M. Van Buren has removed his office from the town of Kinderhook to the city of Hudson." His new residence, a house on Warren Street he purchased along with its land for $1,000, was "nearly opposite the court house." As was the custom of almost all businesses at the time, including those of attorneys, Van Buren used part of the house for his law office and the rest as a family home.[22]

Van Buren's practice flourished in these new circumstances, despite the greater number of attorneys in Hudson and the keener competition. During his first two years, he noted nearly as many new actions in his Legal Record Book as he had noted in the previous two. While the number of cases Van Buren placed on the docket of the Columbia Circuit declined in each of these years, the figure was deceptive because of his additional duties as surrogate.[23]

According to newspaper notices and surviving documents, a considerable increase in official business took place under Van Buren's direction. William W. Van Ness and James Van Alen, the previous surrogates over the past seven years, had infrequently published public notices of estate or inheritance matters. By contrast, Van Buren averaged a new notice almost every two weeks in the *Hudson Bee* and the *Catskill Recorder* of Greene County across the river. Other duties were more extensive, as the few extant records from 1808 to 1813 demonstrate: he filed forty-two guardianships, ninety-five letters of administration, and held surrogate court on eighty-two occasions, several over questions of dower and curtesy.[24]

Fortunately for Van Buren, moving to Hudson lost him few of his old clients. A large number, particularly his Dutch-American connections, continued to consult him about their complex land dealings, or when they had marital difficulties requiring mediation rather than legal resolution. As before, the majority were freehold farmers, but he also added some Hudson businessmen. With a few exceptions, the types of his cases were generally the same. While most were still small civil causes, Van Buren gained new ones that dealt with debts and promissory notes.

Real estate was another constant in Van Buren's endeavors. At a sheriff's sale, Van Buren acquired about forty acres of farm land in Schodack, Rensselaer County, from two clients who owed him $200 for legal services. Van Buren also bought a Kinderhook lot, located in the Great Possession, for the nominal cost of one dollar, to cover his costs in this continued litigation.[25]

Nor did Van Buren's caseload before the Supreme Court slacken. In twenty nonenumerated pleadings in 1809, he requested and won new trials for his clients. The four Van Buren lost in the August term in Albany were enumerated test cases, again affecting property rights. One, *Jackson, ex. dem. Starr and Wife, v. Richmond*, was perfunctory. Van Buren requested a rule permitting an ejectment proceeding to check the rival claims of two lessors. In overruling him the court said that an ejectment action was an improper remedy.[26]

Three other cases, *Jackson, ex dem. Cantine and Others, v. Stills, (George Clark, tenant), Jackson, ex dem. Cantine and Others, v. Stiles, (Buel, tenant),* and *Jackson, ex dem. Van Gorden, v. Stiles, (Hollenbeck, tenant),* were connected and gave Van Buren an opportunity to lessen the dependency of tenants, widen their opportunities for private economic gain, and weaken landlords. Each action concerned a possible fraudulent colonial land deal of some 100,000 acres that covered most of the modern counties of Schoharie and Greene. Several settlers, who considered themselves freeholders rather than tenants, hired Van Buren and Foote to test if George Clark, their purported landlord, could eject them. Van Buren and Foote argued that the court had jurisdiction over Clark, "a British subject, and not a citizen of the United States." The motion Van Buren and Foote filed, a nonsuit, meant that the court must rule against Clark, because he had not appeared to defend himself in the first two cases when the plaintiffs counterclaimed against his ejectments. Clark's attorneys disagreed. They contended that Clark was an alien who had a choice between federal or state courts under the United States Constitution and pertinent federal statutes, and that Clark favored adjudication in the federal district court. Judge Kent ruled for the majority and granted Clark's motion, but stayed the ejectments until the federal court acted. Clark's claims remained in litigation until the 1840s, when the descendants of the plaintiffs in the original cases won, long after Van Buren retired from the law.[27]

Van Buren's efforts in the November 1809 Supreme Court term in New York City saw him on familiar ground. Again trying to modify the common law, he filed an irregularity motion in *Tobey v. Barber* for a new trial case that began in the Columbia Circuit under Judge Spencer. Spencer had instructed the jury to ignore the oral or parol evidence that Baker had accepted turnpike shares in lieu of money as "an absolute payment" for a lease. Van Buren admitted that under the common law, "parol evidence" was "never admissible to vary the substance of, or to contradict" a written contract. But, he added, "where there was sufficient evidence to show" that the parol evidence was not fraudulent, Spencer should have allowed its introduction, especially to consider intent. In a *per curiam,* the court refused to consider the will theory of contracts, denied the motion, and sustained the common law's "general rule" that a written contract could not "be explained or contradicted by parol."[28]

Another case, *Jackson, ex dem. Van Dusen and Others, v. Van Dusen,* tested an ejectment in Canaan, Columbia County, again over property rights. Van Buren requested a ruling for a new trial based on an irregularity in the interpretation of a will, in order to support the adverse possession claim of a Kinderhook resident who had occupied farm land for more than twenty years. Again, the court ruled against Van Buren, stressing that he had not documented the number of years required to establish a claim under adverse possession.[29]

Not all of Van Buren's affairs met with such negative results. Outside the courtroom, Van Buren's legal flair increased his political importance among fellow Republicans. In late 1808, Francis Stebbins, editor of Hudson's Federalist newspaper the *Northern Whig,* stirred a partisan turmoil. Stebbins charged that Clintonian Sheriff John C. Hogeboom, the party's highest-ranking official in Columbia County, had systematically bilked the public by overcharging fees on writs and executions. Hogeboom immediately brought suit for libel. To his astonishment, he found that Stebbins had hired Williams as his attorney, even though Williams had earlier advised Hogeboom that his fees were legitimate within relevant statutes. At that point, Hogeboom engaged Van Buren. The negotiations that followed reveal a fine example of Van Buren's skills. He started by writing a polite letter for Hogeboom requesting Williams to reaffirm his advice. Van Buren then approached Jacob R. Van Rensselaer, who acted for Williams. They constructed Williams's conciliatory reply reaffirming his initial opinion, though with minor reservations. Shortly after, the three lawyers met to find a resolution entailing the least embarrassment to all the parties, since the issue raised partisan questions about their respective motives. In January 1810, each side published simultaneous but separate public letters. Stebbins acknowledged his error; Hogeboom dropped his suit.[30]

Nevertheless, this episode yielded three losers. Stebbins was the first, because he had forfeited public confidence by admitting to a mistake. Williams was next, for he had tainted his legal reputation. Last was Hogeboom, who did not unequivocally prove his honesty. Only Van Buren emerged with honor. He had displayed his ability to mediate while standing firm, earned Hogeboom's gratitude, and diminished Williams's repute. At the same time, Van Buren fulfilled another of his key legal and political priorities: defending Republican officeholders as representatives of the people.[31]

On other political matters, Van Buren continued to remain circumspect. By early winter of 1809, however, the Embargo and its consequences had widened the chasm among Republicans and further revived the Federalist party. Van Buren knew that he could no longer hedge his bets or tend simply to his professional needs; he accepted an invitation to be the main speaker at a pro-Embargo public rally. Conscious of his role and prepared like a careful attorney, he had arrived with extracts from Republican newspapers and government reports. Although his exact words were unreported, the *Bee* noted that his speech was "of unquestionable excellence," casting "the highest credit upon his talents as an orator" and his "patriotism."[32]

Van Buren's words set off a brief but volatile exchange with the Federalists. The *Northern Whig,* twisting his words, accused him of war-mongering and threatening to "tar and feather" Administration critics, a charge the *Bee* refuted. But the controversy did Van Buren no harm. In defending Jefferson, Van Buren had added to his partisan importance in local politics.[33]

What was less certain was whether or not Van Buren had sorted out his conflicting loyalties to Tompkins and Clinton. Fortunately for Van Buren, the necessity for making such a choice became less of a problem in February of 1809, when Clinton sponsored a set of state senate resolutions that justified the Embargo and attacked Federalists. Along with Van Buren, nearly all Republicans approved Clinton's sentiments, except for the former Burrites, the Martling-Men. They rejected Tompkins's pleas for party unity and demanded Clinton's ouster from Republican ranks. Van Buren had none of this. At another party meeting, he toasted the unity of "the Republican cause," steadfast "in principles as the needle to the pole."[34]

Although the double uncertainty over foreign policy and endemic party factionalism hounded Republicans for the rest of the year, for Van Buren, 1810 was a good year. On February 18, Hannah bore a second child, a second son named John for her father. In the early spring, Van Buren also strengthened his practice. He found a junior partner, Cornelius Miller, already well-established in Hudson and the son of a prominent county politician and banker.[35]

Based on surviving court records and Van Buren's haphazard legal records, he had been quite busy even before this arrangement. In 1809, he had handled fourteen cases in the Columbia Circuit and held five sessions of surrogate court. He also settled twenty-five pending actions in the courts of common pleas and general sessions and began fifty-eight new ones. They typically included actions for assault and battery, debt collection, and ejectment; motions to various courts to collect promissory notes and reduce bails; and several *capias* requests, the process of petitioning the court for writs requiring the sheriff to take defendants into custody or to issue subpoenas for witnesses. How much Van Buren earned was unclear. Remaining a casual record keeper, he listed some fees, retainers, and judgments, but left others unrecorded. Accordingly, his exact earnings are impossible to ascertain, and only indirect evidence indicates the breadth of his old practice and the new firm's business. Yet, based on judgments the new partners secured from the Supreme Court, their income almost doubled within two years. In 1810 and 1811, the firm appeared and won forty-nine actions, with several involving substantial cases worth from $6,000 to $10,000.[36]

During the May 1810 New York City term, Van Buren's growing fame attracted a new type of lucrative commercial client in *Van Alen and Others, v. Vanderpool and Others.* Van Buren filed an *assumpsit,* an extension of trespass, or a motion that alleged that one party had breached an implied or explicit contract or agreed in either oral or written form to pay something of value to another. He contended that Schodack shipowners, in accepting a cargo of

300 bushels of wheat for delivery and sale in the city, took ownership under the will theory of contracts and were responsible for the purchase price, even though the factor to whom they sold the wheat had become insolvent. Based on these conditions, the shipowners' fault to complete the transaction, not the factor's insolvency, governed the case. The court sustained Van Buren.[37]

In making intent the key to the cause, the court endorsed the will theory of contracts and denied to itself the power to stymie a private agreement freely made between equal individuals. As a result, the judges accepted four aspects of Van Buren's reading of classical republicanism: private choice, equality, judicial restraint, and the adaptation of the common law to new conditions. At the same time, this decision opened the way to liberal republicanism through Van Buren's stress on individual rights, unhindered economic transactions, and commercial expansion. Furthermore, the ruling anticipated future developments in tort law. A tort, a private or public wrong in which a defendant harmed a plaintiff's property or person subject to damages, was not yet a discrete field. By accepting Van Buren's brief that the factor's insolvency was not germane, the court began to set in motion the concept that eventually formed modern tort law, that is, the idea that damages were linked to fault and beyond the judiciary's traditional equity jurisdiction.[38]

Van Buren was just as busy advocating three notable actions during the August term in Albany. Another shipping case, *Colt and Colt v. M'Mechan,* involved damages to a cargo and extended the previous finding about the will theory of a contract's validity. Judge Spencer, in the Columbia Circuit Court, had instructed the jury to ignore a change in the wind that prevented the captain from delivering goods. Van Buren, acting with Federalist Josiah Hoffman against Williams, sought a new trial through a bill of exceptions. Spencer's "misdirection" was "against the evidence," they argued, and negated a valid agreement. More to the point, their clients were due "expectation damages," the money they anticipated since both parties to the contract had equality in its formation. Williams countered that a "sudden failing of the wind" contributed to the problem, but the captain was more to blame because he had overloaded the vessel. Van Buren and Hoffman disagreed. The "weight of evidence" proved the vessel was not "overloaded." They also cited a precedent that "the sudden failure of the wind" was "the act of God," not negligence on the captain's part. Thus the court could not mitigate a legitimate contract. The judges ruled for Van Buren and Hoffman on these grounds.[39]

Van Slyck v. Hogeboom, a debt collection case, furnished another example of how Van Buren protected party officeholders. The court agreed with Van Buren that his client, Sheriff Hogeboom, was denied full recovery of a judgment against a debtor because he had escaped as a *non est inventus,* a person not found, before the jury made an award. But the justices decided the issue was moot and refused to grant a new trial since the debtor was insolvent.[40]

In the third and last action, *Denton and Others v. Noyes,* Van Buren tried to

protect a fellow Republican party attorney from possible malpractice and dis-
barment. Williams sought on irregularity to set aside a judgment and quash a
writ of *fieri facias,* which ordered the sheriff to satisfy a judgment levied
against John L. Noyes of New York City, even though the writ had been issued but not served. According to Williams, Hezekiah L. Hosmer, Noyes's
lawyer, had accepted the judgment without consulting Noyes or having his
"power of attorney." Van Buren and John Henry, his associate in many future
cases, contended for the plaintiffs that the judgment and writ were proper.
The court had every right to assume that when an attorney appeared, his
client had given him the authority to act. Judge Kent sustained Van Buren
and Henry, yet sympathized with Noyes and implicitly censured Hosmer.
Nevertheless, he admitted that the vague wordings of relevant statutes prevented any remedy.[41]

Returning to New York City for the November term, Van Buren continued to press his campaign to modify the common law and diminish the
power of landlords. The facts in *Jackson, ex dem. Van Alen and Others, v. Vosburgh*
provided him with such an opportunity. Reviving an earlier evidence question, Van Buren now convinced the judges to accept oral evidence to prove
that his client was a freeholder not a tenant.[42]

Van Buren also triumphed in a second action that reemphasized the will
theory of contracts. Thomas Addis Emmet, an Irish émigré and one of New
York City's leading Clintonian members of the bar, was his co-counsel in
Wendover and Hinton v. Hogeboom and Others, an *assumpsit* about contracting
parties in commercial law. They persuaded the court that "a regular bill of sale
[was] not essential to transfer the property in a vessel, but the same passes by
delivery, like any other chattel." Their clients, the sellers, had by intent completed the "transfer of the property" through "contract and delivery." The
court, through a *per curiam,* agreed.[43]

Van Buren was on less firm ground in *Nichols v. Ingersoll,* which embraced
multiple issues of trespass, assault and battery, false imprisonment, due process,
and civil liberties. An agent of Pierpoint Edwards, a Connecticut resident and
Nichols's bail surety, broke into his home and forcefully attempted to trans-
port him from Greene County to Connecticut. Nichols managed to escape.
At a subsequent trial in the Greene County Circuit, a jury found for Edwards
on his claim that under Connecticut court practices a special bail "might take
their principle when they pleased." In their appeal, Van Buren and John
Woodward, a Federalist co-counsel, offered the argument that the power of
bail was derived not from any agreement between the bail and the principal
but from the court. Since the Connecticut court could not authorize the bail
to seize the principal where it lacked jurisdiction, the seizure was illegal and
ignored the judicial principle of due process. But Justice Thompson, speaking
for the majority, sustained Williams's interpretation of old common law
forms; the power of bail did not depend on the authority or process of the
court. Bails, according to precedent, held "their principle always upon a

string, which they may pull whenever they please, and surrender him in their discharge."[44]

During this busy period Van Buren tended to other needs as well. He continued to invest his professional earnings in Kinderhook real estate and remained an active surrogate. He was also deep in study for admission to the Court of Chancery. According to court regulations, Van Buren had the requisite experience to qualify for an examination, administered by two masters in chancery, to determine if he had "sufficient learning and ability" to practice equity. On December 15, 1810, after Gerrit Yates Lansing and Isaac Hansen had tested him, Van Buren gained a solicitor in chancery license. With this privilege, the primary step toward becoming a counsellor in chancery, Van Buren extended his practice, although he could only prepare "not plead" causes.[45]

Equity, through a long history of intricate developments drawn from British ecclesiastical antecedents, differed from the common law with its emphasis on court decisions and judgments. Equity involved hypothetical rules of justice and fairness, somewhat analogous to the Roman-Dutch code of ethical conduct. Using remedies where the common law was inadequate to settle issues, the New York Court of Chancery wrote its own rules, had special forms of evidence, motions, and pleadings, and wielded enormous discretional powers through injunctions, restraining orders, and subpoenas. In seeking justice on both sides of litigation, the chancellor, the sole judge who decided cases without a jury, had jurisdiction over a wide range of causes and actions: these included marital relationships; status of minors and widows; disputes over the use, ownership, and foreclosure of mortgaged property; sales by religious organizations; the nature, function, and property of legislative-chartered corporations; rights of the physically or mentally impaired; supervision of specific performances in contracts; depositions that attempted to ascertain fairness; and naming receivers for failed banks. Chancery consisted of one appointed chancellor, a number of administrative registers, clerks, and examiners, along with three masters in chancery who had exclusive rights to examine accounts and "tax costs," depositing them through registers in designated Albany and New York City banks. County sheriffs served as officers of the court and executed chancery orders.[46]

Many New Yorkers viewed the Court of Chancery with more hostility than any other inherited British legal institutions. They believed that chancery was beyond public control, since the court centralized too much power in one nonelected chancellor, and contradicted the basic civil right of a trial by jury to decide issues of fact as well as law. As such, they attacked chancery as a relic of feudalism committed to traditional authority with indeterminate powers and totally out of step with popular sovereignty and procedural due process. While Van Buren shared these objections, he respected chancery as an integral part of the judiciary. Even so, he sought to remedy the scope of equity through statutes formed under legal instrumentalism and the will theory of contracts, much as he attempted to do with the common law.

Yet, as future events proved, his position would spark disagreements with more radical members of his party.[47]

Van Buren delayed appearing in chancery until October 15, 1811, a full eleven months after securing his solicitor's license, because of heavy involvement in the Supreme Court. During that period, he won twenty-five nonenumerated actions scattered in the Albany and New York terms.[48]

At the same time, Van Buren's labor in lower courts enhanced his political prospects. The libel trail of *Thomas v. Croswell* in the Washington County Circuit was such an instance. Roger S. Skinner, who had recently met Van Buren, requested his aid as a co-counsel for Clintonian state treasurer David Thomas. The case, which they won, was less noteworthy than its major consequence. A closeness developed between Van Buren and Skinner, which their mutual partisan affinities helped deepen over the years. This relationship typified how Van Buren's profession accentuated the personal coalitions that would form his Albany Regency.[49]

Van Buren's efforts for Thomas added to his reputation as a defender of party officials in trouble and led to another case associated with an eminent leader, Judge Moses Cantine, his wife's brother-in-law. In the Columbia Circuit, Cantine sued Nathan Elliott, printer of the Federalist *Catskill Eagle,* for libel. "The cause," according to the Republican *Catskill Recorder,* "was managed and argued with much ability on both sides." Williams, Elliott's attorney, again lost to Van Buren who "substantiated his cause."[50]

While Van Buren's law practice still occupied most of his attention, his political passivity had ended. With Federalists gaining strength, due to President Madison's divisive trade sanctions, intraparty factionalism ceased. In the gubernatorial race of 1810, De Witt Clinton endorsed Tompkins's renomination along with John L. Broome's selection for lieutenant governor.[51]

The imperative of party unity now gave Van Buren a plausible reason to support both Tompkins and Clinton, and he managed Tompkins's campaign in Columbia County, much to Williams's chagrin. While scoffing at Van Buren's "inflated" pride and "impertinence," Williams unwittingly paid tribute to Van Buren's ability. He was, Williams wrote, "in comparison to Most of his Co-adjutors" truly "great—if he is able to do anything out of Hudson for his party, he should travel far." With so much at stake, each side engaged in extensive electoral fraud by filing temporary deeds to qualify tenants for voting. But while the Federalists managed to carry Columbia through more effective chicanery than the Republicans, Tompkins scored a decisive statewide triumph with 54 percent of the total votes cast.[52]

By February 1811, however, rancorous political and economic events disordered Van Buren's position when Congress failed to recharter the Bank of the United States. Three groups immediately clamored for state chartered banks to fill the void. The legislature tabled two, a Martling-sponsored bank to counter the Clintonian-dominated Manhattan Company, and the proposed Bank of America, capitalized at $6M, from mainly Federalist stockholders in the defunct Bank of the United States. Instead, the legislature incorporated a third, formed by Albany businessmen. At once, the Martling-Men, without corroborating facts, accused Clinton of double-dealing. Clinton, they said, bartered future support for the Bank of America in exchange for Federalist backing of his bid for lieutenant governor to replace Broome, who had just died. When the legislative caucus did nominate Clinton, the Martling-Men scorned party regularity and selected their own candidate, Marius Willett. In response, the Federalists ran Nicholas Fish.[53]

Van Buren's choice was easy. He championed Clinton, the party's regular nominee, and stressed the need for an outpouring of "manly, vigorous and zealous support." But Clinton's subsequent victory did not ease Van Buren's uncertainty about his own political future. While Tompkins was finally emerging as a power on his own, Columbia Republicans were still Clintonian. Again, the cautious Van Buren avoided an unequivocal position until local voters made their choice. Such indecision, however, left him vulnerable to Clinton's often self-destroying ambitions, especially when the banking question resurfaced.[54]

Van Buren's legal practice, on the other hand, flourished even more. During the winter of 1810–1811, new work came his way through his off-and-on friendship with William Peter Van Ness. When Van Ness's father died, William Peter chose Van Buren to probate the estate, and they began to exchange friendly letters.[55] Van Buren's efforts on behalf of William Peter accrued to Van Buren's benefit through Columbia County's commercial expansion and their mutual connection with the Bank of Hudson, which the Republican party had chartered in the 1806 legislature to counter the Federalist Bank of Columbia. At a time when lending practices hinged on partisanship, the Bank of Hudson was vital for the profitability of local Republican entrepreneurs, the mainly Clintonian businessmen, shipowners, and landowners who were the bank's major promoters and subscribers. They named Hogeboom president; William Peter, now a respectable country squire because of his inheritance, was among the board members. Except for minor changes, the board stayed the same through two annual elections. But problems existed. One group of stockholders, the New York City Phoenix Insurance Company, created trouble for small investors by demanding restrictive lending policies. Other stockholders resented the Phoenix group because it had not paid on fire insurance damages in the county. Still other difficulties surrounded Van Ness. A majority of the board, whom Van Buren labeled "malcontents," scorned William Peter as a Phoenix member and a Martling-Man among Clintonians; in late 1810, they sought to oust him. Van Buren proved to be a friend in need. Cooperating with Van Ness and the Phoenix group, he secured enough proxies to keep Van Ness on the board.[56]

In early 1811, Van Buren utilized Van Ness's gratitude and his partnership with Miller, whose father and father-in-law were on the board, to petition the bank to retain their firm as its sole legal representative. Miller wrote his father that "I wish Van Buren to be appointed, as he would esteem it *honourable* & it would be equally *profitable* to me." Some members refused, due to Van Buren's support of William Peter, and tried to name Miller alone. He declined, calling the offer "a snare to destroy the union between me & V[an] Buren" and an "*infamous treachery.*" Miller's relatives agreed. They convinced the board to put the firm on retainer and deepened Van Buren's connection with wealthy county Clintonians. Van Buren and Miller sprung into action. They listed their first case for the bank, a debt collection, in the August 1811 Supreme Court session in Albany, and had eight more in October and November.[57]

The new year of 1811 had thus begun conspicuously for Van Buren, and it continued auspiciously. It was, in fact, a year that numbered several of his better-known causes. The Supreme Court's February term in Albany saw Van Buren with two cases laden with political dimensions. Continuing what was now a familiar pattern, he opposed Williams in *Maigley v. Hauer,* a property case out of a justices of the peace court. Maigley, a life owner of an estate, swore that he had agreed to "give up the possession to the defendant for life," provided Hauer gave him "one third of the wheat and rye" he raised, plus "victuals" and "clothes." The justices allowed Hauer to present parol evidence that he had made no such promise. Van Buren appealed for Maigley on a writ of *certiorari,* which called on the court to review cases from inferior courts. Conveniently reversing himself, Van Buren argued for the inadmissibility of oral evidence to alter a deed. The court sustained him, ruling that the verdict "was contrary to law," and rescinded the judgment. The reason for Van Buren's shift reflected another of his legal and political commitments: the need to safeguard the justices of the peace system. He believed that justices of the peace, who were residents of the towns they served and were often not attorneys, were "as near to the People as possible." To Van Buren, these justices embodied classical republicanism: they symbolized a decentralized governmental mechanism; understood the local popular will; and allowed citizens individual autonomy, since they could represent themselves in small criminal and civil matters. From a political standpoint, Van Buren valued the justices because their prominence in local communities made them figures of respect who could influence town voters. But Van Buren's defense of the justices contained an inherent flaw. They were not elected but appointed, a factor contradicting his belief in popular sovereignty. This problem would haunt Van Buren in the future.[58]

The case of *Reed v. Pruyn and Staats* gave Van Buren another chance to defend a party official. The facts revolved around whether Clintonian Henry Van Slyck, deputy sheriff of Columbia County, could execute a judgment against a debtor to whom he had lent money, secured by the Bank of Hudson, to pay that judgment. Van Buren argued that the agreement was valid, and that the defendants had promised to repay but had never fulfilled their promise. Chief Justice Kent was unimpressed. While admitting that Van Slyck's "humanity was imposing," Kent ruled that Van Slyck could not recover his loan because it lacked contractual reality.[59]

Van Buren faced a stiffer challenge in March 1811 over the almost perennial question of individual property rights versus feudal land tenures. The situation evolved out of his earlier triumph in *Jackson v. Frier* and marked his first appearance before the Court of Errors.[60] Much of the argument that opposing counsels advanced in *Daniel Frier and Peter Cooper, Plaintiff in Error, v. James Jackson, ex dem. Johannis L. Van Allen and John J. Van Allen, Defendant in Error* cannot be retraced. Johnson's printed report merely listed notations about motions and notices of presentations. Furthermore, he "omitted" the elaborate visual display Van Buren and Federalist Abraham Van Vechten prepared for the defendants that showed the bounds of the area, "as it would not be well understood, without a reference to the maps and diagrams which were produced." But the brief that Van Buren and Van Vechten presented rested on the grounds developed by Van Buren in the original case.[61]

John Lansing, Jr., Chancellor of the Court of Chancery, a dedicated Federalist and long-time advocate of feudal land tenures, dominated the deliberations. Point by point, he examined the case and stated that a number of errors in common law had indeed taken place. Just as minutely, Lansing assessed the various patents and maintained that it was possible that the De Bruyn and Baker-Flodden patents actually did not overlap. In that light, he surmised that Judge Tompkins had compounded his mistakes in declaring Baker-Flodden void because its boundaries were vague and unlocatable. In sum, the patent was legal and still in existence. Of thirty members present during the hearings, fourteen sustained Lansing, six dissented, and ten others did not vote. With the judgment reversed, the court returned the case for a retrial under the common law doctrine of "*venire facias de novo,*" evidence based upon the face of the record.[62]

This decision was a severe blow to Van Buren. In overruling *Jackson v. Frier,* the court embarrassed not only Tompkins but Van Buren as well, since Tompkins had based his jury charge on Van Buren's brief. In a larger sense, the court's acceptance of common law to uphold Baker-Flodden sustained the traditional landlord-tenant system and harmed the basic economic interests of the one group Van Buren could not afford to alienate, small freeholders in Columbia County. As a result, the court's conservative majority countered Van Buren's classical republicanism value of property as the lack of dependency in order to protect landed estates.

Another case, much more sensational and politicized, also reflected the court's judicial policy of conservative restraint of individual liberty. The case had been in litigation since August 1806 when Chancellor Lansing had ordered the arrest and jailing of Clintonian John Van Ness Yates of Albany, a master in chancery, for malpractice and contempt of court. Yates appealed to Supreme Court Judge Spencer, another Clintonian, for a writ of *habeas corpus* and secured his own release. Lansing, who was on vacation, was outraged. When he returned, he ordered Yates rejailed without further interrogation.[63]

Yates promptly began a series of actions against Lansing that found their way to the Supreme Court. After the judges sustained Lansing's powers in the August 1809 term in *Ex parte Yates*, Yates instituted an "action of debt" to recover a penalty of $1,250 under the fifth section of the state's *Habeas Corpus Act*, a mutated version of a similar British law. The statute provided that the chancellor or a Supreme Court judge, while on vacation or between terms, who refused to allow a writ of *habeas corpus*, suffered a forfeiture of $1,250 to the aggrieved party. In February 1810, the Supreme Court again found for Lansing in *John Van Ness Yates v. Lansing*, ruling that he possessed authority to punish Yates for contempt.[64]

Yates answered with a writ of error to the Court of Errors, which led to one of the more intricate and partisan trials in early New York State legal history, *John Van Ness Yates, Plaintiff in Error, v. The People of the State of New York, Defendants in Error*. After an extensive review, a majority reversed the Supreme Court and decided that Lansing had exceeded his authority.[65]

Still smarting over Lansing's disregard of his civil rights, Yates decided to press his suit against Lansing to recover the $1,250 penalty. At this point Van Buren, Yates's distant relative and a political ally, joined his team of attorneys, including Emmet and Daniel Rodman, in *John Van Ness Yates, Plaintiff in Error, v. John Lansing, Jr., Defendant in Error*. Rather than debate the original issues, Van Buren dealt solely with the question of *habeas corpus*. His brief rested on classical republican principles, augmented by legal instrumentalism and legal positivism, the doctrine holding that the law reflected the popular will and that judges should not overrule legislative decisions. Basing his brief on these values, Van Buren emphasized public fears that judges, if they acted out of partisanship, would corrupt republicanism by seeking power without specific authority. Beyond that, Van Buren viewed the case in partisan and personal terms. He wished to diminish Federalists and sought vengeance against Lansing for his efforts in *Jackson v. Frier*.[66]

To those ends, Van Buren and Rodman argued that judges were responsible for the protection of individual liberties and ideally should be left unfettered. But judges could not exceed their judicial authority at the expense of personal freedom and liberty. In the largest sense, judges must honor a prisoner's right to *habeas corpus*, the guarantee of fairness in criminal proceedings. The chancellor had negated Yates's basic rights through arbitrary and capricious rulings. To prove his point, Van Buren cited the fact that the legislature had passed the *Habeas Corpus Act* to promote the security of liberty. Representatives of the people, through legal instrumentalism, had adapted to changing conditions. Specifically, the statute had created a mechanism to set a "prisoner at large," secured by bail and sureties if the issuing judge thought that reasonable doubt existed about the imprisonment's legality, until a trial. Since discharge under the act was a reversal of the commitment order, allowing a recommitment nullified its intent. If that happened, Van Buren said, any prisoner was liable to wrongful incarceration. Such a situation meant that citizens lacked the fundamental protection of liberty, since any judge could destroy a number of similar basic, human rights. Van Buren was adamant. Legislative supremacy under legal instrumentalism and legal positivism limited Lansing's power and made him liable for the penalty.[67]

Lansing's team of lawyers ignored Van Buren's presentation. They reargued the original issue and contended that Spencer, not the chancellor, had breached acceptable legal authority in issuing the writ. They also asserted that Lansing was within the meaning of the law; he was not subject to penalty because he had corrected Spencer's improper action. Emmet answered: extending Van Buren's contentions, he elaborated on the powers of judges to issue the writ and backed Van Buren's point that Lansing had acted autocratically. On April 6, 1811, the Court of Errors reached a decision. Although Senator Clinton agreed with Van Buren, the majority supported Lansing and his leading defender, Chief Justice Kent. Yates paid a stiff penalty. The court ordered him to pay Lansing "his double [legal] costs."[68]

May's Supreme Court term saw Van Buren with two actions far removed from such constitutional concerns, but no less vital in other ways. *Vosburgh v. Rodgers* and *Strong v. Tompkins and Another* were similar debt collections appeals (although the facts differed) against rulings Judge Thompson had made in the Columbia Circuit during 1810. Van Buren stood for the plaintiffs; Williams for the defendants. Both cases involved the negotiability of third-party promissory notes in contracts. In each, Van Buren sought to establish the concept that the current holders of the notes could assign or transfer them to pay debts. But the court ruled on narrow grounds in both and refused to change privity of contracts, a doctrine holding that damages could only be sought if a direct connection existed between a plaintiff or defendant, not by a third party. As a result, Van Buren failed to create three key points necessary for a functional free market economy: equality among the holders of promissory notes; the functions of negotiable instruments in transferring wealth from one party to another party; and, more critically, the rights of a third party who held the original notes. These unresolved issues were also destined to perplex Van Buren and market transactions in the future.[69]

By the mid-summer of 1811, Van Buren's political ambitions remained unrealized. By contrast, his legal career flourished. Clients and other attorneys sought Van Buren's services; his firm's sizeable practice increased; and he was diligently at work as surrogate and in his profession, preparing all types of litigation at every level of the judicial system. Moreover, through an amalgam of classical and liberal republicanism, he had formulated fresh and lasting legal doctrines that defined him as an innovative lawyer. As conspicuous as this work was, however, Van Buren stood on the threshold of two key cases that would further clarify how republicanism articulated his dual career.

*Republicanism
and Property Law*

$\mathcal{I}$n 1811, two land cases and their consequences would prove to be momentous events affecting the development of Van Buren's dual career and the evolution of his republican principles, as well as New York's conservative legal tradition regarding property law. Each centered on the common law's applicability toward the enforcement of colonial manor grants and letters of patent in the Upper Hudson Valley. Years later, when Van Buren wrote his *Autobiography,* he commented that the "incidents" of his "long" practice were best left, with these exceptions, to judicial reports and "traditions of the time."[1]

In the early winter of 1811, a "Committee of Tenants" from the Manor of Livingston, led by Benjamin Birdsall, Jr., approached Van Buren for a legal opinion about the title the Livingston family held on the lands that the committee members and their associates occupied. Van Buren wrote a careful reply. Plumbing their commitment to a protracted and perhaps losing cause, he warned that a case of such magnitude would prove costly in legal expenses and create immense political sensations. He also warned the committee that his personal involvement was delicate. Much of his professional business since becoming an attorney involved similar actions, particularly the next round of the Great Possession. A related case might give Livingston attorneys a plausible means to discredit his views and motives. But while he realized the "unpleasantness" of his situation, Van Buren acknowledged that he shared the committee's unhappiness over the "distressing tenure" under which manorial inhabitants held the land they had improved, and that he was entirely convinced that they had "justice" on their side.[2]

Still cautious, Van Buren then outlined a brief history of the Livingston claims, documented by material "at the office of the Secretary of State." He concluded that the formation of Livingston Manor in 1715, "purporting to be an act of Confirmation" of Robert Livingston's "preceding grants," bore "upon the face of it a palpable falsehood" that could not be "considered as vesting any title" to the area his heirs claimed. Van Buren's analysis was novel. In 1795, he reminded the committee, over 200 manor residents had petitioned the legislature to revoke the 1686 Dongan Charter that set the basis for the Livingstons' claims in Columbia County. But Ambrose Spencer, their attorney, had not raised that point. Another complication existed. The Livingstons had established "good title" because of long adverse possession and an equally long record of tenant acquiescence.[3]

Yet since the Livingstons' original title was based on a faulty "confirmation," Van Buren continued, "I have no hesitation in expressing my deliberate opinion that these lands in law and of right belong to the State." He recommended that the tenants seek legislative redress, however, rather than testing the titles through the conservative judiciary. But he skeptically concluded, "whether the legislature as the Guardians of the Interests of the People will think it just, politic, or expedient to exercise the right which is vested in them" was "impossible" to know.[4]

Shortly later, the tenants did petition the legislature for a full investigation of the Livingstons' title to their "Manor Lands." The outcome proved discouraging. Three Federalist assemblymen, Abraham Van Vechten, Jacob R. Van Rensselaer, and Thomas B. Grosvenor, all devoted to maintaining tenantry, raised procedural questions, blocked legislation, and maneuvered the issue to a different venue. Along with a majority of Federalist and a few remaining Lewisites, they instructed Attorney General Matthias B. Hildreth to prepare a suit for "The People of New York" to test the titles in the friendly judiciary. Two years later, Federalist Attorney General Abraham Van Vechten, Hildreth's eventual successor, reluctantly filed suit. The trial, which Van Buren characterized as an "*ex-parte* proceeding," found for the Livingstons.[5]

Van Buren was discouraged. Given the judiciary's hidebound record of defending landed estates and tenures, he had every reason to interpret its ruling as a triumph for aristocratic landlords over ordinary citizens, a ruling the judiciary would repeat in the future to neutralize popular sovereignty, maintain traditional property law, and keep tenants in a state of perpetual dependency. Even worse, his reluctance to represent the plaintiffs cast doubt on his motives, despite his excuse about avoiding a conflict of interest in the Great Possession. Nevertheless, this episode's political results set off a chain of events critical to Van Buren's dual career.[6]

How much Van Buren threatened the old order crystallized in the spring legislative election of 1811. During Jacob R. Van Rensselaer's reelection bid in his Middle District stronghold, he and Van Buren fell into a nasty confrontation over whether Van Buren had misled the tenants. This confrontation involved the authorship of a letter quoting Van Rennselaer as purportedly saying during assembly debate that the tenants were unfit "to govern themselves, and deserved a Master." Another component was whether or not Van Rensselaer would allow Van Buren to defend himself in a campaign rally that Van Rensselaer had scheduled. The ugliest part of this exchange lay in the authenticity of a damaging letter that Van Rennselaer ostensibly held, one which Van Buren had supposedly sent to Rueben Whallon, a Washington County Republican assemblyman. According to Van Rensselaer, Van Buren had written Whallon to "stave off" action on the committee's request until the next session, which might have more sympathetic legislators. Van Rensselaer's purposes were simple. He intended to prevent Van Buren from campaigning, charging that his compassion for tenants was a cynical political ploy to elect Republicans.[7]

The Federalist *Northern Whig,* edited by Francis Stebbins, picked up where Van Rensselaer ended. Stebbins published an inflammatory editorial contending that Van Buren had duped the committee for electioneering purposes, ran up legal expenses even though he knew the issue lacked merit, and compounded his guilt by remaining mute about conniving with Whallon. Plunged into a controversy he could not ignore, Van Buren had to refute the paper and guard his good name. After denouncing Van Rensselaer through the *Hudson Bee,* Van Buren arranged a counter meeting to answer critics. At the gathering, he found a "very large assemblage," including Van Rensselaer, Williams, several Livingstons, and a few of their agents. Speaking rapidly, Van Buren refuted his accusers in detail, submitting certified copies of the only letters he had written to Whallon, none of which mentioned the manor question. Van Buren then turned the tables on Van Rensselaer, who was standing in the back, and asked him pointblank to prove that the Whallon letter existed. When Van Rensselaer replied with silence, Van Buren shot back that his unwillingness to speak indicated that he had lied. The flushed Van Rensselaer retorted that Van Buren was the liar. Growing angrier, Van Rensselaer challenged Van Buren to settle the question in court, pledging to forfeit a $500 bond if Van Buren won.[8]

The manor issue was now thoroughly politicized and Van Buren found himself in its vortex. Although Van Rensselaer was reelected, Republicans increased their votes in areas that were normally landlord bastions. In its electoral postmortems, the *Northern Whig* blamed Van Buren for the erosion. In particular, Stebbins denounced "the treacherous manner in which the demagogues of the county" electioneered "the Manor towns, by promising to invest them with the right of soil which they now occupy only on lease."[9]

Taken aback by the ferocity of these events, Van Buren wanted to satisfy himself that he had indeed given the committee a correct legal evaluation. With that in mind, he wrote a long and undated appraisal of the Livingston claim. This study was unique since he left no other full example of how he investigated, marshalled, and analyzed evidence, prepared a brief, and used logical thought to summarize a case in the most efficient manner. It was a simple, straightforward technique, without embroidery, diversion, or deceit; a method that contributed directly toward his success as a lawyer, politician, public servant, and classical republican ideologue.

Van Buren's exercise, entitled "Notes on the Livingston Grant," which ran to more than 100 handwritten pages, was indeed thorough. He began by researching the historic circumstances surrounding each grant, the exact boundaries of the properties involved, previous challenges to the Livingstons' titles, their system of quitrents and tenantry, and their various wills passing the land to descendants. Using this method, Van Buren confirmed his initial belief that the Dongan Charter was faulty since it awarded no new titles. Dongan merely corroborated previous grants of "several tracts or parcels lying together," and provided them with clearly defined limits by using natural geographic locations and well-known American Indian monuments.[10]

Van Buren drew a number of conclusions from these facts. The initial grant of 2,000 acres was valid, as was the second of 600. But the Livingstons had planted the seeds for fraud in each because of their positioning of the grants. The first grant lay in a narrow strip along the Hudson and in a parallel area some "twenty miles to the east." The second grant began the fraud since it was supposedly "adjacent" to the first. This chicanery became obvious in the third with the statement that the "several tracts and parcels of land" were contiguous. The Livingstons, Van Buren commented, knew the description was false because of the gap that existed between the first two. No previous grant had given them such a title and made their claims "*ipso facto* void."[11]

The Livingstons thrust the consequences of this "stupendous fraud" upon innocent parties, the tenants, who had justifiably resisted their ostensible landlords in a series of uprisings prior to 1811. Robert Livingston especially, the first "Lord of the Manor," knew "best of all" that a defect existed. But he used extraordinary political influence in numerous legal actions "to cover up, to evade & if possible to cure the defect." In 1715, Livingston capped his subterfuge by securing a new "Patent of Confirmation," largely on his assertion that the monuments were too vague for a clear title. At that point, Van Buren questioned Livingston's hidden agenda in applying for the confirmation. Answering himself, Van Buren surmised that Livingston wanted to establish a specious title to land he knew was not his and to correct the "radical defect" in the third grant.[12]

Livingston, who died in 1728, manipulated his will to link "the disjointed chains of the title." Van Buren found the will ingenious but dubious, "treading a narrow but it was doubtlessly supposed, a safe course." Yet by combining the different grants into one, Livingston locked his descendants in an untenable position. Their title was "insecure" and directly responsible for "popular out-breaks" among tenants. Over the course of the next few generations, his heirs had aggrandized political, economic, and judicial prerogatives to erect town-ships, elect public officials, and hold court-baron, an old fuedal custom for the maintenance of services and duties imposed for or by the lord of the manor in the disputed area as further evidences of their titles. Finally, his heirs had completed their deception in 1796, through a favorable Supreme Court ruling "upon the ground of possession merely, independent of [official] parchment and paper title." In conclusion, Van Buren reasoned that his first assessment was correct. The Livingstons' possessions rested on an invalid claim, subject to legitimate legislative correction by elective officials who represented the tenants' interests through popular sovereignty.[13]

What use Van Buren made of this elaborate study is impossible to deter-mine. He retained a copy and added some thoughts to it in preparing the *Au-tobiography*. He probably also gave part of it, perhaps all, to the Manor Com-mittee and Birdsall, since their petition to the legislature resembled his reasoning. Whatever Van Buren did, he made the unambiguous point that he supported the manorial tenants and their quest for self-sufficiency; that he had indeed acted as their advocate, despite not representing them in court; that his legal judgment was accurate; and that the Livingstons, given the choice between the public good and their own self-interest, would always choose the latter. Furthermore, as Van Rensselaer rightly conjectured, Van Buren was equally intent on wielding the manorial issue in future elections. He made this position clear in a toast at the Republican party's July 4, 1811 dinner in Kinderhook. Praising the committee, Van Buren said its members had "broken the fetters" that bound them "to unjust domination."[14]

By the August Supreme Court term, Van Buren's life returned to normal. His docket bulged with eleven nonenumerated cases, which he won, and two enumerated. In *Adams v. Supervisors of Columbia County*, Van Buren sought a *writ of mandamus*, an action where the court believed that public officials were not exercising their proper functions, to collect a debt from the supervisors for a local Republican party physician who had treated a pauper. Based on the will theory of contracts, the court sustained Van Buren. *Pugsley v. Van Alen* was trifling. The previous May the defendant, represented by a different attor-ney, had lost a nonsuit. Van Buren moved to quash the execution as "irregu-lar," but the court refused.[15]

Van Buren arrived back in Hudson just as the simmering manorial episode reached a new boiling point. Over the summer, the Livingstons had begun an ejectment against Birdsall as a warning to similar tenants. The threat did not frighten him. Publishing an open letter in the *Hudson Bee*, replete with classi-cal republican ideals, Birdsall cautioned that without impartial justice "the poor and the needy" would fall "beneath the yoke of despotism."[16]

The Federalist *Northern Whig* ignored Birdsall. Rather, Stebbins attacked a bigger target, Martin Van Buren. Arguing again that the alleged Whallon letter existed, Stebbins accused Van Buren of creating an artificial crisis for political gain. Van Buren preferred to let the matter die by not responding, but the manorial committee felt insulted and called a protest rally. Depending on one's point of view, it was either a triumph or a fiasco. Birdsall, the chairman, defended Van Buren. But Stebbins claimed that attendance was sparse and the few who attended refused to pay any of Van Buren's legal fees. "Alas! the mutability of human expectations," Stebbins' editorial ran, "should our little lawyerman, lose not only his men but part of his wages too. What a pity it would be."[17]

This slur stung Van Buren, especially since he had given the committee his counsel free of charge. A few days after the accusation appeared, Van Buren retaliated by calling Van Rensselaer's bluff. Reminding him of his promise to deposit $500 for the proposed test case, Van Buren offered to "facilitate" the "investigation," preliminary to an early jury trial.[18]

While awaiting Van Rensselaer's reply, Van Buren wrote a public letter to the *Northern Whig*. Categorically denying Stebbins' censure, Van Buren maintained that he had not acted improperly nor manipulated Birdsall. Little was settled. Partisans on each side exchanged a war of words about which man was more "depraved" and "contemptible." Van Buren finally decided the issue had gone too far and sued Stebbins for libel. But Williams, acting as a broker, convinced Van Buren to withdraw the suit once Stebbins issued a public apology.[19]

"We have no particular personal enmity against" Van Buren, Stebbins wrote, "nor do we war with his profession as a lawyer," because "it can never cease to command respect." Yet persons such as Birdsall had "disgraced" him, since they "imposed" the false belief on the tenants that they could obtain "the manor lands." Van Buren had had enough. He decided not to respond.[20]

What remained was Van Rensselaers' legal challenge. As Van Buren suspected, Van Rensselaer found an excuse for not depositing the $500. He explained that the "prosecution" had a time limit and the period had long expired. Though no one recalled Van Rensselaer making such a precondition, Van Buren thought he had the last word by publishing their correspondence in the *Hudson Bee*. As events shortly indicated, he was wrong.[21]

At the same time, other imperatives competed for Van Buren's attention. Surrogate business was demanding. In 1811, he held twenty-three court sessions, named eleven guardians for minors, and wrote twenty-three letters of administration. Van Buren and Miller were also busier than ever. The reason lay in a rush of insolvencies, resulting from bleak economic conditions in Columbia due to continued erosions of foreign trade. Handling some of these cases in common pleas, the partners added to their burdens by acting as receivers for failed enterprises and making arrangements with creditors. In one instance, Van Buren personally benefited. He took a mortgage on a farm in Canaan when its owner could not repay a bank loan. Van Buren was also busy with other investments. During September, he completed negotiations to buy a large lot adjacent to the village of Oswego in New York's Military Tract. Over the coming years, Van Buren would continue his real estate interests in the area, both for speculative and political reasons.[22]

In October he was off to New York City for *Jackson, ex dem. Bain and Van Slyck, v. Pulver and Another,* a Supreme Court property case involving several Kinderhook residents who were contesting an unclear deed that denied their claims to the lands in question. Foote and Van Vechten appealed a judgment that Van Buren's clients had won in Judge Thompson's Columbia Circuit. The judges sustained Van Buren. They found that the deed contained ambiguous terms; no indication existed that it was a binding contract, since nothing resembling consideration had been exchanged; and no evidence existed that Van Buren's clients had accepted the deed's conditions.[23]

The end of summer found Van Buren deep in preparation for the plaintiffs in the second litigation that he considered worthy of mention in his *Autobiography,* the Great Possession. In many ways, this litigation in the Columbia Circuit, under presiding Supreme Court Judge John Yates, duplicated the manorial question. While the case was indeed acute in a legal sense, its consequences were even more important to Van Buren's political aspirations.

The defendants employed a galaxy of Columbia's best attorneys: Williams, Grosvenor, and John Suydam, a young and impetuous Federalist. To counter them, Van Buren asked William Johnson for a copy of the Court of Error's proceedings. But Van Buren was disappointed with Johnson's reply. He sent just a skeletal outline containing "the dissenting opinion of Mr. Yates, but the majority of the Court concurred in that of the Chancellor, which is the only written opinion I have, the only one that will be printed." Without an indication of what other members of the court had thought favorable to his cause, Van Buren was forced to develop an alternate strategy.[24]

Rather than retry the old case, he challenged the chancellor's reasoning by stressing Lansing's most equivocal point: his reliance on the fuzzy boundaries of the patents, which had negated property rights. Since a sizeable part of Van Buren's brief rested on conflicting surveyors' reports, his chief tactic was to cast doubt on the veracity of William Dickie, the most recent surveyor, whom Lansing had relied upon. Dickie, a Lewisite turned Federalist, was vulnerable. A previous expert witness for the plaintiffs, he had shifted sides. In his summary to the jury, Van Buren accused Dickie of perjury on the grounds that he had changed his first survey to favor the defendants. "No man," Van Buren said, "in his senses would dare to swear to so flagrant an absurdity." Suydam immediately jumped to his feet and interrupted court protocol. Believing he heard Van Buren say that "no man could swear" to that fact, Suydam shouted that Van Buren misstated Dickie's testimony. Van Buren did not back down and replied that Suydam was "guilty" of "mis-representation." When Suydam continued the harangue, Van Buren called him a liar for abetting "an absolute and unqualified falsehood." At that point, Yates ruled Suydam out of order and allowed Van Buren to finish. The jury found for him and ordered new surveys.[25]

With the boundary issue unsettled, Van Buren spotted the parallel with the manorial question. In both instances, the judiciary was the incorrect venue. Instead, he advised the plaintiffs to seek a legislative remedy to settle the main claims in Kinderhook.[26]

But the disgruntled Suydam thought Van Buren had sullied his integrity, and challenged him to a duel. If Van Buren's historical image as a cool, calculating man who never took chances were true, the incident should have ended at this point, because one of Suydam's friends tried to arrange an accommodation "without discredit to either side." But Van Buren would not back down. He believed Suydam had insulted him, breached legal ethics, and questioned his honesty. As an attorney, Van Buren knew that New York had outlawed duelling and that statute law defined killing an opponent as a capital crime. Yet he lived in a society that regarded dueling as a suitable method among gentlemen to settle matters of honor. Van Buren thus deemed it "indispensable" to his manliness to accept.[27]

Each man posted the other as a coward and sought seconds. Cooler heads intervened. Neither found seconds; friends counseled restraint. Finally, Judge Yates intervened. He put the battling lawyers under court recognizance to keep the peace and forced them to post bonds. Moreover, Yates threatened that he would file criminal charges against both Van Buren and Suydam in the Columbia Court of Oyer and Terminer, which had jurisdiction in such matters, if they ignored him. With that, the duel never took place.[28]

As a whole, the judicial issues in both cases that Van Buren termed so exceptional in his *Autobiography* proved to be more than points of litigation. For the moment, the resolution of the Great Possession rested uncertainly with either another court case or the legislature. As for the Livingstons and Van Rensselaers, Van Buren formulated a new strategy in a variety of future actions that his clients brought against landlords. Instead of directly contesting their titles, which Van Buren realized the courts would sustain, he adopted an oblique approach. In coming litigations, he would challenge the landlords' economic prerogatives under their system of leases to curtail the financial benefits they derived from feudalistic tenantry. This approach, however, did not indicate an ideological retreat on Van Buren's part. From the viewpoint of classical republicanism, he continued his crusade against dependency by using adverse possession to establish a tenant's claim, provided that person had met the twenty-year standard and the landlord's title was unclear. Moreover, Van Buren linked liberal republicanism's emphasis on individual betterment to the tenant's right to achieve personal independence and economic advancement.

From the standpoint of his immediate legal needs in both cases, however, Van Buren had to wait decades for final vindication. Following the "anti-rent wars" of the 1840s, New Yorkers formed a new state constitution in 1846 that abolished feudal tenures and the leasing of land for more than twelve years. Fittingly, John Van Buren, then New York's attorney general, exculpated his father. Cooperating with tenants, the state flooded the courts with suits testing colonial leases. By the 1850s, the Supreme Court adjudicated a number of these actions, endorsed Martin Van Buren's earlier contention that the Livingstons' titles were defective, and awarded the tenants land in fee simple.[29]

Even so, critics argued that Van Buren's efforts in the manor issue and Great Possession were not examples of a lawyer who served the poor against the rich, but that of a callous "pettifogger" and unscrupulous "demagogue" out for cheap political gain. But such censures were unfair; Van Buren was consistent. Ever since his early years in practice, he had been a steady advocate for tenants. The result meant that his championship of tenants' and freeholders' rights associated him in the public mind with an emotional political issue with vast ideological overtones—that is, the determination of a sovereign people to repudiate a landed oligarchy. In both cases, Van Buren had anticipated the Jacksonian attack on artificial privilege.[30]

Both cases also underscored how much Van Buren's ideology guided his legal thinking. By seeking to redefine property law in favor of tenants, he rejected the common law idea of fixed or absolute landownership rights. Instead, he moved against the common law's standard interpretation of property law as a prescriptive doctrine that endowed current holders of colonial manor grants or letters of patent with original, immemorial, and absolute rights. Those doctrines, Van Buren continued to stress, were unjust, because they allowed landlords the monopolistic control of land at the expense of liberty, property, individualism, and equality. As such, he believed that tenants had developed legitimate claims to the homesteads they had farmed for generations through free and honest labor. To assert these rights, Van Buren relied upon a popularly-elected legislature that would use both legal positivism through statute law to curb the judiciary, and legal instrumentalism to meet changing conditions. Overall, Van Buren certified his ideology by a principled view of progress that stressed several classical and liberal republican beliefs: equality of opportunity, antimonopolism, and open competition among competing interests in a free market society—all of which would be future components of Jacksonianism.[31]

By the end of 1811, after seven years of practice, Van Buren had certified his legal credentials. Nothing better illustrated this progress than his advocacy before the Supreme Court. From 1808 through 1811, he received eighty-seven favorable judgments in both enumerated and nonenumerated business worth $84,884.40 in debts, damages, and costs, which covered cases running in value from $33.10 to $10,000. This record, along with his local practice, land ventures, and money-lending, made Van Buren a self-made man. Wealth brought him the confidence that eased the twin embarrassments of his rude class origins and incomplete formal education. Just as satisfying to Van Buren was his ability to run campaigns with his escalating fortune and thus gain political freedom from the traditional dependency of so many other striving young men on great families and their connections.[32]

Van Buren knew from the examples furnished by fellow lawyers that an accomplished private practice opened the door to a political career. He knew that public officials needed legal skills in conducting the everyday business of administrating the state, and that republicanism was a practical guide to decision-making. Attorneys were "conspicuous" in the nation's political life. Since late adolescence, Van Buren had every intention of joining their ranks. Under these conditions, it was bound to happen that he would seek elective public office.[33]

Yet timing was critical. With hindsight, an air of inevitability surrounds his first race for the state senate in 1812. But judging from his *Autobiography*, Van Buren had compelling reasons to avoid any candidacy. He was a young man, barely thirty, with an equally young wife and two children hardly out of swaddling clothes. His "successful and lucrative practice," as he called it, put heavy demands on his time. His words do not represent a man obsessed with officeholding, but a reluctant aspirant.[34]

As the fateful year of 1812 began, Van Buren's routine carried no hint of major change. In early January, he acquired a lot in Troy for $100 when a client defaulted on fees. Later that month, he joined the cream of Columbia's Clintonians as a fellow venture capitalist with his selection to the Bank of Hudson's board of directors. Van Buren's Supreme Court docket listed twenty-eight actions, including nine where the Bank of Hudson was the plaintiff, mainly debt collections, defaulted mortgages, and lapsed contracts. But the one case Van Buren argued, *Jackson, ex dem. Rensselaer et al., v. Thomas Hogeboom and John Hogeboom,* another action about tenants' property rights, once again had important political ramifications. In the Columbia Circuit and then the Supreme Court, Van Buren won verdicts for the Clintonian Hogebooms that prevented the Van Rensselaers from ejecting them. As a result, the Hogebooms, who dominated the local party, believed they owed Van Buren a political debt.[35]

Before they could repay, two developments during the late winter and early spring broke the smooth tenor of Van Buren's life. The first began when the largely Federalist boosters of the proposed Bank of America resurrected their charter application, with apparent Clintonian support. Making the bid almost irresistible, these promoters offered the state what amounted to an unofficial bribe by promising an extraordinary $600,000 bonus for incorporation. According to rumors, they also actually bribed uncertain legislators and politicians, particularly Solomon Southwick, president of the Albany Mechanics' and Farmers' Bank and the editor of the *Albany Register,* a man the public regarded as Clinton's spokesman. At once, latent Republican factionalism again erupted. Governor Tompkins, along with his allies in Tammany Hall, the Martling-Men's successors, believed that a few Clintonians, if not bribed, backed the charter at their leader's secret behest. But before final passage, the measure stalled in an unexpected way. Evidence of bribery was too blatant, chiefly touching Southwick. On March 27, Tompkins prorogued the legislature for six weeks, beyond the coming spring election.[36]

Clinton's unabashed presidential ambition, which surfaced at the same time, was the second development that reshaped Van Buren's life. By 1812, President Madison's floundering foreign policies gave Clinton a plausible reason to run as an alternative Republican presidential candidate. His decision increased already bitter party divisions. Tammany Hall, which was emerging as the key faction within the New York City Republican party through its control of voters, favoritism, patronage, and links to prominent state politicians, was a powerful urban political machine that Van Buren could ignore only at his peril. Fired by a long hatred of De Witt Clinton dating to Burr's heyday, Tammany assailed Clintonians for covert support of the Bank of America to garner Federalist support and urged a prompt state party caucus renomination of Madison, a suggestion Tompkins endorsed.[37]

With so much at stake in the spring elections, each party faction sought its strongest candidates. According to custom in the Middle District, the senatorial nomination rotated by county. Under those terms, the nominee belonged to Columbia.[38]

The following days revealed depths of deception and naked power politics. William Peter Van Ness, a Tompkins Republican, seemingly acquiesced in the nomination of John Hogeboom, the county's leading Clintonian. But Hogeboom demurred because of business and told Van Buren that he and "our friends in Albany," especially Clinton, were "desirous" that Van Buren run. Van Buren tried to squirm out, suggested others, and pleaded that his practice and surrogate commitments were too demanding. But his attitude quickly changed. He discovered that Van Ness was engaged in a clandestine "intrigue" to "break down my influence in the county" in order to help Tompkins and Madison and undercut Clinton. Furious at Van Ness, Van Buren decided to run. At the county convention, Clintonian delegates unanimously selected him, named a correspondence committee, and adjourned without issuing a platform. Remaining Middle District county conventions concurred.[39]

The oddest part of Van Ness's duplicity was that while he labored to destroy Van Buren the politician, he sought to retain Van Buren the lawyer. Van Ness owed $1,750 to Judge Matthew Dorr, the Clintonian Columbia County chairman, who wanted assurances that Van Ness would pay. Writing to Van Buren, Van Ness asked for his mediation, even if it meant a "sacrifice of your feelings to the performance of a professional duty." Van Buren complied by arranging a schedule of payments but again suspended their relationship.[40]

Initially, Columbia voters expected that the banking question and presidential politics would dominate the campaign. But once Van Buren was in the field, his fitness for office became the sole issue. Southwick, writing for the Clintonians, lauded Van Buren's abilities and urged his election. Federalists scoffed. Basing their argument on the manorial issue, they warned that if Van

Buren won he would take his place on the Court of Errors; there he would pose an "insidious" threat "to the rights of property," because he had encouraged the "Livingston tenants" to "Rebel."[41]

Fired by such fears, Middle District Federalists fused with Van Ness's backers, endorsed incumbent Edward P. Livingston, and positioned him as the "official" Republican candidate. On that basis, they claimed Van Buren was an "irregular" nominee who lacked party support, a man too callow and "unacquainted" with vital state needs. Above all, Van Buren's opponents pummeled him with the manorial issue. "Will you vote," Stebbins asked electors, for a man who sought to turn "the seat of justice" into a "den of thieves and robbers" and had misled "honest farmers" on "the Manor of Livingston?"[42]

Van Buren's supporters answered with a mixture of highmindedness and mud-slinging. Dorr reminded voters that Van Buren had "fairly obtained" the nomination through "regular" procedures. Making that point stronger, Dorr issued a joint address with other county chairmen, which emphasized that "respectable" delegates had chosen the "able" Van Buren "without a dissenting vote." Turning to Livingston, they denounced him as a man "destitute" of principles. But these efforts seemed doomed. Tompkins was neutral and created the assumption that he welcomed Van Buren's defeat to rebuke Clintonians.[43]

Across the state, Federalists scored stunning successes in areas where Madison's policies were most unpopular. They did equally well wherever Republicans were factionalized. Few Middle District Republicans expected Van Buren to withstand this tide. By the time the polls closed and election inspectors began to count early returns, Van Buren "conceded" defeat and packed his green bag holding legal documents for the May session of the Supreme Court in New York City. But in a dramatic turn of events, Van Buren, after he boarded the ship, was handed a letter by the captain; Cantine had sent the late totals from Delaware County. Van Buren was elated. He had eked out a narrow victory by the thin margin of 193 votes, 50.5 percent out of 11,1733 cast.[44]

However slight the margin, Van Buren's first election marked the beginning of a new chapter in his life. He had taken his first step toward eventually becoming the eighth president of the United States. As he proudly noted in his *Autobiography,* "from this period" until 1841, "I occupied, without the intermission of a year," a political career involving every great "public question, in conjunction with or in opposition to many of the distinguished public men of the day."[45]

CHAPTER SIX

Distributive Justice
and Legal Instrumentalism

*T*hree new political variables emerged before Senator-elect Martin Van Buren could take his seat. The first developed in June 1812, with the United States' declaration of war against Great Britain. Clinton believed the conflict was unnecessary; Tompkins headed prowar Republicans. Van Buren was caught in the middle. Although he gave a bellicose prowar toast at the Hudson celebration of Independence Day, Van Buren realized that the public could easily confuse his loyalty to Clinton with disloyalty to the United States. The second and third political variables were linked. As a lawyer-senator, Van Buren had to ponder how he could implement distributive justice, which involved the allocation or denial of legislative power to various groups. In a narrow sense, Van Buren understood that this process was a means to gain leverage over his rivals. But ideologically, he also knew that distributive justice dealt with principles and the issues they determined. Van Buren put his trust in legal instrumentalism. This doctrine, which stressed adaptability as circumstances dictated, became his guide to public policy.[1]

With the new legislature set to begin on November 3, Van Buren had six months to formulate his options. In the meantime, he brought his life back under control through the law. After his election, Van Buren filed several new cases in the courts of common pleas and general sessions, wound up others,

settled pending surrogate business, presented seven chancery actions, and prepared seven pleadings for the May Supreme Court. He won three nonenumerated actions, one nonsuit and two affirmed. In open court, he also prevailed in four. The Livingstons were his victims in two, making these
triumphs even sweeter.[2]

Denton et al. v. Livingston, an *assumpsit,* developed from a ruling Judge Yates
delivered in the Columbia Circuit the previous December, about the liability
of a manorial Livingston sheriff for goods he seized under a court order, but
could not fully sell. Van Buren joined Foote in successfully contending that
the sheriff was "answerable for the [total] amount." This judgment was an
embarrassing blow to the Livingstons, who often wielded their own brand of
justice on the Manor.[3]

Knickerbacker v. Killmore bore on a lease. Van Buren's client, a Livingston
tenant, "sold and signed the leasehold" to a third party, but the Livingstons
denied the arrangement's legality and instituted an ejectment. Following his
new strategy to limit Livingstonian economic benefits, Van Buren convinced
the court that the seller could make the sale, provided it was free of all arrears
in rent or other encumbrances.[4]

The two remaining actions indicated Van Buren's principled approach to
contracts and the domestication of the common law. In *Jackson, ex dem. Hall et
al., v. Burr,* his experience as a surrogate proved invaluable. Van Buren argued
that executors could not break Gideon Burr's will if they failed to fulfill
terms directing them to "discharge his debts out of his interest and estate"
and devising the remainder to Burr's heirs. By not following these terms, the
executors had breached Burr's intent. In a *per curiam* that upheld the will theory of contracts, the court backed Van Buren, specifically citing the will's "intent" that any unsold property descended to the "heirs-at law."[5]

The court reversed itself in a related contract case, *Freeman v. Adams,* again
dealing with intent. Roger Skinner was Van Buren's co-counsel. They failed
to convince the court that common law was not applicable to an extension
of time that both parties accepted in a new and modified arbitration contract
when they could not settle their claims.[6]

One week after the Supreme Court adjourned, the prorogued legislature
reconvened and chartered the Federalist Bank of America with heavy Clintonian support. For Van Buren, the most important item did not involve
banking. On June 8, legislators adopted the petition that the plaintiffs' requested in the Great Possession. They chose three commissioners, Jacob Radcliff and David B. Odgen of New York City, and Thomas Rudd of Poughkeepsie, to investigate the titles of all the parties, and authorized them to settle
the entire issue.[7]

Less easily resolved was the rupture over the presidency. The congressional
caucus renominated Madison. But his chief local backers, Tompkins, Tammanyites, and Judge Spencer, who had broken with Clinton, lacked the votes
to halt the party's legislative nominating caucus from making Clinton New

York's favorite son. By mid-September, he was a candidate with feet in two camps. Openly, Clinton ran as a legitimate though insurgent Republican. Secretly, he cooperated with the Federalists by questioning Madison's wisdom in seeking only a military solution against Great Britain.[8]

The question of party loyalty versus loyalty to Clinton redoubled Van Buren's dilemma. He could justify his backing of Clinton, since the state organization had designated him as the regularly-nominated candidate. But other reasons were equally compelling. Van Buren's "personal attachment" to Clinton was stronger than ever, not least because Van Buren was currently engaged as Clinton's advocate in a snarled estate case, *Doe., ex dem. v. Clinton et al., v. Phelps,* over a large tract of land inherited by Clinton's wife, Maria. Moreover, Van Buren was attracted to a sudden opening as the state's attorney general, an office he believed was within Clinton's ability to give.[9]

In July, Van Buren attended the Auburn western circuit court to try *Doe., v. ex dem. v. Clinton et al., v. Phelps* under Spencer, the presiding judge, when all present learned that incumbent Attorney General Matthias Hildreth had just died. At that point, Spencer said to Van Buren, "You ought to be Hildreth's successor." Spencer's candor startled Van Buren. He replied that older lawyer-politicians would feel "slighted" by having Tompkins order the Republican-controlled Council of Appointment to designate "so young a man." When Spencer persisted, Van Buren promised to give the matter more thought.[10]

Spencer's suggestion was less impulsive than it seemed. He knew that Van Buren was one of the state's most eminent lawyers, whether Republican or Federalist. By 1812, New York had slightly more than 1,500 practicing attorneys. Of these, only about 100 appeared as much as once before the Supreme Court in the previous five years. Among this group, less than half had appeared more than four times. The remainder were the court's familiar figures, most from New York City, men whose reputations attracted clients throughout the state. Van Buren belonged to this small, select group. That aside, Spencer also had a more cynical goal. Since the governor made the selection, naming Van Buren might earn his gratefulness and harm Clinton's presidential bid.[11]

Another development also proved promising for Van Buren's prospects. Governor Tompkins had a short list of available choices. Almost all the leaders of the New York bar were Federalists. Only a few Republicans were feasible: Roger Skinner, Thomas Addis Emmet, Richard Riker, the Clintonian recorder of New York City, and Nathan Sanford, the current federal district attorney for the Southern District of New York. Van Buren understood that his legal credentials were as high, perhaps higher, than the others. But he took his first false step in countering his possible competitors. Using Riker as an intermediary, Van Buren informed Clinton about his conversation with Spencer and indicated his willingness to step aside due to his youth or Clinton's desire for someone else to assume the position.[12]

Riker, in turn, relayed to Van Buren that Clinton had given his political blessing for thwarting Spencer. To that end, Riker told Van Buren that he had already contacted William W. Gilbert of New York City, "a particular friend of Mr. Clinton," to press Van Buren's nomination. Yet Van Buren had blundered. While ostensibly gaining Clinton's benediction, Van Buren failed to seek Tompkins's approval, believing that Spencer had spoken for the governor.[13]

The magnitude of Van Buren's mistake became apparent in early August. Van Buren asked a friend to check with Gilbert about his prospects or personally approached Gilbert to probe Clinton's current mood. In either case, Van Buren found Gilbert unwilling to discuss the subject. Knowing Clinton's penchant for self-promotion, Van Buren interpreted Gilbert's reluctance as meanning that Clinton had changed his mind.[14]

As matters turned out, Van Buren's legal assets counted less than his political debits. Quite simply, Tompkins weighed the nature of party factionalism against Van Buren and refused to enhance Clinton's candidacy by tapping one of his more prominent allies. The governor also suspected that Van Buren would drag his feet in prosecuting a bribery case the state was preparing against Southwick for allegedly buying legislative votes for the Bank of America. On top of these objections, the governor indeed "thought" Van Buren was "too young." Naming Emmet made greater sense. An attorney as accomplished as Van Buren, Emmet had an additional credential as the leader of the state's Irish community, a group Clinton courted. By choosing Emmet, Tompkins could disrupt the Clintonians and enhance Madison's prospects more extensively than opting for Van Buren would allow.[15]

Van Buren did not understand Tompkins's calculations and only learned of them some years later. Assuming that Clinton had duped him while covertly backing Emmet, Van Buren overlooked the fact that Tompkins had neared his goal of controlling the party along with Spencer. Instead, Van Buren blamed Clinton. If Clinton had been honest, Van Buren wrote, he would have "consented" to Emmet's appointment. When Clinton said nothing, Van Buren confessed that he was deeply "injured by his silence."[16]

Van Buren's growing disillusionment with Clinton did not sour their legal relationship. Clinton's wife claimed some 5,200 acres of land in Sharon, Schoharie County, through the will of her father, Walter Franklin. In circuit court, Van Buren had presented a strong brief with proof of deeds to 2,800 acres. But he was unable to produce an existing power of attorney authorizing a transfer of another 2,400 acres to Franklin. Judge Spencer, however, recused himself because of his relationship to Clinton, remanding the cause to the Supreme Court. In August, Van Buren reintroduced his brief. The judges found for Clinton in a *per curiam,* which held that Franklin had clear title to his original 2,800 acres. Clinton was so delighted that he sent Van Buren auxiliary documents "to sustain" further "suits" for the remaining 2,400 acres.[17]

While these legal maneuverings preoccupied Van Buren, Madison's clumsy efforts at waging war had severe repercussions. In mid-August, the nation learned about a shameful American defeat, the surrender of General William Hull's army near Detroit. Politicians made the disaster a partisan issue. Administration apologists distanced Madison from Hull and blasted the general as a "traitor" who was solely "culpable" for the disaster. Clintonians came to Hull's defense in a contradictory way. They agreed that he might have been a "weak, trembling coward" unfit for command, but they condemned the Administration for its "pre-disposition to pre-judge" him. The only way to settle the matter was through an unbiased court-martial. Federalists had their own scores to settle. They pointed out that Hull was a life-long member of the Republican party. If he was at fault, so was Madison for putting Hull in "supreme command." Repeating the Clintonian line, Federalists insisted upon an official examination of the evidence.[18]

During these weeks of political posturing and growing alarm over the nation's failed invasions of Canada, Van Buren remained focused on professional work. The firm of Van Buren and Miller brought several cases before the Columbia Courts of Common Pleas and General Sessions and argued an even larger number in the circuit, most stemming from the Livingston family's attempts to eject tenants. As before, the Livingstons targeted Birsdall for retaliation. Rather than contest the Livingstons in circuit, Van Buren decided the solution was a matter of equity and sought an injunction from the Court of Chancery to halt the action.[19]

Van Buren also appeared before the October session of the Supreme Court with nine cases. He won seven nonenumerated actions and argued two that evolved from the December 1811 Columbia Circuit Court under Judge Yates. In *Jackson, ex dem. Livingston and Wilsey v., Wilsey et al.,* a twenty-seven year lease was the focal point. Representing the defendants, Van Buren continued with his new approach toward the Livingstons. Robert Livingston, the "ancestor of John Livingston," the current owner, had granted a life tenure of 75 acres to John Tice Wilsey. Because of the way Robert Livingston drew the lease, Wilsey instead occupied 150 acres. John Livingston now sought to recover the extra 75 acres. In circuit court, the jury had found for him. On appeal, Van Buren admitted that Wilsey had leased only the original 75 acres. He pointed out, however, that Wilsey had paid rent for the whole 150 acres and developed tenure that entitled him to a "notice to quit," a written notice from Livingston to Wilsey informing him that Livingston intended to repossess the demised premises. Yet Livingston never delivered the notice, a procedure integral to due process and the protection of individual liberty. To that end, Van Buren argued that Wilsey had developed a "tenancy from year to year" and was entitled, at the minimum, to the notice to quit. The court assented and ordered a new trial.[20]

The case of *Jackson, ex dem. Van Beuren, v. Vosburgh et al.* centered on the introduction of parol evidence to rule on the will and estate of Johannis Van Deursen of Kinderhook, an alleged incompetent who had died in 1767. The point of law hinged on whether a claimant who abandoned a claim to property in order to seek a better share, could now substantiate a new claim by offering parol evidence that Van Deursen had been incompetent to divide the property. Van Buren and Foote argued that the will and its execution presumably established title for Van Duersen's heirs. Once the plaintiff abandoned his claim, with the excuse that the testator was incompetent, the estate descended only to the heir-at-law, the eldest son. To serve his clients, Van Buren reversed his earlier endorsement of parol evidence and challenged Williams and Van Vechten's reliance on oral testimony about Van Deursen's purported incompetence. Relishing the opportunity to reemphasize the common law, the conservative majority sustained Van Buren and Foote and refused to grant a motion for a new trial.[21]

In spite of these successes, Van Buren's legal accomplishments lost their gloss in the atmosphere of Clinton's presidential ambitions. In particular, Van Buren was dismayed by Clinton's vindictiveness toward Spencer in a series of wounding articles, the "Ambrosiads," that Clinton had either written or authorized. Even worse, Clinton denied to Van Buren any knowledge of its author or authors.[22]

In November, Van Buren rode to Albany from Hudson on horseback, faultlessly dressed, carrying himself in a "jaunty" manner, and looking "more like a sportsman than a legislator." Despite this outward sign of confidence, and the good impression he intended to make as a freshman senator, Van Buren faced his first legislative test with pessimism—the choosing of presidential electors in a joint session of both houses.[23]

Much of Van Buren's dispirited mood stemmed from Clinton's political limitations as a poor organizer with no practical strategy for how to gain those electors. Into this breech stepped the twenty-nine-year-old Van Buren, the second youngest man then elected as state senator; he quickly assumed command over the older and more seasoned Clintonians. Tompkins's supporters, to the surprise of many, allowed this neophyte senator, with the help of an older political veteran, to draft the largely honorific reply to the governor's annual address.[24]

Van Buren's sudden prominence was particularly surprising given that others allowed him to assume that role even though the legislature was fertile with political talent. One reason for Tompkins's flattery was strictly political. He hoped to convince Van Buren to drop Clinton. But more importantly, Van Buren's legal reputation had preceded him as one of the party's most effective lawyer-politicians. At every level across the judicial spectrum, Van Buren's professional work had proven that he possessed all the qualities needed in a legislative chieftain: dispassionate and methodical reasoning, organizational ability, effective republicanism, and the knack to sway juries and judges—or in this instance, hostile legislators. Van Buren was a novice senator only in that this was his first term. Thrust into prominence as a Clintonian senator, Van Buren's legal success marked him as a promising man valued by each party faction.[25]

Van Buren quickly transferred his legal flair into political success. He used a key party principle, the precedent of tying party regularity and discipline to the party caucus, to outmaneuver the Madisonians and secure the electoral

ticket for Clinton. But Van Buren saved Clinton at great personal risk; his tactics estranged party leaders, notably Tompkins and Spencer, and alienated
Tammany Hall. Not everything was adverse, however. Despite the anger of
such men, Van Buren's adept work for Clinton earned their grudging respect.
Nevertheless, Van Buren had to repair this damage, particularly when Madison carried the Electoral College en route to his second term.[26]

When the short session adjourned, Van Buren returned to Hudson to his
pregnant wife who bore their third son on December 30, a new law office at
136 Warren Street, and some semblance of regular life. Immediately, he
plunged into his legal affairs. He arranged a debt collection for a Kinderhook
merchant and sold land for a client. He informed another that the attorney
general had asked for a postponement of his trial. He presided over a few
cases in surrogate court and dealt with William Peter Van Ness about an unpaid note to the Bank of Hudson. All the while, he was getting ready for the
coming terms of the Columbia Circuit and the Supreme Court.[27]

The caseload that Van Buren and his law partner handled continued to
rise. As part of these actions, Van Buren failed to pacify Birdsall about a proposed libel suit he intended to file against Jacob R. Van Rensselaer. Another
complication came from Jacob Radcliff, who found it inconvenient to meet
in snowy Kinderhook for arbitration in the Great Possession matter and suggested a more seasonable and less inclement time. While the commissioners
delayed, other litigation came Van Buren's way from Attorney General Emmet. In August 1812, he had authorized Van Buren "to institute and prosecute
in the name of the People" some ejectments in the "gore," the narrow strip
between the Livingston and Van Rensselaer properties, to test their titles.
Nothing immediate came of this effort. Five months later, the Federalist controlled council removed Emmet, as well as Surrogate Van Buren.[28]

Leaving additional matters to Miller, Van Buren returned to Albany on
January 13, 1813, for the second session of the Thirty-sixth legislature. This
time, Van Buren transformed his legal skills into parliamentary skills. The *Journal of the Senate* revealed a number of the major characteristics that had made
him an eminent lawyer. He was, first of all, tireless. Van Buren sat on thirty-six
select committees, as well as two joint committees and five conference committees. He was by no means the only workhorse in the senate, but few accomplished more. Secondly, Van Buren was knowledgeable. His professional
experience, greater than all but a few fellow senators, made him an irreplaceable member of any committee that considered legal principles and techni-
calities. Thirdly, Van Buren was attentive. The legislature met every morning,
and late on some afternoons for a second session, six days a week for thirteen
weeks. During that period, Van Buren missed only ten roll calls, mainly due to
a chronic bronchial ailment, a precursor of the asthma that plagued him for
most of his adult life. In the fourth instance, Van Buren was efficient. His reports were on time; none took as much as a week to reach the floor. Van Buren was also decisive. He used his knowledge of a subject to make a point; his

votes indicated a tendency to commit himself and to persist in his commitment. Above all, Van Buren was a republican ideologue. But his years of court
work had taught him when to flatter, cajole, or be congenial.[29]

In early 1813, party factionalism entered a fresh round over two key issues:
the selection of a new United States senator and Clinton's renomination for
lieutenant governor. As events played themselves out, these developments became the catalysts for Van Buren's final break with Clinton.[30]

As party factions jockeyed for the Senate seat, Van Buren became convinced
that Clinton had clandestinely thrown his support to the Federalist Rufus
King, the eventual winner. Clinton's actions were dishonorable, Van Buren believed, motivated by an immoral pay back for Clinton's Federalist support during the presidential campaign and, even more, by his Federalist reappointment
as mayor of New York City. When the party nominating caucus met, Van Buren trapped Clinton. In a speech of "considerable length," he urged Clinton's
selection, based on Clinton's own devotion to the precedent of regular nominations. As a result, Van Buren concluded, Clinton would "cheerfully and
heartily" back the ticket, even if Republicans chose someone else.[31]

Which is exactly what happened. The caucus named John Taylor, the senate president, for lieutenant governor. But Van Buren was the real winner. By
nominating Clinton, Van Buren forced him to respect party regularity, the basis of Clinton's presidential challenge, and established the impetus for party
unity in the spring elections. Despite grumbling from Southwick, Van Buren
achieved one of his political goals through distributive justice: the diminishing of a rival. Charles Holt, the editor of Clinton's New York City *Columbian,*
speaking for most Clintonians, acknowledged that they would honor "the
decisions of a majority of the legislature."[32]

Van Buren's transformation from a Clintonian to a Tompkins Republican
was now complete. In the process, Van Buren had demonstrated a means to
end New York's endemic factionalism, by offering up the dual precedents of
party regularity and party loyalty through the caucus system to replace Clinton's erratic politics of personality. Van Buren argued that the caucus system
epitomized classical republicanism, because it represented the popular will
through elected representatives. In addition, he validated himself as the coming man in the state Republican party. As a sign of his fresh status, the Tompkins Republicans selected him, no matter that he was a first-term senator, as a
candidate for the next Council of Appointment. Then they unanimously
named him to the committee of correspondence to prepare an address to
voters and supervise the campaign.[33]

Van Buren, although free from his tangled dependency on Clinton, nevertheless recognized that he still faced formidable problems before becoming
an equal party leader with Tompkins and Spencer. Personally, Van Buren
needed to end skepticism about his position on the war. Politically, he had to
turn the imperfectly articulated Republican party into an effective force, prevent factionalism from shattering its unity, and plan for the party's victory in

coming elections. But Van Buren's most immediate task was to prove that his ideology was a practical means to forge popular programs. His solution to each of these problems, when the legislature turned to questions of practical distributive justice, lay in his training and experience as a lawyer.

Fortunately, Federalist initiatives in the form of grandiose bank projects handed Van Buren his first opportunity to set party policy on an issue of substance. The Restraining Act of 1804, designed to protect existing banks, prohibited banking by unincorporated companies and voided their notes and securities. But by 1813, wartime finances created shortages in operating capital. In response, lobbyists and special interest groups swamped the legislature with petitions for new charters and modifications of previous ones. The Bank of America, as it had before, stirred the deepest passions when it sought to renege on capital requirements and the $600,000 bonus.

Van Buren led the opposition in the senate. Based on his background as an attorney, he chided the Bank of America that it had formed a binding contract with the state. One party to such a contract could not arbitrarily back out without committing a fraud. In the end, the Federalists, helped by a few Clintonians, passed the bill the Bank of America sought. The Council of Revision, consisting of the governor, chancellor, and judges of the Supreme Court, which had the sole power of veto subject to a two-thirds legislative override, concurred amid new suspicions of bribery. While the legislature took no "depositions" about this alleged corruption, Van Buren's firm stance demonstrated his leadership potential in the allocation of legislative economic favors.[34]

Van Buren found that a bill to incorporate a new bank in Catskill was a far better way to enunciate lasting guidelines about the politics of distributive justice, economic development, monetary questions, and legal instrumentalism. Although the report of debates in the *Journal of the Senate* was scanty, he left a memorandum sketching out his thoughts about the bill in his private papers. Van Buren contended that too many banks had created fictitious capital by substituting paper for specie. Such artificial capital increased hoarding of specie, lowered public confidence in the money supply, and distorted real values through inflation. If such inflation in monetary terms and deflation in real value continued, trade would inevitably decline until it reached stagnation. Under those conditions, only specie, which retained its value, proved that its "agents," or banks of issue, were stable. Any destruction of such a source of "confidence" through fresh charters and unlimited emissions of paper currency would depress the value of goods, property, and services, ultimately destroying the monetary system.[35]

At that point, Van Buren shifted his focus and emphasized how classical republicanism shaped his approach toward distributive justice and legal instrumentalism in general and the banking issue in specific. The public was "mistaken" in the belief that the Restraining Act regulated banking. Once the legislature chartered a bank, its board and shareholders were unanswerable to any public agency, and often harmed liberty and equality by concentrating large amounts of political and economic power in the hands of a few men. Proof rested with the improprieties surrounding the Bank of America. As conditions now stood, merchants, workshop owners, artisans, and country people had enough banks to accommodate their needs. The wisest policy to head off imminent statewide economic collapse lay in limiting new banks, specifically the proposed Bank of Catskill, which would restore public confidence in present ones.[36]

Yet Van Buren did not oppose all banks. As part of his evolving attitude toward liberal republicanism, Van Buren interpreted banking, as his growing role in the Bank of Hudson indicated, as a mechanism for capital investment and economic growth. Banks, moreover, if they followed the classical republican idea of equality, gave small depositors and businessmen an opportunity to compete against larger monied interests. But Van Buren believed that economic development through unregulated banks created special privileges for the few and hindered equality for the many. As a legal instrumentalist, Van Buren thought the legislature must indeed adjust to changing conditions. But he had no intention of acting as an apologist for unrestrained capitalism. Rather, his economic program was that of a man whose legal career and private experience confirmed the wisdom of operating within an orderly specie credit system, investing carefully, avoiding insolvency, and accumulating wealth steadily.

For the moment, Van Buren swayed few uncommitted minds. The Catskill bill passed with Federalist and some Clintonian votes. Yet by combining classical republicanism and liberal republicanism with his version of how a free market operated, Van Buren anticipated much of future Jacksonianism: monetary prudence through a specie currency, limitations on the political power of a financial elite, fears about the corruptive power of great wealth, and checks on privilege.[37]

Van Buren used another aspect of distributive justice and legal instrumentalism to redefine his position on the war. In early February, he aligned with prowar Republicans in their attempt to authorize a state loan of $500,000 to the federal government for the military. Before the session ended, he also authored a senate report that defended Madison and Tompkins from Federalist and Clintonian charges that their leadership was incapable of protecting New York City from British invasion.[38]

Van Buren made his prowar position even stronger through the law. Assembly Federalists introduced a resolution that censured the Republican-controlled House of Representatives for discouraging naval efficiency by failing to award the officers and crew of the U.S.S. *Constitution* prize money as one of the fruits of victory. To remedy this slight, they urged the senate to co-sponsor another resolution instructing the state's congressional delegation to introduce a special bill for that purpose.[39]

Republican senators referred the resolution to a committee that Van Buren chaired. The report, which he largely composed, was masterful. Applauding the assemblymen's patriotic gesture, Van Buren employed his professional skills to outline the resolution's technical flaws. The Federalists had mistakenly addressed the expired Twelfth Congress. Since the practice of instructing Congress applied only to future actions not past ones, the resolution was *"ex post facto."* Further, Van Buren undercut the Federalists by pointing out that Congress had already agreed to the prize money. With the issue moot, the senate could not engage in what was a politically-motivated trick against the Administration.[40]

Van Buren's steady climb in the senate was also due to additional qualities. His judicial philosophy, along with the republican principles that sustained his concept of a just society, demonstrated his true leadership. Such values were vital when he sat as a judge on the Court of Errors in *John W. Barry and Samuel Harbeck, survivors of Caspanus Hewson, Plaintiffs in Error, v. Ephraim Mandell, Assignee of Peter P. Dox, Esq. Sheriff of Albany, Defendant in Error.* The case was highly legalistic and best known because it concerned the controversial question of imprisonment for debt, but it actually focused on the validity of an 1809 Supreme Court decision. Here, Van Buren's far-reaching opinion cemented his importance to the party as its key lawyer-senator.

Although the appeal concerned Barry, an imprisoned debtor, and Harbeck, his associate, the major issue was the responsibilities of a sheriff in such instances. On March 30, 1801, the legislature had revised an existing law and allowed an imprisoned debtor to post bond and go "at large," provided the offender remained within prescribed geographic limits. Sheriffs were responsible for the prisoner under "gaol liberty," which retained the common law right to recapture the prisoner, and were protected from negligence charges by the creditor if the prisoner exceeded the limits but voluntarily returned. The act also stipulated that the bond was for a sheriff's indemnity alone.[41]

Barry, while herding a straying cow, walked several feet outside his limits on two occasions but returned, in essence breaking "gaol liberties." Under common law, and prior to the enactment of the 1801 statute, his activities would have been nonactionable because he returned voluntarily. But Mandell, the creditor and also the bail assignee of Sheriff Peter Dox of Albany County, sued Dox on the bond. Mandell's justifications rested on the Supreme Court's February 1809 decision in *Tillman v. Lansing,* as well as a March 1809 statute that permitted the creditor the right to sue for damages. But a complication existed. In April 1810, the legislature passed a new law that reinstated a sheriff's common law defenses of recapture and voluntary return, in direct opposition to *Tillman v. Lansing.*[42]

A jury in the 1811 Albany Court of Common Pleas found for Mandell. On appeal, the Supreme Court affirmed the judgment, but John Henry, Barry's attorney, filed a writ of error. In the Court of Errors, Henry for the plaintiffs and James A. Hamilton for Mandell, presented cogent arguments. Henry relied on common law; Hamilton on the two court decisions and the 1809 statute.[43]

As was Van Buren's custom, he spent long hours researching the question, verifying the facts, and paying close attention to each side. He then issued a lengthy judgment, running to ten pages in *Johnson's Reports*. Van Buren's opinion mirrored five of his basic commitments: partisan defense of office-holders, limited judicial discretion, legislative supremacy over the judiciary through legal positivism, ideological championship of civil liberties, and his Dutch-American ethical code of justice. On one level, Van Buren's effort was notable for his emotional and compassionate criticism of imprisonment for debt, "a practice fundamentally wrong" that penalized honest people "not for frauds," but "for the misfortune of being poor." Yet what gave his reasoning added strength were his professional experience, his principles, and his practical knowledge as a fence viewer in dealing with similar problems concerning straying cows.[44]

These factors were apparent when Van Buren turned his attention to *Tillman v. Lansing*. By citing its several legal defects, he revealed a firm understanding of the common law and a grasp of legal reasoning that was far more acute than that of any other senator. The decision, Van Buren asserted, was "improvident" and "erroneous." In the period before that case and the statute of March 1809, the state's soundest lawyers were under the universal impression that the common law rights of a sheriff, specifically the right of recapture along with deciding the status of an imprisoned debtor's voluntary return, were within his purview. *Tillman v. Lansing* and the 1809 statute shocked the legal profession. Both denied a sheriff any discretion to decide if a prisoner was guilty or innocent, even one who voluntarily returned, or had mistakenly wandered outside the prescribed limit to herd a grazing cow. Worse, both made a sheriff "*ipso facto*" liable to the creditor for the prisoner and divested the sheriff from the common law rights he previously enjoyed.[45]

The Supreme Court then committed an initial error by drawing false inferences about the 1801 statute, which governed the case. The judges indicated that the sheriff's common law rights still existed, but they pronounced that the statute removed those rights. In making such an assertion, the court ignored common law rules regarding the construction of statutes, some of which had become legal maxims. One of these, the key in this instance, held that the court should not presume to make any alterations in the common law beyond what the statute expressly declared. By this standard, Van Buren examined the act of 1801; he searched for but did not find any provisions indicating that it had taken away the sheriff's right of recapture or affected voluntary return. "What cannot be drawn from that source [the judges] seek to make up," Van Buren wrote. The result, he concluded, was that the Supreme Court, in *Tillman v. Lansing,* had established law, not interpreted existing statutes.[46]

The court had further erred in its effort to find justification for the decision by denying the sheriff his equity. This attempt violated two other legal maxims: an obscure statute ought to be construed according to the rules of common law, and an act removing or impeding a remedy that the party held under common law ought never to have an equitable construction. The court, therefore, had negated the most fundamental precepts of justice to reach its decision. While professing admiration for the court, Van Buren continued that judges were, "with the rest of mankind," not "infallible" and "sometimes unavoidably mistake the law." The legislature corrected this fallibility in April 1810 when it secured "to the sheriff his common law rights," virtually repealing the 1809 decision and its related statute. As a result, the legislature had legitimately curbed the court through legal positivism.[47]

The case had another problem as well, one that was more humane and less legalistic: the 1801 statute itself and its interpretation. The legislature had passed it, as the judges had observed, "for humane purposes." The law was a concession made by a society that had previously displayed an inflexible and often foolish attitude confounding "virtue and vice" and destroying "the distinction between guilt and innocence."[48] But the court, in *Tillman v. Lansing,* had not indicated the liberality that the statute suggested. Instead, the judges exacted a price few could pay. Their opinion forced imprisoned debtors, who were generally poor and "too often friendless," into rigorous confinement that required a sheriff to have "the utmost prudence and temperance" in order to obey its provisions. If that rule ever became the established law of the land, no debtor would ever secure bail since no sensible person would come forward.[49]

As for the sheriff, the court injured the operations of his office. The bail might seem secure, but "no subject was more uncertain and deceptive than the solvency of men in business." The decision implied that the sheriff lacked jurisdiction if a prisoner stepped beyond the limits of his liberty, deprived the sheriff of "the security of his *lock and key,*" and hindered his common law right to capture the prisoner. Even if the prisoner voluntarily returned, the sheriff was still liable. Under those conditions, the sheriff could rely only on the prisoner's bond for security. But in allowing the creditor to sue the sheriff for recovery, the statute additionally penalized equity by giving the creditor more security than the sheriff, even before he brought suit for his own indemnification. That placed the sheriff at risk for conditions over which he lacked control, making the attempt to hold him accountable "monstrous."[50]

In conclusion, Van Buren maintained that every point of law led "necessarily and imperiously" to the fact that the Court of Errors must reverse the finding. On March 31, 1813, the court, with the exception of one absent senator, concurred. It ruled that Mandell should receive nothing for his complaint and ordered him to pay Barry and Harbeck full costs and remit their expenses.[51]

The case of *Barry v. Mandell,* sometimes scoffingly called the "cow case," made a lasting impression on Van Buren. On April 2, he introduced a bill "for relief of small debtors." While the senate did not act on this proposal during the session, Van Buren proposed similar bills in succeeding terms and, later, in the United States Senate, adding to his reputation, one admirer noted, as a politician guided by "liberal opinions."[52]

Van Buren revealed a further trait as a political propagandist and strategist of the first rank in the political skirmishing before the gubernatorial election. Whether politicking or addressing juries, he understood that results hinged on numbers, numbers he could sway through advocacy. Van Buren now sought those numbers in an electrifying but demagogic, 6,000-word prowar "Address to the Electors of New York," which defended Tompkins and harshly berated his critics.[53]

Some Clintonians, notably the Hogebooms, resented Van Buren's attitude, but most fell in line out of fear of being branded disloyalists. Election returns produced no mandate. Tompkins won with 52.3 percent of the total vote statewide, and prowar Republicans retained the senate. Yet Federalists kept the assembly. Van Buren was discouraged. New York, he moaned, had to "struggle" with another deadlocked session and lacked "the ability" to give "any essential aid to the public cause."[54]

A large part of Van Buren's snappish mood came from the high price he had paid in his law practice, which he had neglected during this intense period of legislative work. Except for two appearances in the Albany Court of Probates during March and April, his profession was secondary. He did not even prepare the seven cases that his firm listed on the August 1813 Supreme Court docket. Nor did he fully negotiate a small property sale in Kinderhook for a widow. But by mid-summer, Van Buren resumed his normal affairs. In July, he lent Jonathan Dakin $400, taking a mortgage on his property on the De Bruyn Patent, and filed some cases in chancery.[55]

By August, Van Buren reappeared before the Supreme Court. Five nonenumerated causes came from the Bank of Hudson, each a nonsuit in his favor. But four of the enumerated ones held great meaning for Van Buren, because all concerned the key legal issue in his early career: landholding in Columbia County. *Jones v. Gardner* centered on a buyer's refusal to pay a lease due to Robert Van Rensselaer since the description of the property was incomplete. Ruling that Van Buren's client had acted in good faith, the court decided for him. Van Buren also reached some sort of accommodation with the contentious Birdsall and represented him in *Jackson, ex dem. Livingston, v. Baker.* Birdsall had leased land from John S. Livingston and then subleased it to Daniel Baker. Livingston gave Birdsall notice to quit. Van Buren, acting for Baker, objected on the grounds that Baker should have been notified since he had actual possession. But the court backed Williams, who insisted that notice was unnecessary. *Jackson, ex dem. Livingston, v. Kisselbrack* and *Jackson, ex dem. Livingston and Others, v. Sclover* also involved the rights of tenants on Livingston land. In each, the court decided that a Livingston agent had acted incorrectly, giving judgments for Van Buren's clients, who kept possession of their property. In the only unrelated case, the *Matter of Esther Gardenier v. Spikeman,* Van Buren sought to protect a widow's property rights. But the court quashed his appeal against an admeasurement of dower because it was premature.[56]

At the end of the summer, Van Buren once more became enmeshed in the unresolved question of land ownership in the Great Possession when a final settlement seemed ready. The three commissioners, after holding hearings during September 1813, made their "final order, award and determination on the premises." Their decision mainly concerned the southern boundary of the De Bruyn Patent, which they restored to its earlier location while extending the eastern boundary southward. Both awards favored Van Buren's clients and validated his original contentions. The title to one particular piece of land, the Ambler farm possessed by John Niver, was vested in those claiming title under the De Bruyn Patent. The commissioners decided that Niver, on payment of $30 per acre to those claimants, received title "to hold and enjoy forever." These awards should have ended the Great Possession cause. They did not. One group, the Van Alens, Van Buren's kinsmen, decided to contest the finding for Niver. Even so, this favorable settlement further weakened the landed elite in the Middle District and reconfirmed Van Buren's importance as the tenants' champion.[57]

In the fall, Van Buren swung into a vigorous new round of legal business. In October, he boarded the steamboat to New York City for the Supreme Court's term. He had eight cases, five for the Bank of Hudson over defaulted collections. The court upheld him in each, awarding the bank $879.62 for costs and damages, plus the original debts. The rest came from the Columbia Circuit of October 1812 under Judge William W. Van Ness.[58]

Van Buren represented Moses Cantine in *Gunn v. Cantine.* Emmanuel Gunn, an attorney, sued Cantine, also an attorney, for funds he had collected on behalf of Gunn's assignee, Stephen Simmons, but had not distributed to Gunn. Van Buren insisted that "nothing" existed "in the agreement" between Simmons and Gunn, either by intent or agreement, that entitled him "to the money." Until they reached some understanding, Cantine could not legally disburse any funds, because "an attorney can do no act in his own name." A *per curiam* upheld Van Buren.[59]

The case of *The President, Directors, and Company of the Farmers' Turnpike Road v. Coventry* raised the knotty problem of interpreting a legislative charter. In gaining the right to build a road from Troy "to" Hudson, the company received the power to erect toll gates no closer than three miles from each terminal. Van Buren's client, acting for Hudson, removed a toll gate that he contended was less than three miles from the terminal and blocked an old free highway. The issue was relatively plain: where was the starting spot that determined the terminal's location? Was it at the center of the city, the "compact part of the city," as the company held, or at its legal limits, as Van Buren argued the legislature intended? The court found for the company. The governing definition for the word "to" in the charter meant the compact part of each city. By hindering the company from erecting the toll gate, the defendant had committed trespass, a "matter actionable at common law."[60]

This loss confirmed Van Buren's belief that judges were not interpreting the law so much as second-guessing the legislature and ignoring legal positivism. Those harmed by such companies had several remedies: the political process could pass antimonopoly laws; chancery could use fresh tort rules to establish corporate responsibilities for liabilities and damages; or the state attorney general could act for the people based on legislative intent. Eventually, Van Buren would implement each approach.[61]

Another case, *Richmond v. Dayton,* concerned the powers of a justice of the peace and possible false imprisonment. Sylvanus Richmond had asked Henry Dayton, a justice of the peace, about a judgment against him. When Dayton replied that Richmond owed 50 cents, he cursed Dayton as a "damned old rascal" and shouted "many other words" that cast "aspersions" on Dayton's "official and judicial character." Richmond then fled. Dayton immediately issued a warrant for Richmond's arrest; he stipulated that Richmond remain in "gaol" until he had "sufficient security" from bail and until the next general session. When a constable arrested Richmond, another justice took bail and discharged him. Van Buren, again defending a Republican party official, admitted that Dayton was not holding court or acting in an official capacity when Raymond uttered those words. Yet Van Buren maintained that Dayton had the prerogative to bind over all persons who threatened "to break the peace" or spoke "words scandalizing a justice." But the court ruled the issue moot. Dayton had not actually executed the warrant because Richmond was not jailed. Yet the judges did please Van Buren in a roundabout way; they commended Dayton for his lawful manner.[62]

When Van Buren returned to Hudson, he found more business waiting. He collected a debt for his brother, Abraham, a fellow attorney who was in military service. Additional work loomed in common pleas and general sessions, as well as preparation for the next Columbia Circuit and three minor causes in the October Supreme Court. Van Buren also enlisted the help of Comptroller Archibald McIntyre to prevent an effort "by a few individuals to obtain sole" control of the Bank of Hudson in an unfriendly takeover.[63] Amid this business, Van Buren initiated an extensive correspondence with Congressman John W. Taylor of Ballston in Saratoga County. In one letter, Van Buren outlined the breadth of his staggering workload. "I am Judge Advocate in the tedious trial" of Brigadier General William Hull, "a member of the Court of Errors, bound to prepare opinions," a "Legislator obliged to step into the Senate Chamber every two or three hours to stop the passage of some wicked law," and an "Albany counsel in the Supreme Court & Common Pleas & Mayor['s] Court with many great important callings and avocations."[64]

Even for a man with such an obsessive work ethic, Van Buren's burden was indeed heavy. But the most startling part of this load was his sudden connection to Hull's long-awaited court-martial. How Van Buren became a special judge advocate, the government official who advocated the case under the supervision of the court, is uncertain. Originally, Secretary of War William Eustis scheduled the court-martial for February 1813 in Philadelphia, with Alexander J. Dallas as special judge advocate. Dallas methodically prepared the charges and specifications against Hull. But after Eustis resigned in December 1812, the Administration fumbled over a replacement and postponed the prosecution to an indefinite date. On November 17, 1813, the new secretary of war, John Armstrong of New York, an ally of Spencer, cut fresh orders for the court-martial under General Henry A. Dearborn; it was set for Albany on January 3, 1814. Dallas was now secretary of the treasury. As his substitute, Armstrong selected Van Buren. Philip Parker, Spencer's nephew, an attorney who practiced in Hudson and Albany, became assistant army judge advocate. Why Van Buren accepted is difficult to determine. Perhaps he wanted to accentuate his support for the Administration and the war. Or perhaps Van Buren sought to strengthen his alliance with Spencer through Armstrong, even though Van Buren did not trust Armstrong.[65]

Whatever the conjectural motives were that prompted Van Buren's acceptance, they were less important than his self-made quagmire. He agreed to serve on the very eve of the trial. That meant he was unprepared on opening day and immediately following. As he complained to Dallas, "I am considerably embarrassed in making the arrangements preparatory to the trial." While Van Buren's selection accentuated his professional reputation, he stood a good chance of disgrace if he lost. Fortunately, no witnesses of "considerable rank or information" appeared and the court ordered a recess. Van Buren put this time to productive use. Examining more fully the materials Dallas had prepared, he communicated with Dallas and Armstrong about pertinent documents. Yet Van Buren might have been too busy for his own good. Even as he worked up the Hull brief, Van Buren appeared before the Supreme Court in two difficult cases and prepared for the next senate session.[66]

One of these cases, *Jackson, ex dem. Van Rensselaer, v. Collins,* came from Judge Yates's circuit and involved a land dispute in the "gore" among the Van Rensselaer and Livingston families—with Collins, Van Buren's client, crunched between them. Collins had refused to pay Stephen Van Rensselaer rent because Henry W. Livingston challenged Van Rensselaer's title. The issue rested on one point: common law doctrine and statute law required landlords to give adequate notice to tenants for rent due prior to ejectment. Van Buren stressed that these due process protections mandated a demand or a legal request for rent due before ejectment, and that Van Rensselaer had failed to give Collins adequate notice. Williams replied that demand was unnecessary, since Collins had forfeited his lease by nonpayment. Kent for the court ruled for Williams. Collins's refusal to pay the rent amounted to a waiver of the notice requirement. Although Van Buren had a poor case in which to protect the individual liberties of tenants through due process, his approach was consistent with his overall economic tactics against the landlord class.[67]

The second of these cases, *Raymond v. Squire,* a labyrinthine procedural issue of property in Broome County, was equally relevant to Van Buren's concerns. On January 3, 1810, Squire deeded land to Raymond who sold the
premises to Benoni St. John for $2,106. In March 1811, Raymond and St.
John learned that Squire did not own the land. The following July, Raymond
gave St. John a power of attorney to sue Squire in Raymond's name. But in
September 1811, Raymond, without St. John's knowledge, gave Squire a full
release in return for a payment of $1,300. St. John brought suit in Raymond's
name because he wanted his money back. Van Buren for Squire argued that
Raymond had released his client; the power of attorney did not give St. John
the right to sue in Raymond's name. A *per curium* ruled against Van Buren,
listing the common law and several precedents based on the state's statute of
fraud in order to reason that Raymond had obtained the release by fraud and
it was therefore void. The court went on to say that the power of attorney
was a valid assignment of the right to sue and ordered the matter to trial. In
essence, the court handed Van Buren an ironic rebuke. It turned legal positivism against him by emphasizing statute law, rather than the case's facts, as
he contended.[68]

Van Buren had little time to digest these reversals when the legislature
convened on January 25, 1814. It was a time of unmitigated gloom. On the
military front, British invaders threatened New York along its Canadian borders. Public skepticism about the Administration's ability to wage war increased, and Federalists rode the crest of an antiwar tide. More than ever,
Tompkins proved indomitable. In his annual address, he urged the legislature
to expand the militia and fund self-defense through the state treasury, perhaps
by instituting a bond program secured by chartered banks. When state banks
refused to underwrite such bonds without firm collateral, Tompkins made
himself personally liable to financial ruin by endorsing the federal treasury
notes that the state banks demanded for guarantees.[69]

Although the senate honored Van Buren by naming him to a committee
charged with drafting its official reply to Tompkins, Van Buren never participated. The day after Tompkins's message, Hull's court-martial board decided
that it had sufficient witnesses to begin the trail. Over the next three weeks,
Van Buren became "excessively engaged," as he wrote Taylor, in the details of
the examination.[70]

The court had taken several important procedural steps in the interval.
Under General Dearborn's direction, it found a permanent meeting place in
the Supreme Court's Albany chambers. It also permitted Hull to employ
Robert Tillotson and Cadwallader D. Colden, both civilians, as co-counsels.
In addition, the court listed the charges and specifications against Hall. At this
point, civil law diverged from the Articles of War. A court-martial, unlike civil
law, had no permanent existence. The power to convene the court, synonymous with naming a jury, depended on the severity of the charges. In Hull's

case, the court listed three major charges: treason, cowardice, and neglect of duty. Each charge carried explicit specifications: three for treason, four for cowardice, seven for neglect of duty. In military justice, charges were specific accusations and specifications were the alleged facts or events that justified the charges. The court had to determine whether the specifications did occur and if they proved the charges. The court was not permitted to stray from the charges and specifications as written.[71]

These parameters placed Van Buren in an unfamiliar situation. Trained in civilian courts and procedures, he had to learn the provisions of the Articles of War while he acted as the government's advocate. To make Van Buren's situation even more difficult, General Dearborn was hardly impartial. Armstrong had recently removed him from active command for lack of initiative, and he demanded a court of inquiry to repair his name. Dearborn was also Hull's direct superior in 1812. With the case thus politicized and personally charged, an acquittal would implicate Dearborn, President Madison, and former Secretary of War Eustis in what the public viewed as a national shame.[72]

Van Buren's role was no less delicate. In the largest sense a floor manager, his tasks involved ensuring that witnesses were present, that proceedings moved forward, and that a clerk kept a record. Moreover, he was not a prosecutor in the strictest sense, but an advocate bound to present as fully and fairly as possible the factual evidence that supported the government's charges "exhibited" against Hull. The material Van Buren left in his private papers indicates that he prepared in habitual fashion. Beginning with a chronology of events, he noted the points at which problems developed or failures occurred, correlated these with facts that backed the charges, and took testimony from witnesses to "prove" the specifications. He also systematically annotated the printed charges and specifications, consolidated them in a working precis, and revised Dallas's notes on the kind of evidence needed from witnesses.[73]

On January 26, Van Buren addressed the court *in camera*. In his opening statement, he listed an historical account of Hull's entire expedition, starting with the probability of war in the spring of 1812, Hull's subsequent responses, and his surrender. The court had to determine which one, or all, of three probable factors caused his surrender: "the inadequacy" of the military resources the Administration had provided Hull; the "unavoidable discomforture which sometimes attended the best concerted operations in war"; or "the Treachery, Cowardice or Mismanagement of the Commanding General." Summarizing the situation, Van Buren concluded that the disaster lay "exclusively" with Hull.[74]

Van Buren then presented more than sixty documents, mostly letters that passed between Hull and Eustis, to back that conclusion. On January 27, Van Buren began calling witnesses to substantiate the charges and specifications. This process lasted until February 11. The court then allowed Hull a ten-day continuance to prepare his defense. During this recess, Van Buren resumed his senate duties but accomplished little. When the court reassembled on February 21, it was short three members and adjourned for two more days. Proceedings finally moved ahead. Hull took six days to present his defence, calling six subordinates as rebuttal witnesses, along with several civilians and various comrades in arms, who testified about his devotion to duty and good character, his patriotism and courage.[75]

On March 15, Hull delivered his final comments to the court, which admitted the public for the first time, and continued for about three hours a day until Friday, March 18. It was a long, well-prepared statement in which he absolved himself of all specifications and charges, blamed others for the surrender, and alleged that the Administration had promised promotions to many witnesses who perjured themselves in exchange for lying about his conduct. Hull ended with fawning comments about Van Buren: while "I may feel the force of the talents with which he has conducted this prosecution, it shall not make me forget what I owe to his humanity and liberality."[76]

Hull had an ulterior motive for praising Van Buren. Before finishing, he offered the court Colden's written argument against allowing Van Buren's request to summarize the evidence. Past court-martials, Hull claimed, had rarely allowed a special judge advocate, a component part of the prosecution, to go beyond his assigned role of developing charges, presenting specifications, questioning witnesses, and acting as a consultant on points of military law. When that process was complete, his functions ceased. Because of the court-martial's composition, which contained Hull's peers, their judgment was based on factors that only they, as military men, could appreciate. Such judgment did not require the aid of a civilian attorney whose training, talent, and experience were in civil law, and who might use "professional ingenuity" in "a mode of procedure novel and unauthorized."[77]

After deliberating, the court did give Van Buren the final word. On March 23 he started the summation in a systematic, understated way by linking his opening statement to subsequent evidence. After reviewing the historical record again, Van Buren denied the heart of Hull's defense, his placement of responsibility upon the Administration, his troops, and his officers. If facts warranted, Van Buren said, he intended "to refute these odious recriminations and lay the blame where it ought to rest." Then, taking both the court and Hull by surprise, Van Buren abandoned the treason charge "as unsupported and insupportable." Yet Hull still stood guilty of cowardice and neglect of duty. Growing more acerbic, Van Buren claimed that the specifications supported the charges. Hull blundered in his invasion of Lower Canada, misused his resources, mishandled his command, and "abjectly" surrendered his troops to a force inferior in numbers and quality without adequate cause. He submitted to terms "dishonorable" and "injurious" to his nation out of personal fear "and that only." In sum, the specifications, proven by patriotic soldiers, were "creditable to the Government & deplorable to the accused."[78]

On March 25, the court announced its decision. It acquitted Hull of treason on the grounds Van Buren presented. But the next day, the court found Hull guilty of the remaining charges and sentenced him to death by firing squad. In consideration of Hull's "revolutionary services and advanced age," however, the court recommended presidential clemency. Madison agreed.[79]

Van Buren immediately felt relief at the end of a trial he had described to Armstrong as "unpleasant" and "painful." The case had prevented Van Buren from fulfilling his senate duties and "from attending" the Supreme Court where he "had many causes of consequence," resulting in a "serious loss" of income. While he hoped that Madison and Armstrong were content with the results, Van Buren pressed them to recompense his services in a business-like fashion. But the question of "compensation," he added, was embarrassing due to his "ignorance" about such matters. "Some prominent military friends" suggested a $3,000 fee. The strapped government did not meet his terms. After waiting several months, Van Buren received $2,000, a handsome amount, but far short of what he considered adequate.[80]

Yet Van Buren had achieved much. He substantiated his professional reputation and abilities in a difficult case, far distant from his normal practice. His conduct, even if Hull sought to curry favor from the court, was characteristically courteous and kind. He had, for the first time, emerged from the pack of parochial New York lawyers to become a person of national significance. Above all, Van Buren had bolstered the war effort, giving the Administration a political and psychological shot of adrenalin by making Hull and men of his ilk scapegoats for American defeats. Taking these factors into consideration, the trial helped Van Buren approach his next goal, equality with Tompkins and Spencer.

Becoming a Republican State Attorney General

*V*an Buren's ambition to be a true party leader indicated that he was on the threshold of a new phase in his dual career. To achieve his goal, Van Buren realized the need to expand his base in the senate and to acquire an important state office. Once again, Van Buren used his profession as a starting point and began a low-key effort to become New York's attorney general. Almost immediately, however, Van Buren was exhausted by his efforts in the Hull trial. Rest was impossible, though, because the question of distributive justice and legal instrumentalism in relation to banking reappeared in a fresh guise. The problem lay buried in the 1804 Restraining Act, which had not expressly forbidden existing incorporated businesses from engaging in banking and associated functions. Exploiting this weakness, several Federalists and Clintonians floated a number of petitions and bills to grant such mediums banking privileges. During recesses in the Hull trial, Van Buren voted against six. Upon resuming his senate duties, he spearheaded opposition against Morgan Lewis's petition to grant that the New York Coal Company become a bank. Van Buren rejected these attempts for the same reasons he had advanced earlier against the Catskill bank bill, but he added a new wrinkle to the debate under *quo warranto.* Since the Restraining Act had not authorized such privileges, any institution engaging in them usurped a legislative prerogative.[1]

A potentially costly land claim against New York by John Jacob Astor, reputedly the nation's richest entrepreneur, aroused even greater excitement regarding the state's perilous finances. In 1697, King William III had granted Adolph Philipse the Highland Patent of some 205,000 acres, which straddled the future counties of Putnam and Dutchess and reached as far as Connecticut. Philipse died in 1749, leaving his nephew, Frederick Philipse, sole heir. He died two years later, having devised the property to his four children. They, in turn, divided the land. Complications began when one of his daughters, Mary Philipse, who had about 50,000 acres, announced her intention to marry Roger Morris, a British naval officer, whom her siblings feared was a fortune hunter. To protect her, they prepared a marriage settlement in which Mary Philipse relinquished title to her sisters. Upon Mary Philipse's marriage, they agreed to transfer the property back through a life estate, an arrangement that entitled Mary Morris to income from the property for the duration of her life. When she died, the remainder interest reverted to her children. Mary Morris signed the agreement in 1758. But for reasons that are unclear, she did not record the document with proper authorities in Albany, leaving it in the care of her brother-in-law, Beverly Robinson.[2]

During the Revolution, Mary and Roger Morris became Loyalists and fled to Great Britain. The state confiscated their property under an attainder. In 1785, the New York Commissioners of Forfeiture began selling the property in fee simple, unaware that they could not issue complete titles because Mary Morris held a claim only to a life estate. During this period, the British awarded the Morrises compensation for their apparently lost property, but ruled that the terms of the Treaty of Paris protected the remainder rights of her children. Meanwhile, a number of people, including John Jay and Governor William Livingston of New Jersey, had read the marriage settlement and vouched for its authenticity. In 1787, Robinson finally recorded the marriage settlement in the office of the New York secretary of state, explaining that he had waited until the confiscation process was complete in order to protect the Morris's children. With that done, Mary Morris's children, one sister, and Robinson petitioned the legislature for the remainder. A committee, headed by Alexander Hamilton, reported that the judicial process, not the legislature, was the proper venue.

So matters rested until 1809 when Astor, perhaps acting on information that Aaron Burr supplied, learned about the situation. Sensing an opportunity to make a quick killing, Astor bought out the Morris children for $100,000. Astor assumed that since the marriage settlement was not registered until 1787, the attainder applied only to Mary Morris's life estate and did not affect the remainder interest of her children. For the moment, Astor and the Morris children agreed that the claim would remain "inchoate," a contract begun but not completed, until Mary Morris died and ended her life estate. But hoping to recoup his investment and avoid years of protracted court battles, Astor offered New York the property for $300,000.[3]

Van Buren chaired a senate committee that considered the matter. Determined to protect the property of innocent purchasers, he presented a report emphasizing that enough evidence existed to prove that Astor's demand was void, because he had obtained a "pretended title" by violating the statute to prevent "Champerty Maintenance." Champerty was a legal doctrine defined as a bargain by a third party to a suit in which that party undertook litigation at his own cost and risk. Maintenance was the responsibility for undertaking that litigation for others. With this in mind, Van Buren recommended a resolution, which the legislature adopted, requiring the attorney general to defend New York against Astor "in all and every suit or action" for the land that the state had acquired through the attainder and sold to inhabitants.[4]

Other topics on Van Buren's schedule reflected his personal views on distributive justice and legal instrumentalism. Like other senators, he introduced several private bills, amendments, and resolutions to serve his constituents. Late in the session, for example, he sponsored a bill stemming from the "cow case" to define the duties of sheriffs in respect to prisoners. Then there was Burr, who had recently returned penniless from European exile and resumed his law practice. When few clients appeared, Burr tried to augment his meager income; he petitioned the legislature for compensation from the state's military bounty land because of his Revolutionary service. When the Committee on Claims declined, Van Buren took charge. In the senate, he attempted—and failed—to secure a special award allowing Burr 1,500 acres. Even so, Van Buren partially paid a debt of friendship to his erstwhile mentor at a time when few New Yorkers were so forgiving.[5]

Van Buren was just as involved in the Court of Errors. Between his summation against Hull and the legislature's adjournment, he attended three court sessions that considered five cases, voting with the majority in four to reverse Supreme Court rulings. Of these, the most significant was the civil libel suit that Ambrose Spencer brought against Solomon Southwick; the whole court adopted Van Buren's opinion, which set a precedent for similar actions in the future.[6]

Southwick had escaped conviction for bribery during Attorney General Emmet's short tenure, since the state failed to produce adequate evidence of guilt. But during the heat of battle preceding the Bank of America's incorporation, Southwick had attempted to deflect corruption charges. In the *Albany Register,* he alleged that vote-buying was pervasive in New York's political culture. As proof, Southwick wrote that Spencer, when he was a senator in 1798, had deceived the legislature by using "hypocritical cants and practices" in the bill to incorporate Burr's Manhattan Company. The bill contained an ambiguous clause that allowed the company to start a bank. Southwick further accused Spencer of having a "pecuniary" interest in the bank and making an illegal profit of several thousand dollars in stock. Spencer answered with a libel suit.[7]

In October 1812, the Supreme Court heard the first round of *Spencer v.*

Southwick. It decided on narrow procedural grounds that Southwick's plea, his reply to Spencer's declaration specifying the factual reasons for libel, was adequate and ruled against Spencer. During the August 1813 term, Spencer, with the court's permission, responded through a replication, the reply to Southwick's plea. The court again ruled for Southwick on narrow technical grounds. In the process, however, the court listed two differing constructions of libel. Spencer then secured a writ of error, with Emmet as his lead attorney.[8]

Van Buren's opinion in *Ambrose Spencer, Plaintiff in error, v. Solomon Southwick, Defendant in error,* conformed to his usual method. He assembled a well-researched analysis of the legal maneuvers on both sides, the Supreme Court's opinions, and its conflicting constructions of libel. In the first case, Van Buren noted, the judges had limited libel to Southwick's charge that Spencer betrayed his trust as an elected official for personal gain. In the second, the judges had stated that libel was possible in Southwick's accusation that Spencer hoodwinked the public in passing the bill under false pretenses, not mentioning his pecuniary motives. Van Buren insisted that both constructions could not be correct. Of the two, the first was proper. Southwick intended to malign Spencer for lining his pockets with illicit profits.[9]

The court, Van Buren continued, had erred in not making Southwick prove that Spencer had indeed deceived the legislature to enrich himself. Besides, the court's rulings revealed a dangerous doctrine. By allowing a newspaper to make unsubstantiated charges against a person and leaving libel "to the inference of the reader," the burden of guilt rested on the accused, since the accuser did not present compelling facts to back the allegations. Such irresponsible behavior negated Spencer's civil rights, left him "without adequate remedy," and formed "a rampart, from behind which the blackest scurrility and the most odious crimination might be hurled on private character with impunity." The upshot would "render the press both a public and private curse."[10]

By every legal standard, Van Buren concluded, Southwick had libeled Spencer. In the first case, Southwick's attorneys had inadequately answered Spencer's plea for proof of corruption. In the second, they had addressed only the charge of deception and hypocrisy, again avoiding the issue of corruption. Clearly, Southwick meant to impeach Spencer's "official conduct as a Senator" and accused him of "great depravity as a man" because of "mercenary considerations" and "personal aggrandizement." For these reasons, Van Buren urged the Court of Errors to reverse the Supreme Court. The Court of Errors agreed by a unanimous vote, ordering Southwick to pay full damages and costs.[11]

This case, like Van Buren's crusade against landlords, demonstrated the bond between his classical republicanism and his dual career in law and politics. Through *Spencer v. Southwick,* Van Buren reemphasized his commitments to defend party officeholders, guard civil rights, and curb judicial power by legislative review. Earning Spencer's gratitude was an added benefit; the only uncertainty was for how long. In the case of freedom of the press, Van Buren did not advocate prior restraint or the muzzling of newspapers. As a political manager, he valued newspapers as powerful instruments to check entrenched power, educate the public, and instruct party workers.[12]

These four months had been arduous for Van Buren, but he was hardly a drudge. Outgoing by nature, he continued to make "friends"—the contemporary jargon denoting political allies—among other legislators. Some became important members of his future Albany Regency, among them Erastus Root, William C. Bouck, Samuel Young, and John Savage. Van Buren made another key contact when Major General Winfield Scott visited Albany. They formed an enduring friendship, with occasional breaks caused by political differences.[13]

In February 1814, Van Buren's law practice entered a new legal and political stage. The Federalist Council of Appointment reshuffled the judiciary when age limitations forced Chancellor John Lansing to retire. The council chose the Supreme Court Chief Justice James Kent, a Federalist, to replace Lansing. As chief justice, they named Smith Thompson, the senior associate justice, a Tompkins Republican, and Van Buren's friend. As an associate justice, they selected the Federalist Jonas Platt.[14]

But Van Buren could not immediately digest the legal and political implications of these changes because the war dominated everything. In New England, Federalists teetered between constructive dissent and outright treason. Among prowar Republicans, gloom spread as the prospect of achieving military victory grew more illusive. With conditions so baleful, party legislators, along with a large number of voters from across the state, gathered at Albany on April 14, 1814 for a precampaign rally. Van Buren, reflecting his new stature as the party's leading prowar senator and chief campaign strategist, delivered the main, patriotic address. His oratory worked. Party workers left the gathering in "excellent spirits."[15]

The spring elections gave Van Buren all that he wished. Voters, tired of Federalist intransigence, turned them out of office in droves, guaranteeing the prowar Republicans the next council. Their largest majority occurred in New York City. According to the Federalist *Evening Post,* this was accomplished because of what they scathingly called the actions of a few "rotten federalists," the so-called "Coodies," nicknamed after Gulian C. Verplanck's anonymous attack on Clinton under the pen name of "Abimelech Coody." Tied to Rufus King, the Coodies were embarrassed by their party's antiwar stance and repelled by its continual truckling to Clinton. Thus they gave prowar Republicans the critical edge they needed.[16]

An elated Van Buren returned to his law firm, which Miller had managed during the legislative session, in late April. Their practice had continued to burgeon. Van Buren had attracted new clients with the laurels he earned in *Barry v. Mandell,* the Hull trial, and *Spencer v. Southwick.* More importantly, on April 19, 1814, Van Buren met Court of Chancery requirements to practice equity as a counsellor in chancery, the highest position in his profession.[17]

As a solicitor in chancery, Van Buren had prepared a number of actions: generally, protections of mortgages and bonds from creditors; divorce proceedings; and injunctions against property confiscations, usually led by Counsellor John Henry. With his new standing, Van Buren quickly filed five actions. The most important applied to an earlier case, *Keisselbrack v. Livingston.* Chancellor Kent granted Van Buren an injunction that prevented Henry Livingston from selling Keisselbrack's personal property and improvements in real property, pending a full chancery presentation.[18]

May found Van Buren in New York City with four cases. Three were easy collections for the Bank of Hudson. *Jenkins and Others v. Waldron* was out of the ordinary because it mixed racial attitudes, politics, and Van Buren's steady support for party officials. Waldron, a "free man of colour" who had voted in assembly contests for about ten years, tried to cast a ballot in the April 1811 election in Hudson. As the law required, Waldron presented his certificate of freedom, signed by Samuel Edmonds, a Federalist justice of the peace in the Town of Livingston, a sign that Waldron was also a Federalist. The four Republican election inspectors refused to accept Waldron's vote on a technicality. They claimed Edmonds was not a justice of the peace when he had signed the certificate. Federalists retorted that the inspectors were motivated by racial prejudice masked by partisanship and sought redress in the Columbia Circuit. When the jury found for the inspectors, Waldron's attorneys appealed and the Supreme Court issued a *writ of certiorari.*[19]

The brief that Waldron's Federalist attorneys filed held that Edmonds was a *de facto* judge because the council had not removed him from office by a *supersedeas,* a formal notice ordering him to cease exercising his authority. Waldron was thus a legal voter and had an actionable cause against the inspectors. Van Buren, representing the inspectors, maintained that the commissions the council issued to new judges automatically terminated the tenure of old judges. He emphasized that the common law required Waldron to prove that the inspectors had acted "willfully" and "maliciously" with intent to injure. Waldron's lawyers had presented no such evidence. The court, through Spencer, accepted Van Buren's reasoning.[20]

Whether Van Buren acted as a scrupulous advocate, a blind partisan, or simply a racist, is impossible to ascertain. As an advocate, Van Buren was bound to protect his clients in the most effective manner, whatever his personal beliefs. As a partisan, he had no wish to enhance Federalists; his defense of officeholders was limited to Republicans. But Van Buren was also a slaveowner who came from a long line of Dutch-American slaveowners and owned at least one slave as late as December 1824. He did not consider how classical republicanism, or his attempts to modify contracts, applied to statutes that treated enslaved African-Americans as property. This dichotomy in Van Buren's ideology would reappear again, much to his embarrassment.[21]

The dawdling end of the Great Possession posed a different sort of legal problem for Van Buren. Preliminary to the final award, the Van Alens had rejected a survey of Niver's farm and requested a new survey by a neutral surveyor. Van Buren, associated with Peter Van Schaack, approached the commissioners for a postponement. They refused, leaving Van Buren with only an ejectment against Niver as the Van Alens's remedy.[22]

During this period, Van Buren's ambitions, together with his recurrent insecurity about how his limited legal education curtailed those ambitions, took a new direction. In June 1814, he began a transaction to purchase the law library of George Caines, a well-known Catskill attorney and legal scholar, and the appellate system's first official reporter. Caines was deeply in debt. His judicial emolument, $850 a year, had not covered his overhead, particularly stenographic expenses, and ill-health made his practice moribund. For a price, Van Buren was willing to help. By July, they reached an agreement. Van Buren lent Caines $6,000 at seven percent interest, collateralized by his extensive law library. Van Buren was "to have and to hold forever" the books, unless Caines repaid in three years. If Caines defaulted, and if they formed no understanding for Van Buren's purchase of the library, he had the right to sell the volumes, reimburse himself, and remit the "overplus" to Caines.[23]

Van Buren did not buy this material as a speculative venture, nor did he think the impoverished Caines could meet those terms. Rather, the purchase served as the centerpiece in Van Buren's expanding career as a lawyer-senator. He knew that the next council was in Republican hands, which would mean naming a new attorney general. Van Buren had not thus far staked a claim, but the prospect was always in his thoughts. In buying Caines out, Van Buren enhanced his candidacy by gaining control of a personal, ready-made reference library, rare in his time.[24]

The purchase also had additional use. The busy practice of Van Buren and Miller needed associates: young men to handle daily operations, contact clients, and research cases in Van Buren's many absences. For that reason, the partners took on clerks and provided them with formal training, primarily through Van Buren's new collection. Its inventory ran to about 315 titles and over 700 volumes, ranging from nearly every published court report, handbook, attorney's aid, and dictionary, to manuals on ancient and contemporary procedures and practices at all levels of British and American jurisprudence. These works would become professionally irreplaceable to Van Buren and his future associates.[25]

The utility of this library soon became apparent in another way as well. In August Van Buren represented some of the descendants of Abraham Staats, one of Kinderhook's original settlers, in an involuted case, *Jackson, ex dem. A. J. Staats, v. I. and A. Staats,* over the interpretation of a will written in 1731 by the second Abraham Staats. The action itself was less significant than was Van Buren's methodology. In advancing arguments that reflected his new library's resources, his brief contained such a wealth of prolix scholarship and learned references that Johnson refused to record most of it. Although Van Buren lost, his display of professional erudition indicated his qualifications to become the state's official advocate.[26]

The law, however, was hardly Van Buren's exclusive interest in the summer of 1814. The news of war grew more ominous. The British had launched a combined water and land invasion from Canada along the Lake Champlain route and had humiliated American forces defending Washington. As the emergency mounted, Governor Tompkins called the legislature into special session.[27]

Van Buren never wavered. Earlier on Independence Day in Hudson, he had made the principal address at a strident Republican rally. According to the *Hudson Bee,* he delivered an extemporaneous speech "of inimitable effect." In particular, Van Buren called on the "honorable" Coodies to reject "the discipline of party" and join prowar Republicans in defending the nation.[28]

Two weeks before the legislature met on September 26, 1814, Captain Thomas MacDonough's victory on Lake Champlain ended the immediate threat to New York. But the New England Federalists put the finishing touches on the antiwar Hartford Convention. With the crisis hardly eased, Tompkins minced few words in his address. Extraordinary conditions, he announced, demanded extraordinary responses. Van Buren, "Chairman of the Committee on the Governor's Speech," was equally blunt. Demanding united efforts from all Americans to achieve victory, he pledged "prompt and efficacious measures" to solve the emergency.[29]

Van Buren's promise became the legislature's bond. In a blizzard of rapid acts, the Republican party's majority began by setting forth methods for civil authorities to apprehend deserters. They prevented "improper intercourse" with the enemy through cartels, an arrangement authorizing non-hostile trade otherwise illegal in wartime. They exempted militia personnel from civil suits and encouraged the formation of privateer associations. They paid New York's share of the federal direct tax and partially reimbursed Tompkins's personal wartime expenses. They authorized two regiments of "free men of color." They provided payments for militia on active duty and those militiamen who had volunteered. Finally, the legislature set up a joint committee, chaired by Root and including Van Buren, to find a method to secure additional troops.[30]

Immediately, the committee erupted into a "violent debate" between Van Buren and Root over differing methods to raise the men. But Van Buren's plan, the Classification Bill, passed the senate, helped by Major General Scott's lobbying. A draft rather than a volunteer system, the bill authorized the governor to call into two years' service 12,000 able-bodied, free white males, eighteen to forty-five, from the state militia. Van Buren's method for raising and supporting these troops was novel. The governor, with the assistance of the commander of each militia unit whom Tompkins named and the assessors in each town, set up 12,000 classes, each obligated to furnish one able-bodied white man for service. If no member of a class volunteered, any member or group of members from that class could procure such a person at his or their expense, not to exceed $200, to represent the class. The class selected that man either by an election or finding a substitute. If the class failed to agree on the amount, the assessor set a levy on the persons composing the class, and the man chosen received a bounty of $250. The bill's main principle, Van Buren explained, was to create equity among citizens, proportional to their "interests, pecuniary as well as personal." In the assembly, Root's supporters and the Federalists managed to modify only one provision, which the senate accepted—the right of "nominated soldiers" to refuse service outside the state. On October 24, the Council of Revision approved the measure, with Chancellor Kent the sole objector.[31]

Van Buren was proud and remained proud about the passage of each prowar bill, especially his Classification Act. As a whole, this bundle of legislation legitimatized legal instrumentalism by adjusting statute law to serve major demands, created equity through distributive justice, and emphasized Van Buren's position as a co-equal with Tompkins and Spencer in setting party policies. Van Buren even sent a copy of the Classification Act to acting Secretary of War James Monroe as a model for a similar congressional bill.[32]

Public response was not entirely positive, however. The Classification Act angered antiwar Federalists, and many wealthy men disliked the prospect of military service or paying for a substitute. Ordinary citizens, some of them Van Buren's clients, felt that he had betrayed them by allowing richer men to escape the war by paying the commutation fee, a price beyond their means. One person above all, Chancellor Kent, proved the most acerbic critic. Convinced that prowar legislators had illegally passed all the bills, he dropped his usual judicial decorum and issued a blistering attack through Federalist party newspapers under the pseudonym of *Amicus Curiae*. Kent turned his exercise into a lesson in jurisprudence, censuring the legislature for its acceptance of unlawful privateers, wrongful apprehension of deserters without due process, and the unwarranted call for African-American troops. Reserving his most scathing scorn for the Classification Act, Kent excoriated the statute for a lack of equity that made it "contrary to most principles" of "equality" and "justice." To document his strictures, Kent noted that the bill failed to define how the state intended to use the troops, or to include provisions to exempt men with earlier service. Even worse, the act unconstitutionally usurped the Council of Appointment's prerogatives; it gave the governor the sole power to name militia commanders and allowed assessors to levy double taxation on a certain class that might have already paid.[33]

Kent's public stature was a serious blow to prowar Republicans. Although he was a Federalist, citizens did not view Kent as a partisan. Rather, they considered him the state's foremost jurist, a man who was learned, judicious, dispassionate, and unbiased. His opinions were larger than those of his party and his influence was greater. Kent's faultfinding was thus impossible for prowar Republicans to ignore. In addition, Kent's criticisms encouraged Stebbins's

Northern Whig to attack Van Buren as a man "with moral and political vices of the blackest dye."[34]

Van Buren quickly filed suit for libel. But knowing that this litigation would take too long for direct results, Assembly Speaker Young, adopting the name *Juris Consultus,* answered Kent through a series of counter public letters that belittled Kent's strongest suit, his legal reputation. Kent, excessively jealous of his legal scholarship, promptly answered. Protesting that *Juris Consultus* had indulged in a personality attack that ignored the key issues, Kent reiterated his stand.[35]

Van Buren was in a quandary. He liked Kent as a man and respected his legal ability. Since they also had a judicial relationship, that of chancellor and counsellor, Van Buren feared that his practice might suffer unless the public perceived him as a spectator in the affair. Yet Van Buren also appreciated the partisan danger Kent posed. Weighing these factors, Van Buren decided to respond, but also under an assumed pen name.[36]

Never before had the interrelationship between the law and Van Buren's politics been so pronounced. He exhaustively researched his extensive library on public law and the law of nations prior to his appeal to the bar of public opinion as *Amicus Juris Consultus.* On November 29, Van Buren's first letter appeared in the Republican party's *Albany Argus,* bursting with learned references to scores of authorities. He started by chiding Kent's lack of civility and "intemperance" toward legitimate contrary views, a character fault that began when Kent had impeached Judge Thompson's integrity in the Council of Revision for supporting the legislature's right to pass the bills. This statement was a harsh appraisal, likely relayed by Thompson, despite the confidentiality of the council's inner workings, and one designed to knock Kent off his judicial pedestal to his level of self-imposed partisanship. That done, Van Buren adopted Kent's posture as a legal pedagogue. He cited a host of "enlightened jurists" to contradict Kent about the legality of the legislature's actions. Van Buren even charged that Kent, as a partisan, was a deficient legal scholar whose vast antiwar prejudices warped his judicial judgment.[37]

Kent accepted the challenge. Dropping the pretense that he was not *Amicus Curiae,* Kent replied in another public letter. He protested Van Buren's revelation that he had used "offensive language" in the council and asserted that he would persist in doing his duty "independently, frankly and firmly."[38]

But Van Buren was not finished. Brushing aside Young's advice to answer Kent's attacks on the Classification Act, Van Buren hammered at Kent's legal posture on the war in the next letter. Van Buren ended with a question that troubled the public. Considering the confidence people placed in the state's highest judicial officer, he asked if Kent might have served the citizens better by not using "his official weight and character" for partisanship. By doing so, Kent had injured himself and lowered the public's respect for the law's dignity.[39]

This war of words was not over. Kent published a response in the *Albany Gazette,* in which he accused Van Buren of a malicious intent to disrupt the harmony of the judicial system. Van Buren answered by branding the charge "an unfounded imputation." If discords existed, he asserted, Kent was to blame. As his parting shot, Van Buren advised the chancellor to stay out of politics and confine himself to his official functions, his true "element." Van Buren was just as brusque in private. "The Chancellor," he wrote Taylor, "suffers much but not more than he deserves."[40]

Kent did exactly what Van Buren suggested. In a private letter to a friend, Kent promised to avoid all future participation in party politics. For his part, Van Buren, who was not usually unkind or vicious, endeavored to repair his damaged personal relationship with Kent. It worked. Some years later, the chancellor assured Van Buren "of my constant respect & esteem." In the long run, this incident had more important ramifications for the state's legal system. It became a step in the long road toward Van Buren's goal of diminishing the judiciary's partisanship and power through legislative supremacy.[41]

Even Van Buren's libel suit against Stebbins ended on a quiet note. On December 27, 1814, Stebbins halted his long and acrimonious hostility toward Van Buren by retiring from the *Northern Whig.* In a final show of bravado, Stebbins claimed that he had won all past libel suits (though at great legal expense), except for the recent action of Van Buren, whom he challenged to a showdown in court. But with Stebbins's withdrawal, Van Buren dropped the suit.[42]

Van Buren somehow fit three Supreme Court cases into his schedule during this hectic session and its aftermath. Each reflected his overall commitments. The main issue in *Whitbeck v. Van Ness* marked important progress in the evolution of commercial law, particularly the negotiability of a note signed by a third party. Justice Spencer accepted Van Buren's contention that a third party note was negotiable, even though its second holder had defaulted, if no evidence existed that it was fraudulent and if the purchaser had not misrepresented the solvency of the maker, unless "the contrary be expressly proved."[43]

Henry Livingston, by his next friend, Mary Livingston, v. Haywood was a property action. Henry Pitcher, a tenant on Livingston Manor, held a lease from Henry W. Livingston with a covenant preventing Pitcher from cutting, taking, or carrying away more timber than he actually used on the premises. The lease further prevented Pitcher from committing or allowing any waste, a common law tenet that prohibited unreasonable injury to the leasehold. When Henry W. Livingston died, his will devised the premises through a life estate to Mary Livingston, his wife, and after her death, to Henry Livingston, their minor son. Following Henry W. Livingston's death, Pitcher permitted Haywood to cut fifty loads of wood and carry them from the premises. The plaintiff, represented by Williams, sued Haywood for trespass. Van Buren for Haywood held that trespass was the wrong remedy. The plaintiff should have brought the action against Pitcher; Haywood was a "stranger," a third party who had no standing in the suit. Justice Thompson ruled for Van Buren, again limiting the Livingstons' economic gains.[44]

Watts v. Coffin resembled both the preceding case and *Jackson v. Collins,* although the facts differed. In 1774, John Van Rensselaer leased land in what became the city of Hudson to Jacob Herder. The lease contained a number of clauses. Herder's heirs and assigns paid rent to Van Rensselaer's heirs, executors, administrators, and assigns. In return, Herder, his heirs, and assigns, had "reasonable estovers" that allowed Herder to cut only sufficient timber for buildings, fences, and repairs on the property. Herder could also use common pasture on part of the manor in Claverack. Coffin, Van Buren's client, was Herder's assign; Watts, represented by Williams, was Van Rensselaer's assign. The central issue was that Coffin had withheld rent on two connected grounds: residents in Hudson had cut all the timber the original lease had guaranteed, and pasturage on the manor was equally unavailable because the land had been developed. Williams contended that the lease and all its provisions were still in effect. Van Buren argued that Herder's right of reasonable estovers and pasturage were parts of the same lease. Because Coffin could use neither, he was within his right to withhold rent. Judge Van Ness issued a long opinion that dismissed Van Buren's contentions as ones that "cannot be sustained." Knowing that Van Buren had essentially challenged the legality of long-term leases once land development had eroded their terms, Van Ness held that Coffin had breached the lease and must pay the rent. In so doing, Van Ness contravened Van Buren's tactics against the landlord system.[45]

With the legislature ended and the court term over, Van Buren returned to Hudson and much uncompleted work. Some clients were displeased that he had either dallied with their cases or not collected judgments. New causes in the Supreme Court and chancery awaited further research. Worse yet, Van Buren had still one more strenuous action to consider when he accepted an appointment as special army judge advocate for the court-martial of Brigadier General James Wilkinson, scheduled for January 1815 in Utica. The cumulative result of these cares placed Van Buren on a precarious balance. After juggling the law and politics for so long, he was physically and mentally weary. In that mood, he wrote Taylor "I am sick of the circuit which has been a busy one."[46]

The Administration's motives for selecting Van Buren for the Wilkinson case were as conjectural as they were in Hull's court-martial. Maybe Madison indirectly made the choice to aid Monroe, who was both secretary of state and acting secretary of war. To lift Monroe's burden, Madison had offered Tompkins the state department. He refused. Tompkins feared a renewed British invasion of New York in 1815. He also thought that his chance for the presidency in 1816 was best served by staying in Albany and finishing what he had begun. Perhaps, then, Madison convinced Monroe to name Van Buren, the governor's staunchest ally, as a sign of the Administration's regard for Tompkins. Or Monroe might have thought that Van Buren, fresh from his victory in the Hull trial, was best equipped to prosecute the wily Wilkinson.[47]

Van Buren received the offer at an awkward time. He was deep in the Columbia Circuit's "session," he wrote Monroe, and equally busy preparing for the Supreme Court's "commencement" where he had "several interesting causes for argument." After acknowledging to Monroe that "the pressure of my business would have induced me to decline" the appointment, Van Buren acceded, for his "duty" to the Administration made him "sensible that my declining" at such a late date would "have produced an embarrassment." Van Buren took charge of the court-martial on December 14, 1814, less than two weeks before the trial opened.[48]

Van Buren's acceptance worried Wilkinson. No one in the army had his instinct for self-preservation, or was more alert to personal danger. He knew that Van Buren would put his life, or at least his career, in jeopardy. When the court-martial convened, Wilkinson's attorneys protested Van Buren's presence. They reasoned that a section in the federal statute of January 11, 1812, which covered the case, prevented Monroe from designating a special judge advocate without the Senate's advice and consent, an authorization Van Buren lacked. Taken aback, Van Buren let the court decide. After deliberating, it accepted Wilkinson's objection and ended Van Buren's participation. He was well rid of a burdensome task. The trial lasted until the end of March 1815 and resulted in Wilkinson's acquittal.

Van Buren was nonetheless professionally rattled. The dismissal, he wrote Taylor, was "extremely trouble some" and "mortifying." Van Buren also complained that he had forfeited substantial anticipated income when some judges refused to grant continuances in several of his scheduled cases. To make up for these lost receipts, Van Buren billed the government $3,000. Nearly a full year later, Secretary of the Treasury William H. Crawford authorized $1,000 less, the same as for Hull, but Van Buren was still professionally unsatisfied. What Van Buren did not appreciate was how much his dismissal from the court-martial ultimately benefited him.[49]

To begin with, Van Buren now had ample opportunity to complete pending legal business, starting with William P. Van Ness. Old wounds had healed. Van Buren arranged, as he frequently had on earlier occasions, the postponement of another of Van Ness's recurring debts. For the moment, Van Buren avoided any proceedings in chancery, since he was uncertain if he could yet trust Kent. But Van Buren did have the time to appear before the January Supreme Court in *Jackson, ex dem. Gouch, v. Wood,* which touched on the familiar issues of adverse possession and common law procedures. Gouch owned a tract of land he had inherited in Onondaga County; Wood laid claim to a portion. Van Buren represented Wood, disputing Gouch's title by Wood's adverse possession for over twenty years and through purchase. The complication was that Wood's deed did not contain an official seal, required under common law usage and a pertinent British statute the state had adopted. The court ruled against Van Buren on those points, concluding that the common law mandated that the seal was "indispensable."[50]

Above all, not being confined to Utica galvanized Van Buren's legal and political career when he resumed his senate duties on January 31, 1815. The heated political battles of wartime had suddenly ceased. The Treaty of Ghent that ended the war, along with Andrew Jackson's astonishing victory at New Orleans nearly three weeks earlier, made the Hartford Convention irrelevant and ushered in a new political world, a world that Van Buren found even more compatible with his ambitions and talents. Displaying the flexibility of a legal and political instrumentalist to adapt to new circumstances, he had moved ever upward over the last three years. Beginning in obscurity as a local Columbia County courtier of De Witt Clinton, Van Buren was now the leading lawyer-senator in his party's ruling triad, which included Tompkins and Spencer. Van Buren counted on his reward. He believed he deserved the council's appointment as state attorney general.[51]

During yearly changes in the council, Albany was accustomed to a few days of intense personal politicking, politicking Van Buren would have missed if he had prosecuted Wilkinson. Under these circumstances, the jousting between Van Buren and Spencer for the ultimate appointive power over a host of major and minor offices reached new levels of intrigue. In an intense intra-party battle that tested older alignments and fresh individual relationships, Van Buren gained Tompkins's support, routed Spencer, and won the coveted attorney generalship.[52] These developments opened a new chapter in New York politics. Spencer, enraged at both Van Buren and Tompkins, split with them and sought new allies. Tammany Hall further disrupted the party when it forced the council to remove Clinton as mayor of New York City. Tompkins followed his own star. Weary from the burdens of office, he worried that the state might not honor his wartime indebtedness and mulled over the idea of running for President. As a result, Tompkins acted as the party's corporate front, but Van Buren was its chief operating officer. All these factors meant that Attorney General Martin Van Buren had begun the third stage of his dual career as the party's leading lawyer-politician. This transition placed him on the threshold of a momentous change in the life of his party, his state, and his profession. No longer merely a member of the Republican party, he was potentially *the* Republican party. But three imponderables blocked his path, his efficiency as attorney general, his effectiveness as a lawyer-politician, and the yet formidable De Witt Clinton.[53]

CHAPTER EIGHT

Republicanism
and State Attorney General

Phase One

The state constitution and statutory law mandated a simple duty to Attorney General Martin Van Buren. As New York's *defacto* official advocate and legal adviser, he prosecuted and defended "all cases where the people of this state shall be interested." On closer inspection, however, the office held breathtaking responsibilities. The 1813 revised code listed the attorney general's multitudinous obligations in twenty-seven scattered chapters, located on seventy-four separate pages.[1]

To start with, Van Buren had broad supervision over local and state instrumentalities, including elected and appointed officials. He scrutinized the operations of town, county, and state governments for possible malfeasance. He served on the board of inspectors of state prisons and protected American Indians on designated reservations. He ruled on the legality of bail sheriffs granted in certain instances. He also regulated public auctioneers, checked proper allocations of common school funds, and sued town clerks or school trustees for delinquencies. And he ensured that chartered corporations operated according to pertinent statutes.

Acting as the legal agent for the comptroller and surveyor general, Van Buren recovered all funds due on public land sales and collected fees that such debtors owed. He deposited these moneys, plus costs and damages, with the state treasurer. At the request of the comptroller or the surveyor general, Van Buren prepared contracts and other legal instruments for the state. He also gave the oath of office to assemblymen and supplied the legislature with legal opinions.[2]

Van Buren's trial work was equally extensive. He instituted suits for the comptroller and surveyor general against nonpaying mortgagees who bought public land. He also filed suits for banks in which the state had investments but received no dividends, as well as for local agencies that received a variety of public funds but had not accounted for spending, nor reimbursed the treasurer on demand. Van Buren prosecuted county supervisors for dereliction of duties and institutions that breached their charters. He indicted and tried duelists, arraigned any person accused of attempting to bribe a state official, and brought impeachment charges against alleged corrupt officeholders. When required by the governor or a Supreme Court justice, Van Buren further litigated major criminal cases, usually connected to murder, treason, or high misdemeanors, in special courts of oyer and terminer. County assistant "attornies general," named by the Council of Appointment, could request Van Buren's assistance in trials that dealt with attainders and outlawries. These referred to alleged offenses that resulted in the loss of civil rights due to treason or felony and carried the death sentence, or to instances in which a prisoner had escaped and was declared an outlaw. Van Buren also rode the circuit once a year to check court operations.[3]

Land issues by far dominated the attorney general's attention. Under the surveyor general's purview, Van Buren was an *ex-officio* member of the Land Office, along with the governor, lieutenant governor, assembly speaker, comptroller, and treasurer. The board investigated claims to public land, checked the validity of surveys on such property, authorized warrants for collections, and evaluated payments of mortgages. In each instance, Van Buren could choose a variety of writs, normally through sheriffs, to enforce Land Office directives. If these failed, he prosecuted lawbreakers. Without Van Buren's approval, the state could neither commence ejectment proceedings on land it owned nor foreclose without his consent. In escheat, when property reverted to the state if a person died without heirs, Van Buren reviewed administrators' accounts, dispositions issued by the courts of probates or the Court of Chancery, and the amounts due the state treasurer. If faults existed, Van Buren sued appropriate officials. He also defended the state and recovered any money from Connecticut land claims. If separate litigations involved several plaintiffs in similar actions, Van Buren could, with the defendants' permission, consolidate the actions to save court costs.[4]

Being attorney general proved to be a financial bonanza for Van Buren. His annual salary was $2,000, paid quarterly, plus $5.50 a day for official duties, "besides all charges and expenditures" the comptroller deemed reasonable. Van Buren's total emoluments, including the $4 per diem he earned as a state senator, reached an estimated $5,000 a year. Van Buren at least tripled that figure through his general practice, appellate pleadings, and private real estate investments and loans. The office provided two additional features of importantance to Van Buren's aims. With so many of his state duties centered in Albany, Van Buren could use the attorney generalship, along with his senate seat, to direct the Republican party on a daily basis and prevent Clinton from regaining power. The attorney generalship also gave Van Buren the unique opportunity to implement his basic legal beliefs. The office had only one drawback; Van Buren's demanding schedule forced him to dissolve his partnership with Cornelius Miller.[5]

Understandably, Van Buren faced a dizzying schedule. Starting slowly in May 1815, he presented only fifteen cases in the Supreme Court for "The People of the State of New-York" during the remainder of the year. Although Van Buren's predecessor, Abraham Van Vechten, had prepared these cases, Van Buren was now in charge of their advocacy, as well as that of a host of new ones he had formulated (twenty-nine alone in January 1816). A far better gauge of Van Buren's activities in 1815 may be found in his in-coming mail. This correspondence—ninety-six letters in all—revealed a great deal about his work. Some forwarded information about coming suits, names of heirs or intestates, actions on writs, discontinued litigations, missing offenders, Land Office affairs, and lapsed mortgages. Others complained about unjust ejectments, dunnings on clerk's fees, unrecorded payments of mortgages, and slow reimbursements of advertising fees from newspaper editors for publishing mortgage sales. Still others inquired about Van Buren's opinion on points of law from various state officials, allowable advertising rates, receipts to prove liquidations of mortgages, methods to delay debts, and requests from attorneys for conferences.[6]

Although most of Van Buren's replies to these queries have not survived, the "Attorney General's Case Register" reveals the nature of many such actions. Van Buren collected various clerks' fees and sued for debts on mortgages, bonds, covenants, and common school loans; he foreclosed mortgages and authorized special bail and ejectment; he wrote pleadings and appeared before chancery; he arranged trials, checked escheat and courts of probates' proceedings, and investigated operations of incorporated businesses; he deposited funds with the treasurer and attended Land Office meetings; he joined the comptroller and surveyor general to certify land titles and sales, especially in Military Bounty Land; he visited prisons; and he probed fraudulent purchases involving American Indians. Van Buren generally used special orders to expedite litigations through a variety of *capias* writs to sheriffs. Among these were demands that sheriffs confine defendants prior to trial, recover judgments, seize goods and chattels, secure or sell property of debtors to satisfy judgments, and protect either defendants or plaintiffs from false claims.[7]

Many of the cases Van Buren pursued in 1815 were perfunctory and nonenumerated. In a typical case, *The People of the State of New-York v. Artemis Aldrich,* Van Buren cited merely the facts in a printed, two-page Supreme Court form. Aldrich had defaulted $150 on a mortgage; Justice Thompson authorized Van Buren to make the collection, plus costs and interest. Others, equally unreported, were more demanding. *The People of the State of New-York v. Robert Archibold* addressed a broken covenant of $1,100; Van Buren's brief ran to seven handwritten pages. He listed the evidence, the attempts a previous attorney general had made to collect the debt, and the legal points sustaining the suit. In an unsigned judgment, the court ordered Archibold to pay $1,600.39, which included the debt, interest, and costs.[8]

Despite the ease of these pleadings, Van Buren was at a disadvantage, because he lacked a permanent staff of competent lawyers and clerks to research and prepare his briefs. Nor did any continuity exist between officeholders. In the thirteen years since Clinton and Spencer had forged the Council of Appointment into a patronage engine, seven men served as attorney general, one for only seven months. Professional courtesy often fell victim to political antagonism, and incumbents gave successors little aid during the transitional period. Van Buren's role as a lawyer-politician created another problem as he tried to strike a balance between his private practice, senate duties, state responsibilities, and politics. He needed someone to help shoulder the load. Luckily, Van Buren found such a person in Benjamin F. Butler, an exceptionally able young clerk. The son of Medad Butler, the owner of a tavern in Kinderhook Landing, Butler had already read law in the office of Van Buren and Miller. Barely twenty in 1815, and not yet admitted to the bar, Butler had nevertheless earned Van Buren's complete trust and respect, nearly becoming a surrogate son. He handled much of Van Buren's everyday work in the attorney general's office, sometimes even writing formal pleadings. Butler idolized Van Buren. In a letter to his fiancee, Harriet Allen, Butler gushed that Van Buren's "politeness, vivacity and good nature," coupled with his "integrity" and "powers as an advocate & his merits as a man," proved his "talents as a statesman." This admiration went both ways. Van Buren found Butler so invaluable that he devised various stratagems to delay Butler's marriage.[9]

Senate duties dealing with distributive justice made Van Buren's life even more frenetic, beginning with his service on twenty-four select, standing, and joint committees. Some of the legislation before these committees seemed prosaic in comparison to the excitement of the last session. Chartering stage lines or drafting legislation for inspectors of beef and pork stirred few political juices. In some instances, however, Van Buren's voting reflected his legal instrumentalist belief in molding legislation to solve pressing problems. For example, he approved raising the threshold of personal property exemptions for tenants when sheriffs seized their property for failing to pay rent. Other bills of substance dealt with the consequences of the war. Prompted by Comptroller McIntyre, Van Buren urged the senate to allow Tompkins some reimbursement from all wartime state expenditures "properly chargeable to the United States." Van Buren also managed the passage of a bill for the back pay of militiamen, as well as a measure empowering the comptroller to borrow $1.6M in federal treasury notes to fund wartime appropriations that had been unauthorized by existing statutes. Van Buren, still a scrupulous financial watchdog of the public's money, fastened a four mill tax on real and personal property assessments to underwrite the loan.[10]

Yet Van Buren did not shape all legislation. In one such instance, he could not contain his party's ethnic and racist divisions over a bill to speed the pace of gradual emancipation. To please his Dutch-American slaveholding neighbors, Van Buren sought to delay the process of freeing enslaved African-Americans. Interregional conflicts over reapportionment, based on the state's 1815 census, proved equally thorny. Van Buren failed to convince a joint committee to realign the legislature in a way that favored the Republican party.[11]

When the session ended, Van Buren returned to Hudson for the spring election. Despite his accumulated power and influence, he curiously avoided any campaigning. Returns jarred the Republicans. They kept the senate by a reduced margin, but the count was different in the assembly. The Republicans claimed control, but the Federalists tallied a one-vote majority in their favor. The discrepancy lay in a contested seat. The significance of these outcomes placed Van Buren's position in jeopardy. If the Federalists indeed had the assembly, they held the coming Council of Appointment with Clintonian support and could oust him as attorney general after only one year.[12]

Van Buren described the situation as "remarkable," then dismissed it for the moment. The explanation for his odd apathy soon came into focus. Hannah Van Buren was in poor health. She was suffering from the first sign of the tuberculosis that would shortly end her life. Furthermore, the birth and death of her recent baby, named in honor of Winfield Scott, was an emotional and physical trauma. Her decline alarmed Van Buren. During the height of the campaign, he took his wife on a recuperative vacation for several weeks and left politics alone.[13]

Returning to Hudson by late June, Van Buren engaged in no overt political activity, except for delivering a short oration at the Independence Day celebration. Instead, he cared for his wife, using his free moments to read large chunks of his library that related to attorney general's matters. By August, Hannah Van Buren's recovery reached a point where he could travel to Albany. Starting a new round of official duties, Van Buren presented two winning cases in the Supreme Court. Both deviated from his accustomed causes, because they concerned interpretations of criminal statutes. Since each remained from Van Vechten's tenure, Van Buren merely presented the briefs and did not offer oral arguments.[14]

Three months later, during the New York City Supreme Court term in October, Attorney General Van Buren was on his own for the first time in *The People, ex relatione Wilson, v. the Supervisors of Albany*. The issue pertained to whether the court, through Van Buren on Constable Wilson's behalf, would issue a *mandamus* that forced the Albany Board of Supervisors to reexamine Wilson's costs for removing paupers from Albany to adjoining towns. The board had awarded Wilson $28 but rejected his additional demand for $74 as excessive. Justice Spencer refused to grant the *mandamus,* ruling that the board had employed a valid discretionary power.[15]

Van Buren also represented a private client, Jesse Buel, the editor of the *Albany Argus,* with Robert Tillotson as co-counsel, in the libel case of *Sumner v. Buel.* On August 19, 1814, Buel had published a report that certain unnamed militia officers refused a presidential call for military service outside the state. Sumner, an ensign and one of these unspecified men, claimed that Buel had libelled him. Sumner won in circuit, receiving six cents in damages, but Van Buren and Tillotson moved an arrest of judgment. Although the facts were different from *Spencer v. Southwick,* the arguments were somewhat similar. Tillotson emphasized that Sumner lacked an action because Buel made no "personal allusion" to him. Van Vechten countered that the libel was inherent, as Van Buren had argued in *Spencer v. Southwick.* Van Buren, determined to protect Buel as the chief editorial mouthpiece of upstate Republicans, now reversed himself. He contended that Sumner lacked a remedy because he suffered no "private injury." Judge Thompson spoke for the majority. In setting aside the judgment, Thompson underscored the "general rule" that "no writing whatever is to be deemed a libel, unless it reflects upon some particular person."[16]

While this decision did little to define the actionable nature of libel, the case was notable for the way the judges divided along partisan lines. Three Republicans, Yates, Thompson, and Spencer, voted for Buel, while the two Federalists, Van Ness and Platt, voted for Sumner. This split was both partisan and philosophical, and foreshadowed new problems for Van Buren and the entire judicial process. Federalists considered the court their last stronghold and used the judiciary as a political weapon against Republicans. The division also represented a serious divergence in views of the law. More than ever, Federalist judges continued their undeviating application of the common law as a bulwark against change. By contrast, Republican judges, along with Van Buren, urged flexibility through legal instrumentalism.[17]

These actions signaled the end of Van Buren's rather quiescent activities due to his wife's illness. By the end of October, he had travelled to his office in Albany several times, readied twenty-nine cases for "The People," and started ten litigations in chancery, a few for the state, but most on behalf of his clients. Two were especially meaningful to Van Buren's legal and ideological beliefs. Representing wives who sought divorce based on their husbands' adultery, the sole grounds for divorce in New York, Van Buren received injunctions that prevented the husbands from hiding or disposing of marital property. This effort again illustrated the way Van Buren melded classical and liberal republicanism. Treating divorce not so much as a question of morality as an economic arrangement, Van Buren rejected old common law adages that a husband and wife were of "one flesh," with the husband dominant. Instead, Van Buren advocated the concept that divorced women had the same individual property rights as their husbands. By protecting the assets of such divorced women, Van Buren sought to guarantee their equal share of marital property, secure their economic maintenance, and free them from dependency.[18]

Van Buren was far less successful in the skirmishing surrounding the party's 1816 presidential nomination. In the Republican party's legislative caucus, his wing "recommended" Tompkins. Clinton, seeking to revive his career through the sponsorship of a "Grand Canal" from Albany to the Niagara River that would become the Erie Canal, favored Secretary of State James Monroe. Spencer backed Secretary of the Treasury William H. Crawford of Georgia.[19]

Many historians have analyzed Van Buren's actions and inactions over the issue of presidential nomination and concluded that he meant to undermine Tompkins and back Monroe from the start. But a different interpretation exists. Van Buren was confused and remained confused. If anything, he approached this question fatalistically, letting events take their natural course. Furthermore, with his party so divided, Van Buren's chief priority was local not national politics.[20]

Van Buren was especially worried about who might replace Tompkins as governor if he became President. Clinton thought he fit the bill. Although Clinton claimed that the canal was nonpartisan, voters in the central and western districts linked its fate to his political success and further strained the party's interregional divisions. As a holding action, the New York Republican legislative caucus renominated Tompkins, just before the congressional caucus choose him as Monroe's vice-presidential running mate. Nevertheless, the organization persuaded Tompkins to remain in the gubernatorial race, with the understanding that he would either retain both offices, or resign in favor of Lieutenant Governor John Taylor if the national ticket won. Reacting at once, the flexible Spencer wrote Armstrong that he was working out the "prospect" of an accommodation with Clinton.[21]

Throughout all these twists and turns, Van Buren spent the majority of his time practicing the law. Ever since the spring election of 1815, he had grown progressively concerned that the coming council would remove him as attorney general. Under these conditions, Van Buren's main preoccupation was to protect himself, not make Tompkins President. To that end, Van Buren laid out a two-pronged plan: prove that he was an efficient attorney general, then wield raw political power to retain the office. Concentrating first on the law, Van Buren won twenty-six of twenty-nine nonenumerated cases for the state in the January 1816 Supreme Court term, most dealing with defaulted mortgages in central and western counties. The three cases that were reported were interpretations of criminal statutes: the rights of witnesses in cross examinations; a delay in a trial for assault and battery; and the disposition of stolen promissory notes. Johnson did not record Van Buren's briefs, but in each the justices sustained him. All told, Van Buren collected $23,358.21 for the state, an impressive figure that polished his credentials.[22]

To exhibit further his professional acumen, Van Buren won two private cases at the same session. *Bennet v. Jenkins and Others, Executors of Jenkins* centered on Van Buren's winning request for the court to award damages to his client, a tenant, because a sheriff had evicted him due to a faulty deed. *Haywood v. Sheldon* related to a $50 bet on a horse race that Sheldon made for himself and several friends with Haywood. When Sheldon lost, the stakeholder paid Haywood. Sheldon was a spoilsport. He retained Van Buren, who brought an action of debt through an act to prevent horse racing. Based on that statute, Van Buren stressed the doctrine of legislative supremacy and argued that contracts for money bet on a horse race were void. A bettor was entitled to recover his money according to the provisions that prevented excessive and deceitful gaming. The act also stated that a loser in any game, if the sums were excessive, could sue for and recover the amount lost or paid by a simple action of debt, without spelling out the nature of the debt. The court decided for Van Buren, noting that a bet on behalf of others, according to the governing statute, had determined their ruling.[23]

The pace of arriving mail further attested to Van Buren's abilities as attorney general. In January 1816 alone, he received twenty-six letters. Although most were similar to earlier ones, others bore a new tone. The largest portion came from attorneys, court clerks, and sheriffs who were paying pending bills, asking for postponements, or relaying the results of various writs. Butler again proved his worth. Under Van Buren's direction, he dispatched bills, interviewed clients, discussed cases with lawyers, and drafted briefs for the Supreme Court, chancery, and the circuit.[24]

Van Buren also appeared twice in chancery. One action was minor: a master's report that awarded his client full costs and interest in a disputed contract. The second, between Henry Platner and two Van Rensselaers, Robert H. and Henry, was more substantial and involved a contested will. Van Buren, Platner's lawyer, began the first phase of a protracted litigation when Kent supported Van Buren's motion to refer the matter to a master in chancery in order to ascertain "the amount due to the complainant."[25]

The Court of Errors proved to be equally time-consuming during February, when Van Buren played his usual forceful role. Ignoring his apparent conflict of interest as a private lawyer, attorney general, and constitutional judge, he advocated, but did not vote, in two long and lucrative actions. The first, *Jackson, ex dem. Brockholst Livingston, and Others, Plaintiff in error, v. Ann Delancy and Abraham Russell, Defendants in error,* revolved around two sets of wills over rival ownership of a large tract in the old Hardenbergh Patent.

During the course of an erratic life, Lord William Stirling ran up a series of high debts, some to Mrs. Ann Waddell. In 1770, Lord Stirling gave her mortgages in several counties that included all his patent lands, tenements, and heritable rights as security for repayment. The following year, she obtained a judgment foreclosing the mortgages and secured the property under the common law for nonpayment of dormant debts. Mrs. Waddell died in 1773. Her will directed the executor to collect all "outstanding debts," then sell her estate, including the Hardenbergh Patent, for equal division among her five children. In 1787, Lord Stirling died. His will gave his wife a life estate with the remainder interest to his two daughters. To protect themselves, the Waddell heirs sought and received a *scire facias,* which repealed Lord Sterling's letter patent and denied his heirs any stake in the property because of nonpayment of the dormant debt. Tenants at once petitioned and received an attornment, which transferred and acknowledged their obligations to their new landlords.

Acting on these judgments, the Ulster County sheriff sold several properties that belonged to Mrs. Waddell's estate. Brockholst Livingston, an associate justice of the United States Supreme Court, was the trustee for Mrs. William Duer, Lord Sterling's only living heir and the wife of a prominent Federalist. To test one of the sheriff's sales prior to challenging the Waddells' entire claim, Livingston's attorneys won an ejectment in the state Supreme Court. This judgment returned 1,000 acres of the property to Mrs. Duer, on the grounds that Mrs. Waddell's will did not give the sheriff the specific right to sell any property. The court also ruled that the *scire facias* was improper because it limited Mrs. Duer's remainder. The Waddell heirs then moved a writ of error.[26]

Both sides realized the vast financial stakes at risk and employed two teams of the best available lawyers. Van Buren, with Thomas Oakley, stood for the Waddell heirs; John Duer, the son of Mrs. Duer, and John Henry represented Livingston. In their brief, Duer and Henry reargued the ejectment, emphasizing that the Supreme Court's opinion was correct. Van Buren and Oakley answered that Mrs. Waddell's original judgment against Lord Sterling was the ruling decision under *stare decisis,* that the Waddell heirs further controlled the estate through long adverse possession, and that the statute of limitations negated Livingston's case. Turning to the will, Van Buren and Oakley declared it binding. They did concede that Mrs. Waddell had not specified the sheriff's right to sell but held that was her intent. In an argument emphasizing legal positivism, they also claimed that the attornment fell within a state statute that allowed a landlord or lessor to enter such an agreement once a mortgage was forfeited. Chancellor Kent, speaking for the unanimous court, sustained Van Buren and Oakley. Concentrating on the common law and British precedent, Kent ruled that Mrs. Waddell's will was valid because Lord Sterling had indeed forfeited his claim due to nonpayment of a dormant debt.[27]

This finding made Van Buren a major winner. The Court of Errors had essentially established a key precedent in declaring colonial letters of patent not to be absolute. Van Buren also sustained adverse possession and legislative supremacy over those patents, each a major triumph in his effort to expand tenants' rights and end the state's feudalism. Lastly, although Van Buren left no record of its amount, his clients likely paid a handsome fee.

David Gelston and Peter A. Schenck, Plaintiffs in error, v. Gould Hoyt, Defendant in error was a case that was just as complex as the last, further revealing Van Buren's aptitude in commercial law. In 1810, Gelston, collector of the port of New York City, and Schenck, surveyor of the port, had seized Hoyt's ship and cargo, alleging that he violated federal law by loading the vessel with war materials for a purported civil war in Santo Domingo. Hoyt won in federal district court. He recovered his vessel and cargo on the grounds that he had not committed an overt act and that Gelston and Schenck had exceeded their authority. Hoyt then sought damages through a trespass action against them in the state Supreme Court. In sustaining and awarding Hoyt $107,369.20, the court overruled his opponents' main defense that they were not liable personally because they had acted as government agents. Gelston and Schenck then appealed on a bill of exceptions to the Court of Errors. Van Buren and Emmet defended Hoyt; Harmanus Bleeker was the lead attorney for the defendants.

Each side debated several remedies touching on maritime law, the plaintiffs' liability, and Bleeker's attempt and failure to introduce evidence not presented in the Supreme Court. Kent, again speaking for the unanimous judges, agreed with Van Buren and Emmet that while Hoyt, a private citizen, could not sue the government, he had an action against its public officers if they lacked proof that a civil war was taking place in Santo Domingo. The only remaining point was the amount of interest due Hoyt, since the Supreme Court's verdict stood. But the Court of Errors did not specify this amount, informing Van Buren and Emmet that their remedy lay in chancery.[28]

With these cases successfully dispatched, Van Buren set the stage for the second phase in his plan to safeguard his position as attorney general. When the legislature opened in the first week of February 1816, the Federalists asserted that they controlled the assembly because their candidate had legally won the contested seat. Ignoring what turned out to be a legitimate claim, Van Buren used ruthless methods to organize both legislative branches and form a new Council of Appointment before Federalists could react. Van Buren later confessed that he had acted in an unbecoming manner. He could afford the apology, since the council reappointed him to another term. The Federalists were not so magnanimous. Justifiably outraged, they decided not to provoke a constitutional crisis by seeking to overturn the council. Rather, they directed their wrath on Van Buren himself. William L. Stone, the new editor of the *Northern Whig,* was especially scathing in his criticism. He coined a phrase destined to become synonymous with Van Buren forever. To Stone, Van Buren was "one of the greatest magicians" in Republican ranks.[29]

After this episode, Van Buren fell ill with an asthmatic attack in early February. Returning a week later, he gave the official reply to Tompkins's annual message, outlining the main thrust of the governor's reelection campaign. In particular, Van Buren rhetorically waved the American flag by lauding

Tompkins's extraordinary contributions to victory during the "difficult and trying periods of the great war."[30]

Van Buren received another means to win the loyalty of small freehold farmers on Tompkins's behalf when John Jacob Astors pressed the Morris claim. The previous legislature had followed Van Buren's advice that the attorney general must defend the property owners who had purchased the land from the state. But Attorney General Van Vechten dallied, possibly reasoning that Astor had the law on his side. The new senate again sought a legal opinion, this time from Attorney General Van Buren.[31]

Although familiar with the situation, Van Buren made a fresh investigation. While he avoided issuing an opinion in his report about title to the land, since he concluded that it was a judicial matter, he did observe that Astor's "exhibits of title" were hardly sufficient. Even so, Van Buren recommended forming a special commission to gather evidence as a further means of protecting lawful purchasers against "Mr. Astor."[32]

Van Buren, in his efforts to secure his power, stumbled over only one key issue: the canal commission's request to authorize the first step in Clinton's pet project, a bill to implement a survey of "internal navigation" prior to construction. Van Buren realized the canal's political potential and tried to stymie Clinton. Defying Tammany's adamant refusal to even consider building the canal, Van Buren suggested that the commissioners delay until they provided the legislature with exact details. Eventually, a modified bill passed along these lines. But Van Buren was trapped. He had neither placed building the canal above party, nor blunted Clinton's mounting popularity.[33]

Van Buren's supporters were nevertheless impressed by these efforts. To show their regard, they elected him a regent of the University of the State of New York in a highly politicized joint ballot over William W. Van Ness. Although the position was largely honorific, Van Buren compensated for his own lack of academic credentials by conscientiously fulfilling his duties. The Middle District Republicans were just as impressed. They renominated him by acclamation for another four-year senate term.[34]

The election campaign fell along lines of personality. In a typical editorial, Stone's *Northern Whig* vilified Tompkins as a public thief who had misspent $400,000 in unaccounted treasury notes. "Little Matty," infamous "in the annals of the MANOR CONSPIRACY," was equally guilty for abetting Tompkins's "criminal" behavior. Even more, Federalists, with Spencer's covert assistance, raised troubling accusations about Van Buren's conduct as attorney general. They alleged that he had callously multiplied the number of suits against debtors.[35]

Although Van Buren considered a libel suit against Stone, his supporters concentrated on the governor's wartime achievements and their association with him, contrasting it to the Federalists' sorry history. As for himself, Van Buren relied on his friends to defend his record, scoffing at a Federalist demand that he withdraw from the senate election.[36]

As in his three previous gubernatorial races, Tompkins coasted to an easy victory with long coattails. Republicans retained the senate by capturing all eight seats at stake, including Van Buren's, and won nearly two-thirds in the assembly. The result elated Van Buren. Compared to 1812, when he squeaked to victory by a scant 133 votes, his margin of 1,017 represented the largest Republican party majority in the Middle District since 1807.[37]

Van Buren now decided that the time was ripe for a decision he had contemplated for some time—moving his family and professional business to Albany on a permanent basis. Politically, relocation made sense, because he would now be at the hub of party developments. Equally important, from a legal standpoint, Van Buren's responsibilities as attorney general mandated close contact with state officials and Albany courts for major portions of the year. Then, too, his private practice had changed. Earlier, his specialization derived from issues in the circuit and appellate business. But now his docket swelled with increasing litigations in the Court of Chancery that was also located in Albany. Albany, the state's second most populous city, also had more potential clients than Hudson, a point equally attractive to Van Buren. The hours he wasted in travel alone sealed this decision. In 1816, a trip from Hudson to Albany amounted to a good day.[38]

In late July, Van Buren rented a four-story house on State Street near the Capitol, but kept his official residence in Hudson to maintain voting requirements. Furnishing the house became the Van Burens most engrossing summer project. Despite their Dutch-American thrift, they spent freely from funds deposited at the Albany Farmers' and Mechanics' Bank and the Bank of Hudson.[39]

The move symbolized something even larger. Van Buren still sought to balance the law and politics, but with Clinton's fortunes on the ascent, Van Buren gradually found that politics dominated the law. For the time being, however, he was secure in his second term as attorney general and attacked his duties with fresh exuberance. Butler tried to maintain that pace, marveling at Van Buren's "industrious habits" as the statesman diligently assembled litigations, orally tested causes before delivering them, carried on an extensive correspondence, and bargained with other attorneys.[40]

Butler aptly described Van Buren's daily schedule. From February to December 1816, eighty-seven letters spilled onto his desk from lawyers, clerks, sheriffs, state officials, and mortgagees from nearly every county, all asking for advice, relaying payments, seeking continuances, finding plaintiffs, or sending results of sundry writs. The Supreme Court also saw much of Van Buren. In May, he won twenty-six nonenumerated cases for New York and deposited $15,472.80 with the state treasurer. Van Buren's August docket was less full but just as gratifying. He triumphed in ten more state actions, worth an average of slightly over $1,100 per case. He also joined Root in a private action, *Pain v. Parker,* to secure a change of venue for a libel trial from Delaware to Albany County. If these were not enough, Van Buren listed ten new chancery causes, spent mid-summer touring circuits, and participated in a Regents' meetings.[41]

Continuing at this tempo, Van Buren was in Hudson during September for criminal trials at the request of Moses Cantine, the assistant district attorney for Columbia and Greene counties. Their docket was exceptionally crowded and attracted "uncommon" interest, due to Van Buren's presence. He helped Cantine prosecute six criminal cases: alleged grand larceny, slander on a sodomy charge, counterfeiting, rape, seduction, and murder.[42]

By October, Van Buren was back before the Supreme Court in New York City. He argued two private causes, both connected to land claims, the kind at which he excelled. *Jackson, ex dem. Livingston, and Others v. Hallenbeck* was a typical case containing a colonial patent, wills and deeds in conflict, amounts of inheritance in dispute, and land held in adverse possession. Chief Justice Thompson decided the issue in Van Buren's favor, once again harming the Livingstons' economic interests. *Jackson, ex dem. Valkenburgh, v. Van Buren* was a case within Van Buren's collateral family, with Van Vechten representing one member and Van Buren another. Like the first, it touched on a patent, the De Bruyn, and its interpretation. Van Buren won by emphasizing his cousin's right to the land in question through adverse possession.[43]

But new political developments tarnished Van Buren's professional accomplishments. Over the preceding six months, Clinton had managed to merge his personal identification with the Erie Canal in order to build momentum as Tompkins's logical successor. Political machinations accelerated on November 5 when the legislature convened. Van Buren controlled the party caucus and denied Clinton a spot as an elector-at-large, in effect repudiating his legitimacy as a regular Republican party member. Yet Van Buren's coup proved to be merely the opening round in a decade-long political war between the two, one that had a profound effect on the politics, legislation, and economy of New York and the nation.[44]

During this short session, Governor Tompkins issued a succinct address. Avoiding the question of the canal, he concentrated on the postwar economic downturn and the necessity of improving the business climate. Tompkins underscored a major point: the lack of specie was a stubborn by-product of the war and inhibited economic growth. As conditions grew more menacing, some corporations and banks issued rapidly depreciating promissory notes, payable at some future date, in lieu of specie. Even worse, New York City banks had stopped redeeming their paper money in specie but promised to make good at some unspecified time. Because of that pledge, their paper became the main source of circulation. Smaller country banks scrambled to acquire those resources and were forced to pay a premium because of increased demand. In response, some country banks started printing "faculty bills," unbacked paper that circulated in local communities for short durations. City banks disliked faculty bills since they lessened demand for their money and sought to demonetarize them. Van Buren faced a quandary. As a hard-money, deflationary conservative, he was on record against inflation. But as a director of the Bank of Hudson, which issued faculty bills, he recognized that currency expansion, no matter the means, was a practical way to spur a faltering economy.[45]

One institution, the Utica Insurance Company, had its own expedient. Even though it lacked legislative permission, the company printed and circulated paper money in the form of loans for business transactions. Soon, "a great portion of the money" was scattered around the state to the relief "of many useful merchants, farmers and mechanics." This practice infuriated many incorporated banks. Their spokesman, Federalist Senator Abraham Van Vechten, introduced a resolution that called on Van Buren as attorney general to investigate the Utica Company's charter and to ascertain if it had the right to conduct "banking operations." If not, Van Vechten urged immediate action as Van Buren "shall deem proper." He took the resolution seriously. In December, Van Buren informed the company of his intention to seek an injunction from the Court of Chancery the following month in order "to restrain you from the further exercise of Banking powers."[46]

At the short session's end, Van Buren's trip home was a matter of minutes, both to his new office and a household grown large. Hannah Van Buren was again pregnant. The noise of three active sons filled the air. Mrs. Hoes, the "old grandmother," was spending the winter with them, along with Hannah's eldest sister. Butler, now twenty-one, lived on the first floor, still functioning as Van Buren's office manager, confidant, and bill collector. Butler also devoted much of his time to studying the "forms and practice of the law" in the library to prepare for his bar examination.[47]

Butler's distraction hindered Van Buren because his state burdens, along with his private practice, had escalated. During November and December, he received numerous communications questioning the legality of "this New Stuff called Faculty bills" for payments to the state treasurer, as well as his willingness to accept promissory notes based on them for mortgages. Others sought information about bail, injunctions, lapsed default judgments, and unreported payments. Some of Van Buren's previously filed cases in chancery neared resolution: a divorce for adultery, a master's reports on a will in conflict, and a wrangle over a land contract. More legal work filled Van Buren's hours well into the Christmas season of 1816: he advised Comptroller McIntrye to secure either a *mandamus* or legislative action to force Ulster County supervisors to repay a loan; he met with private clients; and he settled a dispute with Francis Silvester over an old debt.[48]

In the January 1817 Supreme Court term, Van Buren had only one action: the Great Possession's final disposition. The Van Alens still disputed the commissioners' finding that awarded thirty-seven acres to John Niver. In October 1814 Van Buren had secured an ejectment from the Columbia Circuit Court. Niver appealed to the Supreme Court in *Jackson, ex dem. Van Alen and Van Alen, v. Ambler.* Opposing advocates represented an odd alignment. Van Buren, in association with Federalist Van Vechten, contended against Thomas

Emmet, a Republican stalwart, and Elisha Williams, a devout Federalist. Van Buren repeated his circuit court contentions. The commissioners had mistakenly conceded the land of one party, the Van Alens, to another, Niver, without considering that the property lay outside the De Bruyn Patent. Judge Spencer for the court sustained Niver, ruling that the commissioners acted within the powers the legislature had granted.[49]

Although the result disappointed Van Buren, too many other vexing problems clamored for his attention. Hannah Van Buren bore another son, named Smith Thompson in honor of their friend the chief justice. As she convalesced, Van Buren's fatigue and recurrent bouts with asthma reduced his normal stamina. He kept Butler close at hand, reading and talking, as both studied material in the library for the injunction against the Utica Insurance Company, which the Court of Chancery heard on January 24, 1817.[50]

Van Buren began *The Attorney General v. The Utica Insurance Company* with a review of the state's fundamental legal and economic reasoning in seeking the injunction. The 1813 legislature had modified the 1804 Restraining Act, he pointed out, specifically to prevent "unincorporated banking associations" from "transacting" business as incorporated banks. In 1816 when the legislature authorized the Utica Insurance Company, its charter lacked terms that allowed "banking operations of any kind." Yet the company ignored legislative intent; it conducted "moneyed concerns usually performed by incorporated banks" by illegally claiming that privilege through "the provisions of the act of incorporation."[51]

Van Buren's brief was novel for its day in how he sought a remedy for this purported usurpation of power. Since the Supreme Court ordinarily heard such a case, he had to convince Kent that jurisdiction lay in chancery. To that end, Van Buren argued that it was customary for chancery to take cognizance where the remedy was "for prevention only," in forcing the company to cease financial practices, "not for the punishment of an offence." Shrewdly employing the case book authority and precedent that Kent cherished, Van Buren stressed that the British Court of Chancery normally tried "the rights of the subject in hostility to the crown." In this instance, the company, by extending powers beyond its franchise, placed itself in conflict with the state. Thus, an injunction ordering the company to answer by what authority it engaged in banking was a *quo warranto* proceeding commonly used in Supreme Court criminal cases. But it was also a "civil proceeding" within the New York Court of Chancery's scope, which did not regularly deal with criminal matters. Van Buren concluded that Kent could avoid issuing an indictment because no injury had occurred, generally a procedure integral to equity. British precedent, however, gave Kent "visitation" and "supervisory" authority over corporations. In short, he had the jurisdiction to determine whether the Utica Company had breached its franchise.[52]

Kent was impressed with Van Buren's legal scholarship, but withheld approval of his reasoning. To Kent, if the company exceeded its chartered power,

New York had an adequate remedy through the 1813 statute. The method was indeed *quo warranto,* under which the issue was "strictly a criminal proceeding, being for the usurpation of a state prerogative," a fact Van Buren proved. Under those conditions, Kent denied Van Buren's motion. But, Kent continued, the Supreme Court did have jurisdiction in the matter, because "the whole question, upon the merits, is one of law, and not of equity." On that basis, Van Buren prepared a *quo warranto* action to the Supreme Court.[53]

This legal setback was the first in a series of disasters that made the next two years the bleakest in Van Buren's career in law and politics. Still hampered by illness, he found the next legislative session highly politicized over two related issues: a replacement for Tompkins, when he resigned as governor after receiving official notice of his vice-presidential election, and Clinton's personal identification with the canal, which made him Tompkins's logical successor. In fact, the groundswell for Clinton had become so insistent that Van Buren could not stop the legislative caucus from nominating him. Tammanyites were furious. They urged Van Buren to run "an opposing candidate." He refused. Loyal to the point of obsession with the precedent of regular nominees, Van Buren was forced to support a gubernatorial candidate he distrusted.[54]

Van Buren's years of discontent had just begun. His efforts in three cases before the March Court of Errors were failures. *Lyon v. Tallmadge* involved confused, fraudulent, and almost collusive activities surrounding a prisoner's escape, the sheriff's responsibilities, and a suit for recovery of damages against the sheriff. As in the earlier "cow case," Van Buren voted to relieve the sheriff of responsibility. Yet, unlike his previous thoughtful review, he did not write an opinion and joined only one other senator in the minority. *Franklin v. Osgood,* an appeal from chancery in which Kent sustained Clinton's land claim, was an extension of the case that Van Buren had earlier won for Mrs. Clinton. The court upheld the decision, but the voting pattern was politicized. Pro-Clinton senators unanimously backed Kent, opposed by an equally firm bloc of anti-Clintonians. Van Buren refrained from an opinion because of a possible conflict of interest due to his representation of the Clintons. Yet his marked lack of vigor in either action spoke volumes about his dark emotional mood.[55]

Van Buren was at his worst as the advocate for the plaintiffs, the executors of Isaac Clason, against a number of defendants in the final case in error. The facts "were very plain" about a contract Clason had formed, in which he added a written memorandum to employ an "authorized agent" to buy a quantity of rye for future delivery and sale. The agent carried out these terms, but Clason "refused to accept and pay for" the consignment. The merchants then sold the rye at auction "at the best price" they could get, suing Clason for the difference. When the Supreme Court upheld the defendants, Clason's attorneys filed a writ of error. Van Buren's brief for Clason was defective and, for him, slipshod. Using a specious line of reasoning, he maintained that the contract was illegal. A "sufficient memorandum in writing" did not exist "within the statute of frauds," because Clason and the agent had signed the agreement in lead pencil, which could be altered, rather than pen and ink. Kent, writing for the majority, hardly concealed his disdain. The contract, he lectured, was binding. The lead pencil was immaterial, since the statute did not specify the type of instrument with which the contract was to be written. With only two senators dissenting, the court gave Van Buren a stinging rebuke.[56]

At this juncture, Van Buren faced his key moment of truth over the canal bill. As he had so often before, he formulated a position based on political calculation, professional dispassion, and principle. In a speech lasting almost two hours, he said that the canal was feasible from an economic standpoint, and that his vote for the bill, the most important "he gave in his life," would benefit the entire state. Ending with a gesture stemming from classical republicanism, he exhorted his colleagues to accept the popular will by backing his position.[57]

By adapting to the canal, Van Buren emphasized the flexibility inherent to legal instrumentalism. But as far as the jury composed of his fellow Republicans was concerned, he failed. When the bill passed both houses, infuriated Tammanyites raged against Van Buren's "betrayal," rejected his leadership, and refused to support any measure that enhanced Clinton.[58]

Van Buren was dismayed but philosophic. Two weeks were left in the gubernatorial campaign when the legislature ended, and he kept a low profile. Not that he could have accomplished anything. Clinton swept to an easy triumph, running poorly only in the Southern District, Tammany's bailiwick. With the aid of his Federalist allies, the "Swiss Federalists," so-called because of their purported willingness to be bought by Clinton's control of patronage, Clintonians also dominated the coming legislature and, apparently, the next council. With this stunning victory, Clinton confirmed how much he had shifted the state's political fulcrum and put Van Buren's next reappointment as attorney general at risk.[59]

Van Buren anticipated these events and was neither shocked nor surprised. Deciding to let time and reason mend his fracture with Tammany, he accepted the inevitable and turned his attention for the rest of 1817 to the law. But Van Buren found that the strains from Clinton's victory were acute, both in his political life and his practice of law, and each continued to suffer.[60]

In the May Supreme Court term, Van Buren won two nonenumerated actions for the state. But other losses mounted. In *Kidzie v. Sackrider and Others,* an appeal from the Delaware County Court of Common Pleas, he overlooked a chance to score a vital precedent. The case originated when Kidzie, a justice of the peace, found Sackrider and several others guilty of diverting an ancient waterway. Sackrider's original attorneys convinced the Supreme Court to issue a *certiorari.* But Kidzie won because he had supplied the court with what Sackrider termed false information. Sackrider then resubmitted his cause to the Supreme Court on the grounds of falsification. The court reaffirmed the previous judgment. Sackrider tried another tactic. He brought an action in trespass against Kidzie, which claimed damages because Kidzie had engaged in unlawful interference with Sackrider's property. The circuit court sustained Sackrider, and Kidzie appealed to the Supreme Court. At this point, Van Buren entered. He contended that Kidzie had indeed harmed Sackrider's property, giving him an actionable cause and the right to damages. But in a *per curiam,* the judges sustained the circuit court.[61]

While the justices ruled for Sackrider on only trespass, the case touched the larger question of riparian rights, a major issue in coming economic developments. In shunning this question, Van Buren did not address the issue of whether the flow of water from upstream gave those living downstream a prescriptive remedy to create an easement in its usage. Worse, Van Buren, perhaps to serve his client's interests, contradicted liberal republicanism. He neglected to consider how his defense of Kidzie limited commercial growth through the potential establishment of a monopoly that would hinder individual enterprisers.[62]

These litigations marked no obvious change in Van Buren's normal professional load. But something happened shortly after this term that indicated how much his political needs were preempting his private practice. In mid-May of 1817, Van Buren inspected a newly-purchased farm near Middleburgh in Schoharie County, inviting Butler along as his companion. Along the way, Van Buren took an important step into the future. In order to devote more time to politics, he offered Butler, who had just passed the bar, a partnership. This offer was so appealing that Butler could hardly wait to write Harriet Allen. Van Buren, he exulted, was "really & truly a gentleman & a man of refined generosity, and liberal feeling." The partnership encompassed all of Van Buren's "private business," work in chancery, and "in the Supreme & Common Pleas courts." Knowing the practice was still suffering from Van Buren's neglect, Butler anticipated that his income would be low for a while, but believed his long run prospects were "excellent, perhaps lucrative." On June 3, the *Albany Argus* announced the new arrangement. With that, Van Buren began his next phase as a lawyer-politician, a period in which politics gradually became dominant.[63]

The following weeks presented no immediate change in Van Buren's routine. With his family on vacation, he used this opportunity to settle some private concerns. He purchased 150 acres of land in Kinderhook for $1,100 at a sheriff's sale. He also advised his wife's rather irresponsible younger brother about personal finances. Otherwise, Van Buren fastened his attention upon "attorney general business."[64]

From January through August 1817, he had received ninety-six letters dealing with state business. A few concluded unresolved matters but most required further research. In chancery, Van Buren filed four new cases and anticipated decisions in several earlier ones; he brushed up on equity principles for coming actions and drafted briefs for twenty-five cases scheduled for the August Supreme Court.[65]

On July 1, Van Buren's plummeting political fortune reached a new low when Clinton took office. Hoping to start his administration on a positive note, Clinton used an intermediary to propose a truce with Van Buren. Clinton implied that Van Buren could remain as attorney general in exchange for his political cooperation, or at least acquiescence. Van Buren decided to make inactivity a virtue. If Clinton supported only measures that satisfied "our friends" and sustained the Republican party, Van Buren promised to make himself "useful."[66]

But Van Buren's losing streak, both in politics and law, only accelerated. On July 19, he joined John Woodworth in the well-publicized chancery action of *Hart v. Ten Eyck and Others,* a case in litigation for several years. It tested whether Abraham Ten Eyck, the last surviving executor of the Hart estate, had misappropriated moneys that resulted in depleting the legacy of the sole heir, a minor.[67] In 1816, Chancellor Kent issued an order to Ten Eyck that directed him to provide all books, papers, and writings in his "custody" dealing with the estate for a master of chancery's inspection; he also required a sworn affidavit before a notary public that they were accurate. The process, a discovery, was a pretrial procedure in which parties to a lawsuit asked for and received such information.[68]

While the master deliberated, Van Buren and Woodworth sought to modify Kent's order by limiting the discovery to only those papers that Ten Eyck had "referred and admitted" in previous litigations. In response, Kent noted that court rules protected a litigant from discovery only if it would expose him to penalties and criminal prosecution. Since the motion was "not against any particular interrogatory or examination" but "against the order itself," Kent denied the motion. The case was far from over. Much to his later chagrin, Van Buren continued to represent Ten Eyck in several related actions.[69]

In August, Van Buren scored a partial comeback by winning twenty-four cases for the state in the Supreme Court, mostly nonenumerated debt collections. But in *The People v. Anderson,* his ineffectiveness continued regarding the question of what rights Anderson had to a lost trunk he had found on a public highway. Van Buren maintained that Anderson was guilty of larceny because he "took up the trunk" with intent to steal. Anderson's attorneys replied that British precedent and common law stressed that larceny hinged on whether the "*taking* was felonious." Even if a person converted the goods "to his own use," larceny had not taken place, provided "the first taking is lawful." Van Buren countered that the common law did not apply, since it related only to treasure-troves, "derelict" goods abandoned by the owner. A split court under Spencer gave Van Buren another rebuff, both in his effort to modify the common law and as attorney general. Spencer ruled that Van Buren had misread the law. The court would not make an "innovation" in the criminal code by considering this case as larceny, because the state had not proven Anderson guilty of a "premeditated or already formed intention to steal."[70]

In September and October, Van Buren was back in chancery for two cases. His losses continued to mount. In *Moody v. A. and H. Payne,* he could not

convince Kent to maintain an injunction that prevented three insolvent partners from settling their individual and joint debts. Kent also declined to grant
Van Buren a discovery to aid the plaintiffs in *McIntrye and Others v. Mancius
and Brown,* because he had not provided sufficient reasons why the motion
"would be proper and material."[71]

As any good lawyer would, Van Buren tried to take these reversals in stride,
but his reaction indicated that his political problems were getting the best of
him. How much his mental state had affected his physical health was impossible to gauge, but he became "considerably ill" in early October, forcing the
unprepared Butler to "rush up" and take over his work in Albany Common
Pleas. Ten days later, Van Buren was still so "extremely ill" that Butler doubted
whether Van Buren could appear at all in the coming Supreme Court session.
Sick or not, Van Buren went to New York City for five cases.[72]

His decision proved professionally sound and briefly lifted his spirits when
the court sustained him in three nonenumerated state actions and two private
cases. *Jackson, ex dem. Wynkoop, v. Myers* provided Van Buren with customary
footing by defending a tenant in Greene County over the exact boundaries
of his farm and convincing the court to overrule his ejectment. *Caswell v.
Black River Cotton and Manufacturing Company* was also familiar. In 1814, the
company had sold Caswell fifty acres for $3,600 in Watertown, Jefferson
County. The premises were part of a larger tract the company bought, but
Caswell's purchase was encumbered by a defaulted mortgage, which he knew
existed but had accepted. After holding and using the land for three years,
Caswell decided that his deed was improper and sued for the return of his
money. Van Buren's brief for the company was short and clear. Caswell had
known about the defaulted mortgage. He needed "to show either a breach of
contract by the defendant, or fraud to recover." The contract may have been
unfair, but Caswell had accepted its terms and the court was confined to the
intent of each party. In upholding Van Buren, the court agreed that under the
will theory of contracts a buyer was responsible for his purchase, provided his
intent was to accept a contract. If Caswell had any remedy, the court continued, it lay in chancery.[73]

With his health recovered by January of 1818, Van Buren was back before
chancery, but again with mixed results. *Denning and Others v. Smith and Others*
saw him depart from his usual defense of officeholders because of his Dutch-
American sense of ethical justice. Kent agreed to overrule two land commissioners in Greene County who had rigged advertisements in their favor and
failed to give Van Buren's clients a fair notice to purchase the property. Yet Van
Buren lost *A. Van Bergen v. H. Van Bergen,* another action in which he avoided
riparian rights. His client had erected a new mill and dam downstream that
impeded an older mill and dam upstream. Van Buren sought an injunction
against the upstream operation as a public nuisance. Kent ruled that chancery
lacked jurisdiction to grant the injunction, unless the older dam and mill hindered the right of a long-established enterprise. Van Buren's client was in the

wrong, because he had erected a new dam and mill to hinder another.[74]

In the January Supreme Court, Van Buren rebounded with a stunning triumph in *Jackson, ex dem. Woodruff and Others, v. Gilchrist*. The action dated back to 1711 when Mrs. Ann Bridges, a wife of one of the thirteen original Dutch owners of the Kayaderosseras Patent in the future Saratoga County, had sold her share to Peter Fauconier, a New York City merchant. By 1771, the patent had been partitioned, evidence of Ann Bridges's sale was recorded with the secretary of state, and Fauconier's heirs filed deeds to show proof of "acts of ownership and assertion of title." In 1816, her natural heirs, the Woodruffs and others, tried to recover the land, which had become quite valuable, from the heir of Peter Fauconier's assign, John Gilchrist, on the grounds that the deed was void since Ann Bridges had no legal standing to market the property. At the Saratoga Circuit, the court ruled for the plaintiffs, subject to Supreme Court review.[75]

This reconsideration presented a fascinating analysis of the history and application of the common law in New York, specifically the rights and legal status of women. John Henry, the Woodruffs' attorney, based their claim on the precedent in the common law that denied Ann Bridges, a *feme covert,* or a married woman, the right to alienate landed property in her possession, even with her husband's consent, without a private examination before a magistrate, which had not taken place. The provision was intended to protect a woman against her husband's undue influence or coercion, especially if he might have forced her to alienate the property. But to make this doctrine effective, Henry needed to prove that the common law was operational in New York as of 1711.[76]

The task was not easy, because the Dutch had settled first in New York and their singular legal system governed New Netherland until 1674. To that end, Henry argued that the English had legitimately claimed territory from the 38th to the 68th parallel based on discoveries that John Cabot made in 1497. The area between the 34th and 45th parallels was also English because of Virginia Patents. Each of these areas encompassed New York and predated Dutch settlement of New Netherland. The territory was thus always English; the Dutch were "intruders." Although distracted by civil war, the English finally resumed control and took possession "in full sovereignty." This meant that English laws had always prevailed in New York. Not all the laws, Henry admitted, but such as were applicable to the situation in the province. Yet in this case, "the law of *descents,* the law as to *baron* and *feme,*" did specifically apply. The Charter of Liberties and Privileges, granted by the Duke of York in 1683, confirmed the fact, particularly the provision based on common law declaring "that no estate of a *feme covert* shall be sold or conveyed but by deed acknowledged by her in some Court of record." But Ann Bridges had not acknowledged her action in a proper court of record, making the sale void. As a result, she had no right to sell the property, which still belonged to her natural heirs.[77]

Van Buren and Van Vechten, his co-counsel, ignored this attack on their common Dutch-American heritage. Instead, they presented a different version of history, predicated on the contention that no precedent existed in the province at the time of sale concerning *feme covert*.

Van Buren and Van Vechten argued that Ann Bridges had full individual authority to engage in a personal legal transaction, and they implied further that she possessed that right under Dutch-American concepts of communal property, mutual wills, and a partible division of assets. As for Henry's contention, they emphasized that the colony had been Dutch until the English conquest of 1674. But they also explained that the common law did not automatically supplant Dutch-American law when "the deed was executed" in 1711. Those older statues remained until they were "actually changed and new laws imposed." The 1683 document did have a provision about *feme covert,* they conceded, but it "never had the force of law." The "first colonial legislature" of 1691, under William and Mary, denied the document's authority. In fact, the legislature disavowed "all the acts of the Duke of York, as such, or as James II., after he came to the crown," and passed a new bill of privileges. Although this bill was "afterwards repealed by the king in 1697," that act did not create the common law. In 1710 and in 1752, various legal scholars published digests of the province's laws. None took notice of the Duke's charter and revisions, nor did Peter Van Schaack's 1773 "edition of laws," which the legislature had authorized to "revise, digest, and collect all the laws in force in the colony" back to 1688. From this historical review, Van Buren and Van Vechten concluded that there was "no act, statute, or charter existing in the colony, regulating the mode of conveyance by a *feme covert.*"[78]

Turning to the state constitution, they maintained that the "framers," in Section 35, did accept certain parts of the common law and legislative statutes that "formed the law of the colony" prior to independence. But the "framers" recognized and adapted these colonial laws; "they never meant to re-enact them." Where, then, they asked, "are we to look for the constitution of the colony?" Where did "Courts of justice derive their powers?" "Surely not" the "charter of liberties granted by the Duke of York." The answer was "from the common law," which they defined as "custom and usage." But, they added, "the common law may be altered by statute" through legal instrumentalism. Over Henry's objection, Van Buren and Van Vechten maintained that the governing statute in this case came from the legislative act of 1771, which had voided any "claim to real estate" that "any person is now actually possessed, whether as tenant in common, or otherwise, upon the pretense that the *feme covert* granting the same had not been privately examined before any of the public officers or magistrates."[79]

Chief Justice Thompson delivered the court's unanimous opinion. After lauding both sides for their "able and elaborate" presentations, he declined to rule on the main question about the common law's applicability. But Thompson, in accepting the Van Buren-Van Vechten brief, did so rule by inference. He backed their interpretation that the common law concerning the alienation of property by a *feme covert* was not in effect at the time Ann Bridges conveyed her property to Peter Fauconier. And the court went even further. The 1771 act did govern the case; under those conditions, the judges confirmed Gilchrist's property rights. While this decision was admittedly narrow, Van Buren and Van Vechten indirectly made an important advance in the legal status of women, in particular, by including women within classical republicanism by emphasizing that they enjoyed full individual property rights and contractual freedom. Moreover, the case allowed Van Buren to reassert both legislative supremacy over the judiciary and strict construction of the constitution. He had also won another round in his effort to end feudal relics that were embedded in the common law.[80]

By January 27, 1818, when the legislature gathered for its Forty-first session, Van Buren's professional and political troubles were far from over. With Clinton still too popular for direct assaults, Van Buren realized that, strategically, he needed to develop new skills in opposition, while still playing a constructive role in the legislative process. Tactically, he also understood that he needed to preserve his constituency and mobilize the political organization he had so carefully built during his years before the bar, one fabricated of the human conglomerates of the court system: judges, fellow attorneys, clerks, sheriffs, justices of the peace, and numerous grateful clients. Once this base was secure, Van Buren had to reach out to peripheral groups. For the moment, however, peace reigned. Each side honored President's Monroe's "Era of Good Feelings" and pledged mutual unity. To symbolize this attitude, the council renamed Van Buren attorney general for a third term.[81]

Van Buren, the leader of Republican "Bucktails," the term they adopted to differentiate themselves from the governor's supporters, set his new tactics in motion. Van Buren found both the law and his background as attorney general to be invaluable as he laid out a positive program of distributive justice and legal instrumentalism, principally by seeking to modernize the judiciary. To that end, he sought to enlarge the jurisdiction of justices of the peace courts. He supported a Supreme Court initiative to prevent attorneys from buying bonds and promissory notes for collection and urged the expansion of circuit courts. He also backed an effort to hold a session of the Court of Errors, which had met exclusively in Albany, in New York City. Van Buren's most important achievement concerned assistant district attorneys. Ignoring accusations that he was only interested in aiding "pettifoggers" and finding a fresh source of patronage, he sponsored the passage of a bill that allocated an appointive district attorney to each county. This streamlining of the judiciary branch replaced the older, often ineffective process, in which an assistant district attorney usually prosecuted cases in small, multiple counties, resulting in delayed justice due to an excessive workload.[82]

As attorney general, Van Buren asserted himself just as successfully. In the January and May Supreme Court terms, he won eighteen state actions, collecting the impressive sum of $32,446.97. His office received almost a letter every other day. Most paid debts without court action in answer to earlier demands, returned previous writs, corrected defective titles, or sent copies of deeds to verify property holdings. Out-going mail concerned new suits, orders to county sheriffs, and notices to newspapers to advertise sales of foreclosed mortgages. Equally helpful, the legislature called on Van Buren, as attorney general, to investigate and prepare opinions concerning the legality of several claims on state lands involving escheat, as well as the possible prosecution of contractors who failed to fulfill their obligations. The most intriguing subject Van Buren studied for prosecution was an alleged forgery of deeds purportedly recorded in 1711 with the secretary of state. Swinging into action, he instituted suits against several claimants and contractors and reported that he was convinced the deeds were forged, an opinion that led to further investigations.[83]

When the legislature adjourned on April 21, Van Buren had every reason to feel satisfied with his accomplishments. But he labored under an illusion. True to his pledge to Clinton, Van Buren had sought party unity. Yet he had not weakened the governor, nor repaired his crumbling base, especially among Tammanyites who continually bickered with him.[84]

Political realities in the spring elections mortified Van Buren and accentuated the difficulties involved in unseating Clintonians. Still enjoying popular approval, they won enough votes to control the legislature and the coming council with their Swiss-Federalist allies. Putting Van Buren on notice that his days as attorney general were numbered, the Clintonian *Utica Patriot* editorialized that he, not the governor, was the chief source of party divisions. In a blunt warning that party unity was over, the paper continued, all lessons from history proved "That a house divided against itself cannot stand."[85]

CHAPTER NINE

Republicanism and State Attorney General

Phase Two

*V*an Buren kept his political career alive during these discouraging days of Clinton's ascendancy through the only public position within his grasp, attorney general. This was the post, after all, that the Clintonian state senator and future historian Jabez Hammond affirmed as "one of the most important, influential and at that time lucrative offices in the state." During 1818, Van Buren proved that Hammond was correct. Adopting a tireless routine, Van Buren issued writs, deposited fees, checked tax collections, received and answered up to 704 letters for the year, and prepared a cluster of state actions for the Supreme Court and chancery. In May, as part of this process, Van Buren won nineteen nonenumerated Supreme Court actions worth $24,358.19 for the state.[1]

Van Buren also finished the groundwork in his most meaningful action as attorney general, the Utica Insurance Company case. On May 16, 1818, he filed a *quo warranto* in the Supreme Court. Asserting that the company had illegally acted as an incorporation bank and "usurped" legislative authority, Van

Buren demanded the company "answer" to the "people by what warrant" it claimed to "enjoy the liberties, privileges and franchises" of "a bank."[2]

The People of the State of New-York, ex relatione The Attorney-General, v. the Utica Insurance Company headed the docket for the August term in Albany. The press followed the case closely, an indication both of the stakes involved and the reputations of the opposing counsels: Van Buren for New York, and Emmet, Nathan Williams, and Richard Harrison for the company—a line-up of the best legal talent in the state.[3]

Van Buren developed his brief according to a logical progression. He began that nothing within the statute passed on March 29, 1816 that established the company, either by intent or implication, had allowed banking. Shrewdly, Van Buren anticipated a likely rebuttal that since the legislature had not specifically prohibited a bank, the company had that right. He emphasized that the Restraining Act of 1813 had explicitly denied such functions to incorporated institutions. The company, circumscribed by legislative intent, was a corporate body, which thus had no rights beyond those its charter distinctly granted. Such a corporate body could only operate under the statutory design of its creator.[4]

Harrison and Emmet replied that *quo warranto* was an improper remedy. Tracing the motion back to British origins, they explained that *quo warranto* sprang from the royal prerogative or franchise. Since the company had not usurped such a franchise, the writ was inadequate, and they asked the court to declare that it lacked jurisdiction. Emmet hammered away at that point, declaring that the legislature had approved numerous charters since 1813, but each contained a specific clause deterring banking. These exclusionary limitations were the strongest evidence the legislature recognized that banking was not a franchise. On the contrary, it existed "at large" in every citizen and could be freely used, unless the legislature categorically denied that right. The 1813 Restraining Act had therefore taken a basic right from citizens. True, Emmet noted, the legislature did not give the company such a franchise. But its charter contained a clause that the object of incorporation "ought to be liberally encouraged"; it also listed a number of prohibitions and restrictions that governed the company. Yet the statute left the company free to employ surplus money "in any manner" it deemed beneficial. Banking was thus a matter of its own discretion, not the state's.[5]

Van Buren answered by first addressing the issue of jurisdiction. He stressed that when the Court of Chancery heard the case on a motion for an injunction, the defendant's counsels had objected to the court's authority on the grounds that there was an adequate remedy at law, the very *quo warranto* that they now found objectionable. Aside from such inconsistency, Van Buren pointed out that counsels who customarily challenged the jurisdiction of a court offered a substitute. They had none. Van Buren continued that the 1813 Restraining Act made banking a franchise only "derived from the grant of the Legislature." If this statute was breached, the state had the right to pursue a "remedy" through "the public prosecutor in the Supreme Court." There was no question that a franchise was "a liberty" or "a privilege," or that a distinction existed "between *royal* and *common* franchises." But through public law passed by representatives of the people, the state defined privileges and franchises as a government function. Citizens could not arbitrarily ignore such public law, unless the legislature included a specific clause to that affect. Whether that right was a franchise in Great Britain was immaterial; it was in New York. The company was not a private individual, but a creature of the state, which conducted banking in violation of statute law.[6]

Van Buren capped his argument with a review of the company's charter and the question of legislative intent. Only by the wildest stretch of the imagination could anyone suggest that the statute allowing the company to use its surplus was synonymous with authorizing a bank. "If that privilege was intended, why not say so in express terms?" Why should that authority "be left to be made out by implication and inference?" Answering himself, Van Buren concluded that the company lacked such a right. Based on these facts, he asked the court for a judgment that barred the company from banking and confirmed that the state had the lone power to grant such privileges.[7]

All the participating justices supported Van Buren's *quo warranto,* but they were divided about the company's prerogative to create a bank. Chief Justice Thompson spoke for the majority. Admitting that banking had once been a common right belonging to individuals, he nonetheless agreed with Van Buren that the legislature had the authority "to regulate, modify, or restrain this right." The sole issue rested on whether the company's charter granted that right. Thompson found it "a little extraordinary" that the 1816 act did not employ the customary phraseology of a banking charter; he observed that only the "hands of a skillful workman" could "frame anything like a plausible appearance of a banking statute." On that basis, the court confirmed Van Buren's contention that the state alone had the right to grant such privileges and enjoined the company from future banking.[8]

Van Buren's memorable victory came at a fortunate moment. As a lawyer, his innovative use of *quo warranto,* the first instance of its application against a corporation, confirmed his legal sagacity. As a politician-lawyer, his triumph further demonstrated his effectiveness as attorney general and made his possible removal more difficult. Equally significant, Van Buren's brief, continuing the arguments he had first made against the Catskill bank, again anticipated many key economic ideas in Jacksonianism: a hard money currency, restricted banking, deflation, and the state's right to regulate private corporations in the public interest. As a future Jacksonian, Van Buren also asserted his classical republican beliefs in legislative supremacy, strict construction of constitutional power, state control of banking, and the principle that government must protect liberty by denying special privileges to corporations in order to ensure equal opportunity.[9]

Before the month was out, Van Buren was back in chancery with *Lansing v. McPherson and Others,* another action defending small freeholders. In this instance, Van Buren petitioned Kent to set aside a foreclosure decree on McPherson's lapsed mortgage. McPherson, Van Buren argued, had misconstrued his legal position and failed to bid for his property at a sheriff's sale. As a remedy, Van Buren requested Kent to issue a decree in equity to reopen the bidding. Kent rejected the petition because too much time had elapsed. But he accepted Van Buren's remedy by allowing McPherson an opportunity to make a new bid.[10]

Other litigations beckoned in September. The Court of Errors, which usually met concurrently with the legislature, held a special three-week tribunal to adjudicate seventeen cases it had set aside to avoid interfering with the regular session. Surprisingly, Van Buren neither represented anyone nor offered opinions. Something was amiss in his personal life. In August, Hannah Van Buren became ill, "dangerously so" he admitted. As she grew worse, friends noted his distraction and realized that her "indisposition" was the "cause."[11]

Van Buren devoted the late summer to her care. But in the midst of her convalescence, his professional duties grew more intense. Besides the familiar but demanding volume of normal official business, he was committed to represent the state in a murder trial and prosecute a case in the Albany Court of Common Pleas that grew out of his investigation of forged deeds. Nor could he avoid advocating twenty-eight cases before the October Supreme Court in New York City. While twenty-five of these were undemanding cases for the state, Van Buren's main reason for attending lay in two appeals from the Columbia Circuit connected to his closest supporters and the Livingstons.[12]

Although Van Buren won each action for the state, *Jackson, ex. dem. William J. Livingston, v. Barringer* was more complex. Livingston had sought to eject Barringer from a portion of land he had held dating to 1773 on a three-lives lease. The sticking point was that one section of the lease described Barringer's tract in "metes and bounds," but another clause indicated that the farm contained "eighty acres in one piece," which made the whole area 149 acres. Barringer had fulfilled the agreement, paying rent for forty years on the entire parcel. For that reason, the Columbia Circuit found for him on a special verdict. Livingston appealed. In the Supreme Court, Williams asserted that Livingston could eject Barringer because the operative words in the lease were "eighty acres." Van Buren responded that Barringer had held in "undisputed possession" all the land for forty years and paid rent, during which time the Livingstons had not raised a prior objection. The lease's intent, then, covered the entire area and "must prevail." Judge Thompson delivered the court's opinion. Endorsing Van Buren's stress on the will theory of contracts, Thompson wrote that the lease's "presumed intention" covered "the whole of the farm."[13]

Four male Livingstons, and Catherine Livingston and her husband John C. Stevens, were central to *Decker v. Livingston.* In circuit court, Stevens, acting for his wife, had won an ejectment of Decker for alleged nonpayment of a long-standing lease he held as an assign. On appeal, Van Buren, acting for Decker, termed the proceedings "irregular," because the seizure was based on rents due for years prior to Catherine Livingston's marriage. Under these conditions, she ought to "be joined in the action." Additionally, Van Buren emphasized that Decker had "rendered" payments all the preceding years and that the Livingstons had accepted the money. Aaron Vanderpool, a rising Kinderhook lawyer, disagreed. Catharine Livingston Stevens was not a party because her husband held the estate in her name. Speaking for the majority, Spencer noted that Decker had paid his rent, raising the assumption that his lease was sound, unless the Livingstons offered compelling evidence indicating otherwise, which they had not. Just as important, Spencer cited a "well settled" point of law that a wife involved in a "cause of action accruing before marriage" must be "joined with her husband in [the] suit." Since she was absent, the ejectment was illegal.[14]

Van Buren's final cause, *Commissioners of Highways of the Town of Kinderhook v. Claw and Another,* a *certiorari,* reflected his commitment to legal positivism. The central issue concerned whether "the 36th section of the act to regulate highways" gave Claw the right to appeal a judgment against him for interfering with the commissioners' attempt to construct a highway through his property. Van Buren, representing Claw, insisted that Claw had complied with the statute, which governed the case. Judge Van Ness ruled against Van Buren, supporting Vanderpool's contention that the commissioners had not denied Claw due process. Even so, Van Buren was satisfied; he had once again reasserted legislative supremacy.[15]

In November, as Hannah Van Buren's condition grew more ominous, President Monroe precipitated a further crisis in Van Buren's life by offering Chief Justice Thompson the post of secretary of the navy. Thompson was receptive. He wrote Van Buren that he would accept the position, raised the question about the best moment to resign, and asked if Van Buren wished to replace him. Van Buren was tempted, but faced a dilemma. From a personal standpoint, the seat would cap his professional career. But he also feared that "the pecuniary sacrifice would be considerable." Additionally, Van Buren had to weigh several political implications that weighed heavily on his mind. Clinton might indeed choose him to deprive the Bucktails of their chief strategist. Even if Clinton did not, he could select a Swiss Federalist and harm the Bucktails just as much. On top of those considerations, some Clintonians introduced another imponderable factor. They sought legislation to name two additional Supreme Court judges. Van Buren found this objectionable, since the appointments might destabilize the court if the men appointed were either Clintonians or Swiss Federalists. For the moment, he was paralyzed with indecision. In this impasse, Thompson accepted Monroe's tender in November, but withheld resigning.[16]

Van Buren continued his law practice in the meantime. *Troup v. Sherwood and Wood,* part of the long delayed and lucrative Platner cause, raised a question about the purposes of a deposition. Van Buren and Henry filed a motion in chancery to prevent Abraham Van Vechten, their opposing counsel, from gaining the court's approval to make known information he had taken in depositions from three witnesses, which he conducted without Kent's permission. Van Buren and Henry protested that the depositions impeached the credibility of their witnesses in an action that the court had not yet heard. Kent allowed Van Vechten to use the information, if it were confined to "the general character" of the witnesses' "veracity," and provided that the facts gathered were not material to the case. But to protect Platner, Kent also ordered a delay until Van Buren and Henry assessed the depositions.[17]

A few days later, Van Buren teamed up with John Woodworth in chancery; they acted as co-counsels for Peter and Henry Ham, against Henry and Van Vechten, who acted for Rensselaer Schuyler and others, in a major case testing long-term leases. According to the brief that Van Buren and Woodworth prepared, the Hams' grandfather, Casper Ham, received a 300-acre lease, subject to a quitrent, in 1730 from the "proprietor of the manor of Rensselaer." In 1764, the proprietor transferred the property to his sister, Elizabeth, the wife of Abraham Ten Broeck, who eventually became sole owner at her death. After the transfer, the then current "proprietor" assured Casper Ham that he retained the farm, but must pay rent to Ten Broeck. Casper Ham continued in possession and made valuable improvements on the property until he died in 1777, when his only son and heir, Paul Ham, assumed possession. Paul Ham built a new house, made further improvements, and paid the same rent. In 1787, Ten Broeck formed an agreement with him to convert the rent from in-kind to money. That understanding lasted until Paul Ham died in 1807.[18]

Prior to Paul Ham's death, Ten Broeck promised him a durable lease in fee, tantamount to a perpetual lease, but never recorded this pledge. Yet Peter Ham continued in possession, believing that he had an interest in the farm protected by law and equity for as long as he paid annual rent. As proof, Van Buren and Woodworth noted, Ten Broeck allowed Peter Ham to sell fifty acres of improved land for $250, which Ten Broeck deducted from Ham's rent. When Paul Ham died, he willed his farm into five parts among his sons. Until Ten Broeck's death in 1810, they paid him the same rent.[19]

Ten Broeck's will reshaped the situation. He devised the premises to his daughter, Margaret. She, in turn, recorded a will devising all her real estate to her sister, Elizabeth, the wife of Rensselaer Schuyler, during her life, and to Elizabeth's children, if any, or to her brother, Dirck Ten Broeck and his children, if Elizabeth had none. In January 1813, the Schuylers, her heirs, sold 645 acres, including the premises of Peter Ham, Jr., and Henry Ham, to James Kane. The Hams objected by citing the promise that Ten Broeck had given their father. The defendants, denying any knowledge or belief in the lease arrangement that the Hams alleged, brought an ejectment.[20]

Van Buren and Woodworth asserted that the facts offered sufficient evidence to presume that an agreement existed between the proprietor and Casper Ham for a durable lease in fee, one merely modified by a mutual shift in the method of payment. Nor did fraud exist in the Hams' claim, a charge that they thought might arise, because the Hams had consistently improved the property and sold a portion with Ten Broeck's knowledge. At the minimum, the Hams deserved to finish a three-lives lease. Finally, Van Buren and Woodworth emphasized that the defendants, as a matter of justice and equity, were responsible to pay the Hams for their improvements if Kent found against them.[21]

Henry and Van Vechten disagreed. They argued that the defendants had an absolute right to the property under the colonial leasing system. The plaintiffs lacked documentary evidence from either the proprietor or Ten Broeck to substantiate the purported promise. Furthermore, since the rent was nominal, the Hams had no equitable claim for the improvements.[22]

Kent withheld his opinion for almost two months, perhaps because he had trouble suppressing his anger. When he issued his finding, Kent's words crackled with indignation. Repeating the line Van Buren and Woodworth had developed, Kent ruled that the evidence proved that the Hams "occupied and cultivated" a farm "under a steady and uniform rent." The defendants' allegation that the Hams were "mere tenants at will" was "utterly incredible." In fact, the Hams had a "permanent interest in the soil," as their "expensive improvements" attested. If any fraud existed, the defendants were guilty, because they had permitted Ham and his heirs, over a course of fifty years, to expend their money and labor for the benefit of the estate and then arbitrarily voided their rights. As his remedy, Kent ordered the defendants to execute a lease in fee simple to the Hams, supervised by a master in chancery.[23]

This decision marked a vital ideological, legal, economic, and political achievement for Van Buren, especially when connected to the Great Possession and the manorial question. By dealing the feudalistic colonial leasing arrangement a severe blow that limited the power the landed aristocracy held over tenants, Van Buren renewed his importance as the exponent of their rights and solidified the constituency he needed against Clinton.[24]

Yet two worrisome problems remained for Van Buren. His wife's health was still precarious, and Thompson pressed him to make a decision about the Supreme Court's vacuum. In that vein, Thompson wrote that the choice might be easier if Van Buren knew that the "respectable part of the Bar" wanted him "to take a seat on the Bench." But Van Buren remained undecided, turning instead toward the next legislative session.[25]

The selection of the assembly speaker completed the disintegration of Van Buren's old Republican party. Rejecting the choice of the party caucus, Clintonians selected Obadiah German, a former antiwar Federalist, now a Swiss Federalist. Van Buren, infuriated with the governor's "treachery" toward a traditional party precedent, introduced a set of resolutions at another caucus that condemned Clinton for placing himself above the organization.

But before a vote was taken, Clintonians moved for a week's recess.[26]

At the same time, Van Buren strove to make himself indispensable to the rank and file as its leading politician-lawyer. As a result, his labors during January of 1819, while normal for a man accustomed to a killing pace, far surpassed anything he had done in the past. Even as he fretted about his wife's sudden turn for the worse, Van Buren served on multiple senate committees and continued his enormous correspondence regarding the legal business of the state. Moreover, his Supreme Court docket reached epic proportions with forty-six actions. He secured judgments in forty-three for the state, calculated at $44,007.96. His single loss occurred in *The People v. The Supervisors of the County of Ulster.* Van Buren filed a *mandamus* against the defendants for failing to levy a state-ordered tax on the county, in order to recoup a $17,500 defalcation made by a previous supervisor. But the judges refused, since the statute of limitations had passed.[27]

The two cases remaining from Van Buren's private practice contradicted both his past efforts in property law and his evolving liberal republicanism. *Livingston v. Ten Broeck,* another confrontation with Williams, who represented Henry Livingston, concerned an ejectment against Ten Broeck, Van Buren's client. The action raised two issues. One rested in the wording of the original deed of 1694 from Robert Livingston to Derick Wessels, Ten Broeck's forbear. The deed, conveying a large but imprecise tract, gave Ten Broeck the right to pasture his cattle on manorial land and contained a clause for "cutting and hewing timber for building or firewood." Ten Broeck alluded to that clause in order to build a fence. Williams maintained that Ten Broeck had breached the deed since the clause did not specify such use. Van Buren noted, however, that Ten Broeck and his ancestors had cut wood for fencing "on the premises conveyed, for as long time back as the memory of man can reach." Then, Van Buren cited numerous authorities maintaining that where the language of "ancient deeds" was obscure or doubtful, courts had allowed "continuing usage" or intent as the "best practical exposition on the meaning of the parties." The second issue was less clear, however. In 1796, Ten Broeck sold 446 acres in fee simple. Williams again said that this action canceled Ten Broeck's right in common to cut and hew timber. Van Buren demurred. Such a right in common was "not extinguished by the severance of the premises." The court should accept "parol evidence of usage" as "the best practical exposition of the meaning of the parties."[28]

Led by Spencer, the court noted that precedent suggested that the right of common became "extinct" if the holder sold all or part of the land out of which common was taken. But a snag existed. The original deed was unclear about the size of Ten Broeck's tract, and neither side could prove if its intent included the 446 acres. Since the case "wholly turns on [this] fact," Spencer granted Van Buren's motion for a new trial.[29]

Livingston v. Potts touched a somewhat similar point. Van Buren appealed a trespass action, which Williams had won in the 1816 Columbia Circuit. The only question was whether Potts, Van Buren's client and Livingston's lessee "for two lives," had surrendered his right in common when he accepted a new lease from Livingston for three lives. In a *per curiam,* the court ruled that Potts, by giving up the old lease, had indeed forfeited his right in common.[30]

These two cases had wide implications. In both, Van Buren had stressed four familiar points to assert tenants' rights: classical republicanism's definition of property as the lack of dependency; parol evidence; the will theory of contracts; and his standard tactic to limit landlords' economic benefits. But in each case Van Buren had contradicted these commitments through his argument that courts could not modify "ancient" leases. In essence, the court's rulings had actually given landlords new chances to maximize their economic holdings in the future by substituting a fresh lease that benefited them for an altered one, which limited their interests. Van Buren might be excused in that he sought the best legal remedies for his clients on a case to case basis. In that way, he did defend Ten Broeck's and Pott's short-term needs. But Van Buren's overall strategy of not contesting landlords' titles actually enhanced their economic positions by giving conservative judges a means to continue "ancient" leases under a new guise. Just as significantly, Van Buren's line of reasoning in each case negated liberal republicanism. By defending his clients through classical republicanism in property law, he failed to appreciate how much liberal republicanism could contribute to the area's economic development and expand tenants' opportunities to achieve material progress.[31]

Meanwhile, each passing day brought Hannah Van Buren closer to death. Staying with her as much as possible, Van Buren curtailed most of his activities. During this period, he missed the last attempt to refashion the party around his caucus resolutions. Worse, because he was absent, the internecine war among the Republicans grew more intense over the selections of a new United States senator and a Council of Appointment.[32]

Three candidates vied for the Senate seat. The Bucktails nominated Samuel Young. The Clintonians selected John C. Spencer, the judge's son. High Minded Federalists—including the Coodies, who were distinct from the Swiss Federalists because of their hostility to Clinton and their defense of old party policies—ran Rufus King, the eminent incumbent. From Washington, Thompson informed Van Buren that some High Federalists hinted that "if you would make [King] Senator, you could have the Council," provided Van Buren avoided any semblance "of an understanding or bargain with" them. But at this point, Van Buren's options were limited. His championing of party purity precluded a sudden accommodation with the High Minded Federalists. He was also far too distracted because of his wife. With no side willing to budge, the legislature was deadlocked; they rescheduled the choice for the following December. Other political events increased Van Buren's unease. Clintonians, with the aid of Swiss Federalists, organized the new Council of Appointment and signaled that the ouster of Van Buren as attorney general only involved a question of timing.[33]

Van Buren broke out of his self-imposed isolation only twice during this period. He was present during the last joint vote for Senator and supported Young. Van Buren had also promised to advocate two substantial cases in the Court of Errors. Since he did not believe he could serve his clients fairly by seeking continuances, he tried the cases.[34]

Van Buren, as co-counsel with George Griffin, represented two American citizens, Nathaniel L. Griswold and George Griswold, over an issue of international law against Joshua Waddington and his brother, Henry Waddington. The Griswolds wished to collect about £3,600 sterling in an account they had accrued by depositing bills of credit with Henry Waddington in London before and during the War of 1812. The Supreme Court had denied them relief since their actions, trading with the enemy, was illegal.[35]

On appeal, Van Buren and Griffin explained that the Waddingtons, both naturalized American citizens, were partners in two firms prior to the war. Joshua Waddington operated one in the United States; Henry Waddington the other in Great Britain. Neither partnership dissolved during or after the war. According to Van Buren and Griffin, the war did not annul preexisting civil contracts; it only suspended their enforcement. Their aim was to prove that the double partnership was responsible for the activities of each. Furthermore, under Van Buren's theory that courts must honor a contract's intent, the Waddingtons were responsible for the debts Henry Waddington owed the Griswolds.[36]

Van Buren and Griffin also addressed a related but equivocal distinction about the nature of wartime commerce. They held that Congress's declaration of hostility lacked an "express prohibition of individual intercourse and trade." Conceding that the war made such trade illegal, they argued it applied only to tangible goods, not the deposits of bills of credit that were promises to pay in the future. To validate that point, they observed that the American government had sanctioned the remittance of bills of credit to Great Britain through a cartel. In 1813 and 1814, the belligerents formed this arrangement, which authorized non-hostile intercourse otherwise illegal in wartime. George Griswold travelled to Great Britain as a cartel and conducted business with Henry Waddington in accordance with this agreement.[37]

Despite their ingenious presentation, Van Buren and Griffin went against three facts that Kent noted in a closely-reasoned forty-page opinion in *Johnson's Reports.* The war had made the two governments and their citizens enemies, and the war automatically terminated normal commercial intercourse. The war had also dissolved all contracts, including partnerships, not only between citizens of the two nations, but even between men residing within the separate jurisdictions of those warring governments. With only two dissenters, the Court of Errors affirmed the Supreme Court, ordering the plaintiffs to pay "costs and charges."[38]

It was an ironic moment. On one side, the Griswolds had two Republican party attorneys, Van Buren and Griffin, who had supported the war and tried to prevent trading with the enemy. As advocates, they aided clients who had broken the law to recover money from the same enemy. On the other side were two Federalist attorneys and one key Federalist jurist who had opposed the war and whose political colleagues had condoned, if not supported, commerce with the enemy. They now upheld the principle that such trade with the enemy was illegal. To make the irony more painful, a majority of the participating senators agreed with Kent, including most Republicans. If Van Buren was embarrassed, he hid his mortification. As a lawyer, he was a true advocate, no matter the unpopularity of his clients' cause. Additionally, he raised a critical but unaddressed question about the federal government's constitutional right during wartime to void a valid business arrangement made before the declaration of war. This failure perplexed New York merchants when Southerners refused to honor contracts as the Confederate States of America took shape.[39]

Jackson, ex dem. Livingston, v. Delancy, Van Buren's second case, came from Catherine Nelson, the daughter of Lord and Lady Stirling, who attempted to reverse the Supreme Court's judgment that she had lost three years before. Her counsels said that her mother had a life interest in the estate; the court had ignored Catherine Nelson's remainder interest. Van Buren and Samuel Jones insisted that this line of appeal was "immaterial." The Supreme Court had heard the case "on its merits," and Catherine Nelson could not introduce new issues, even collaterally. Kent again issued the main opinion, sustained the defendants, and ruled that Catherine Nelson should have raised the issue earlier. More to the point, the statute of limitations had expired, and she had no case. The Court of Errors voted unanimously to affirm the judgment, awarding costs to Van Buren's clients.[40]

Van Buren came home to a hushed house. Over the last few days, Hannah Van Buren's feeble body had no longer rallied. She died on February 5, 1819, nearly a month short of her thirty-sixth birthday, leaving behind a somber thirty-seven year old husband and four sons under twelve. The cause of her death was unrecorded, but it was probably tuberculosis complicated by pneumonia.[41]

Worn and exhausted, Van Buren took off for the quiet friendship of Kinderhook, but he did not recover quickly. Finding himself overly weak and his health "much more delicate" than he had supposed, he wrote Butler that he could not resume normal activities. He asked him to obtain a continuance in a case scheduled in a few days in Schoharie County, or to find a replacement. Beyond that, the intensely private Van Buren left no immediate hint of his inner feelings.[42]

Whatever his psychological state, Hannah Van Buren's death forced him to reorganize his personal life. First came his children. Fortunately, the older ones, Abraham and John, were enrolled as day students in the Albany Academy. Christina Hoes Cantine, Hannah Van Buren's sister, took the younger two, Martin and Smith, to Catskill. Shortly later, her teenage daughter moved to Van Buren's Albany home as a surrogate mother.[43]

Van Buren had to reorganize his professional and political life as well. Butler, who finally married Harriet Allen in 1818, had received a tempting offer
from Jacob Barker, a New York City venture capitalist and private banker, to
become the president and cashier of a proposed new bank at Sandy Hill,
north of Albany. At first, Butler refused. Van Buren, Butler explained, "desires
to keep me because he can't do without me at present." But by mid–February
1819, Butler accepted the positions once the bank was incorporated. He
ended his partnership with Van Buren largely because he thought his "professional business" would decline if Van Buren accepted the Supreme Court slot.
Butler's desertion, coming on the heels of his wife's death, devastated Van Buren. Reluctantly, he groomed Jesse Hoyt, his senior clerk, for more responsibilities. But politics complicated Van Buren's professional adjustments. With
the law growing secondary to politics with each passing day, he found Butler
irreplaceable.[44]

Nonetheless, Van Buren attempted to stabilize his life within the friendly
confines of the courtroom. The opportunity came through a sensational
murder case the press called the "most atrocious" that had ever occurred in
Orange County. Richard Jennings, a local farmer, had disappeared. The sheriff discovered his bodily remains one week later. Investigations revealed that
Jennings, a man of "deceitful arts," had argued with three persons over a piece
of land that legally belonged to none of them: James Teed, his nephew; David
Conklin, his assign; and David Dunning, his tenant. Further evidence uncov-
ered allegations that they, along with Teed's pregnant wife, had hired Jack
Hodges to kill Jennings. When the sheriff arrested Hodges, he implicated the
others. Hodges swore that he had shot and wounded Jennings, but Dunning
bludgeoned him to death. A grand jury indicted Hodges for murder and the
others as accessories to murder before and after the fact. In early March, the
trials took place in a special Court of Oyer and Terminer at Goshen, under
Supreme Court Judge William Van Ness.[45]

Attorney General Van Buren headed the three-man prosecution team and
labored with "great effectiveness." Justice was swift. The jury found Hodges
guilty and sentenced him to death. To lighten the sentence, he agreed to tes-
tify for the state about the plan the others had hatched to murder Jennings.
Van Buren was most effective in utilizing this admission to hammer at Teed in
a trial lasting eighteen consecutive hours. Teed, Dunning, and Conklin were
all found guilty and received death sentences. As for Mrs. Teed, Van Buren accepted a *nolle prosequi,* meaning that he would not prosecute Mrs. Teed due to
her pregnancy, provided she served thirty days in jail.[46]

Van Buren found solace in senatorial duties as well. Considering the re-
alignment taking place in New York politics, the legislature reached unexpected consensus over a variety of economic issues. This remarkable armistice
between Clinton and Van Buren raised new questions about his removal.
Spencer, whether seeking Van Buren's support for his son's bid for the still

open United States Senate seat, or motivated by respect for Van Buren's handling of the office, or truly interested in healing the party, approached Van Buren and suggested that the council might reappoint him for the sake of party harmony. But Van Buren placed the onus for the party's disintegration squarely on Clinton and refused to cooperate. As for the position of attorney general, Van Buren said he "regarded the loss of my office" as inevitable once Clinton had regained control of the council.[47]

Van Buren was far more passionate in private. Believing, as did other Bucktails, that Clinton had destroyed the New York Republican party for his own gain, Van Buren let his anxieties ignite a personal vendetta against the governor. Writing to Gorham Worth, a close friend, Van Buren denigrated Clinton as a man and as a politician and swore to drive Clintonians "from power."[48]

Van Buren put these words into action during the most important political vote of this session. When an opening on the canal commission developed in 1819, Clinton proposed a man whom the High Federalists abhorred. Van Buren, in a stunning agreement with them, successfully substituted the Bucktail Henry Seymour. With a 3 to 2 majority on the board, the Bucktails now controlled the canal's vast patronage, mostly in the form of profitable construction jobs and contracts. They thus neutralized Clinton's main power base, while gaining more "patronage and power" from the board than Clinton "obtained" from the council.[49]

Completely shocked by this turn of events, Clinton lashed back with his patronage axe. Meaning to rebuke Van Buren in the most personal way, the council settled the Supreme Court vacancy by shifting Spencer to chief justice; they appeased the Swiss Federalists by selecting Woodworth for the open slot. Van Buren was hardly offended. Perhaps content that Clinton had made the decision for him, Van Buren had no comment.[50]

With all signs indicating that his dismissal was next, Van Buren needed allies from groups on the periphery in order to lay a solid foundation for rebuilding the party. The High Federalists fit his needs. In early 1819, they had founded the *New York American* to counter Clinton and secure King's reelection. Yet while these men shared the same enemies as those of the Bucktails, they put Van Buren on notice that he could not automatically gain their support.[51]

These developments set the bounds for the spring elections of 1819. The results gave the Bucktails the senate, but neither faction held a working majority in the assembly. Holding the balance of power were forty-three former Federalists, split between Swiss and High Minded. But a closer analysis indicated an optimistic trend favoring the Bucktails. The Clintonians ran poorly in the populous Southern and Middle Districts, and the Bucktails made significant inroads in the governor's strongest bastions, the Western and Northern, because of controlling the canal board. These factors indicated that the governor might be vulnerable in the coming 1820 election.[52]

Van Buren waited until after the polls closed to take the steamboat to New York City for the May Supreme Court. Ready for the worst, he presented and won his largest docket for the state, forty-four nonenumerated cases, worth $44,008.66. He lost a private cause again, however, in *Jackson, ex dem. Troup and Others, v. Blodget.* This action tested whether Blodget, a Revolutionary War veteran, could legally convey his right to bounty land to another person before the state had granted his title. But the facts were against Van Buren and Henry, Blodget's attorneys. Spencer ruled that Blodget lacked a legal title and, therefore, could not form a binding contract to property he did not own.[53]

By early June, Van Buren was back in the city for a Court of General Sessions' case dealing with John W. Thorn, Valentine N. Livingston, and Henry D. Tracy, three upper-class, High Minded Federalists. The Clintonian District Attorney Pierre C. Van Wyck, who requested Van Buren's aid as attorney general, had secured an indictment against them for conspiring by "unlawful and fraudulent" means "to obtain and convert to their own use" about $100,000 from the Merchants Bank of New York. Because of the amount of the money involved, and the defendants' family connections, the trial drew sufficient attention to gain space in the nationally-circulated *Niles Weekly Register.*[54]

Under Van Buren's lead, the five prosecutors keyed their brief to Thorn's written confession. But when Van Buren offered the confession as evidence, he faced an obstacle. The defense objected that Richard Varick, the bank's president, had coerced Thorn by holding him a virtual prisoner in Varick's home (with a constable's connivance) and intimidating him with an indictment, while promising immunity if he signed an affidavit that implicated the others. The judge ruled that the confession was inadmissible. With the foundation of his argument thus undercut, Van Buren said, "he had no other evidence sufficient to make out the charge." The jury, without leaving the box, acquitted the defendants. Nevertheless, the case's consequences were far from over.[55]

By now, the suspense about Van Buren's continuance as attorney general had reached its peak. In private, supporters admitted what the public believed: his dismissal would happen "eventually." Yet Clinton played a cat and mouse game, and even Van Buren chafed at the delay. Slowly, matters clarified. Shortly after the Thorn case, Clinton requested that Van Buren travel to Delhi in Delaware County to prosecute the "laborious and difficult" murder trial of Nathan Foster, who was accused of killing his wife. The order nettled Van Buren, although he allowed that the governor could designate him as the state prosecutor in a special Court of Oyer and Terminer. But Van Buren suspected that Clinton was using the trial as a ruse to isolate him while the council, scheduled for a July meeting in New York City, would finally make its decision.[56]

The circumstances facing Van Buren were burdensome. The trip to Delhi took nearly two days from Albany. The selection of jurors, the examining of witnesses, the summing up by counsels, the jury deliberations, and the sentence of death for Foster, all lasted over one week. Once the trial ended, Van Buren rushed to New York City for news of the council's decision. German was there and offered Van Buren a deal. Whether speaking for himself or for Clinton, German assured Van Buren that he could retain the office if he accepted a truce with the governor. Van Buren's reply spoke volumes about his exasperation. The only truce that was possible, Van Buren replied, was if Clinton accepted an ambassadorship and left the country. The council responded at once. On July 8, 1819, Clinton replaced Van Buren with Thomas J. Oakley, a well-connected Swiss Federalist and a man "particularly obnoxious" to the Bucktails and the High Minded.[57]

Van Buren took the removal in stride. Nor did other Bucktails whine. Instead, they praised Van Buren's professionalism in office, explaining that his firing was not due to "malconduct" or "dereliction of principle," but to his "want of confidence in the political integrity of De Witt Clinton." High Minded Federalists were just as complimentary; they warned their erstwhile Swiss colleagues that "the voice of Mr. Oakley is the voice of Mr. Clinton." Van Buren appreciated these sentiments and turned them to his own benefit. Within days, he was on the road again, organizing young lawyers, seeking allies among High Federalists, and trying to establish Bucktail newspapers.[58]

In marked contrast to his predecessors, Van Buren's transition of his office to Oakley was proper and thoughtful, especially when he assigned Hoyt the task of completing "every thing that is necessary to be done to make Mr. Oakley perfectly acquainted with the business." Following these instructions, Hoyt labelled each action to make them identifiable, gave Comptroller McIntyre "all the Bonds & Mortgages except those which are now in suit," along with a "list of those left with Mr. Oakley," and "settled the account with the Treasurer," making sure that he received a full "statement of all monies due & paid."[59] In retrospect, Van Buren could take justifiable pride in his tenure as attorney general. Like any effective advocate, he was competitive. By that token, his record was impressive. During his fifty-three months in office, the second longest up to that time, Van Buren won 254 actions and secured $279,482.92 for New York. Some were small causes, less than $100, but others, such as the Utica Insurance case, significantly benefitted "The People." These achievements further confirmed Van Buren's status as the state's leading Bucktail politician-lawyer and demonstrated his future qualities as a public official: personal integrity, honesty in carrying out official duties, and fidelity in working for the state's best interests. Then, too, the attorney generalship gave Van Buren one constant to shore up his fluctuating political fortunes against Clinton: the practical application of the principles of classical republicanism and liberal republicanism through the law for the public good. In this regard, Van Buren promoted legislative supremacy under legal positivism, made adjustments in public polices by legal instrumentalism, modified the common law, and fought for antimonopolism and equal opportunity in economic concerns, despite his blundering over riparian rights and his mishandling of the actions involving Ten Broeck and Potts. Yet these achievements were incomplete. Clinton had ended the middle phase of Van Buren's dual career. Success in the law no longer satisfied his inner drives. Political matters, particularly the need to organize the Bucktails and ostracize Clinton, now became Van Buren's chief obsessions.[60]

CHAPTER TEN

Republicanism in a New Era

efeating Clinton was the least of Van Buren's concerns during the late spring of 1819. The first tremors of a spreading depression had already sent shock waves across the state. By June, some New York City banks had suspended specie payments, and hard times spread into the Upper Hudson Valley. Nervous depositors withdrew funds from local banks, borrowers defaulted on loans, and businesses neared ruin.[1]

Van Buren was caught in these financial straits. The imminent collapse of the Bank of Hudson, in which he was a stockholder, director, and legal advocate, lowered his supply of ready cash. Other complications existed. With his law practice still in disarray after Butler's departure, Van Buren found that the upkeep of his young family drained his disposable resources; he could no longer depend on the sizeable income that the attorney generalship generated to counter the shortfall. In this unaccustomed pinch, Van Buren suspended his political activities and concentrated on his profession.[2]

During the late summer and early fall, Van Buren informed colleagues that he welcomed new business. He pushed older cases, chiefly that of Henry Platner, through clogged court channels, and he cut operating costs. Delinquent clients, and even fellow lawyers, found fresh dunning bills in their mail. Fortunately, Van Buren's backlog of cases solved his short-term needs. In August, he and Butler, whose banking business was also near collapse, gained favorable verdicts in two chancery cases. Better still, Kent ordered both sets of losers to pay full costs and damages.[3]

Van Buren was equally active in other venues. After winning a few minor causes in the Columbia and Western circuits, he filed several motions in the Court of Errors and finally litigated the chancery action of *Troup v. Wood and Sherwood,* an extensive and remunerative property case for Platner.[4]

The cause started as a simple effort by Robert Troup, the Holland Land Company's long-time resident agent, to recover two lots located in Onondaga County's military tract. Troup believed that he had acquired them from Platner, a Columbia County resident, through a legitimate purchase carried out by attorneys William Wood and Samuel Sherwood. Van Buren had a good case, one that aroused his Dutch-American sense of justice. The story he unfolded, assisted by Butler and John Henry, revealed a wide chain of sordid transactions. A group of Platner's relatives, friends, and their lawyers had knowingly committed a "premeditated fraud," Van Buren charged. In systematic fashion, they had executed illegal "conveyances" that bilked Platner of his real property "lying in five counties," purportedly worth $409,000. Platner was unaware of these transactions because he was serving a seven-year jail term for forgery. Once he gained his freedom, Platner sought to regain his property. Van Vechten and Williams, for the defense, accepted the point that the transfers had taken place. But they held that Wood and Sherwood were blameless intermediaries. Kent sustained Van Buren's argument that they had cooperated in the gross fraud, mandated appropriate restitutions and damages to Platner, and, in ordering a master of chancery to investigate the entire episode, opened the possibility that Van Buren could gain additional fees in future recovery actions.[5]

Van Buren's professional business, however, did not last beyond August. Putting the law on hold as much as possible, he poured his energies back into politics. The prospects seemed bright. Monroe, prodded by Thompson, began awarding the bulk of federal patronage to the Bucktails, and the High Minded Federalists seemed on the verge of an alliance. Finding a suitable gubernatorial candidate was Van Buren's next task. The still popular Tompkins, who was unfulfilled with the vice-presidency, seemed the best choice.[6]

The extraordinary events that unfolded over the next six months revealed that Van Buren's mania to defeat Clinton knew no bounds. After securing Tompkins's agreement to run, Van Buren discovered that Tompkins was an alcoholic. He considered dropping him from the ticket when other Bucktails thought Tompkins's addiction made him unsuitable. He then spent considerable time researching and writing a pamphlet that defended Tompkins from charges that he had misused government funds during the war. Finally, he led a long and acrimonious debate in the senate to settle Tompkins's accounts. At the same time, Van Buren intensified his courtship of High Minded Federalists by co-authoring another pamphlet, with the assistance of the young and able William L. Marcy, to bolster Rufus King's reelection. To thwart any suspicion that he favored party amalgamation or "a political bargain," Van Buren wrote that King could remain a Federalist, but a special anti-Clintonian Federalist, not a renegade Swiss Federalist who sold his soul for Clinton's political handouts.[7]

Van Buren spent even more time dissuading some Tammanyites, along with their counterparts in the South, that King's reason for opposing the extension of slavery into the proposed state of Missouri was not a "plot" to form a new national party and run Clinton for the presidency in 1820. Van Buren had powerful reasons, beside his commitment to King, to deter such suspicions. The use of slavery was a part of his Dutch-American heritage and a long tradition within his family, including his own ownership of a slave. Moreover, his reluctance to criticize white Southerners was critical to the national Republican party's Virginia-New York axis. Yet Van Buren's support of King implied a defense of Clinton, who favored blocking "the progress of slavery." But Van Buren could hardly disown King, given the imperative of electing Tompkins. In the end, Van Buren managed to hold Tammanyites in line. Clinton had to back King after endorsing his stand over Missouri, and King was reelected with only three dissenting votes on a joint legislative ballot.[8]

Even with this matter settled, Van Buren's strained political workload hardly loosened. His schedule was more frenetic than ever, aggravated by what he called laboring "with holy zeal and almost more than human industry" in directing the campaign and fulfilling his senatorial duties. To make matters worse, Van Buren's asthma left him listless and irritable.[9] Under these conditions, it was not surprising that Van Buren paid little attention to his practice. Breaking his streak of fourteen years of consecutive appearances in each Supreme Court session, he advocated no cases in the January 1820 term. Even his work in chancery was limited to two perfunctory contract cases, both of which he won.[10]

Even if Van Buren entertained thoughts about balancing politics and law during the campaign, Clinton's genius at self-survival precluded such work. In the past, various reform-minded groups had urged a revision of the outmoded state constitution. The depression spurred this effort, mainly among debtors and nonfreeholders who lacked the ability to protect their interests because of suffrage limitations. To capture this popular question, Clinton advocated a limited convention confined to abolishing the Council of Appointment and whatever other amendments the legislature saw fit. Van Buren wanted no part of any reform; he feared introducing an unpredictable issue so close to polling. The upshot was that the legislature could not find a compromise and revision faded as an election issue.[11]

By late winter, Van Buren, this seemingly inexhaustible man, at last reached the limits of his physical and emotional endurance, particularly when the campaign degenerated into mutual recrimination and invective. In April 1820, Van Buren confided to King that for the past ten days he "scarcely had time to take regular meals" and was "pressed by at least a half dozen unfinished concerns growing out of this intolerable political struggle." Yet the effort seemed worth the cost. The Bucktails, under Van Buren's instruction, fanned out teams of speakers to every district, city, ward, and town in the state. Forty-nine High Minded Federalists also paid their debt to Van Buren when they issued an address that criticized Clinton. Van Buren supplied the only unanticipated factor. Bone-weary and perhaps unwilling to risk his reputation by losing to the alliance of the Clintonians and Swiss Federalists in the Middle District, he declined renomination for a third senate term.[12]

As the election neared, Van Buren was so optimistic that "our election is safe" in "all branches of Government" that he took a brief vacation in Kinderhook. He partially deceived himself. Clinton won by the narrow margin of 1,457 out of 94,894 votes cast. To make Tompkins's defeat less bitter, the Bucktails swept to impressive majorities in legislative races and secured the next council. Nonetheless, Van Buren was not yet satisfied. With Clinton still governor, he wrote Worth, victory was not secure.[13]

Van Buren's displeasure did not obscure his remarkable recovery from the depths of two years before. While Clinton remained a formidable foe, his moment was on the wane. Despite his electoral success, he was only a one-man operator of a personal faction. By contrast, the future belonged to Van Buren and his brand of organized politics through the emerging Albany Regency. During those two years, Van Buren had worked steadily to create this unified, state-wide political apparatus, directed by an inner circle of his trusted lieutenants that functioned as a coordinating board, based on ideological principles that determined public policies, the use of subsidized newspapers to set the party line, practical mechanisms to mobilize voters, and bound by party loyalty, regularity, caucuses, and patronage.[14]

This innovative political organization, so admired by Van Buren's contemporaries for its efficiency and ultimate mastery of state politics, did not spring full blown from his imagination. The Regency germinated from the years Van Buren had spent doing the law as a practicing attorney, working in the circuit, conducting appellate business before the state's highest courts, appearing in chancery, and cultivating fellow lawyers.

Van Buren transferred this legal experience, along with its classical and liberal republican principles and his Dutch-American ideals, into politics. Legal instrumentalism, distributive justice, legal positivism, and the Americanization of the common law became Van Buren's guides for how a political party can set substantive public policies, adhere to principles, and accommodate change. Those cases, dealing with commerce, contracts, third party negotiable notes, and property law, along with legal instrumentalism, helped Van Buren appreciate how politicians must adapt to shifting conditions, especially in a free market. The will theory of contracts applied equally to politics. Bound by popular intent, politicians nominated candidates and formed platforms that were founded upon a communal commitment to legislate ideological values and guarantee the government would not interfere with questions of private choice. The caucus system, which Van Buren made the center of his Regency operations, represented the popular will. As in his legal practice, Van Buren sought to end individual dependency by using the power of the masses to end elitism.

The men Van Buren groomed for higher office were also similar to the clerks Van Buren trained in his law office. Butler, Marcy, Samuel A. Talcott, Silas Wright, Azariah C. Flagg, and Churchill C. Cambreleng, among others, were destined to dominate state politics for the next three decades. Their political rise paralleled Van Buren's own progress from his lower class origins to professional prominence and wealth. His method of citing precedents in briefs, defending elected officials, and shielding party newspapers from libel, formed the basis for running campaigns, educating voters, and carrying elections—chiefly through the caucus system, regular nominations, and party loyalty. The courteous way Van Buren treated clients and opposing attorneys established the means for political consensus building. Even being an agent of the court gave Van Buren lessons in constructing a political bureaucracy that functioned as an instrument of popular sovereignty, administered the state, and ensured equal justice. Above all, the practical way Van Buren implemented classical republicanism and liberal republicanism through the law forged the basis for party principles and programs, many of which anticipated Jacksonianism. In short, whatever Van Buren achieved in politics was impossible without his life in the law.

These efforts bore heavy costs, however. The searing personal price Van Buren had paid after his wife's death, added to his almost pathological crusade against Clinton, was incalculable. Nor did Van Buren's choice to put the law on hold leave him much freedom to relieve his financial shortfall. While he had plentiful assets in tangible land holdings and savings, Van Buren lacked sufficient liquid capital, a condition aggravated by the Bank of Hudson's final collapse. Taking these factors into consideration, Van Buren sought piddling settlements from clients because he was "hard pressed for money to perform promises." Even in the next phase of the Hart cause, Van Buren demanded a $300 advance and warned that his advocacy without the proper retainer might "well brook inattention in the particular."[15]

Despite these financial constraints, Van Buren remained adamant about avoiding the law until after the election. During the April session of the Court of Errors, however, he could not avoid one scheduled professional commitment that he had joined five years before, *John K. Beekman, Appellant, v. Josiah Frost, Eli Goddard, Philo Goddard, and Jesse Kellogg, Respondents.* The issues were clear; their resolution hinged on the relevance of the old concept of *caveat emptor* in a modern free market. In May 1803, Beekman had mortgaged a lot to Henry Corlin in the town of Marcellus for $3,000, due with interest in May 1808, and registered the agreement in Onondaga County. Before the mortgage reached maturity, Corlin sold the lot to Frost and Martin Goddard, who in turn conveyed part of it to Kellogg, Eli Goddard, and Philo Goddard; Corlin then vanished. When the respondents discovered the original mortgage and offered its redemption, Beekman refused because the property had increased in value. In 1814, the case reached chancery. Kent accepted their contention that they bought the lot in good faith, honored their request to pay the mortgage, and ordered Beekman to deliver the deed. Instead, he appealed to the Court of Errors and hired Van Buren and Emmet.[16]

Van Buren's brief rested on the will theory of contracts. He asserted that Kent had erred because the defendants lacked a right to relief in equity. Rather, they were bound by the intent of each party. To prove his contention, Van Buren cited a number of precedents to stress that the mortgage was duly registered, that the defendants were obligated to search the title, and that Beekman retained the right to foreclosure without Kent's interference. Further, Van Buren insisted that Kent should have dismissed the case, leaving the parties to their private "remedies at law." Even so, Beekman had the greater equity; his innocence was purer. He had the legal mortgage.[17]

Only Chief Justice Spencer offered a written opinion. He disagreed with Van Buren that the defendants had no right to proceed in chancery, but concluded that Kent was faulty in decreeing a redemption of the mortgage. Citing the precedents that Van Buren had noted, which endorsed the will theory of contracts, Spencer concluded that the defendants were not entitled to any relief and thought that the court should reverse Kent. The majority concurred.[18]

Even with this success, Van Buren had a nagging feeling that things were amiss in his life as a politician-lawyer. Sometime over the past winter he had become "heartily sick" of the "thousand vexations" of public life that "wore upon my health and spirits." In that vein, he decided, once Tompkins won, "to confine my future exertions to my profession." Yet in trying to sort out his emotions, Van Buren's specific plans for the future veered between confusion, vexation, and exhaustion. In February 1820, he entertained the idea of a fresh start in New York City, maybe with Butler. During the session, Van Buren left for the city to take his soundings of a possible move, but concluded that relocating was not feasible. By March, his turmoil took a new turn. Butler was in Albany on bank business and Van Buren "urged" him "to stay two or three weeks." But Butler was unwilling to leave his wife and young child in Sandy Hill and had no desire to move to New York City.[19]

By early June Van Buren's thinking clarified. He decided to restructure his dual career by forming a new partnership with Butler in Albany and withdrawing from politics. Butler hesitated, unsure of Van Buren's sincerity. But after discussing this misgiving with Van Buren, Butler excitedly wrote his wife that Van Buren "says he will continue in his profession four or five years at least—certainly 3. He has no inducement to leave it, but every motive to continue in it." Van Buren's offer was enticing and duplicated their prior arrangement. He pledged Butler one half of all litigation, including chancery, which produced the greatest income, and lent Butler $50 to "pay some bills." Butler found the offer and the prospect of study in Van Buren's "splendid library" irresistible. By the middle of June, the *Albany Argus* carried a notice that the reconstituted firm was operating in fresh quarters on the lower floor of John V. N. Yates's house at 107 State Street. Van Buren took the front room with the library; Butler, the back. Four clerks scurried between them.[20]

The partnership picked up where it had left off. Apparently true to his word, Van Buren seemed done with politics. He entrusted Butler with several Supreme Court and chancery suits, particularly the next round of the Platner case in which, Butler observed, Van Buren "expected our pay to be very liberal." As a further sign of his intentions, Van Buren made Butler his co-counsel in two additional actions before Kent.[21]

Because of their industry and previous success, the partners swiftly rebuilt their practice into one of "the most distinguished law firms in the State." Some business came from older contacts, mainly in circuits throughout the state. Others were new clients attracted by Van Buren's political fame. Through it all, Van Buren, according to Butler's metaphor, steered with the dexterity of a master helmsman, while he himself worked at the "laboring oar." Butler was fascinated by Van Buren's "concise, elegant, and convincing arguments," and wished that he was truly done with politics and would indeed concentrate on the law to reinstate his luminous reputation as a great trial lawyer. Yet while the firm's professional repute soared, cash flowed in slowly since the depression still throttled the economy. "Fifty and hundred dollar fees," Butler lamented, "were very scarce." To keep Butler happy, Van Buren continued to press Ten Eyck for a retainer through Gerrit Lansing, the master of chancery in charge of Ten Eyck's funds. The delay, Van Buren complained, deprived him of substantial anticipated income. If the situation continued, "it is not probable that I could be of much use to [Ten Eyck] thereafter, as good feeling is an indispensable requisite between client and counsel."[22]

In October, Van Buren reappeared in the Supreme Court. But instead of his usually laden docket, he left the bulk to Butler and advocated just one cause, *Fleming v. Slocum,* a contract case with racial dimensions from the Columbia Circuit. Williams stood for Fleming, who charged that Slocum was guilty of fraud in the sale of an enslaved African-American. In circuit, Judge Van Ness ruled a nonsuit, since Williams had not proven his case. On the appeal, Johnson did not record the briefs Van Buren and Williams filed, but Justice Spencer sustained Van Ness's ruling.[23]

Despite all this legal activity, Van Buren deceived Butler and even himself about confining his energies just to the law. As an attorney, Van Buren needed Butler. Still not physically sturdy, Van Buren had collapsed after a long trial and spent three weeks recuperating. Even so, his obsession against Clinton was too ingrained for any permanent withdrawal; and Tompkins's defeat meant that the Albany Regency could not dispense with Van Buren's leadership. But Butler had also fooled himself. As he implicitly acknowledged to his wife, Butler was thoroughly disillusioned with banking and had no option other than the partnership.[24]

By July, hardly one month after he had made his agreement with Butler, Van Buren took part in a politically-related matter, the sale of Jesse Buel's

Albany Argus to Moses Cantine and Isaac Q. Leake, Tompkins's former private secretary. They worked out a $7,000 purchase, paid in four equal installments with interest to Buel. In turn, Van Buren, who may have overstated his financial crunch, and Peter J. Hoes, a Kinderhook merchant and Hannah Van Buren's brother, pledged up to $1,500 each for any sum Cantine and Leake fell short.[25]

Once the paper was secure as the Regency's official journal, Van Buren ended his brief retreat to the law and opened a new era in state politics. During his hiatus, Clintonians questioned what "scheme" Van Buren, "the puny ape and disciple of Aaron Burr," had in mind. Van Buren did not keep them guessing for long. His supporters were already busy sowing the ground for his selection as New York's next United States Senator. While Van Buren wrote in his *Autobiography* that he "neither solicited the place" nor took "a single step" to promote the process, he did not discourage the meticulously orchestrated bursts of resolutions and accolades flowing from party meetings. By September 1820, his candidacy had become common knowledge, mentioned in private letters and trumpeted by party newspapers.[26]

Tammany greeted Van Buren's bid with silence. Instead, the Hall riveted public attention on the need for thorough constitutional reform. Van Buren became a selective convert. While fearful that delegates might tamper with too many existing institutions, especially the court system, he concluded that a modified broadening of property requirements for voting, not universal suffrage as Tammany wished, would benefit the Regency. As Van Buren explained years later, he wanted to advance the right to vote "step by step" and to enfranchise new voters "as we should find ourselves justified by experience." With that in mind, he used the Kinderhook Independence Day celebration to signal his cautious position: "The elective franchise—Existing restrictions have proven to be as impolitic as they are unjust. It is the office of wisdom to correct what experience condemns."[27]

While Van Buren and Tammany Hall agreed on the need for revision, they were split over the extent of that revision. The Clintonians tried to widen the rift. To prevent Van Buren's election to the Senate, they charged that he was doubled-crossing Tammany by seeking to replace incumbent Senator Nathan Sanford, one of its own and a stalwart Bucktail.[28]

The Clintonians found another means to hammer at Van Buren's integrity. In mid-October, their *New York Statesman* carried an anonymous letter insinuating that Van Buren, while attorney general, had purposely mishandled *The People v. Thorn* two years earlier to curry favor with High Minded Federalists. The charge was serious, and the *Albany Argus* treated it seriously. Cantine and Leake reminded readers about the inadmissability of Thorn's confession and wrote that nothing "in the remotest degree" could "sully" Van Buren's "honorable" reputation.[29]

The Thorn prosecutors were equally intent on preserving their good names. James A. Hamilton, their leader prior to Van Buren's appearance, wrote a public letter explaining their legal reasoning and defending Van Buren's actions. Van Buren was relieved and grateful for this support. The "base" attack, he admitted to Hamilton, had vexed him. Yet interest in the matter quickly faded, either because the issues were so obtuse; or, as Hamilton suggested, because "the calumny was destroyed by light"; or, more likely, because the question of revising the constitution dominated the political stage.[30]

When the legislature met, the popular demand for a constitutional convention peaked. Clinton, who favored only limited revision, now committed a critical blunder. He opposed a bill, written by Tammany Assemblyman Michael Ulshoeffer and calling for unlimited revisions, but hoped to avoid a public stand. The bill passed both houses with heavy majorities and moved to an uncertain fate in the Council of Revision, which included Clinton. But the council deadlocked, 2 to 2. The most unfathomable vote belonged to Clintonian Supreme Court Justice John Woodworth, who supported the bill. At last forced to reveal his position, Clinton cast a veto because of the bill's broad nature and created the impression that he and Kent, who wrote the veto message, had connived against the popular will.[31]

As howls of outrage rumbled through the state, Ulshoeffer pounced on the magnitude of Clinton's blunder. With Van Buren's tacit backing, Ulshoeffer moved a new bill that met the council's specifications. It was overwhelmingly approved by a special statewide election.[32]

Paradoxically, Van Buren arrived late and hesitant in this showdown that finally discredited Clinton. Yet Van Buren adapted to this new circumstance by seeking to guide the coming convention. Writing to King, Van Buren confided that he was "timid in all matters of innovation." He further assured the conservative King that the Regency, which represented the "Yeomanry of the State," posed no threat to "generally approved parts of the Constitution," particularly "the rights of property."[33]

But Van Buren, like Clinton, could not control the forces that constitutional reform had unleashed. Despite his words to King, Van Buren was indeed an innovator. As a classical republican in legal matters, Van Buren had consistently sought to broaden tenants' rights and form new departures in all aspects of the law to ensure the values of classical republicanism. His means lay in fresh interpretations of public and private law affecting procedural and substantive jurisprudence, notably the will theory of contracts, legal instrumentalism, and legal positivism. In the process, Van Buren had also accepted the liberal republican ideas of individual gain and personal advancement, mainly in contract, property, and commercial law. Van Buren tempered such innovations, however, by stressing classical republicanism's self-restraint, through communal virtue and statute. These guides checked the most selfish aspects of liberal republicanism's unlimited commitment to human progress—which might negate communalism, such as in the Utica Insurance action and the cases involving Ten Broeck and Potts.

Yet Van Buren had a deep conservative streak on other aspects of the law. As a classical republican and strict constructionist who believed that the people's representatives had created a workable judiciary, he shared the misgivings of many Clintonians and High Federalists about radical attempts to restructure the court system. Then, too, Van Buren had no quarrel with a system that had given him prestige and wealth. Above these issues, Van Buren failed to appreciate advancing democratic forces. Distrusting universal suffrage, he put his classical republican faith in a restricted electorate comprised of the propertied agrarian class and real property taxpayers from both rural and urban areas, whom he considered independent individuals free of deference. In sum, the convention posed as great a threat to him as it did to Clinton.[34]

The furor Clinton and Tammany raised over Van Buren's candidacy for the United States Senate compounded his troubles and tested the Regency's strength. At first, Clinton tried, but made little headway, to diminish Van Buren's standing by accusing the Monroe Administration of unconstitutionally interfering in state politics at Van Buren's behest. Clinton then sought to marshal public opinion against Van Buren in another way. Using the pseudonym of "*Heraclitus*," Clinton published a series of public letters that traced the "vainglorious" Van Buren's "contemptible cunning and duplicity" to the traitorous Burr. Again the effort fell flat. The *Albany Argus* replied that such sentiments denigrated the office of governor and countered that New York needed Van Buren, "the *statesman,* the *patriot* and *the philanthropist,*" in the Senate.[35]

Clinton tried other tactics. In the legislature, his allies vilified Van Buren for "timidity" and "cowardice," because he was running away to the "secure harbor" of Washington instead of staying at home to protect the men who had "enlisted under his banner and who now wanted their rewards." On a more practical level, the Clintonians seconded Tammany's efforts for Sanford and maintained that his long record of "unimpeached service" deserved better than being cast aside for Van Buren's mean ambition. This, too, died. Van Buren held an insurmountable caucus majority, 58 to 24 over Sanford, and Tammanyites agreed to make the vote unanimous. On February 6, 1821, the legislature voted on joint ballot to send Van Buren to the United States Senate.[36]

Senator-elect Van Buren had to wait nearly eight months before taking his seat. Putting this time to productive use, he tended to his neglected practice. One civil case in the February 1821 Court of Errors, *Woodworth v. Bank of America,* in association with Talcott for the plaintiff against Josiah O. Hoffman and John Henry, was first on Van Buren's docket and indicated how much he used the law to advance his political agenda.

In April 1817, Judge Woodworth had endorsed a sixty-day, $2,500 promissory note for James Kane, payable in Albany. When Kane sent Woodworth the note for endorsement, he withheld information "as to where it was to be sent." Kane had good reason for secretiveness. He had tendered the note to the Bank of America in New York City to settle a debt. Without Woodworth's permission, Kane further wrote and signed a notation in the margin that the note was payable at the bank's home office. When the note matured, the bank demanded the money from Woodworth under those terms. He refused, claiming that he had not signed the provision and that a demand at the place designated for payment by the marginal memorandum was insufficient. The Supreme Court ruled for the bank, but granted Woodworth "leave" for a special verdict in the Court of Errors.[37]

Johnson did not publish the arguments of opposing counsels, merely listing the cases and authorities they cited, therefore it is not possible to determine the emphasis on either side. Some hints, however, were present in the opinions offered in the judge's decision. Kent, using the Hoffman and Henry citations, concluded that the bank had a right to assume that Kane made the marginal notation on the note with Woodworth's knowledge. Even if he had not done so, the note was still valid. The bank could call on Kane for payment at its office and, once transferred, "look to the endorser," Woodworth. In contradicting Kent, Regency Senator Roger Skinner copied Van Buren and Talcott. Skinner followed the "reasonable maxim" that Woodworth was not responsible, because every alteration in the endorser's contract "in a part which may become material, without his approbation, shall discharge his liability." Thus Kane's intent was not to honor the contract but to breach its terms. The court backed Skinner, 17 to 9, with every Clintonian voting to sustain the judgment; all Regency senators save one voted for a reversal.[38]

While this action was mainly, as Van Buren commented, "a dry mercantile point of law," the case spawned significant political consequences because of Woodworth's relationship with Clinton and Van Buren. The *Statesman,* expressing what many New Yorkers believed, editorialized that Woodworth, a Clintonian, had conspired with Van Buren to support Ulshoeffer's convention bill in the Council of Revision as a bribe for the Regency's backing in the Court of Errors. Van Buren shrugged off this charge. For the small price of defending Woodworth in a case where he was on solid legal ground, Van Buren solidified his reputation as a political manager, since the *Statesman's* assessment was correct, again validated the will theory of contracts, and watched in satisfaction as the alliance between Clintonians and Swiss Federalists frayed over whether Woodworth had indeed betrayed the governor.[39]

Van Buren also showed his sagacity in chancery with two other actions, neither so politically charged but likely more well-paying. *Higginbotham v. Burnet* regarded a bill for discovery and a motion for an injunction concerning mortgages held in a part of the military bounty land near Manlius. Calling on his experience as attorney general, Van Buren noted that his client had followed proper statutory forms and convinced Kent to quash both requests. *Westcott and Others v. Cady and Others* touched a will including a life estate and the administrators' obligations in overseeing its disposition. Van Buren, once more using his background, in this instance as surrogate, convinced Kent to allow a master in chancery to investigate the administrators' handling of the entire estate before issuing a ruling.[40]

By May 1821, Van Buren continued to focus on earning money through the law until the coming Congress. "We are doing hardly any business—what we have is in chancery," Butler fussed, "and the expenses are so heavy and the proceeds so long in coming that my present hopes are confined to a bare subsistence." For that reason, Van Buren paid minimal attention to the spring election and spent his time preparing three cases for the Supreme Court's May term. Nevertheless, he watched with paternal pride as the Regency thrashed the Clintonians.[41]

Mills v. Martin pitted three Swiss Federalists, notably Williams and Thomas Oakley for Mills, against three Republicans, including Van Buren and Talcott for Martin. In May 1818, a court-martial had convicted and fined Mills, a member of the New York Militia, for failing to obey an allegedly lawful order issued under the authority of President Madison, Governor Tompkins, and various congressional acts, to enter the United States military service. Martin, a federal deputy marshal, seized two of Mills's oxen to cover the fine. Mills denied the court's jurisdiction and sought to recover the oxen and receive damages from Martin.[42]

Mills v. Martin had wide possible ramifications, both nationally and locally. Many militiamen, not only in New York but in other states, had disobeyed such orders and refused to enter federal service during the War of 1812. By direct extension, the case raised the issue of a President's constitutional authority to nationalize a state's militia. As a result, the case provided Mills's attorneys with a means to justify their antiwar conduct and tarnish prowar Republicans, especially Madison and Tompkins. By contrast, the case gave Van Buren an equal opportunity to defend their record.[43]

Neither side addressed these larger questions. Williams and Oakley based their defense on the narrow idea that the congressional acts applied only to militia in actual federal service. Since Mills had never been on such duty, the laws did not apply and made the court-martial illegal. Van Buren also took a narrow approach. Martin was not liable because he had acted under the belief that the court-martial was legal. Platt, a former Federalist speaking for the justices, ruled against Martin. The court-marital had no jurisdiction to try Mills for his purported disobedience. Martin was a trespasser when he took Mills's oxen, and Mills had a right to recover damages. Under this ruling, the justices and both sets of attorneys avoided the major question of executive authority in similar instances, leaving the issue unresolved until 1827 when the United States Supreme Court, in another New York case, *Martin v. Mott,* upheld the President.[44]

Van Buren opposed John Henry in *Whallon v. Kaufman,* an action over two conflicting interpretations of covenants where the land title was unclear. Henry said that a general covenant, which referred to a modifying agreement in a deed that a creditor held covering all the property in question, took precedence when a sheriff illegally ejected Whallon from a portion of the land. Van Buren countered that Whallon held that land under a special covenant, which had precedence over a general covenant, and that Kaufman had acted in a legal manner. The court, through Woodworth, backed Van Buren and noted that a deed's special covenant restrained a general covenant.[45]

Manahan v. Gibbons and Others dealt with a more elaborate commercial question and underscored Van Buren's abilities in contract law. In 1814, Manahan, Gibbons, and their associates had secured a judgment for $10,000 against two debtors, which the sheriff of New York County executed against their property. The partners, with Manahan the sole dissenter, signed a statement that the sheriff had discharged the debt, except for "some 400 or 500 dollars." Manahan, who believed he had not received the same compensation in proportion to the debt as the others had, sued to secure his due. An Albany Circuit jury agreed and awarded him $1,067. The others appealed through an *assumpsit*.[46]

John Henry, representing the plaintiff, maintained that the defendants were jointly answerable for Manahan's share. Van Buren disagreed, listed a string of precedents that indicated his clients had no joint liability, and pointed out that they had made no mutual contract or promises with Manahan. Spencer issued a mixed opinion. He agreed with Henry that Manahan deserved recompense in ratio to the amounts owed. But he supported Van Buren's position that his clients were unaccountable jointly since no such agreement was in force, and that Manahan should have joined them in the initial recovery.[47]

At this point, the law played an unanticipated role in Van Buren's political needs. He had little hope of victory in the June 1821 special election for convention delegates, considering the strength of the Clintonian-Swiss Federalist alliance in Albany, his home county, or Columbia, his official residence. Fortunately, Regency supporters in Otsego County solved this problem. Besides being a large landowner in the county, Van Buren was hard to miss. At that very moment he was trying a case in the local courthouse. Otsego Bucktails named him, Van Buren recalled, "without even appraising me of their intentions." In the ensuing contests, voters gave Regency candidates, including Van Buren, a ringing endorsement. They gained 110 out of 126 seats in comparison to 13 for old-line Federalists and 3 for Clintonians and Swiss Federalists. Yet this overpowering victory was too complete. Van Buren now carried the heavy burden of preventing this majority from splitting into competing ideological factions.[48]

When the delegates gathered in Albany on August 28, 1821, Van Buren was at home in more than one sense. Not only did the members include the state's ablest and most competent men, but they debated familiar issues that formed a critical intersection with both his ideology and his double career as a lawyer and politician. Van Buren understood that these men had their own principled commitments and would consider matters of deep conviction, matters that he could not finesse by political management. At first, all went easily for him. The Regency elected Tompkins the presiding officer, 94 to 8 over King, with power to select the chairmen and members of ten select committees. Tompkins gave Van Buren a choice of chairmanships. He opted for the one that would determine the Council of Appointment's fate.[49]

Serious deliberations started regarding the alteration of the executive branch. To create an effective separation of government power similar to that of the federal Constitution, Van Buren voted with the majority to abolish the Council of Revision, provide the governor with a veto subject to a two-thirds legislative override, and eliminate the governor's power to prorogue the legislature. Van Buren also convinced the delegates to fix the governor's term at two years, rather than the one year Root proposed to punish Clinton.[50]

These alterations represented practical refinements in government operations. As delegates moved to more contentious issues, however, they scattered into four blocs. Led by Root, a "radical" left wing, largely from the state's rural districts and augmented by most Tammanyites, favored extensive reforms, mainly concerning suffrage and the judiciary. Privately, Van Buren called them "madcap democrats." On the right, conservatives under Spencer and Kent were bent on both preventing any democratic expansion and preserving the judiciary. A center group, captained by Van Buren, pushed for moderate alterations capable of winning broad public support. Floaters, mercurial types who often shifted with each issue, made up the fourth bloc. As these divisions became more pronounced, many Regency delegates became increasingly independent and radical, forcing Van Buren on the defensive and into alliances with conservatives.[51]

Sanford's report on suffrage set these forces into motion. His committee proposed to expand voting to include every tax-paying white male, twenty-one years of age, who had resided in the state for at least one year and in a town for six months preceding elections. If a white male did not meet those standards, he could still vote if within that year he had labored upon a public highway, or commuted his labor, or served in the militia. A strong racial and political division immediately erupted. Sanford had specifically excluded free African-American voters, who had met previous requirements but usually voted Federalist. When conservatives introduced an amendment to secure equal voting for such taxpayers, Van Buren sided with them in a persuasive speech for ethical and ideological reasons. Depriving those who had voted in the past and paid taxes was unfair, he said, and he urged delegates to accept the proposal. It passed with the backing of most conservatives, centrists, and floaters. But the victory proved short-lived. Later, radicals introduced another amendment to place a $250 freehold requirement on free African-American voters. A new rupture arose. Conservatives still opposed the measure, but the centrists and floaters split, and the maneuver won. Van Buren accepted the amendment, explaining that the provision did not explicitly deny equal suffrage since it allowed taxpayers voting privileges. Even so, Van Buren's qualified commitment to expanded democracy became clearer, as well as his inability to control the convention.[52]

Further signs of Van Buren's slippage surfaced when Spencer introduced another amendment to the Sanford report retaining the $250 freehold requirement for the senate. Kent supported him in a forcible speech that defended property rights as the basis for civil government. In the process, Kent also revealed a harsh antiurban bias when he denigrated universal suffrage as a calamity, which meant that "men of no property" would "govern the state."[53]

Van Buren allowed others to counter before presenting a lawyer-like brief against Spencer and Kent. Turning to precedent, Van Buren indicated that other states had eliminated freehold requirements and that even the United States Constitution lacked such a provision. Yet Van Buren did not wish to extend the electorate indiscriminately by abolishing all property qualifications. Articulating the classical republican belief that only those who were economically independent would be politically independent, he argued that Spencer's amendment penalized small, freeholding, real and personal taxpayers who lacked the $250 threshold. This group, the state's "bone, pith, and muscle," deserved better. In the past, their representatives in the assembly had shunned making "an unjust distinction between real and personal property." Why should delegates "alarm [them]selves" by false fears that these men now endangered property? Put that way, the delegates supported Van Buren's position and defeated Spencer's amendment, 100 to 19.[54]

Van Buren's adamant defense of limited suffrage alarmed many of his political friends. But he was consistent. Van Buren supported another conservative attempt to confine the franchise for the senate merely to real or personal property taxpayers, thereby eliminating those with no property. After radicals rejected this effort, Van Buren grew more censorious. "The people are not prepared" for universal suffrage, he said. When Root demurred, Van Buren retorted that not even twenty members of the convention would vote to "cheapen this invaluable right" to either "black or white." While favoring "rational liberty," he refused to "undervalue" that "precious privilege."[55]

There was no question that the convention was divided and confused. Delegates rerouted the issue to a special committee for thorough reexamination. When it returned, members basically recommended the original plan, followed by some amendments from the floor. To please Van Buren, this new approach included a provision to award the franchise to all white males over twenty-one who paid taxes on real or personal property. Even this partial gain that eliminated some nonproperty owners and nontaxpayers left Van Buren dissatisfied. As a principled classical republican who valued property ownership as the main prop of effective civil government, he duplicated Kent's antiurban bias. Astounding Tammanyites, Van Buren called attention to the "many evils" universal suffrage would produce, making elections a "curse" that penalized the "hardy sons of the west" and giving real power to "the worst population" of New York City. As debate ended, Van Buren bowed to the inevitable. When a few centrists and floaters appeared ready to join the radicals, he accepted the modified report. Under this plan, white male voters over twenty-one had to meet one of two cumbersome conditions. They gained the right to suffrage if they had lived in the state for one year, in their towns for six months, and paid a property tax or served in the militia. For those potential voters who had not paid a property tax nor served in the military, suffrage requirements consisted of having lived in the state for three years or in their towns for one year, or having worked on a public highway or commuted their labor.[56]

Van Buren's inability to sway delegates became more pronounced on appointments. Fellow committee members, and even Tompkins, labored under a misapprehension. They believed that Van Buren valued the Council of Appointment as an indispensable political tool and would preserve its patronage in some form.[57]

Van Buren did nothing to discourage these assumptions. He insisted that all members of his committee write a report before he summarized their views. This procedure allowed him to hold the Regency together and anticipate possible rebuttals. Then he made a breathtaking proposal, which the committee and delegates backed, ending the council and dividing most previous appointive offices among voters, the governor, legislature, and militia units. He seemed equally in command pinpointing the elimination of specific offices. Van Buren said that he cut "14,943 appointments" that the council had made to 453 under the remaining "appointing power" and left the rest to popular elections. This part of his report drew warm support from the floor.[58]

But Van Buren lost control of his committee and the convention when he turned to preserving the appointment of judiciary officials and protecting his profession from radical onslaughts. Rather than allowing popular elections of all judicial officers, he proposed to divide their selection between the governor, courts of common pleas, and appropriate county courts. His most controversial proposition dealt with justices of the peace. Based on long familiarity with those courts, Van Buren knew that justices were the most powerful persons, both legally and politically, in each of the state's 639 towns. In line with classical republicanism, Van Buren also believed that the justices were closest to the people and understood the popular will. Moreover, they and their dependents, mainly constables and lawyers, formed the Regency's grassroots base. To perpetuate this system, Van Buren wanted county supervisors and judges, with the governor's approval, to appoint all the 2,556 justices, four to a town. His committee opted for popular elections.[59]

Van Buren's self-appointed role as the guardian of justices of the peace turned the convention into turmoil. Delegates again split, but in an altered form. Most conservatives, generally old-line Federalists apart from King, supported democratically-elected justices because the committee's insistence on popular elections benefitted them in the towns they controlled. King objected that Van Buren's proposal politicized the justices too much and might lead to the election of "demagogues." Radicals were torn. Some demanded popular elections; others, dropping their democratic principles for opportunism, backed Van Buren. Floaters remained characteristically unsure.[60]

Forced on the defensive, Van Buren denied that his proposal entrenched legal elitism at the expense of democracy. Drawing on his years as an attor-

ney, he remarked that an elective justice could count votes and would "be acquainted with all, who opposed and supported him." How might a party to a
suit "get his facts" before "a jury" if a justice were biased? Is not the "court
the crucible through which" parties passed to secure justice? Did anyone
doubt "that in civil cases the court can in almost every case regulate the verdict of the jury by the exclusive power it possesses to decide the questions of
law?" As for politics, he conceded that the governor, county supervisors, and
county judges would likely choose men with similar views. But in a ringing
defense of classical republicanism through a viable party system that also foreshadowed Jacksonianism, he added that these officials would use that power
not for themselves, "but to secure to the people that control and influence" to
which "they are justly entitled."[61]

Van Buren's efforts destroyed the aura of infallibility and respect he had
earned during the war against Clinton. The New York *American* denounced
his plan as "anti-democratic," while Tammany shot back that Van Buren
strengthened "the federal party." Even some dispirited Clintonian journals,
previously silent about the convention, chided Van Buren for fastening a new
brand of aristocracy on the state.[62]

As the volume of criticism mounted, Van Buren tasted defeat when the
delegates, led by radicals, voted his scheme down. But ever the practical
politician, he called a party caucus to find a consensus. An unwieldy middle
ground emerged, which retained limited appointments and gained ultimate
approval. Under this plan, county judges and county supervisors would name
the justices; the governor would make the final choice if they disagreed. But
Van Buren had discredited himself. To get this formula, he made a bargain
with the radicals for the popular election of sheriffs and county clerks. Beyond that he refused to barter and blocked a radical initiative for the election
of common pleas judges.[63]

Above all else, a far-reaching restructuring of the judiciary, which came
from Peter Jay Munro's committee, posed the greatest threat to Van Buren's
profession and the entire structure of law he respected. Blending useful reforms with antilawyer prejudices, Munro first rearranged the Court of
Chancery's traditional method in judging equity. The chancellor, along with a
new vice-chancellor and a second vice-chancellor if the legislature believed
one was necessary, now shared equity matters. Appeals derived from the vice-
chancellor, but the chancellor heard them. Munro further reshuffled the
Supreme Court by creating a superior court of common pleas made up of a
chief justice and three associate justices who had almost concurrent jurisdiction with the present Supreme Court. This provision, however, essentially created a muddled question of where that jurisdiction actually rested. Additionally, Munro added the new vice-chancellor and judges of the superior court
of common pleas to the Court of Errors, formed a series of new county
courts, altered the way circuits operated, and abolished surrogates by transferring their functions to common pleas. In short, Munro had fundamentally

destroyed the old judiciary, created unanswered issues of where adjudication rested, shifted the nature of equity, and destabilized Van Buren's profession.[64]

The full convention decided that the report was "too detailed" and "too complicated." But Root stirred further confusion when he moved a more extremist substitute. Reform of the judiciary was never far from radicals' minds. They objected to expensive litigation in chancery; to the low number of cases the Supreme Court heard because of circuit duties; to the blatant partisanship of appointed judges; and to the growing class of wealthy, elite lawyers, Van Buren among them. To "emancipate" the state from this "judicial thralldom," Root urged a set of revisions that abolished the old Supreme Court and formed another under new judges, increased the authority and scope of circuit courts, and destroyed the Court of Chancery by transferring equity to common pleas. As his justification, Root said the time was ripe to democratize the judiciary by replacing the old elite with men "who would restore the law to the standard of common sense" and reduce the "enormous costs and expenses" of litigation.[65]

Conservatives offered strenuous objections, but they were suspect because of their seeking to block the convention and generally being Federalist. Instead, Van Buren led the major thrust against Root, especially after he gratuitously remarked that his critics were "chancery lawyers in favor of a mother who had bestowed upon them so much nutriment." Reacting to this attack on his profession, Van Buren retorted that only shortsighted men wanted to "commit to the winds a system which had justly been considered the proudest pillar in our political fabric." After more bitter debate, conservatives, centrists, and floaters defeated Root's substitute. Other plans surfaced, including one by Van Buren to expand circuits but leave the Supreme Court, chancery, and the Court of Errors untouched. These and the original report failed. Faced with multiple and conflicting suggestions, the convention referred all substitutes to a new committee under Munro, with Root and Van Buren among its members.[66]

The next day, Munro presented a report that basically kept the old appellate system and judges, with a proviso for legislative discretion in filling in the blanks for inferior courts. Van Buren interjected a motion to postpone, but he could not find a second. Stirring further agitation, Tompkins, who up to this point had taken little part in debate, offered a friendly amendment that called for the removal of incumbent Supreme Court judges. To his great embarrassment, Van Buren found himself at odds with Tompkins. Making his last major speech at the convention, Van Buren stressed that throughout his political career opponents had assailed him "with hostility, politically, professionally and personal." But "as a representative of the people, sent here to make a constitution for them and their posterity," he would not "indulge [his] individual resentment" to destroy private and political adversaries. Such an extreme partisan measure, he ended, would ruin the delegates' mission to forge a workable constitution. Van Buren carried the day. Tompkins's motion went down.[67]

After more debate, the eventual solution in the constitution's fifth article gave Van Buren as much as it took. Accepting his classical republicanism, the constitution permitted voters, through the legislature, "as the public good may require," to increase circuits to "not less than four, nor exceeding eight." Moreover, another section endorsed Van Buren's plea to maintain the current Court of Errors. But other provisions displeased Van Buren. Ignoring his desire to preserve the Court of Chancery in its present form, a majority of delegates basically adopted Root's idea to allow the legislature to invest equity in circuit judges or "subordinate" courts, subject to the chancellor's "appellant jurisdiction." In another blow to Van Buren's desire to maintain the customary legal system, a further provision authorized a new Supreme Court and reduced its members to three, a chief justice and two associate justices, appointed by the governor and subject to senate approval. In reforms equally disillusioning to Van Buren, the refashioned Supreme Court was now left with significantly reduced appellate jurisdiction and less power to issue sundry writs, and shared authority with district judges to hear nonenumerated business and hold trials in courts of oyer and terminer. Despite Van Buren's best efforts, then, the delegates had fabricated a complete overhaul of the state judiciary, limited the tenure of judges who supported Van Buren, and shifted the nature of his appellate practice.[68]

In the convention's concluding days, Van Buren was often remote, except for a clash with King and Williams over reapportioning the legislature, and took little part in deliberations as delegates fine-tuned their work before adjourning on November 10. His detached mood continued in the short campaign that resulted in the document's ratification. Late in December, Van Buren put matters in perspective in a letter to John Van Ness Yates. Voters appreciated, Van Buren wrote, "that those who were the least violent in the convention were the most prudent."[69]

Van Buren's analysis was correct. The convention represented an historic moment, not only for himself but for the state. While it was true that he faltered on some occasions and did not appreciate the growing democratic impulse, he used his full repertoire of skills as a moderate centrist, bending on issues he could not influence, tasting defeat on others, cajoling and leading delegates along the broad middle acceptable to most New Yorkers. The new document was not his master plan, nor did he placate everyone, but it created a practical legal, constitutional, and political structure that balanced conservative fears of extreme democracy with radical concerns for increasing popular participation "in the management of public affairs." In that sense, Van Buren needed no apology. A shrewd and astute consensus builder who understood far better than most of his contemporaries how to play the politics of his age, he displayed tact and skill in not disturbing the critical mass of voters while defending his brand of republicanism and maintaining the basic integrity of his political organization and profession, no matter how much delegates had changed the judiciary. Just as important, the Regency had basked in public

approval for instituting popular constitutional reforms, while Clinton's political prestige plummeted even more.[70]

The convention had an additional meaning for Van Buren. Over the
course of the last year, his absorption with political and constitutional issues,
his readiness to shunt aside his monetary problems, his willingness to shelve
the law for politics coupled with assigning the bulk of his practice to Butler,
indicated a new phase in his career. As Van Buren moved to a larger plateau
than New York, he was no longer the lawyer-politician. He was now simply
the politician.

The Dual Career Ends

an Buren signalled that his career as both a lawyer and politician had entered its final stage in a long letter to Butler filled with detailed instructions about settling professional and business affairs. This "statement of demands" proved that Van Buren's financial embarrassment was over and perhaps had been exaggerated. Debts receivable from fifty-five clients and several stipends the state owed for attorney general services came to $7,605.54, more than the equivalent of three years of Van Buren's Senate salary. A few "demands" were in arrears since 1809; others were fees in the form of promissory notes ranging from $10 to $1,500, plus interest; and more than twenty appeared with unspecified amounts. In some instances, Van Buren was pessimistic about collections, but he authorized Butler to pursue delinquents with vigor and threats "of prosecution."[1]

Van Buren also personally contacted one major defaulter, Abraham Ten Eyck, whom Van Buren had represented in several cases connected to the still unresolved Hart legacy. While records listing charges to clients during his partnership with Butler have not survived, Van Buren's letter somewhat clarified this fee structure. Billing out $2,500 for preparation and litigation, Van Buren noted that the total approximated his income from three summers in the "Western Circuit." But with politics now his main priority, Van Buren further instructed Butler to "take the charge" of his current cases "& push them out of the way by compromise or arbitration."[2]

On December 3, 1821, the Seventeenth Congress opened, and Van Buren took the oath as New York's junior Senator. Placed on the judiciary and finance committees, he found a marked departure from his background in the New York senate. The rules were more rigid, the proceedings more ceremonial, and debate more deliberate, with fewer Saturday sessions and more time for leisure.[3]

Even before the session began, Van Buren had formed an audacious plan for an as yet untested freshman Senator. Appalled at "Monroe's Heresy," the consensus politics that blurred party distinctions and typified the Era of Good Feelings, Van Buren believed that the Republican party lacked consistent policies and a bedrock ideology. As a remedy, he sought to revive the old New York-Virginia axis (which had been the key to the party's control of the federal government since 1800) and to refurbish the organization's ideological commitments around issues that reflected republicanism. Playing for such high stakes, Van Buren's efforts during this session became a crucial testing time for all his future prospects.[4]

By happy coincidence, Van Buren's professional sagacity proved that he possessed all the qualities needed in a national politician. The situation started with an issue that bore a remarkable resemblance to his experience with the Livingstons. Early on, Senator Nicholas Van Dyke of Delaware introduced a bill with supporting documents seeking approval for a claim made by Tench Coxe of Philadelphia to the vast Maison Rouge tract near Fort Miro, Louisiana, worth some $500,000. Coxe's justification stemmed from two alleged grants, one in 1795 of 8,000 acres, and a second in 1797 that covered a further 210,000 acres.[5]

Van Buren, whose legal background with property titles exceeded that of any other Senator, studied the problem, took voluminous notes, and decided the claim was faulty. But when he began to make his maiden speech, his mind went blank. Somewhat apologetically, he remembered that his "unaffected timidity" and "respect for the body of which he was so new a member" created too stressful a moment. Louisiana Senator James Brown, a Coxe supporter, pounced on Van Buren's stage fright to lecture him in "irritating condescension" and sarcastically pointed out the differences in civil law between New York and Louisiana.[6]

Everything Van Buren wanted hung in the balance. Any more fumbling would destroy his nascent dreams and turn him into a laughing stock. Anxiously, he awaited his turn to reply. Some days later, his moment came. Speaking in a characteristically rapid delivery, he said that Coxe's claim was fraudulent because neither grant had legal foundation. For proof, Van Buren presented evidence that the certificates confirming the "grants" were either forgeries or written after the purported confirmations were made. When he finished, the Senate's most venerated member, Nathaniel Macon of North Carolina, congratulated Van Buren for "the service [he] rendered to the public." This accolade was the first indication that he would be as successful in

Washington as in Albany. With that encouragement, Van Buren began to implement his ideological and partisan goals.[7]

At the same time, Van Buren completed his career as a politician-lawyer in the politicized New York Supreme Court case of *Van Ness v. Hamilton and Others*. On January 26, 1820, the New York *American* had published a report that unearthed old scandals surrounding the Bank of America. Editors James Hamilton, Johnston Verplanck, and Charles King, acting as the ethical watchdogs of High Federalists, lay bare a sleazy story. In 1812, they alleged, the bank had bribed Elisha Williams, Jacob Van Rensselaer, and Supreme Court Judge William Van Ness to use their influence to secure the hotly-contested charter. As their pay-off, the bank deposited a $150,000 loan in the Federalist Bank of Columbia for fifteen years at six percent interest, but half of that interest accrued to the three for their personal use. The following year, Williams, Van Rensselaer, and Van Ness again served the bank. They illegally convinced the legislature and the Council of Revision to modify the Bank of America's original charter by cutting capital requirements and lowering the bonus the bank had promised to the state for incorporation. Once both laws passed, the directors of the Bank of America reneged and offered Williams, Van Rensselaer, and Van Ness $20,000 for their "double services." Williams purportedly received the money but refused to cut the others in until they threatened him with public exposure. He relented, but not before forcing the directors to give an unnamed fourth person an "equal share of the spoils."[8]

The editors placed the brunt of guilt on Judge Van Ness, because he was then a member of the Council of Revision, which held a veto over both pieces of legislation. Hoping to avoid libel, the editors denied any "malice or personal hostility" toward the judge, but trusted that his sense of honor "would spare us" from publishing the details. Yet the implication that there had been a "cause and effect" relationship was inescapable. Judge Van Ness had influenced political matters "foreign to his duties, and degrading to the character of his station." Although lacking direct proof of his guilt, the editors ended, "if this inference is unavoidable, then it is a public benefit to drag such an offender from the bench."[9]

Assemblyman Erastus Root cited this article to launch a special committee investigation, preliminary to filing articles of impeachment against the judge. Partisanship blinded the proceedings. Swiss Federalists and Clintonians permitted Judge Van Ness to cross-examine the editors, but refused them counsel, and accepted Williams's deposition denying bribery. When the committee reported, minus Root's concurrence, it absolved the judge, since there was "no *direct, positive testimony*" to prove guilt. The full house was more thorough, allowing the editors counsel, but split along party lines over impeachment before reaching an impasse.[10]

To clear his name, Judge Van Ness filed a libel action and shrewdly hired two distinguished Republican advocates, John Henry and Thomas Emmet.

The defendants, who needed equally outstanding attorneys, were just as cal-culating and approached Van Buren to join John Duer, a High Minded Fed-eralist. To strengthen his bonds with Rufus King, Van Buren accepted. Once committed, he took customary care, drafted a forty-three-page memoran-dum, and presented a long brief with specific facts that asserted the paper had published the truth. Unlike the precedent that defined libel as insinuation that he had established in *Spencer v. Southwick* eight years before, however, Van Buren avoided citing that case in order to duck the question of intent and li-bel by insinuation. In rebuttal, Henry and Emmet filed nineteen demurrers.[11]

Johnson did not publish the arguments either side presented, only printing Spencer's "opinion of the Court." Noting that "a decided distinction" existed "between words spoken, and written slander," Spencer identified the main issue as "the import and meaning of the libel." Using that standard, he turned the ta-bles against Van Buren. The precedent that Van Buren established in *Spencer v. Southwick* indeed "laid down" the "principle" that libel was "not necessary" in proving "criminality; but that if it necessarily implicates the conduct of the party concerned, it is libellous." Yet in finding for Judge Van Ness, Spencer de-nied him any monetary award since his attorneys had not established damages. In addition, Spencer gave the defendants the option for a new trial to present evidence more specifically demonstrating the judge's culpability.[12]

Van Buren also concluded with mixed results. On the negative side, he technically lost the case, cast doubt on the precedent he won in *Spencer v. Southwick,* and bolstered suspicions that his earlier defense of Spencer was less righteous than he claimed. More positively, Van Buren reaffirmed his alliance with the High Federalists and blackened the reputations of three of his most implacable political and judicial enemies, because Spencer did not exonerate them. In addition, Clintonians and Swiss Federalists lost more credibility.[13]

The case had another dimension as well. It indicated that while Van Buren's chosen destiny lay in national affairs, he could not ignore his state power base, especially during the November 1822 elections in which the Regency la-bored for a complete victory. In the gubernatorial race, Clinton, staggering under the load of having opposed the convention, chose a face-saving retire-ment rather than confront humiliation. For the Regency, Van Buren seemed its most "available" candidate for the gubernatorial race. He refused. Even so, he guided the Regency from Washington, adjusted differences between radi-cals and moderates, backed the gubernatorial nomination of Joseph C. Yates, an associate Supreme Court judge, and directed his campaign. The results confirmed Regency aims. Yates won easily, the Regency had an insurmount-able majority in the legislature, and three of Van Buren's protégés—Jesse Hoyt, Jesse Buel, and Azariah Flagg—won seats in the House of Representatives.[14]

Despite unexpected bickering with Governor Yates over spoils, the Re-gency put the finishing touches on its mastery of New York politics by awarding patronage to party workers in proportion to their efforts during the campaigns against Clinton. The same spirit touched the judiciary. By 1823,

Van Buren's familiar legal world underwent a transformation, because of the new constitution's provisions and subsequent legislation. The remodeled three-man Supreme Court functioned under Chief Justice John Savage and Associate Judge John Sutherland, two of Van Buren's allies, and Associate Judge John Woodworth, his sometime rival who was now in Van Buren's debt. Equally satisfying to Van Buren, Samuel Talcott, one of Van Buren's brightest lieutenants, became attorney general. Partisan considerations also molded the circuit courts. The legislature fixed the number of courts at eight. Yates, with Regency advice, selected men who were Van Buren's "friends," people he respected, or individuals he needed to flatter. Similar motives affected the superior court of common pleas and inferior courts. As for chancery, James Kent's forced departure due to age allowed the Regency to pacify Tammany by naming former Senator Nathan Sanford the new chancellor. But the Regency was not finished. Using party regularity as a litmus test, it followed recommendations of local county caucuses and selected a panoply of dependable local judicial officers. Although Van Buren was not personally involved in each decision, he set policy. The result was that for the first time since he became an attorney, Van Buren saw either his friends or dependents at every level of the bench.[15]

For the moment, Van Buren had no equal in the state and could plausibly claim that he was the only man capable of reviving the Republican party for the 1824 presidential election around the candidacy of William Crawford. Yet Van Buren's distraction with national events proved costly. Swift-breaking local events proved that the Regency was ill-equipped to cope with new political developments, and it floundered without Van Buren's hands-on direction.[16]

These political matters lay in the future. When Congress adjourned in May 1822, Van Buren returned to Albany and a law partnership in flux. Because of his fixation with becoming a national powerbroker, Van Buren had neglected his clients, and some had drifted to other attorneys. But Butler was content to remain a lawyer. Starting with their earliest association, he and Van Buren had differed about the role that law and politics played in their respective lives. While still a law clerk in 1817, Butler informed Harriet Allen that he preferred practicing law and found politics distasteful, even though he realized that the law, as in Van Buren's case, "*drives* one into political life" and "*compels* him more or less to engage in political concerns." Butler's antipathy to politics perplexed Van Buren. As late as 1828, he urged Butler "to play deeper" in politics. Revealing much about his own priorities, Van Buren asked Butler whether it was possible "to be anything in this country without being a politician?"[17]

Although Butler did become a valued if reluctant member of the Regency, he also became the firm's managing partner and rose to the top of his profession. Butler's emergence was most noticeable in appellate work, where he litigated a large number of cases that Van Buren would have normally advocated. In 1822, Butler became district attorney of Albany County, although he found criminal prosecution offensive to his religious scruples. Four years later, Butler's legal knowledge led to his appointment as one of the revisers of the state's statutes.[18]

Van Buren was content with these developments. He was still determined to devote the majority of his time to politics and curtail his practice. Under these conditions, Van Buren took on only a few uncomplicated circuit cases during the five months after he returned from the Senate in 1822. But one thing remained constant. A prudent manager of his own finances, he was implacable in hounding debtors and hired Arent Van der Poel of Kinderhook, to whom he offered from one-quarter to one-half of any debts gathered, as his collection agent. Moreover, Van Buren continued to badger Ten Eyck, even going fruitlessly to his home "with a view to a settlement of my demands."[19]

Appellate and chancery business provided the most dramatic sign of how deeply Van Buren's political priorities eroded his work before the bar. Over the next six years, he took cases selectively, based on the time needed to prepare and argue them and whether or not they intruded on his political ends. For those reasons, Van Buren, unlike other eminent attorneys who served in Congress, among them Daniel Webster and Henry Clay, never appeared before the United States Supreme Court.[20]

Van Buren handled only one case for the remainder of 1822, a November appeal to the Court of Errors from chancery. The case of *Jonathan J. Coddington, and Joseph C. Coddington, who were impleaded in the Court below with John F. Randolph, and Josiah Savage, Appellants, v. Thomas Bay, Respondent* epitomized the troubled commercial relationships during the recent depression. The case also duplicated earlier actions where Van Buren had sought fresh departures in contract law applicable to a new market economy through liberal republicanism.

Thomas Bay of Hudson had sold a vessel through two New York City agents and partners, John F. Randolph and Josiah Savage, for six negotiable notes. Before turning the notes over to Bay, their business failed and they transferred the notes, worth about $3,500, to Jonathan and Joseph Coddington. The notes were "security for an antecedent debt" that Randolph and Savage owed the Coddingtons but had not yet paid. In chancery, Kent reasoned that the Coddingtons were unentitled to the notes, because they had not received them in the proper "course of trade" nor received "consideration." In ruling for Bay as the lawful owner, Kent ignored the question of possible fraud and accepted the notion that notes in payment of antecedent debts were not negotiable.[21]

On behalf of the Coddingtons, Van Buren and Emmet appealed. Their presentation was difficult. It hinged on the common law contract precedent against them that favored the appellants, if the notes were given in the course of a normal business transaction and they had received something of value in return. Van Buren, in trying to mitigate those points, contended that the notes were negotiable instruments held by Randolph and Savage, the "lawful holders." As "holders in due course," they had the right to "pass them away, for a valuable consideration that a *bona fide* holder of a negotiable note, without notice, is entitled." Van Buren argued that giving the notes as additional security on an antecedent debt constituted valuable consideration. "The tree must be as it has fallen," he ended. "The money is in the possession of the appellants, and cannot be taken from them, without showing fraud" or bad faith. Seven senators agreed; the antecedent debt was a consideration. But the three Supreme Court justices and twenty-two senators supported Samuel Jones, Bay's attorney, that precedent in contract law made a distinction between present and past consideration. Sustaining Kent, they ruled that the transaction did not come under the ordinary definition of "course of trade," and that security for the previous debt could not be considered something of value.[22]

In the short run, this ruling humbled Van Buren. Not only did the court compel the Coddingtons to pay Bay's full legal costs, but New York judges and courts in other states depended on the opinion for a number of years to rule that a holder in due course of notes for antecedent debts lacked an absolute right of recovery, and that equities between original parties remained in force. But as similar cases developed, many attorneys and jurists became convinced that this ruling inhibited commercial transactions in a complex, growing economy. During the long run, Van Buren did achieve important results. In the 1842 United States Supreme Court case of *Swift v. Tyson,* Justice Joseph Story began an effort to establish a uniform commercial code, including the definition of a holder in due course. By overruling Kent, Story justified Van Buren and set in motion the formation of the modern Uniform Commercial Code, applicable to all the states, which recognizes additional security on an antecedent debt as sufficient consideration to sustain a holder in due course. As a result, Van Buren indirectly created a precedent that the legality of such negotiable instruments changed the nature of chancery equity, since the agreement between the original buyer and seller was no longer germane. Van Buren, again indirectly, also achieved other long-sought ends, modifying common law and contract law through legal instrumentalism and the will theory of contracts. Just as significant from a liberal republican outlook, Van Buren's interpretation of a holder in due course had the potential to stimulate commercial growth throughout the nation.[23]

By December of 1822, when Van Buren returned to Washington, he had set a lasting pattern in public affairs, a pattern that a number of historians have analyzed with thoroughness and sophistication. Van Buren championed his ideology, both in New York and Washington. Often pragmatically shifting on divisive issues, such as the tariff and internal improvements, he still strove to resuscitate the party's traditional credo and elect a president who shared his principles and the issues they generated. Seeking to balance the competing demands of sectionalism and nationalism with the realities of a new market economy, Van Buren's ratio of triumphs to defeats fluctuated from year to year.[24]

During 1824 and early 1825, Van Buren's political hopes bogged down with depressing regularity. Despite Van Buren's stress on the congressional caucus to select Crawford as the party's official nominee, other candidates remained in the field. Then Crawford, who suffered a stroke during the campaign, trailed Andrew Jackson and John Quincy Adams in the Electoral College and no one received a majority. The House of Representatives made the decision and chose Adams under suspicious circumstances. In New York, the Regency lost focus. Motivated by spite, Van Buren's lieutenants removed Clinton from his last public office as canal commissioner. A resultant backlash revived his career. Clinton reclaimed the governorship in 1824 and continued to disrupt the Regency until his death on February 11, 1828.[25]

But where others saw only the ashes of defeat, Van Buren saw opportunity. From 1825 to 1828, he chartered a steady ideological course, played a significant role in the Senate's daily operations, repaired the Regency's damaged base, and avoided a direct confrontation with Governor Clinton. Van Buren's most important activity during those three years, however, was weaving the discordant elements of the shattered Republican party into a new alignment with Andrew Jackson and his followers that ultimately became the Democratic party. From the outset of this effort, Van Buren employed the same legal techniques and ideological principles that had proved so effective in his formation of Albany Regency—order, discipline, structure, precision, harmony, and cohesion—to become one of Jackson's key tacticians in opposing President Adams.

Van Buren's alliance with Jackson started as a marriage of convenience. Jackson needed Van Buren's skills as a political manager; Van Buren needed Jackson to start a national party system to replace President Monroe's consensus politics. Van Buren's tactics were productive, because he and Jackson shared a common ideology and issues it generated. Many of the classical republican and liberal republican themes Van Buren had emphasized as a lawyer-politician thus became associated with Jacksonianism. Legal instrumentalism, distributive justice, legal positivism, and the defense of party workers became guides to public policies including adaptation to changing circumstances, manipulation of patronage, judicial restraint, and legislative supremacy. The Americanization of the common law merged with Jacksonian nationalism. The will theory of contracts fit the Jacksonian commitment that government would be based on the popular will and would not interfere with privatism, notably that of Southern slaveholders. Van Buren's championship of tenant's rights also complemented Jackson's belief in individualism, the lack of dependency, expanded democracy, and equal rights. Van Buren's use of party newspapers became powerful instruments that Jacksonians employed to attack Adams. Even the men Van Buren recruited for Jackson paralleled the persons Van Buren had groomed as clerks. These legal and ideological principles further helped to define many Jacksonian public policy initiatives—limited government, minimum taxation, antimonopolyism, strict construction of the Constitution, antielitism, state control of economic growth, a hard money currency, and low tariffs.

Above all, Van Buren gave Jackson a means to justify party politics at a time when many Americans considered partisan strife as the antithesis of national unity. As Van Buren noted in a letter to Thomas Ritchie, an influential Virginian Jacksonian newspaper editor, "political combinations" were "unavoidable" in a free, republican society. By "substituting *party principles for personal preferences,*" a two-party system was an irreplaceable instrument of self-rule that could broker sectional differences and could supply stability in an era of instability. By doing so, a political party moved from the realm of self-interest and expediency to the realm of morality. This alliance between Van Buren and Jackson grew stronger as a bond of friendship developed between them when they discovered that they shared other traits. Each lacked extensive formal education. Both were eminent lawyers in their respective states. Each rose to power as self-made men without important family connects. By 1828, Van Buren had completed the groundwork for the new Democratic party by restoring the old Jeffersonian New York–Virginia alliance that became the basis for the new Democratic party and became Jackson's campaign manager in his successful presidential race.[26]

Van Buren wavered from this pattern only once. In February 1823, Brockholst Livingston of New York, an associate justice of the United States Supreme Court, died. To keep sectional balance, President Monroe offered the vacancy to Secretary of the Navy Smith Thompson. But Thompson, pleading ill-health, delayed acceptance and offered to step aside in Van Buren's favor.

Duplicating his reaction four years earlier over the state Supreme Court, Van Buren was once more tempted for several reasons that may be conjectured. Perhaps his disillusionment with exhaustive everyday politics again overcame him; perhaps he wanted the position to symbolize his professional eminence; or perhaps he believed that the slot was the best way to check Chief Justice John Marshall's "consolidationist" interpretation of the Constitution. The willingness of King and Secretary of State Adams to petition Monroe on his behalf was also flattering. But Van Buren slowly recovered his equilibrium. He realized that Thompson, smitten by the presidential virus, was trying to swap the seat for New York's nomination. Similarly, King thought that Van Buren's removal from active politics would aid Adams's election, because Van Buren could no longer control the New York Legislature, which named presidential electors. In addition, Van Buren knew his criticism of Monroe made the selection highly unlikely. Indeed, the President had no intention of naming a man so opposed to his policies and put the appointment on hold. By June, Van Buren returned to normal. He assured Thompson that he harbored no grudges if he accepted the seat. When Thompson did, Van Buren turned back to politics.[27]

Less well known than these political actions was the pattern Van Buren stitched in the law. He continued as an advocate for the next six years, but only a part-time one, with a practice diminishing yearly in scope as almost an afterthought between senatorial sessions, elections, and political maneuvers. Nonetheless, from this point on, Van Buren's routine did not vary. Each year following Senate adjournment, he hurried home to New York for work in the circuit and took on select appellate cases. True to this criterion, Van Buren spent the better half of September and October 1823 "most laboriously engaged" in three causes before the Court of Errors, each of which dealt with legal principles he valued.[28]

Wilkes v. Lion, a case worth a purported $500,000, hung on a will and originated from the estate of Medcef Eden, a New York City brewer, who had died in 1798 and left extensive properties in Manhattan and Westchester counties to his two natural sons, Joseph and Medcef, Jr. According to the will, if either died "without lawful issue," his "share" went to the "survivor." If both died "without lawful issue," the estate reverted to John Eden and Hannah Johnson, their father's brother and sister. The language in the will generated a number of legal proceedings as to what interests the sons exactly held, particularly since both were spendthrifts. They borrowed heavily from New York City banks, mainly the Bank of New York, secured by promissory notes from money-lenders at usurious rates. Gradually, both brothers lost the bulk of their holdings through sheriffs' sales and foreclosures. In 1812, Joseph Eden died without lawful issue, and his estate reverted to his brother Medcef, in accordance with the terms of their father's will. Three years later, Aaron Burr entered the mix. Eager to find clients, he discovered Medcef Eden mired in debt and living in Westchester. With nothing to lose, Medcef entrusted Burr with his fate. For the next decade, Burr adopted the legal strategy of retrieving Eden's property on a parcel to parcel basis.[29]

In January 1819, Burr won a favorable ruling in the Court of Errors that overturned a finding by Chancellor Kent. *Anderson v. Jackson* held that Medcef Eden had become the owner of the property in Westchester after Joseph's death, even though the Bank of America had taken title to the land under a foreclosure against Joseph. The court ruled that Joseph did not hold the land in fee simple, an estate limited absolutely to one person. Nor did the land involve an estate tail, which was limited to his "lawful children," especially since a 1786 New York statute abolished entails. Joseph's interest was contingent; it depended upon whether or not he had lawful children. As such, he had no right to encumber the land, thereby voiding the bank's lien. The court made no determination of Medcef Eden's precise interest in the land, except that his inheritance was legal. With this, Burr began ejectments in Westchester, chiefly against persons who purchased land from the Bank of America. More complexities surfaced. On July 16, 1819, Medcef Eden died without lawful issue. His will named his wife executrix, and Burr became the guardian of Medcef Eden's stepchildren. After Eden's death, the Bank of America again challenged the original will on the same issue as in *Anderson v. Jackson.* This time the bank contended that it held an enforceable lien against the property because Eden had died without lawful issue, therefore extinguishing his interest. The Supreme Court ruled against the bank, which appealed to the Court of Errors.[30]

These actions were now more than Burr could handle. But they were the least of his worries. With his name still anathema to most New Yorkers, he had few resources to research the appeal and even fewer friends. Van Buren was one. Possibly out of gratitude to what the younger and yet unblemished Burr had been to him, Van Buren agreed to act as Burr's co-counsel; Butler prepared much of their *Wilkes v. Lion* brief. But Van Buren was not an innocent where Burr was concerned. In lieu of a retainer, Van Buren bought twelve acres from Medcef's estate for $1,000, a price far below their market value.[31]

Wilkes v. Lion hinged on the extent of Medcef Eden's interest in the properties. Delving into "general" common law precedent, which Van Buren called the most "intricate in the law," he asserted that the Bank of America had no legal redress against the estate. Van Buren maintained that Medcef's interest was in fee simple, not "a fee-tail," or a limited freehold. That distinction was not "open" to further discussion, because the Court of Error's ruling in *Anderson v. Jackson* was settled law under *stare decisis*. Furthermore, Van Buren cited his precedent in *Frier v. Jackson* that the Edens established good title through adverse possession, adding that the state Statute of Wills, based on the 1786 law, converted fee tails to fee simple. On those grounds, Van Buren concluded that Medcef Eden's interest was in fee simple, with the remainder to John Eden and Hannah Johnson if Medcef died without lawful issue. In short, two doctrines, which Van Buren had long championed, laid "down the rule which governs this case": continuous possession through adverse possession and legislative supremacy over the judiciary. The full court agreed. The Bank of America lacked actionable grounds until John Eden and Hannah Johnson were located.[32]

Van Buren stressed another of his legal principles, the will theory of contracts, in *Nicholas I. Roosevelt, Appellant, v. Dale & Wife, Executors of Robert Fulton, Respondent*. This case related to an appeal from chancery over a contract Fulton had made with Roosevelt for the purchase of land along the Ohio River. Believing Roosevelt's assurances that the property included a coal mine, Fulton had paid him $4,400 with an "annuity of $1,000" for twenty years. When the mine proved contrary to Roosevelt's description, Kent granted Fulton a permanent injunction that prevented Roosevelt from collecting the annuity, but noted that "it did not appear [he] had been guilty of fraud." In the Court of Errors, Roosevelt denied any misrepresentation, swore that both parties executed the contract in good faith, and contended that Kent erred in supposing that "a valuable coal mine" might not have possibly existed under the Ohio River, or at least "above the tide water." Van Buren insisted that Roosevelt had purposely hoodwinked Fulton. Emphasizing intent, Van Buren stressed that whether Roosevelt had committed a purposeful "moral fraud" or a "mistake" was not his to judge. But Roosevelt's "actions" had the same "effect upon the contract." Above that, Roosevelt's supposition that coal rested under the river was a diversion. The Ohio River was a public highway, not private property. The court sustained Van Buren's reading of the will theory of contracts, 18 to 6, and ordered Roosevelt to pay costs to Fulton's estate.[33]

The case of *Sarah Wilson and Others, Appellants, v. Robert Troup and Others, Respondents,* also an appeal from chancery, gave Van Buren a further opportunity to formulate a liberal republican line of reasoning. The case concerned the development of the law about the respective rights of a mortgage holder and a borrower in the event the borrower defaulted. The central issue was the right of Troup, the "agent" of the mortgage holder, to market the property without filing a foreclosure suit in chancery, the traditional remedy, by using a "special power of sale" contained in the mortgage. This power of sale was a summary foreclosure if a borrow defaulted. The case was further complicated by the fact that Wilson, the borrower, gave a general power of attorney to a third party to execute the mortgage on her behalf; however, this power of attorney did not specifically contain authority to sign a mortgage with a power to sell. Troup had two remedies: the power of sale, which was more expedient because he could merely declare a default and sell the property without going to court; or a foreclosure action in chancery, which was a lengthy process. Troup chose the power of sale and sold a number of properties. Wilson then filed but lost a motion in chancery to redeem.[34]

On appeal, Harmanus Bleeker, Wilson's lawyer, developed the point that the court must deny the power of sale, because the power of attorney did not have specific authority to sign a mortgage containing a power of sale provision. In reply, Van Buren reiterated the will theory of contracts by asserting that "no doubt" existed that the power of sale "must be construed according to the intent of the parties." Under the mortgage contract's terms, "a good and sufficient mortgage was intended, and an express clause was inserted, sanctioning every act necessary to complete the security of the purchase power." More important, all mortgages had a power of sale. For proof, he cited a statute passed in 1788 that legitimatized the execution of this power of sale. The court unanimously sustained Van Buren.[35]

This ruling had important ramifications for emerging rules dealing with defaulted mortgages. In the past, a mortgage holder had to file a foreclosure suit in chancery against the borrower if the borrower defaulted. The borrower had a certain time to redeem. But under this decision, the power of sale gave the mortgage holder the right to sell the property without filing a foreclosure action in chancery if the borrower defaulted. Nor did the borrower retain a time limit or the right to redeem. As a result, Van Buren helped change the older protective cannon that foreclosures belonged exclusively to chancery and reasserted the will theory of contracts and legal positivism. Equally important, Van Buren aided the possibility of commercial expansion by treating the power of sale as an individual, liberal republican right in a free market economy stripped of traditional equitable mortgage doctrines.[36]

Over the next two years, Van Buren paid minimal attention to other aspects of his practice, except for inescapable matters. When Moses Cantine died in December 1823, Van Buren helped Butler probate the estate. Since Van Buren and Peter Hoes were responsible to Jesse Buel "for $1500 of the last payment" in the purchase of the *Albany Argus,* Van Buren redoubled pursuit of Ten Eyck and instructed Butler to find collectors for other debtors. Yet too much was happening politically for Van Buren to aid Burr's continued quest for the Eden estate. During the height of congressional intrigue over the unsettled presidential election, Van Buren took precious time to assure Burr of his willingness to find other attorneys to help him, promised assistance "by way of conference," but avoided other involvement.[37]

Van Buren's legal pattern persisted in 1825 and 1826. Collecting fees remained another constant. He badgered slow-paying clients and empowered Butler, Hoyt, and Van der Poel as his agents, often seeking mediation if debtors were reasonable, or threatening foreclosures if they were stubborn. Van Buren's money-lending continued, as well as additional real estate purchases. Yet despite his constant bleating about unrecoverable debts and the impression that he was perpetually short of cash, Van Buren was simply following the Dutch-American trait of thrift and his belief that an honest day's work was worth proper recompensation. In a revealing letter to Cambreleng in 1827, Van Buren wrote that he wished to stay at his house in New York because "I cannot afford to pay $2 a day for a room." But Van Buren added that he would supply the wine for "a dinner to all the young Jackson Bloods in the city."[38]

Living in such comfortable economic circumstances, then, Van Buren could afford the luxury of picking and choosing his legal actions, less for their monetary values than their intrinsic challenges. With that in mind, he concluded his legal career with three such causes in 1827 and 1828.

Perhaps the cruelest personal and professional setback Van Buren encountered occurred in the preliminary stage of the action that evolved into the United States Supreme Court case of *John Inglis, Demandant v. The Trustees of the Sailor's Snug Harbor in the City of New York.* Captain Thomas Randall, "one of the most noted sea captains of his day" before and after the American Revolution, had died in 1797 and willed his property to three children, Robert R. Randall, Paul R. Randall, and Catherine Brewerton. Robert Randall received the most valuable part of the estate, four lots in the city's first ward. While his siblings became Loyalists and fled to Great Britain, Robert Randall was "a Patriot." In 1790, he bought the "Minto Farm," which consisted of "twenty-one acres" of land in upper Manhattan. Eleven years later, Robert Randall died a wealthy man. His estate included the Minto Farm, stocks valued at about $10,000, and the lots in the first ward. In his will, Robert Randall left small annuities to "the legitimate children of my brother, Paul R. Randall," but devised the largest part of his estate to a trust for the establishment of "an Asylum or Marine Hospital," the "Sailors' Snug Harbour," to maintain and support "aged, decrepit and worn-out sailors." Robert Randall's legacy became a prize another way. The mounting worth of his property in the first ward, Manhattan's most commercially rich area, burgeoned the net worth of Robert Randall's bequest into millions of potential dollars.[39]

This bonanza proved too lucrative for one possible distant heir to ignore, John Inglis, Bishop of Nova Scotia. He demanded a right of inheritance to the lots in the first ward passed through several generations from "common ancestors" to Paul Randall and then his daughter, Margaret, who was Inglis's mother. John Inglis's interest had two defects. The evidence was debatable if he was a legitimate claimant to the "real estate by inheritance." Although born an American citizen, Inglis had become a Loyalist and a British citizen, subject to property confiscation under New York statute. In addition, Inglis's stake rested on his inheritance through Paul Randall. But New York had declared him "an absent debtor" in 1784 and confiscated his property through proper channels. The key issues in the complex case rested on whether Robert Randall made a "valid devise" that deprived Inglis of "his legal estate," and if the trust was legal.[40]

The first round of this case began in the circuit court of the United States for the Southern District of New York in November 1827, with Judge Thompson presiding. Attorney General Talcott and Emmet represented the state. Van Buren was Inglis's lead advocate. Proceedings went badly for Van Buren from the start. Inglis could not prove that he was an American citizen, New York statutes regarding attainder and debtors weighed heavily against him, and Van Buren failed to convince the jury that the will was defective. But other disturbing circumstances shook Van Buren to the bottom of his soul. Emmet, his colleague and friendly rival in so many legal and political forays, suffered a cerebral hemorrhage during the trial and died. A grieving Van Buren served as one of his pall bearers. Just as shattering, Van Buren discovered that Talcott was often "unfit" to "come into court" because of the acute alcoholism that would shortly take his life. Political concerns forced Van Buren to withdraw from further appeals. He left the matter in the hands of Webster, who later noted that he made "greater exertions" in this case than "any since [Dartmouth College] v. Woodward—& that is probable I shall ever make in any other." Despite Webster's efforts, the United States Supreme Court in 1830 ruled for the trust.[41]

The November 1827 case of *James Jackson, ex dem. Theodosius Fowler and Others v. James Carver* stemmed from Van Buren's 1815 senate report and subsequent opinion as attorney general that John Jacob Astor's claim to the Morris estate was without merit. Astor had no intention of backing down. After Mary Morris's death in 1825, Astor reasserted his right to the remainder interest and informed the legislature that he was willing to settle for a reasonable sum. Since Astor and his associates were so powerful, the state senate formed a special committee to ascertain the property's exact value. It estimated that Astor's alleged ownership of 48,472 acres was worth more than $600,000, and that he and his associates had invested an additional $350,000 in the properties. On April 6, 1827, New York offered Astor $450,000 in state stock, plus $250,000 if the United States Supreme Court ruled in his favor. But before paying, the state stipulated that Astor had to establish ownership by winning three of five test cases in federal circuit court. Moreover, the state gave him a deadline of October 6, 1827 to comply.[42]

This solution did not apply to ejectments begun prior to that date. In 1826, Astor hired a team of skillful lawyers, including Emmet and Thomas Oakley, to confirm his title. New York was equally careful. The state designated Attorney General Talcott as its lead advocate and hired Webster to address the jury. Van Buren joined them as New York's most experienced authority on the case.[43]

In May 1827, Astor's lawyers filed an ejectment in the Circuit Court for the Southern District of New York under Justice Thompson to prove "complete title." They insisted that they could use the Morris heirs' remainder interest to certify Astor's rights and that a "subsisting title in the premises need not be shown." Van Buren countered by reviving the doctrine of champerty and cited the commissioners of forfeiture's action to contend that the Morrises "had no interest in the premises at the commencement of suit nor at this time, and their names had been used without any authority from them." Beyond that, Van Buren asserted that Astor lacked legal title to the property and that the current occupants owned the land through adverse possession. In finding for Astor, Judge Thompson dealt the state an ominous blow. The ejectment could proceed. Astor's "power to use" the Morrises' title was derived from the deed their children sold him, undercutting Van Buren's earlier opinions and destroying the property rights of the blameless people he had sought to protect.[44]

By November 1827, Astor had not accepted New York's time limit, but the first test trial under that formula went forward in *Jackson, ex dem. Theodosius Fowler and Others v. James Carver.* Oakley opened with evidence about Adolph Philipse's will. He also presented certified copies of the 1753 deed that divided the estate among his children; the Morrises' marriage settlement recorded in 1787; the provisions for a life-estate and the remainder interest; and a certified copy of the transaction Astor made with the Morris children. Talcott answered for New York. Stressing that proper proceedings had legally "attained and convicted" Roger and Mary Morris "as Loyalists," he emphasized that the state correctly declared all "their estates, real and personal," were forfeited "to the people of this state" for sale. Van Buren followed by questioning the "authenticity of the marriage settlement on which the claim of the plaintiff was founded." Above that, Van Buren maintained that the holder of a life estate was legally obligated to refrain from any action that might devalue the property. But the Morrises, during the seventeen years they were "in continued possession and use of the property," had leased lots, sold others, and recorded deeds "in which they guaranteed that they were possessed of the property in fee simple." Thus, by their own admission, a life estate never existed, the Morris children had no remainder interest, and Astor held no legitimate title.[45]

In his summary, Webster castigated Astor's ethics, emphasized the points Talcott and Van Buren raised, and ended with emotional praise for the state, which sought "justice" for innocent, hardworking farmers. Emmet closed for Astor. No doubt existed, Emmet said, that the marriage settlement was "executed and delivered." Moreover, British precedent held that the attainder did not affect the remainder interest.[46]

Judge Thompson's instructions to the jury essentially gave the case to Astor. Thompson asserted that, in his opinion, the attainder only affected the life estate and that "no legal impediment" existed against the remainder interest. Using this guide, the jury returned a verdict for Astor. The next day, Van Buren and Attorney General Talcott indicated that the state would "carry up the case" to the United States Supreme Court.[47]

Although the litigations in the "Astor Cause" indeed reached the United States Supreme Court, Van Buren's role had ceased. While he and Webster did consult as co-counsels as late as September 1828, Van Buren again turned to politics and left Webster in charge. In 1831, the Supreme Court found for Astor and New York began settlement payments.[48]

This opinion was a hard loss for Van Buren. In deciding between conflicting property rights among two sets of entrepreneurs, one market-orientated agrarians, the other commercial speculators and developers, the legal system upheld presumptive evidence. It treated this evidence as true unless rebutted by other evidence, in order to destroy the titles of blameless buyers, deny them compensation for their improvements, and negate legislative supremacy because the attainder was inoperable. Only Astor and his associates were satisfied.

Ironically, Van Buren left his profession just as he had started: an extended member of what was now truly Burr's Little Band. In 1827, Burr had won another action, *Stephen Waring, Plaintiff in Errors, v. James Jackson, ex dem. Medcef Eden and Another, Defendants in Error,* in the United States Supreme Court, which upheld the original will. With that as his justification, Burr instituted ejectments in Manhattan. Richard Varick, a defendant in one of these suits, had purchased a lot from John Wood, Jr., one of Medcef Eden's creditors, made valuable improvements, and contested the ejectment. In 1827, the state Supreme Court sustained a circuit court ruling for the estate. Varick and his agent appealed to the Court of Errors in *Varick and Bacon, Plaintiffs in Error, and Jackson. ex dem. Eden and Wood, Defendants in Error.*[49]

Van Buren had shunned these actions, largely because Varick was a valued political ally. Van Buren also knew Burr was operating on a shoestring and was remiss paying fees. "Do me a favor," he wrote Gorham Worth in March 1828, "to call on [Burr] personally & get the cost out of him before the matter gets cold." But the adult Van Buren could hardly resist the charming Burr any less than he could as a callow apprentice lawyer. In June 1828, Van Buren wrote the reporter of the United States Supreme Court for all the material on the Eden Case and gave Burr his best effort.[50]

This case was based mainly on the rights of an owner to devise his property by will if he was not in possession of the property at the time of his death. To start with, Van Buren stressed that the plaintiffs did not have good title, since the person from whom they received the title had no right to convey that property. But there was more. Van Buren's brief epitomized many of the larger themes that he had developed during his legal career. The plaintiffs, he pointed out, relied on British precedent, British statute law, and British common law to define the nature of inheritance. Yet New York's "statute of wills and the English statutes on the same subject are not alike." In particular, "the principles" behind the British method "derived" from "the feudal system." These were "inapplicable" in the United States. Thus the case rested on the "battle between" New York's "fair and liberal construction of the Statute of Wills" and "the contracted and illiberal construction" in British courts. Returning to ideas he employed against landlords, Van Buren argued that individuals in New York owned property in *"pure allodium,"* land held in one's own individual name, not the British custom of *"free and common socage,"* the epitome of feudalism. As a result, the state's Statute of Wills "in relation to property is a system of right, sustained by reason." By those terms, Medcef Eden held the estate in fee simple; "his representatives might recover" the property for his heirs "if the title was a subsisting one;" and the court had decided "the question now in controversy" under *stare decisis* in "the causes" of *Anderson v. Jackson* and *Wilkes v. Lion.* The judges, in a unanimous decision, sustained Van Buren and ordered the plaintiffs to pay costs.[51]

Taken as a whole, Van Buren's efforts in the Eden cases meant more than his mere attempts to save Medcef Eden's estate, or a simple boon for Burr. In the broadest sense, Van Buren had used an instrumentalist approach to readjust traditional common law doctrines and techniques and to graft liberal republicanism onto American institutions. To be sure, he accepted the fact that the common law molded American law. But Van Buren also recognized that some of the common law proved inadequate in the new society that it served. From this point of view, Van Buren stressed utilitarian liberal republicanism in the Eden cases to reflect a new distribution of economic and political power in a free market economy; modification of the common law by eradicating its feudal character; enlargement and definition of individual property rights; the salience of American judgments through native *stare decisis;* justice based on legal positivism made by elected representatives of the people; and legal instrumentalism in response to novel conditions.

That fall, Van Buren resisted Regency pleas to accept a gubernatorial nomination and cautiously weighed party needs against his desire to stay in the Senate. At the eleventh hour, he did become a candidate. Seeking his first statewide elective office, Van Buren tried to prove his personal political popularity to

Jackson, clinch the state for Democrats, and earn an eventual seat in the cabinet. Election returns in New York were slow and wrenching. Jackson eked out a narrow victory, by a margin of merely 5,350 votes out of 276,176 cast. Van Buren won by 30,350 over his nearest rival in a split field. Yet if the total vote of his two opponents were combined, he actually had less than a plurality, only 49.5 percent, and would have lost. In explaining both his and Jackson's embarrassing results, Van Buren blamed old enemies, the reappearance of "old 98 Federalism," and the sinister forces that the "manor influence" still wielded in the Upper Hudson Valley. Yet Van Buren did not dwell on the past for long. In becoming governor, he had started down the avenue leading to the presidency.[52]

As this new phase began, an older one ended. After a quarter of a century of mixing law with politics, one admirer wrote, Van Buren's "absorbing work" as a politician took him "from the bar all too soon." He left, another noted, "before he was forty-six" with "a competence fairly earned" and still "in the early ripeness of his powers." Even so, yet another explained, Van Buren's profession laid the basis for all of his accomplishments: "Such and such only was the magic by which he rose to eminence." With these accolades, Van Buren ended his dual career.[53]

Martin Van Buren's Legal and Political World

By 1828, Governor Martin Van Buren had reached a point in life when his formative years were over and his qualities fully developed. But while his physical frame had matured from that of a slender youth to the more rotund features of middle age, many of the distinctive traits that had molded his beginnings endured.

Van Buren began his dual career as lawyer and politician with a Dutch–American heritage and classical republican principles that he augmented with an evolving set of liberal republican values. These constructs shaped his ethical view of the world, provided a host of lasting values, and helped Van Buren achieve ambitious goals: professional distinction, financial independence, personal recognition, and political renown. Now standing on the threshold of true national power as President-elect Andrew Jackson's chief tactician, Van Buren was widely recognized by both admirers and critics as a master politician, one who shaped the nation's first mass political party through his organizational skills, tact in harmonizing conflicting sectional and group interests, ideological principles, and adaptation to the rising democratic spirit of the age.[1]

So seemingly inevitable were Van Buren's achievements that his contemporaries neglected to ask: What were the ingredients behind his political rise

and mastery? Shortly after Van Buren's death in 1862, William A. Butler's eu-
logy added some depth to William Holland's initial explanation, twenty-
seven years earlier, that Van Buren's work as a lawyer was the most salient reason for his success in politics.

Subsequent historians echoed this axiom. Van Buren's years of advocacy,
they pointed out, resulted in public visibility, produced a sense of personal security and self-esteem, secured the loyalty of a dependable constituency,
achieved freedom from dependency on traditional political leaders, and
earned the wealth to finance campaigns. Furthermore, travel on the circuit
and appellate pleadings widened the circle of "friends" he used to build the
network for the Albany Regency. But outside of Donald M. Roper's sugges-
tive 1982 article in the *Journal of the Early Republic*, none of these historians
clarified *how* the law in general, and Van Buren's brand of republicanism in
specific, forged his dual career.[2]

Van Buren lacked three qualities valuable to the making of a great advocate. As a young lawyer, his practice was circumscribed by sharp class and social stratifications in the Upper Hudson Valley. "My business," he wrote in the
Autobiography, came from the "publick at large, having received but little from
the Mercantile interest or from Corporations, and none from the great
landed aristocracies of the county." Additionally, Van Buren was not a polished
orator and shunned the ornate phraseology and classical allusions so prized
among his fellows to sway impressionable jurors. Van Buren was also poorly
educated compared to many of his peers and suffered pangs of insecurity.[3]

Van Buren was correct in that his early practice typified his time and place,
centering around small actions and the daily uninspiring work of an all-purpose lawyer. During this period, Van Buren was indeed a people's lawyer, one
who never forgot that the law began with human beings and their problems.
Yet even if many of these initial clients were not from the elite, they did represent the core of an upwardly striving agrarian class determined to secure
their rights through the legal system. Their agrarianism was not, however, a
nostalgic longing for an imagined past, nor were they subsistence farmers.
With land as their main form of enterprise in a preindustrial economy, and
with their dependence on a fairly undeveloped credit system, they were businessmen intent on abolishing all remnants of feudal prerogatives. Van Buren
served them through classical republicanism, particularly with new departures
in property law, to end dependency and create equal individualism, liberty,
and freedom. Moreover, Van Buren recognized the utility of liberal republicanism to achieve their ends by applying its principles in practical matters involving land titles, claims, ejectments, and debt collections. Van Buren's practice shifted when modernized commerce and finance fostered fresh sorts of
litigation that demanded skilled advocates. After securing his professional credentials in appellate courts, he attracted wealthier clients, often from the very
propertied groups, mercantile interests, and corporations that purportedly
scorned him. As a result, Van Buren aimed classical republicanism and his

evolving liberal republicanism toward gaining a wide distribution and allocation of opportunity, in order to ensure equality and to give fellow Americans similar means to participate in economic betterment.

Even Van Buren's lack of education needs clarification. In the *Autobiography,* he acknowledged little interest in literature and habitually read "light matters" for amusement. Giving the impression of superficiality, he wrote that he shrugged off "weightier matters of law, as well as those that appertained to public affairs" until the moment "it became indispensable to grapple with them." But these remarks had a ring of forced modesty and mirrored his determination "to check the indulgence in egotism, to which human nature is so prone."[4]

Van Buren was not a dilettante. His hard-driving work habits, incessant preparations, and competitiveness were ingrained character traits. Such attributes gave him a critical edge over more self-indulgent opponents. Furthermore, as much as he denigrated his general and professional education, his practice proved that he was an accomplished professional who perfected his standing before the bar through constant self-improvement and studiousness, as well as by his direct experience learning the law by doing the law. These efforts also applied to politics. Without such obsessive labor Van Buren could never had been so successful.[5]

These qualities were most pronounced in Van Buren's legal problem-solving. Combining native intelligence and thorough analytical skills, he organized each cause to determine the central issues, examined the factual background on both sides, arranged evidence in a logical progression, and supported his briefs with relevant points of jurisprudence and casebook authorities. In lower courts, Van Buren was cautious and prudent by presenting all the evidence in the event of appeal. Equally important, he used tact and charm toward opposing witnesses and counsels and rarely turned cases into personal confrontations. Such an approach made more friends than enemies and helped Van Buren develop a reputation as an effective, unemotional evaluator of character and a scrupulous litigator with statewide prominence.[6]

As for his speaking style, Van Buren was most comfortable and effective in appellate advocacy before a bench of judges. His appellate record was striking. Over a span of twenty-five years, Van Buren represented 255 clients in all types of litigations, winning nearly 89 percent, sometimes in association with James Van Alen, Cornelius Miller, John Henry, Thomas Emmet, and Benjamin Butler, against the state's best legal talents. While sole advocate for "The People" when he served as attorney general, Van Buren triumphed in another 258. In the Court of Errors, he handled twenty-one cases, gained favorable verdicts in eleven, and wrote fifteen opinions while a senator-judge. Furthermore, Van Buren advocated fifty-four actions in chancery and triumphed in thirty-eight.[7]

At the same time, Van Buren's legal career illustrated profound changes in his profession. Although he charged clients standard statutory fees, he demanded and received larger rates than the law allowed through retainers, as in the Ten Eyck case, and accumulated a fortune when market conditions set compensation. With many clients willing to pay a premium for effective advocates, lawyering became less a calling and more an enterprise geared to what clients were willing to pay in ratio to the value of their causes. Van Buren was thus a transitional figure who spanned two legal worlds, the elitist and privileged sort that typified the eighteenth century, and the bustling, upwardly mobile, achievement-oriented one of the nineteenth.

Van Buren was a consummate lawyer, one of the best if the not the busiest, in a brilliant field of New York attorneys. Even granting that his record-keeping was incomplete, his partnership with Van Alen attracted approximately 300 clients from 1804 to 1809. Van Buren and Miller added another 238 from September 1807 to June 1810. As for Van Buren and Butler, no exact figure is extant. Whatever the actual total for Van Buren and Butler, these clients likely represented a valid statistical sampling of Van Buren's Middle District constituents, the volume of his practice, and a fair deduction about his docket in other venues. Over the course of his legal career, then, Van Buren participated in a host of high profile cases, faced hundreds of other lawyers, examined thousands of witnesses, and won the gratitude of numerous clients. All of these activities indicated Van Buren's illustrious reputation as the leading attorney of his era in the Republican party and among the elite practitioners of the New York bar.[8]

If Van Buren had been content just to practice the law, his career would have merely provided useful insights about legal developments in the nation's most important state during the formative years of the early nineteenth century. But, as other commentators have properly noted, Van Buren's lasting prominence lay in politics. Nevertheless, the indispensable way in which Van Buren integrated classical republicanism and liberal republicanism into his early career as both a lawyer and a politican remains the least investigated but most significant part of his legal and political world.

Yet a problem exists in regards to determining the significance of republicanism in his career. Republicanism, as an historical concept, is a multifaceted term that denotes a variety of meanings to diverse groups. As a consequence, republicanism seems lacking in clarity because it was not a fixed ideological series of axioms, but a flexible instrument of policy subject to multiple interpretations.[9]

But Van Buren's commitment to republicanism was neither imprecise nor one-dimensional. On one level, he defined his principles in purely classical republican terms. Under this approach, Van Buren stressed that republicanism meant a government with limited powers, restrained by statutes and constitutional arrangements, and resting on civic-minded virtue, propertied independence, popular sovereignty, personal liberty, freedom, equality, and privatism. Furthermore, classical republicanism employed those values as a bulwark against aristocratic privilege, tyranny, concentrations of wealth, and arbitrary government. But as Van Buren's dual career evolved, he also selected other ideological ingredients from liberal republicanism: equal opportunity; human improvement through private acquisitiveness, much as he himself had achieved; personal security, upward mobility, competitiveness, and self-reliance in a free market economy; and individual freedom, both material and political. In the process, Van Buren wove this synthesized republicanism into the law and politics, thus giving his contemporaries a means to reconcile his nation's basic ideology of republicanism with self-seeking political parties in the quest for a just society.

As both an attorney and a politician, Van Buren implemented his brand of republicanism into a coherent system. The judiciary, he believed, was an equitable and moral vehicle in private and public law, much along the lines of his ethical Dutch-Americanism, which safeguarded republicanism. In practical terms, Van Buren stressed procedural guarantees of substantive due process to foster civil liberty and to ensure individual freedom. Van Buren found the logical political extension of these beliefs to be especially appropriate to an emerging democratic society. For that reason, he valued legal positivism as the embodiment of the public will and defended officeholders as tribunes of the people. Van Buren was also a committed legal instrumentalist who used the law and politics as adjustable policy-making mechanisms that adapted to their times. Additionally, republicanism checked judges by making them accountable to the public through legal positivism, and set the bounds for public and private law through fresh rules of procedural law and substantive law. The same reasoning applied to distributive justice. Voters, in electing legislators, weighed and allocated the benefits of economic growth, mainly over chartering and supervising banking in a free market economy. Lawyers and politicians implemented justice in another way. Van Buren recognized that those in authority, symbolized by the elites of wealth, birth, and deferential politics, inevitably attempted to increase their own power by limiting republicanism. Lawyers and politicians restrained this elite by becoming the guardians of liberty.

Van Buren further interpreted his republicanism in other areas of the law and politics. He embedded freedom, liberty, and individualism in contract law to enunciate the principle of intent under the will theory of contracts as the basis for economic bargains, not the outmoded and abstract rules of equity. Similar values applied to the emerging field of torts. Rather than considering damages to be a matter of traditional equity, Van Buren urged a new method based on fault as the standard for compensation. Freedom, liberty, and individualism shaped the nature of negotiable instruments as well, particularly those involving a third party, in a free market economy based on private choice. Van Buren also applied these concepts to women. While he was not a crusader for women's suffrage, Van Buren advanced the idea that a woman enjoyed the individual economic right to dispose of property without the approval of a male, that she deserved the law's protection of her property and family in divorce, and that the traditional doctrines of dower and curtesy were inapplicable to an emerging liberal republican culture.

Van Buren's republicanism further molded his attitude toward the common law. After the American Revolution, surging growth in self-government, new state constitutions and statutes, along with bewildering social and economic dislocations, forced many New Yorkers to ponder the viability of inherited British legal institutions. Van Buren joined them through legal instrumentalism when he questioned some of the common law's applicability to energetic American realities. The result placed him among a group of innovative attorneys and judges who thought that many of the common law's procedural methods fell short of substantive needs in evolving civil, equity, property, and commercial matters. While Van Buren accepted the fact that the common law was the foundation of American law, his success as a litigator recast many of the common law's procedures in both private and public law as the means to achieve his republican ends.

Most important, Van Buren applied his republicanism to redefine property law in a long crusade against the prevailing landlord system in the Upper Hudson Valley, with all its vestiges of feudalism. He stood in the vanguard of New York attorneys who attacked older views toward the sanctity of vested property rights, chiefly the perpetuation of restrictive colonial land-ownership based on outmoded feudalistic customs. Holding the belief that manorial grants and letters of patent unfairly awarded land in perpetuity and posed a threat of continuous dependency through restrictive covenants on individuals, Van Buren diagnosed republicanism to mean establishing fee simple as the property norm for an independent yeomanry, free of dependency, whom he considered the basic building bloc of meaningful liberty and freedom.

This conception posed considerable political risk to a budding politician. Van Buren's melded republicanism concerned political power and economic possibilities between traditional leaders intent on maintaining unlimited landed rights and perpetual tenantry, or a dynamic view of equal opportunity in a new market economy that adapted to shifting conditions. As his battles with the Livingstons, Van Rensselaers, and their sympathizers demonstrated, Van Buren never hesitated. This choice bore important dividends. He indelibly associated himself with burgeoning democratic forces in New York and the liberal republican, entrepreneurial free market he associated with these yeomen-businessmen.

Taken as a whole, Van Buren's republicanism set the parameters for his two careers. To be fair, he was a partisan and did not hesitate in bending the law to serve political ends, as in the libel suit involving Ambrose Spencer, or the William Van Ness action. Even so, Van Buren saw no basic contradiction between the law and politics. Both functioned to achieve a larger end, the creation of a functional republican nation in all its forms.

At times, Van Buren seemed inconsistent in blending his republicanism to his legal and political goals. Although differing from many Federalists who valued the law as the sum of human wisdom and experience, he occasionally supported their view of institutional arrangements in ways that apparently contradicted republicanism. The most striking example occurred at the state convention of 1821. Van Buren struggled against equalitarian attempts to liberalize equity and democratize circuit courts because of the need to defend his profession. For similar reasons on appellate affairs, he strove to preserve the Supreme Court's composition and scope, despite its politicization and failure to adjudicate many disputes. Van Buren's republicanism also ostensibly fell short when he echoed conservatives' alarms about urbanism and, for political reasons, accepted their support to retain appointive sheriffs and justices of the peace. As for universal, white male suffrage, his version of republicanism apparently rejected the ability of the masses to govern themselves.

Van Buren's republicanism seemed contradictory in other ways. In his speeches, writings, and presidential addresses to Congress, he conveyed a classical eighteenth-century agrarian image in opposition to the growing commercialization of national life with all its ancillary factors, such as urbanization, institutional banking, corporations, stock-trading, and artificial monopolistic privilege created by an extension of government power to spur economic growth.

Van Buren apparently put his classical republican faith in an agrarian nation, composed of virtuous citizen-farmers, determined to protect their values from the encroaching business world of the nineteenth century. Van Buren seemed clear on this point. The "landed interest," he wrote in the *Inquiry,* "will secure to our people the blessings of republican government as long as it remains the predominant interest in this country." Van Buren appeared just as contradictory when he either failed or underestimated the anxieties that the new market economy produced.[10]

But during his professional life, Van Buren emphasized a blend of classical republican and liberal republican ideas, which indicated that he was far less a dogmatist than an advocate of prudent change. As an innovative lawyer, he accepted commercialization and enunciated legal principles that strengthened rather than scorned an equalitarian free market economy and a business culture. His efforts to establish the will theory of contracts, new types of contract arrangements in property law and commercial law, along with altering equity and the negotiability of notes, aimed to open opportunities for private initiative. As a classical republican ideologue, he did fear the corrosive power of landed and moneyed elites. But he emphasized both sets of republican principles to guarantee equalitarian competitiveness through an organized political system that used legal instrumentalism and distributive justice to achieve measured, stable economic growth that would not destroy civic virtue. Moreover, Van Buren was just as consistent in dealing with universal suffrage; he shared the classical republican bias against urbanism and defended small versus large property owners, not the propertyless against the propertied. Whatever his deficiencies in this regard, Van Buren did articulate a major principle rooted in classical republicanism: the fear that voters without property would remain dependents and could not exert a check on powerful elites.

In short, Van Buren cannot be categorized as either an agrarian reactionary or the agent for capitalist advances. Rather, he was a lawyer and politician with both conservative and innovative traits who incorporated his evolving republicanism into a complex era of economic and political developments. Seen in that light, Van Buren's republicanism was not contradictory. Throughout his legal career, he stressed three principled themes to alleviate human anxiety and to adjust material progress with disparities in wealth, property, and opportunity: personal liberty, private choice, and equal justice. Van Buren added another theme through politics. "The disposition to abuse power," he noted, was "deeply planted in the human heart." Consequently, an institutional party system was a "necessity" in a free country. As such, Van Buren believed that a party's ideological functions were interrelated with the law. These functions meant "the maintenance of order," the protection of "civil and political rights, and the management of public affairs in a spirit of equal justice to all men."[11]

The question of power that Van Buren expressed in his republicanism, its allocation, location, justice, and institutional arrangement, was central to understanding his career as a lawyer-politician. He did not draw a dichotomy between the law and politics. Both operated according to classical republican and liberal republican precepts, keyed to fulfilling private, individual, and group needs. Van Buren recognized, however, that classical republicanism, liberal republicanism, and Jacksonianism did not always mesh. Like any political program, this ideological approach was plagued with ambiguities, problems, and inconsistencies. Because of these realities, Van Buren rejected some features of liberal republicanism that became entrenched in the new Whig party—unrestricted private accumulations of wealth that created a monied aristocracy, protection of corporations, government stimulation of the economy, moral reforms that impinged on privatism, protective tariffs, judicial supremacy, centralized banking, and growing economic inequalities. In reconciling his definition of classical republicanism with liberal republicanism and Jacksonianism, Van Buren sought a middle ground, keyed to fulfilling private, individual, and group needs. As a result, Van Buren warned that the Whig brand of liberal republicanism ran the risk of creating unremitting class warfare unless it duplicated the classical republican and Jacksonian concern for a social conscience and the placement of human rights, except regarding enslaved African-Americans, over property rights. In that manner, Van Buren sought to harmonize classical republicanism, liberal republicanism, and Jacksonianism to create a just society of free and independent citizens.

Van Buren's political career reflected these legal commitments. At times, this relationship was crude and bordered on expediency. For instance, he sometimes wielded his legal talents to defend questionable party officials or campaign workers. Worse, Van Buren, either consciously or unconsciously, revealed racist tendencies by failing to appreciate how his republicanism failed to serve African-Americans and American Indians, or fell short of their needs.

However, Van Buren's construct of how an effective republican legal and political culture operated did serve a number of his partisan goals. The principles Van Buren enunciated determined his stand on national issues, mainly state's rights and weak central government, nationalism, executive restraint, curbs on the federal Supreme Court, silence on slavery, and state controlled economic development. On the local level, Van Buren thought the legislature, chosen by the popular will, should set statutes through majority rule. Lawyers were part of a republican government bureaucracy that implemented this theory. Local judicial officers, notably justices of the peace, the courts that were closet to the people and humanized the legal system, formed another part of his republican bureaucracy.

During his twenty-five years before the bar, Van Buren moved between two worlds, the law and politics, before settling in as a full-time politician by 1828. Yet throughout this dual career, and later when President, he thought and acted as an attorney by using the methodology, work habits, techniques, and cast of mind of an expert lawyer.

The factors that made Van Buren a great lawyer made him a great politician. His major political contribution to his era, the formation, operation, and justification of political parties, developed out of the process of preparing briefs geared on precedent and the law's formalism. As a result, the law gave him a sense of order that influenced party functions to proceed on an organized and regularized basis. The need to obey court decisions set the standard for his concept of party discipline. The methods of dealing sympathetically with clients and his judgment of them contributed to his political tact. The bonds of friendship he formed with other attorneys laid the foundation for the basic notion of loyalty that was central to the Albany Regency's mechanism. The need to advocate the best interest of clients, along with legal instrumentalism, formulated his political mixture of idealism, principle, and opportunism. The partisanship of the bench sharpened his ideas about the importance of patronage. The necessity of paying close attention to opposing counsels in court made him a good listener, a trait invaluable in a politician, because it taught him when to heed contrary views, when to be persuasive, when not to disturb public opinion. The nature of appellate litigation accentuated his cautious approach to politics—one which sometimes bordered on expediency—by waiting until all the evidence was accumulated and dispassionately scrutinized before acting. Van Buren may have achieved his political goals without the law through his innate talents, but the process would have been less sure.

Nowhere was this relationship between the law and politics more revealing than with Van Buren's contributions to the Jacksonian Movement, his alliance with Andrew Jackson, and the emergence of the Democratic party. As a legal and political innovator, Van Buren anticipated the Jacksonian concerns for individualism bounded by the institutional constraints of party, the accountability of judges in carrying out the public will, the expansion and enhancement of property rights to eliminate political deference and entrenched elites, majority rule, the sovereignty of the people, and the legislative supremacy over the judiciary. In the same way, Van Buren's Dutch-American sense of ethics as manifested in the law prefigured the Jacksonian commitment to civic betterment through the extension of personal liberty. By that standard, Van Buren advocated the abolishment of imprisonment for debt, the elimination of all relics of feudalism, and the implementation of democratic procedural modifications in the common law, such as adverse possession, due process, the sanctity of *habeas corpus,* easing restraints on bail, and shielding the rights of women. Likewise, when Van Buren served as a state senator and attorney general, he anticipated later Jacksonian beliefs in measured economic growth by individual entrepreneurs, anti-monopolism, fiscal restraint, state control of banking, equal opportunity, and ending unfair privilege.

But Van Buren's conservatism contravened other aspects of Jacksonianism. Because of his commitment to preserving certain parts of the existing judicial system, Van Buren's support of appointive justices of the peace and incumbent Supreme Court judges countered the Jacksonian faith in popularly-elected public officials and rotation in office. By contrast, Van Buren's conservativism did reflect the Jacksonian stress on maintaining the Jeffersonian principles of states' rights, frugal government, racism, executive restraint, and strict construction of the Constitution.

Van Buren's twenty-five-year career as first a lawyer, then a lawyer and politician, reveal his place as a transitional figure in ideology, law, and politics. His ultimate legacy to Andrew Jackson, Jacksonianism, and the Democratic party blended the classical republican and liberal republican characteristics that typified his professional life.

In the final analysis, Alexis de Tocqueville put Van Buren's overlapping life in ideology, law, and politics into perspective. "The government of democracy is favorable to the political power of lawyers," he observed. When mass voting excluded traditional leaders from governing, lawyers took "possession," because "they are the only men of information and sagacity, beyond the sphere of the people, who can be the object of the popular choice." Without "this admixture of lawyer-like sobriety with the democratic principle, I question whether democratic institutions could long be maintained."[12]

Martin Van Buren's dual career proved de Tocqueville was correct. By linking classical republicanism and liberal republicanism with political equalitarianism, majoritarianism, and the viability of a party system, Van Buren created the possibilities for a democratic government and an expanding economy, no matter their imperfections. In this process, Van Buren irrevocably intertwined ideology, law, and politics as he began the next phase of his life, which led to the White House.

Glossary of Legal Terms

These definitions are adapted from *Black's Law Dictionary*. Other definitions are supplied in text.

Adverse possession   A doctrine that allows a person, who has lived on another's real property without challenge for a statutory period, to acquire title to that real property.

Alienate   The transfer of title to real property.

Appellant   A party who seeks to reverse a finding through an appeal to a higher court.

Appellant brief   A written statement that a counsel prepares and files with an appellant court; it explains why a trial court has acted correctly or incorrectly on points of law.

Appellate court   A higher court that has jurisdiction on points of law in cases of appeal and review.

Assign   The transfer or designation of interest in real property to another.

Assignment   The transfer to another of an interest in real property, personal property, or a negotiable instrument.

Assumpsit   A common law action in which a party seeks damages for failure to fulfill an expressed or implied contract; for default of a promise to pay moneys due; or for the failure to perform a legal contract.

Attorn   An agreement in which a tenant transfers and acknowledges obligations to a new landlord.

Bail   The monetary amount set by a judge as a condition for a pretrial release of a prisoner to ensure future appearance in court, with the stipulation that the prisoner remain within court jurisdiction.

Bill of Certiorari   A procedure filed in chancery that seeks to remove an equity suit in an inferior court to chancery, on the grounds of inconvenience to the parties or the inferior court's incompetency.

Bill of exceptions   A written statement that seeks review by an appellate court on the basis of irregularity; it contains all circuit court proceedings and the ruling purporting to be grounds for error.

Cartel   Agreements formed by belligerents authorizing nonhostile intercourse otherwise illegal in wartime.

Certiorari   A discretionary writ in which a superior court requires a review of proceedings in an inferior court; it includes a full record of the inferior court's proceedings.

Complaint   A civil law legal document filed by a plaintiff that alleges damages or liabilities against a defendant; a civil law legal document filed by a plaintiff that accuses a defendant of a criminal act.

Consideration   The inducement of a contracting party to form a contract; something given in return for a service.

Conversion   The wrongful taking of ownership rights to tangible goods that belong to another for one's own use.

Damages   The compensation, usually monetary, that may be recovered through courts by any person for some injury.

Deed   A written legal document, fully executed and recorded, that conveys real property from one party to another.

Defendant   The party required to answer in a suit at law; the accused in a criminal case.

Demand To make a formal claim; to assert a legal right; to petition a court for relief; to require a party to refrain from some unlawful activity.

Demurer A pleading filed to dismiss a case, because the opposite party lacks insufficient grounds in law to proceed.

Deposition Part of discovery; the taking of sworn pretrial oral or written interrogatories from a witness.

Devise The disposition of real property through a will.

Devolve Denotes the passing or transfer of an estate from one party to another; this usually applies to real property passed or transfered through a will.

Discovery A pretrial procedure to ascertain facts in a suit at law previously unknown or hidden.

Distributive Justice The obligation of the community or a legislative body to an individual or groups of individuals in the allocation of risks and benefits; involves a fair distribution of common duties and common burdens.

Distraint A landlord's inchoate right under the common law to seize the property of a tenant located on the landlord's property.

Distress A landlord's right under the common law to seize a tenant's goods and chattels, without court approval, to satisfy back rent.

Dower A provision that allows a widow to receive interest in her husband's real property or estate for her support and her children's nurture as long as she lives.

Due process The constitutional guarantees in the Fourth and Fifth Amendments that outline the process necessary before a person is deprived of life, liberty, or property.

Ejectment A common law action to recover the possession of land and to claim damages for the wrongful use by another.

Entail A process to limit the devolvement of real property to certain heirs.

Equity The jurisdiction, paralleling the common law, that encompasses a variety of procedures to provide equitable rather than legal solutions to conflicts. In New York, the Court of Chancery, under an appointive chancellor, heard cases in equity.

Estate in fee tail A freehold estate that passes to a donee's lawful children and, through them, to his grandchildren.

Estoppel A motion to prevent a party in a suit at law from denying or alleging a fact, which the other party had relied upon and which contradicted those alleged facts.

Escheat Property reverting to the state when a person died intestate.

Estovers The right or privilege of a tenant to cut a certain amount of wood from a demised premise for own use as fuel, fences, or other agrarian needs.

Fee simple A freehold estate in which a person holds an absolute interest.

Femes covert A married woman, whose legal rights and property are merged with her husband.

Femes sole A single woman, either unmarried, divorced, or widowed.

Freehold An estate, either in land or real property, held for life or in fee.

Ground rent The rent due a landlord for a tenant's use of real property, usually involving a three-lives lease, with the landlord retaining title to the real property.

Injunction A Court of Chancery judicial order commanding a person to perform or cease an act.

Indictment A formal accusation, presented by a grand jury, that charges a person with committing a criminal act.

Interrogatory Related to discovery; written questions that a counsel presents from one party to another party, witnesses, or those who have an interest in the suit at law.

Intestate A legal condition in which a person dies without recording a will.

Irregularity Improper procedure during a suit a law; grounds for an appeal.

Lease An agreement that sets the formal terms for the rental of real property.

Leasehold The real property that a tenant holds under the terms of a formal lease.

Legal Instrumentalism A doctrine that judges the law as an instrument of policy, adjusted to changing conditions, not a set of immutable principles.

Legal Positivism A doctrine holding that the law should reflect the majority will; that the legislature, chosen by the people has supremacy over judges; and that judges must interpret statutory law, not make law through their opinions.

Libel A type of defamation that appears in some printed form.

Life estate An estate in real property of limited duration, possessed during the lifetime of the person who holds it, or some other person; the legal arrangement under which the beneficiary is entitled to income from the estate for the duration of that person's life.

Livery of seisin A formal ceremony for the conveyance of property by a grantor to grantee.

Mandamus A writ issued by a superior jurisdiction ordering the performance of some public duty required by law.

Mandate A court order, either in written or oral form, that a person or persons must obey.

Negligence The failure to perform an act that a reasonable and prudent person would do or, conversely, what a reasonable and prudent person would *not* do; a breach of duty; the obligation of a person to use reasonable care and not injure another.

Negotiable Instrument A written and signed unconditional legal instrument, such as a check or bond, with transferability from one party to another; the second or third party holder holds the same rights as the original holder.

Nonsuit The judgment against a plaintiff unable to prove a suit at law; a court order terminating a suit at law without prejudice.

Parol Evidence Oral or verbal evidence.

Per curiam A court decision rendered under the authority of the whole court rather than an opinion issued by one judge.

Personal recognizance Common law forms that allow a sheriff to release an accused prisoner from custody, before a trial is held, without requiring a money bond or some other form of security.

Plaintiff A party who brings a suit at law; a party who seeks relief for some wrong.

Plea A common law form in which a defendant first answers a plaintiff's declaration and demand; in criminal law, the accused party's answer to a charge or indictment.

Pleadings A written statement prepared by advocates in a cause at law that contains the respective claims and defenses to be presented in a trial.

Power of attorney A written statement in which one party appoints another as his or her agent and gives that agent authority to act on his or her behalf.

Power of sale A summary foreclosure by a mortgage holder if the borrower defaulted.

Praecipe A writ that commands a defendant to perform some act, or to show cause for not performing that act; drawn as an alternative that gives an option or choice; includes an order to a clerk of courts to execute a judgment previously decided.

Precedent A court decision that furnishes the authority for subsequent identical or similar questions of law; it sets the basis for ruling on cases based on principles laid down in prior cases.

Prior restraint A form of censorship that requires a public official either to clear or eliminate material in a newspaper prior to publication.

Private law That part of the law that defines, regulates, enforces, and administrates relationships among individuals.

Procedural law That part of the law that prescribes the manner in which a person may exercise rights and responsibilities enforceable in a court.

Proceeding The regular and orderly form of conducting judicial business in court or before a judicial officer.

Public Law That part of the law that concerns the rights, obligations, and capacities of the state in its political and sovereign character.

Pure allodium Land absolutely held in one's own right.

Quit A notice to a tenant to surrender the premises.

Quitrent A fixed payment that a tenant under socage makes to a landlord in goods or services as commutation from certain feudal obligations.

Quo warranto A common law writ ordering a defendant to show cause under what right that party exercises a franchise or liberty; to prevent an exercise of power not conferred by statute.

Recapture A sheriff's retaking of a accused prisoner under common law forms.

Remand An appellate court's action to send a case back to the trial court for new hearings or a new trial.

Remainder interest That part of an estate that passes from a holder of a life estate to a third party after the death of the holder of the life estate; a future interest in a life estate.

Remedy A means under which a right is enforced, or a wrong is prevented, corrected, or compensated.

Replication A formal reply to a plea.

Replevin A legal action to recover goods and chattel from a person who has wrongfully converted such goods and chattel.

Seisin The possession of real property held through absolute title under a freehold.

Settlement An agreement between contending parties to adjust disputed matters.

Severalty An estate held as freehold personal property without another sharing in the ownership.

Socage The form of feudal tenure under which a tenant held land in consideration of certain services, duties, rents, or obligations due a landlord.

Substantive law That part of the law that deals with the nature and substance of law.

Surety A bondsman.

Special verdict A jury finding based on the facts in a trial, but which allows the court to determine a difficult point of law.

Stare decisis A judicial policy to abide by precedent laid down in previous decisions in which the facts are substantially the same; to adhere to previously determined cases.

Supersedeas A formal common law writ that contains an order to stay proceedings in a suit at law; a command from an appellate court to a trial court to suspend the execution of an judgment under appeal.

Tenure A system of landownership resulting from feudalism in which real property was held by a superior over an inferior.

Title The formal ownership of property in real property law.

Trespass A common law action brought to recover damages to one's person or property.

Trover A common law action to recover the value of goods or chattels wrongfully converted to another's use.

Venue The particular geographic place for a trial held by an appropriate court with the proper jurisdiction.

Waste A tenant's action, inaction, or spoilation in causing unreasonable harm to a landlord's material interest in that property.

Will Theory of Contracts A legal doctrine that stresses intent as the key to forming and implementing contracts; it assumes that equity exists between the private parties who made a contract, and that courts should not be concerned with equity in the contract.

Writ of error A mistaken application of the law, or an irregular interpretation of the law, about the facts in a suit at law, which furnishes ground for review.

Notes

ABBREVIATIONS

AHR	*American Historical Review*
AJLH	*American Journal of Legal History*
CU	Columbia University, New York, N.Y.
JAH	*The Journal of American History*
JAS	*The Journal of American Studies*
JER	*The Journal of the Early Republic*
JSNY	*Journal of the Senate of the State of New-York*
LC	The Library of Congress
MHS	Massachusetts Historical Society, Boston
MVB	Martin Van Buren
NYH	*New York History*
NYHS	New-York Historical Society
NYHSQ	*New-York Historical Society Quarterly*
NYPL	New York Public Library, New York, N.Y.
NYSA	New York State Archives, Albany, N.Y.
NYSL	New York State Library, New York, N.Y.
PNYH	*Proceedings of the New York State Historical Association*
SAQ	*The South Atlantic Quarterly*
VBA	"The Autobiography of Martin Van Buren"
VBL	The Papers of Martin Van Buren, Chadwyck-Healy Microfilms
VBLC	Martin Van Buren Papers, Library of Congress

1: THE MAKING OF A REPUBLICAN DUAL CAREER

1. John Niven, *Martin Van Buren: The Romantic Age of American Politics* (New York: Oxford Univ. Press, 1983), 215–222; John S. Jenkins, *The Lives of the Governors of the State of New York* (Auburn: Derby & Miller, 1852), 374.

2. John C. Fitzpatrick, ed., "The Autobiography of Martin Van Buren," *Annual Report of the American Historical Association for the Year 1918* (Washington, D.C.: Government Printing Office, 1920), II: 21, hereafter cited as *VBA*.

3. Arnold J. F. Van Laer, ed., "Some Early Dutch Manuscripts," *PNYH* 20 (October 1922): 229–230; Frank J. Conkling, "Martin Van Buren, With a Sketch of the Van Buren Family in America," *New York Genealogical and Biographical Record* 28 (July and October 1897): 124; Harriet C. Peckham, *History of Cornelis Maessem Van Buren . . . and His Descendants* (New York: Tobias W. Wright, 1913), 7–620; Alice P. Kenney, "Private Worlds in the Middle Colonies: An Introduction to Human Tradition in American History," *NYH* 51 (January 1970): 3–31; Alice P. Kenney, *Stubborn for Liberty: The Dutch in New York* (Syracuse: Syracuse Univ. Press, 1975), 86–89, 96, 104, 127; Donald C. Cole, *Martin Van Buren and the American Political System* (Princeton: Princeton Univ. Press, 1984), 11.

4. Peckham, *Van Buren,* 233–365; Conkling, *Van Buren,* 210; William M. Holland, *Life and Political Opinions of Martin Van Buren, Vice President of the United States* (Hartford: Belknap & Hammersley, 1835), 2–3; Denis T. Lynch, *An Epoch and a Man: Martin Van Buren and His Times* (New York: Horace Liveright, 1929), 28; *Hudson Weekly Gazette,* Dec. 6, 1791, Feb. 17, 1792; Cole, *Van Buren,* 12–13; *VBA,* 10–11.

5. Bureau of the Census, *Heads of Families at the First Census of the United States Taken in the Year 1790: New York* (Washington, D.C.: Government Printing Office, 1908), 67–70; *VBA,* 10; William L. Mackenzie, *Life and Times of Martin Van Buren* (Boston: Cooke, 1846), 18; Holland, *Van Buren,* 14; Peckham, *Van Buren,* 88, 90, 99; Cole, *Van Buren,* 10–11.

6. Henry W. Scott, *The Courts of the State of New York: Their History, Development and Jurisdiction* (New York: Wilson Publishing, 1909), 3–126; Paul M. Hamlin and Charles E. Baker, *Supreme Court of Judicature of the Province of New York, 1691–1704* (New York: NYHS, 1952), 3–77; Michael G. Kammen, *Colonial New York: A History* (New York: Charles Scribner's Sons, 1975), 129–130; Donna Merwick, "Becoming English: Anglo-Dutch Conflict in the 1670s in Albany, New York," *NYH* 61 (October 1981): 389–414; Donna Merwick, "Being Dutch: An Interpretation of Why Jacob Leisler Died," *NYH* 70 (October 1989): 373–404.

7. Alice P. Kenney, "Dutch Patricians in Colonial New York," *NYH* 49 (July 1968): 383–407; Donna Merwick, "Dutch Townsmen and Land Use: A Spatial Perspective on Seventeenth-Century Albany, New York," *William and Mary Quarterly,* 3rd ser., 37 (January 1980): 53–78; David S. Cohen, "How Dutch were the Dutch of New Netherland?" *NYH* 62 (January 1980): 43–55; Thomas E. Burke, Jr., *Mohawk Frontier: The Dutch Community of Schnectaday, New York, 1661–1710* (Ithaca: Cornell Univ. Press, 1991), 196–222; Joyce D. Goodfriend, *Before the Melting Pot: Society and Culture in Colonial New York City, 1664–1730* (Princeton: Princeton Univ. Press, 1991), 20–21, 187–221; David S. Cohen, *The Dutch-American Farm* (New York: New York Univ. Press, 1992), 65–148.

8. J. E. Crowley, *This Sheba, Self: The Conceptualization of Economic Life in Eighteenth Century America* (Baltimore: Johns Hopkins Univ. Press, 1974), 76–124; John J.

McCusker and Russell R. Menard, *The Economy of British America, 1607–1789* (Chapel Hill: Univ. of North Carolina Press, 1985), 82, 115, 191–188; David A. Armour, *The Merchants of Albany, New York: 1686–1760* (New York: Garland, 1986), 106–243; Milton M. Klein, "From Community to Status: The Development of the Legal Profession in Colonial New York," *NYH* 55 (April 1979): 132–157.

9. Horatio Gates Stafford, *A Gazetteer of the State of New York* (Albany: H. C. Southwick, 1813), 70–224; Stephen B. Miller, *Historical Sketches of Hudson, Embracing the Settlement of the City, City Government, Business Enterprises, Churches, Press, Schools, Libraries* (Hudson: Bryan & Webb, 1862); Franklin Ellis, *History of Columbia County, New York, with Illustrations and Biographical Sketches of some of Its Prominent Men* (Philadelphia: Everts & Ensign, 1878), 127–219; Dixon R. Fox, *The Decline of Aristocracy in the Politics of New York, 1801–1840* (New York: Columbia Univ. Press, 1919), 39–40; David M. Ellis, *Landlords and Farmers in the Hudson-Mohawk Region* (Ithaca: Cornell Univ. Press, 1946), 6–36; David M. Ellis "The Yankee Invasion of New York, 1783–1850," *NYH* 32 (January 1951): 1–17; David G. Hackett, *The Rude Hand of Innovation: Religion and Social Order in Albany, New York 1652–1836* (New York: Oxford Univ. Press, 1991), 57–75.

10. *Hudson Weekly Gazette,* May 18, Sept. 20, 1786, Apr. 26, Dec. 6, 1787, Jan. 20, April 7, 28, 1789, Feb. 7, 1788, Feb. 28, 1793; Edward Collier, *A History of Old Kinderhook* (New York: G. P. Putnam's Sons, 1914), 205–210, 324–332.

11. Oliver A. Rink, *Holland on the Hudson: An Economic and Social History of Dutch New York* (Ithaca: Cornell Univ. Press, 1968), 94–136; Sung Bok Kim, *Landlord and Tenant in Colonial New York: Manorial Society, 1664–1775* (Chapel Hill: Univ. of North Carolina Press, 1978), 3–128.

12. Beverley W. Bond, Jr., *The Quit-Rent System in the American Colonies* (New Haven: Yale Univ. Press, 1919), 254–416, 433, 444; Jeannette B. Sherwood, "The Military Tract," *PNYH* 24 (1926): 169–179; Ulysses P. Hedrick, *A History of Agriculture in the State of New York* (Albany: J. B. Lyon, 1933), 40–63; Alfred N. Chandler, *Land Title Origins: A Tale of Force and Fraud* (New York: Robert Schalkenback Foundation, 1945), 164–220.

13. Charles W. Spencer, "The Land System of Colonial New York," *PNYH* 16 (1917): 150–164; Don R. Gerlach, *Philip Schuyler and the American Revolution in New York, 1733–1777* (Lincoln: Univ. of Nebraska Press, 1964), 324–327; Patricia U. Bonomi, *A Factious People: Politics and Society in Colonial New York* (New York: Columbia Univ. Press, 1971), 179–228; Kammen, *Colonial New York,* 34.

14. Robert L. Fowler, *History of the Law of Real Property in New York: An Essay Introductory to the Study of the New York Revised Statutes* (New York: Baker, Voorhis, 1895), 118; Kim, *Landlord and Tenant,* 137–280; Young, *Democratic Republicans,* 97, 262–267; Irving Mark, *Agrarian Conflicts in Colonial New York, 1711–1775* (New York: Columbia Univ. Press, 1940), 202–206; Edward Countryman, *A People in Revolution: The American Revolution and Political Society in New York, 1760–1790* (Baltimore: Johns Hopkins Univ. Press, 1981), 221–251; Edward T. Price, *Dividing the Land: Early American Beginnings of Our Private Property Mosaic* (Chicago: Univ. of Chicago Press, 1995), 211–244.

15. Fowler, *Real Property,* 40–42; Mark, *Agrarian Conflicts,* 85–106; Peter C. Hoffer, *Law and People in Colonial America* (Baltimore: Johns Hopkins Univ. Press, 1992), 1–72; Cynthia A. Kierner, *Traders and Gentlefolk: The Livingstons of New York, 1675–1790* (Ithaca: Cornell Univ. Press, 1992), 92–95, 201–251.

16. Milton L. Klein, "Democracy and Politics in Colonial New York," *NYH* 40 (July 1959): 221–246; Nicholas Varga, "Election Procedures and Practices in Colonial New York," *NYH* 46 (July 1960): 249–277; Mark, *Agrarian Conflicts,* 131–163; Chilton Williamson, *American Suffrage, from Property to Democracy, 1760–1860* (Princeton: Princeton Univ. Press, 1960), 27–29; Kim, *Landlord and Tenant,* 281–415; Kierner, *Traders and Gentlefolk,* 110–119.

17. Ellis, *Landlords and Farmers,* 34–35; Kierner, *Traders and Gentlefolk,* 247.

18. *Daniel Frier and Peter Cooper, Plaintiff in Error, v. James Jackson, ex. dem., Johannis L. Van Allen and John J. Van Allen, Defendant in Error,* William Johnson, *Cases Argued and Determined in the Supreme Court of Judicature and in the Court for the Trial of Impeachments and Correction of Errors, of the State of New-York* (New York: Banks & Bros., 1863), 8, 496–520 (1811), hereafter cited as *Johnson's Reports; Hudson Weekly Gazette,* Feb. 18, 1790; Collier, *Old Kinderhook,* 28–30, 44–85; S. G. Nissenson, "The Development of a Land Registration System in New York, *PNYH* 37 (January 1939): 26–27; Kim, *Landlord and Tenant,* 8–30. Various published cases in *Johnson's Reports* were inconsistent in capitalization; to avoid confusion, I have used the upper case. *Johnson's Reports* cited the term ex. dem. as an abbreviated form of ex demissione—a phrase that signified an ejectment action. In the judgment rolls prior to 1830, the Supreme Court used fictitious terms in an ejectment. "James Jackson" was the fictitious plaintiff if the actual defendant won the ejectment. If the actual plaintiff won, the judgment roll recorded either the defendant's real name or the fictitious "John Stiles."

19. *Map of the Division of the Kinderhook Patent Granted in 1686,* NYSL; Deed of Dirck Wessels Ten Broeck, April 18, 1711, NYSL; *Hudson Balance,* Jan. 5, 12, 19, Feb. 2, 9, 16, Mar. 2, 1802; Ellis, *Columbia County,* 15–23, 220.

20. Edward B. O'Callaghan, *Documentary History of the State of New-York* (Albany: Weed, Parson, 1849), 3: 615–627, 644–50, 680, 690–702, 834–839; Lawrence H. Leder, *Robert Livingston, 1654–1728, and the Politics of Colonial New York* (Chapel Hill: Univ. of North Carolina Press, 1961), 23–53.

21. Copy of a Petition from Freeholders and Inhabitants of Kinderhook to the General Assembly of the Colony of New York, Dec. 23, 1769, NYSL; Collier, *Old Kinderhook,* 72–79.

22. Ellis, *Columbia County,* 211; Collier, *Old Kinderhook,* 81–82; Alice P. Kenney, "The Albany Dutch: Loyalists and Patriots," *NYH* 42 (October 1961): 331–350; Cynthia A. Kierner, "Landlord and Tenant in Revolutionary New York: The Case of Livingston Manor," *NYH* 70 (April 1989): 133–151.

23. *Hudson Weekly Gazette,* Sept. 20, 27, Dec. 6, 1787, March 13, 20, June 17, 24, Sept. 9, 1788, Feb. 17, 24, Apr. 21, 28, 1789, June 3, 1790, Apr. 21, Nov. 10, 1791, Feb. 28, July 19, 1792, March 7, 1793, Feb. 20, 1794; Fox, *Decline of Aristocracy,* 39–46, 237, 266; De Alva S. Alexander, *A Political History of the State of New York* (New York: Henry Holt, 1906–1924), 1: 28–39; *VBA,* 18–19; Linda Grant De Pauw, *The Eleventh Pillar: New York State and the Federal Constitution* (Ithaca: Cornell Univ. Press, 1966); Alfred F. Young, *The Democratic Republicans of New York: Their Origins, 1763–1797* (Chapel Hill: Univ. of North Carolina Press, 1967), 71–72, 85, 87, 133.

24. Jabez D. Hammond, *The History of Political Parties in the State of New York, From the Ratification of the Federal Constitution to December, 1840* (Albany: C. Van Benthuysen, 1842), 1: 1–93; Young, *Democratic Republicans,* 109–412; Nobel Cunningham, *The Jeffersonian Republicans: The Formation of Party Organization, 1789–1801* (Chapel Hill: Univ. of North Carolina Press, 1957), 3–115; Cole, *Van Buren,* 15.

25. *Hudson Gazette,* Apr. 10, 1799, Mar. 24, Apr. 14, 21, Aug. 1, 22, 1801; *VBA,* 13–14; Holland, *Van Buren,* 50–56; Jenkins, *Governors,* 353; Shepard, *Van Buren,* 39–40.

26. *VBA,* 9, 112, 185–187; Martin Van Buren, *Inquiry into the Origin and Course of Political Parties in the United States* (New York: Hurd & Houghton, 1867), 233–272, hereafter cited as *Inquiry.*

27. Holland, *Van Buren,* 34–50; Max Mintz, "The Political Ideas of Martin Van Buren," *NYH* 30 (October 1949): 422–448; Marvin Meyers, *The Jacksonian Persuasion: Politics and Belief* (Stanford: Stanford Univ. Press, 1957), 143–162, 280–282; Joseph G. Rayback, "Martin Van Buren: His Place in the History of New York and the United States," *NYH* 64 (April 1983): 122–123; *VBA,* 502.

28. Kenney, *Stubborn for Liberty,* 4, 43, 229, 265–266; *VBA,* 8, 9, 19, 34, 139–140, 400, 509, 678, 772.

29. Hendrik Hartog, *Public Property and Private Power: The Corporation of the City of New York in American Law, 1730–1870* (Chapel Hill: Univ. of North Carolina Press, 1983); James A. Henretta, "The Slow Triumph of Liberal Individualism: Law and Politics in New York, 1780–1860," in *American Chameleon: Individualism in Trans-National Context,* ed. by Richard O. Curry and Lawrence B. Goodheart (Kent: Kent State Univ. Press, 1991), 87–106.

2: LEGAL TRAINING, THE DUAL CAREER, AND REPUBLICANISM

1. *VBA,* 11; Milton M. Klein, "Prelude to Revolution in New York: Jury Trials and Judicial Tenure," *William and Mary Quarterly,* 3rd ser., 17 (October 1960): 439–407; Milton M. Klein, "New York Lawyers and the Coming of the Revolution," *NYH* (October 1974): 383–407; Cole, *Van Buren,* 14–15; Kermit L. Hall, *The Magic Mirror: Law in American History* (New York: Oxford Univ. Press, 1989), 22–23.

2. James Willard Hurst, *The Growth of American Law: The Law Makers* (Boston: Little, Brown, 1950), 249–252, 377–375; Maxwell Bloomfield, *American Lawyers in a Changing Society, 1776–1876* (Cambridge: Harvard Univ. Press, 1976), 32–58.

3. Anton-Herman Chroust, *Rise of the Legal Profession in America: Revolutionary and Post-Revolutionary Era* (Norman: Univ. of Oklahoma Press, 1965), 2: 3–91. See for example, *Laws of the State of New-York Passed at the Session of the Legislature Held in the Year 1801, Being the Twenty-Fourth Session, Including the Acts Commonly Called Revised Acts of that Session* (Albany: Weed, Parsons, 1887), 5: chap. 190, 553–571.

4. Erwin C. Currency, "The Lawyer and the American Revolution," *AJLH* 8 (April 1964): 125–132; Daniel H. Calhoun, *Professional Lives in America: Structure and Aspirations, 1750–1850* (Cambridge: Harvard Univ. Press, 1965), 9–10, 179–181; Maxwell Bloomfield, "Lawyers and Public Criticism: Challenge and Response in Nineteenth-Century America," *AJLH* 15 (October 1971): 269–277.

5. Holland, *Van Buren,* 27–28; Edward M. Shepard, *Martin Van Buren* (Boston: Houghton, Mifflin, 1899), 19; Collier, *Old Kinderhook,* 88–124, 390–444; Milton M. Klein, "The Rise of the New York Bar: The Legal Career of William Livingston," *William and Mary Quarterly,* 3rd ser., 15 (July 1958): 334–358.

6. *VBA,* 12–13.

7. Holland, *Van Buren,* 14–16; Collier, *Old Kinderhook,* 284; George R. Howell

and Jonathan Tenney, *Bi-Centennial History of Albany, History of the County of Albany, N. Y., From 1609–1886* (Albany: W. W. Munsell, 1886), 135; *VBA,* 11; Niven, *Van Buren,* 7; Cole, *Van Buren,* 14.

8. Lawrence M. Friedman, *A History of American Law* (New York: Simon and Schuster, 1973), 20, 275–280.

9. Holland, *Van Buren,* 25–26; Adrian Hoffman Joline, "Martin Van Buren, Lawyer," *The Autograph Hunter and Other Papers* (Chicago: Alderbrink Press, 1907), 51–92; Niven, *Van Buren,* 8.

10. Nathaniel H. Carter, William L. Stone, and Marcus T.C. Gould, *Reports of the Proceedings and Debates of the Convention of 1821, Assembled for the Purpose of Amending the Constitution of the State of New-York: Containing All the Official Documents, Relating to the Subject, and Other Valuable Materials* (Albany: E. and E. Hosford, 1821), 18–19, hereafter cited as *Proceedings and Debates;* Charles A. Collin, "Statutory Revision in New York," *Albany Law Journal* 49 (January 1894): 72–76; Mark De Wolfe Howe, "The Process of Outlawry in New York: A Study of the Selective Reception of English Law," *Cornell Law Quarterly* 23 (June 1938): 559–563; Benjamin F. Butler, John Duer and John C. Spencer, *New York Commissioners to Revise the Statute Law of the State of New-York,* 3 vols. (Albany: Packard and Van Bethuysen, 1829).

11. Carter, Stone, and Gould, *Proceedings and Debates,* 3; John T. Kirkpatrick, "The Revised Statutes of New York," *Law Library Journal* 19 (March 1926): 72–79; Paul M. Hamlin, *Legal Education in Colonial New York* (1939; reprint, New York: Da Capo Press, 1970), 120–130; Elizabeth G. Brown, *British Statutes in American Law, 1776–1836* (Ann Arbor: Univ. of Michigan Press, 1974), 69–72.

12. Hamlin, *Legal Education,* 132, 216.

13. Ibid., 131, 214; John Theodore Horton, *James Kent: A Study in Conservatism* (1939; reprint, New York: Da Capo Press, 1976), 99.

14. Holland, *Van Buren,* 25; Henry C. Van Schaack, *The Life of Peter Van Schaack, LL.D.* (New York: D. Appleton, 1842), 443–444; Lynch, *An Epoch and a Man,* 33; Holmes Alexander, *The American Talleyrand: The Career and Contemporaries of Martin Van Buren, Eighth President* (New York: Harper and Bros., 1935), 28; Bloomfield, *American Lawyers,* 1–31; *VBA,* 11.

15. Holland, *Van Buren,* 25–26; *VBA,* 13–14; Shepard, *Van Buren,* 16.

16. Hamlin, *Legal Education,* 40–41; Lynch, *An Epoch and a Man,* 35.

17. *VBA,* 13; William A. Butler, *Martin Van Buren: Lawyer, Statesman and Man* (New York: D. Appleton, 1862), 7–8; Hamlin, *Legal Education,* 56–72; John H. Moore, "One Hundred Fifty Years of Official Law Reporting and the Courts of New York," *Syracuse Law Review* 6 (spring 1955): 273–279; Julius Markle and Richard Sloane, *Legal Research and Law Library Management* (New York: Law Journal Seminars-Press, 1982), 43–53; Frederick Kemplin, Jr., "Precedent and Stare Decisis: The Critical Years," *AJLH* 3 (January 1959): 28–54.

18. William Wyche, *Treatise on the Practice of the Supreme Court of Judicature of the State of New-York in Civil Actions* (New York: T. and J. Swords, 1794); Thomas Spencer, *The New Vade Macum; Or Young Clerk's Magazine* (Lansingburgh: Silvester Tiffany, 1794); Charles R. Webster, *The Clerk's Magazine* (Albany: N.p., 1800); Herbert A. Johnson, "Civil Procedure in John Jay's New York," *AJLH* 11 (January 1967): 79–80.

19. Shepard, *Van Buren,* 17; Niven, *Van Buren,* 8.

20. Holland, *Van Buren,* 15, 23; *VBA,* 11.

21. Alden Chester, ed., *Legal and Judicial History of New York* (New York: Na-

tional American Society, 1911), 1: 346; Hoffer *Law and People,* 7–10, 26–27, 37, 66.

22. Holland, *Van Buren,* 26–28; Levi Beardsley, *Reminiscences, Personal and Other Incidents; Early Settlement of Otsego County; Notices and Anecdotes of Public Men; Judicial, Legal and Legislative Matters; Field Sports; Dissertations and Discussions* (New York: Vinten, 1852), 184–190; Lynch, *An Epoch and a Man,* 35.

23. Alexander, *American Talleyrand,* 33; *VBA,* 11.

24. *Albany New-York Statesman,* Dec. 26, 1820.

25. Charles Edwards, *Pleasantries about Courts and Lawyers of the State of New York* (New York: Richardson, 1867), 172; Shepard, *Van Buren,* 17; Howell and Tenney, *Bi-Centennial History,* 135; Joline, *Autograph Hunter,* 58.

26. Butler, *Van Buren,* 10; *VBA,* 13; David Hackett Fischer, *The Revolution of American Conservatism: The Federalist Party in the Era of Jeffersonian Democracy* (New York: Harper & Row, 1969).

27. Cole, *Van Buren,* 15.

28. *Hudson Gazette,* Sept. 15, 22, Nov. 10, 1801; Hudson *Balance,* May 4, 1802; Holland, *Van Buren,* 52; Niven, *Van Buren,* 8–10; *VBA,* 13–14.

29. *VBA,* 14; MVB to William P. Van Ness, Sept. 28, 1802, VBL; MVB to John P. Van Ness, Dec. 3, 1802, VBL; Cole, *Van Buren,* 16–17.

30. Information derived from Van Buren's letters to Van Ness, cited above.

31. MVB to John P. Van Ness, Dec. 3, 1802, VBL.

32. MVB to John P. Van Ness, Dec. 27, 1802, Jan. 6, 1803, Jan. [n.d.], Apr. 1, May 3, 21, 26, 30, Sept. 10, 1803, VBL.

33. MVB to John P. Van Ness, Dec. 3, 27, 1802, Apr. 1, May 3, 21, 30, Sept. 10, 1803, VBL; John P. Van Ness to MVB, Jan. 6, 1803, John Van Alen to MVB, May 26, 1803, VBLC.

34. MVB to John P. Van Ness, Dec. 3, 27, 1802, VBL.

35. MVB to John P. Van Ness, Dec. 3, 27, 1802, VBL; *VBA,* 14–15.

36. MVB to Francis Silvester, Dec. 12, 1802, John C. Hogeboom to MVB, Mar. 14, 1803, VBLC; MVB to John P. Van Ness, Apr. 1, May 21, 1803, VBL.

37. MVB to John P. Van Ness, Dec. 3, 1803, John P. Van Ness to MVB, Jan. 6, 1803, VBLC; Cole, *Van Buren,* 17.

38. MVB to John P. Van Ness, Jan. [n.d.], May 3, 1803, VBL.

39. MVB to John P. Van Ness, Jan. [n.d.], 1803, VBL; *Hudson Gazette,* May 3, 1803.

40. John C. Hogeboom to MVB, Mar. 14, 1803, VBLC; MVB to John P. Van Ness, Dec. 27, 1802, Jan. [n.d.], 1803, VBL.

41. Aaron Burr to Edward Livingston, Feb. 12, 1801, Aaron Burr Papers, NYSL; Burr to Albert Gallatin, Feb. 12, 25, 1801, Albert Gallatin Papers, NYHS; Nathan Schachner, *Aaron Burr: A Biography* (New York: Frederick A. Stokes, 1937), 188–209.

42. Hammond, *Political History,* 1: 79–82, 83–86, 152–153, 155–160; Charles Z. Lincoln, *Constitutional History of New York* (Rochester: Lawyers Cooperative Publishing, 1906), 1: 191, 178–191; Howard McBain, *De Witt Clinton and the Origins of the Spoils System in New York* (Columbia Univ. Press, 1907), 35–42, 83–96; Milton Lomask, *Aaron Burr: The Years from Princeton to Vice President, 1756–1805* (New York: Farrar, Straus, Giroux, 1979), 262–265, 301, 304–5; Craig R. Hanyan, *De Witt Clinton: Years of Molding, 1769–1807* (New York: Garland Publishing, 1988), 174–226.

43. John P. Van Ness to William P. Van Ness, Apr. 2, June 9, 1802, John Swartwout

to William P.Van Ness, Feb. 9, 1803,Van Ness Papers, NYPL.

44. John Quincy Adams, *Memoirs of John Quincy Adams: Comprising Part of His Diary from 1795 to 1848,* ed. by Charles F. Adams (Philadelphia: J. B. Lippincott, 1877), 7: 272.

45. *VBA,* 15; Holland, *Van Buren,* 83; Lynch, *An Epoch and a Man,* 53.

46. MVB to John P.Van Ness, Jan. [n.d.], 1803, July 20, 1803, May 31, 30, Sept. 10, 1803,VBL.

47. MVB to William P. Van Ness, July 23, 1803,VBL; MVB to William P. Van Ness,Aug. 20, 23, 1803,VBL.

48. MVB to William P.Van Ness, July 20, MVB to William P.Van Ness,Aug. 23, Sept 10, MVB to John P.Van Ness, Sept. 10, October 26, John P.Van Ness to MVB, Nov. 11, 1803,VBL; *VBA,* 15.

49. MVB to John P.Van Ness, Sept. 10, Oct. 26, Nov. 25, 1803,VBL.

3: THE DUAL CAREER BEGINS

1. *VBA,* 21; Sean Wilentz, *Chants Democratic: New York City and the Rise of the American Working Class, 1788–1850* (New York: Oxford Univ. Press, 1984), 49–51, 401–402.

2. *Hudson Gazette,* May 3, 1803; *VBA,* 21–22; Shepard, *Van Buren,* 30–31; Payton F. Miller, *A Group of Lawyers of Columbia County, New York* (Hudson: De Vinne Press, 1904).

3. Statement of Van Alen and Van Buren's business from the Commencement of Firm until Mar. 19, 1805,VBLC.

4. Ibid; William P.Van Ness and John Woodworth, *Laws of the State of New-York, Revised and Passed at the Thirty-Sixth Session of the Legislature, with Marginal Notes & References, Published by the Revisors, William P. Van Ness and John Woodworth, Esq.* (Albany: H. C. Southwick, 1813), 2: chap. 65 (R.L.), 141–149.

5. Memorandum of Debts Due US and Debts Due, Mar. 19, 1805,VBLC; *VBA,* 22–24; Kinderhook Law Society, 1805, VBL; Columbia County Common Rule Book, Court of Common Pleas, 1804–1805, Hudson County Court House; Docket for Clerk of Circuit Court, Hudson County, Hudson County Court House.

6. Memorandum, Mar. 19, 1805,VBLC. Descriptions of actions derived from Henry C. Black, *Black's Law Dictionary,* 6th ed. (St. Paul:West Publishing, 1990).

7. *VBA,* 21; Statement of Van Alen and Van Buren, Mar. 19, 1805; Memorandum of Debts, Mar. 19, 1805,VBLC.

8. Accounts with the proprietors of the Great Possession, [1804–1808],VBLC; MVB to Manor Committee, Jan. 28, 1811,VBL; Ellis, *Columbia County,* 38–43, 220; Collier, *Kinderhook,* 50–79; Niven, *Van Buren,* 19.

9. Joline, *Autograph Hunter,* 51–92; Cole, *Van Buren,* 22–25. Inferences about Supreme Court cases based on *Johnson's Reports.*

10. Butler, *Van Buren,* 7, 8.

11. *Hudson Gazette,* Feb. 8, 1803; George Clinton to De Witt Clinton, Feb. 25, Sept. 7, Oct. 31, 1803, De Witt Clinton Papers, Butler Library, CU; Gallatin to Jefferson, June 16, 17, July 2, 1803, Thomas Jefferson Papers, LC; MVB to William P.Van Ness,Aug. 23, MVB to John P.Van Ness, Sept. 10, 1803,VBL; Hammond, *Political Parties,* 1: 91–185; Robert Ernst, *Rufus King: American Federalist* (Chapel Hill: Univ. of

North Carolina Press, 1968), 43–279.

12. Thomas Tillotson to James Madison, Dec. 2, 1803, James Madison Papers, LC; *New York Morning Chronicle,* Feb. 24, Apr. 18, 1804; John R. Livingston to Robert R. Livingston, Jan. 20, 1804, Livingston Family Papers, NYHS; *Poughkeepsie Journal,* Mar. 27, 1804; *Hudson Balance,* May 21, 1804.

13. *VBA,* 15–16; William P. Van Ness to MVB, Feb. 22, 1804, MVB to William P. Van Ness, Mar. 13, 1804, VBL; *VBA,* 15–16.

14. *Hudson Bee,* May 8, 1804, hereafter cited as *Bee; Hudson Balance,* May 21, 1804; *New York Republican Watch Tower,* June 13, 1804; *New York Evening Post,* Feb. 25, 1806, Mar. 24, 27, Apr. 3, 18, 1807; Matthew L. Davis to William P. Van Ness, Jan. 21, 1807, Van Ness Papers, NYPL; *New York American Citizen,* Feb. 17, March 19, 1807; Hammond, *Political Parties,* 1: 210–265.

15. MVB to William P. Van Ness, July 15, 1805, VBL; *Bee,* Apr. 21, 1806; *VBA,* 17; Niven, *Van Buren,* 20–21.

16. *Bee,* Mar. 2, 9, Apr. 2, May 14, 1805; Elisha Williams to Ebenezer Foote, Apr. 17, 1805, Ebenezer Foote Papers, NYSL.

17. *Bee,* July 16, 1805.

18. Charles Foote to Ebenezer Foote, Apr. 20, May 18, 1806, Foote Papers; *Bee,* Apr. 22, May 13, 1806; *Albany Register,* June 10, 1806.

19. De Witt Clinton to MVB, May 29, 1806, Martin Van Buren Collection, MHS; *Republican Watch Tower,* May 12, June 16, 1807; *Bee,* May 13, 1807.

20. *Bee,* Dec. 16, 1806, Jan. 20, 24, Mar. 17, Apr. 14, 21, 1807; *Republican Watch Tower,* Mar. 20, 1807. For examples of Van Buren's mature ideas on political organizations, see Robert V. Remini, *The Election of Andrew Jackson* (J. B. Lippincott, 1963), 18–19, 33–179; Alvin Kass, *Politics in New York State, 1800–1830* (Syracuse: Syracuse Univ. Press, 1965), 28–54; Niven, *Van Buren,* 65–69, 109–110.

21. Van Ness and Woodworth, *Laws of the State of New-York,* 2: chap. 35, 125–136; Thomas F. Gordon, *Gazetteer of the State of New York* (Philadelphia: T. K. & P. E. Collins, 1836), 157–162.

22. *Hudson Balance,* Apr. 8, 1806; Minutes of the New York State Supreme Court of Judicature, 2: Feb. 10, 11, 14, 1806, 392–393, 400, 403, NYSA; New York Supreme Court of Judicature, Docket of Judgements (Albany), 1806, Box 3, Vol. 4, Box 5, Vol. 5, NYSA.

23. Charles Foote to Ebenezer Foote, Oct. 17, 1805, Foote Papers; De Witt Clinton to MVB, May 29, 1806, Martin Van Buren Collection, MHS; Peter Van Schaack to MVB, Oct. 28, 1806, William Peter Van Ness to MVB, Feb. 21, 1807, VBL; Legal Record Book and a Statement of Van Buren's Notes, [Dec. 24, 1808], VBLC. Newspapers carried some evidence of Van Buren's practice at Hudson and Claverack.

24. Legal Record Book and A Statement of Van Buren's Notes, [Dec. 24, 1808], VBLC.

25. Butler, *Van Buren,* 12; Catherina Van Rensselaer Bonney, *A Legacy of Historical Gleanings* (Albany: J. Munsell, 1875), 2: 170; *VBA,* 21–22.

26. Figures derived from Memorandum of Debts, 1805, and Legal Record and Statement, [Dec. 24, 1808], VBLC; *Laws of the State of New-York, Containing all the Acts of the Thirtieth—and the Public Acts of the Thirty-first and Thirty-second Session of the Legislature, 1810, 1811, 1812* (Albany: Webster and Skinners, 1812), 6: chap. 238, 590.

27. Deed for House and Land in Kinderhook, New York, from John C. Hogenboom to MVB, Oct. 13, 1806, VBL; Indenture between Tobias D. Van Buren, Harmen

Vosburgh, and MVB, Oct. 16, 1808, VBL.

28. *VBA*, 26–27; Collier, *Kinderhook*, 82–84; *Frier and Cooper v. Jackson, ex dem. Van Allen and Van Allen*, 8 *Johnson's Reports*, 496–506 (1811).

29. Ibid.; Morton J. Horowitz, *The Transformation of American Law, 1780–1860* (Cambridge: Harvard Univ. Press, 1977), 43–47.

30. *Frier and Copper v. Jackson, ex dem. Van Allen and Van Allen*, 8 *Johnson's Reports*, 507.

31. *Bee*, Mar. 1, 1808; *Albany Argus*, Feb. 9, 1819, Apr. 19, 1830; Lynch, *Epoch and a Man*, 73; Cole, *Van Buren*, 20; Laura C. Holloway, *The Ladies of the White House, Or In the Homes of the Presidents* (Philadelphia: Bradley, 1881), 138, 140, 143, 317.

4: REPUBLICANISM IN LAW AND POLITICS

1. *Bee*, Mar. 1, 1808; Charles P. Daly, *History of the Court of Common Pleas for the City and County of New York* (New York: Smith's Common Pleas Reports, 1855), 51–57; Charles P. Daly, *The Nature, Extent and History of the Jurisdiction of Surrogate's Courts of the State of New York, Opinion of the Hon. Charles P. Daly* (New York: John A. Gray, 1863); Royden W. Vosburgh, "Surrogate Courts and Records in the Colony and State of New York, 1664–1847," *PNYH* 20 (1922): 108–117; Henry W. Scott, *The Courts of the State of New York: Their History, Development and Jurisdiction* (New York: Wilson, 1909), 361–363; Chester, *Legal and Judicial History*, 1: 357–360.

2. *Laws of the State of New-York Passed at the Sessions of the Legislature Held in the Years 1785, 1786, 1787, 1788, inclusive, Being the Eighth, Ninth, Tenth and Eleventh Sessions* (Albany: Weed, Parsons, 1885), 3: chap. 38, 419–24.

3. *Laws of the State of New-York Passed at the Sessions of the Legislature Held in the Years 1789, 1790, 1791, 1792, 1793, 1794, 1795, 1796, and 1797, inclusive, Being the Twelfth, Thirteenth, Fourteenth, Fifteenth, Sixteenth, Seventeenth, Eighteenth, and Nineteenth Sessions,* (Albany: Weed, Parsons), 4: chap. 25, 56–57; *Laws of the State of New York Passed at the Session of the Legislature Held in the Year 1801, Being the Twenty-Fourth Session, Including the Acts Commonly Called Revised Acts of that Session* (Albany: Weed, Parsons, 1887), 5: chap. 190, 569–570.

4. Ibid.; Franklyn Setaro, "The Surrogate's Court of New York: Its Historical Antecedents," *New York Law Forum* 2 (July 1956): 283–304.

5. Carter, Stone, and Gould, *Proceedings and Debates*, 3; Scott, *The Courts of New York*, 239–248; Lincoln, *Constitutional History*, 1: 181–182; Harold Weintraub, "Mandamus and Certiorari in New York from the Revolution to 1800: A Chapter in Legal History," *Fordham Law Review* 32 (May 1964): 681–748; James D. Folts, *"Duely and Constantly Kept." A History of the Supreme Court, 1691–1847 and An Inventory of Its Records (Albany, Utica, and Geneva Offices, 1797–1847)* (Albany: N.p., 1991), 2–30.

6. Ibid., 41–72.

7. Ibid., 24–26, 75–80.

8. Ibid., 11–30, 19, 30, 62–65, 58, 97, 98.

9. Ralph Lockwood, *An Analytic and Practical Synopsis of all the Cases Argued and Reversed in Law and Equity in the Court for the Correction of Errors of the State of New York from 1799 to 1847, with all the Names of Cases and a Table of Titles* (New York: Banks, Gould, 1848); Scott, *The Courts of New York*, 393–396; Francis Bergen, *The History of the New York Court of Appeals, 1847–1932* (New York: Columbia Univ. Press, 1985), 7–9.

10. Supreme Court Common Rule Books, Box 31, Book, 82; *Peter Vosburgh v. Abraham Vosburgh,* Supreme Court of Judicature Docket of Judgements (Albany), Box 3, Vol. 5.

11. Ibid., 4–5, 28–29; William Coleman and George Caines, *Reports of Cases of Practice Determined in the Supreme Court of Judicature of the State of New-York; From April term, 1794, to November Term, 1805, Both Inclusive. To Which is Prefixed all the Rules and Orders of the Court to the Year 1808* (New York: Banks & Bros., 1883), 1–37; *Johnson's Reports,* vi–viii; William Kent, *Letters and Memoirs of James Kent, L.L. D.* (Boston: Little, Brown, 1898), 117–128; Alden Chester, *Legal and Judicial History of New York* (New York: National Americana Society, 1911), 105; Horton, *Kent,* 149–152, 200–201; Moore, "Official Law Reporting," 271.

12. Donald M. Roper, "Martin Van Buren as Tocqueville's Lawyer: The Jurisprudence of Politics," *JER* 2 (spring 1982): 170–189; Cole, *Van Buren,* 22–25.

13. *Wilson and Gibbs v. Ephraim Reed, 3 Johnson's Reports,* 175–178 (1808).

14. Ibid., 177, 178.

15. Hall, *Magic Mirror,* 121.

16. Joyce O. Appelby, *Capitalism and a New Social Order: The Republican Vision of the 1790s* (New York: New York Univ. Press, 1984); Robert E. Shalhope, *The Roots of Democracy: American Thought and Culture, 1760–1800* (Boston: Twayne, 1990), 44–52, 119–125; Daniel T. Rodgers, "Republicanism: The Career of a Concept," *JAH* 79 (June 1992): 11–38; Barry Alan Shain, *The Myth of American Individualism: The Protestant Origins of American Political Thought* (Princeton: Princeton Univ. Press, 1994), 23–150.

17. *VBA,* 28–29.

18. *Bee,* July 14, 21, 18, 1807, Nov. 10, 29, 1807, Jan. 5, 24, Apr. 5, 12, May 14, June 14, Aug. 16, 1808; *American Citizen,* Dec. 3, 12, 16, 24, 1807, Sept. 19, 1808, Jan. 6, Feb. 4, 13, 15, 16, 1809; Tompkins to De Witt Clinton, Jan. 7, Feb. 13, De Witt Clinton to George Clinton, Apr. 3, 1808, Clinton Papers, CU; *Evening Post,* Jan. 31, Sept. 1, Dec. 22, 26, 1808; Ray Irwin, "Governor Daniel D. Tompkins and the Embargo, 1807–1809," *NYH* 22 (July 1941): 309–320; Ray W. Irwin, *Daniel D. Tompkins: Governor of New York and Vice President of the United States* (New York: NYHS, 1968), 54–56.

19. Van Buren to Clinton, Apr. 16, 20, 30, 1808, Clinton Papers, CU; *Bee,* Apr. 19, May 10, 1808; John P. Van Ness to William P. Van Ness, Oct. 24, 1808, Van Ness Papers, NYPL.

20. *Jackson, ex. dem. Whitbeck and Gardiniere, v. Deyo, 3 Johnson's Reports,* 422–423 (1808); *Jackson, ex. dem. VanDeuzen and Others, v. Scissam,* ibid., 499–505 (1808).

21. *Bee,* May 31, Dec. 7, 1810; Niven, *Van Buren,* 22–23.

22. *Bee,* Dec. 15, 1808, January 3, 17, 1809; *Hudson Northern Whig,* Jan. 19, 1809; George Chittenden to MVB, May 18, 1809, VBL; Columbia County Deed Book, BK, May 18, 1809, C. 120, Columbia County Archives.

23. Legal Record Book, VBLC. Columbia County Common Rule Book, Court of Common Pleas, 1807–1810, Hudson Court House; Docket for Clerk of Circuit Court, Hudson Court House. Other unsorted papers in the basement files of the Clerk of Columbia County in Hudson reveal Van Buren's additional legal actions beyond those listed in his Legal Record Book.

24. For a representative sample see: *Bee,* Jan. 10, 21, Apr. 4, 25, June 6, 13, 27, 1809, June 9, 15, 24, Aug. 11, Nov. 23, 1810, Apr. 15, May 31, June 17, July 5, Oct. 22, Nov. 19, 1811; *Catskill Recorder,* Apr. 5, 22, May 31, June 21, 26, 28, 1809. See also

Surrogate Order Book, D, Surrogate's Office, Columbia County, New York. Aug. 7–Nov. 8, 1809, VBL; Appointment of Administrators, 1803–1813, Appointment of Guardians 1808–1813, Book of Orders, 1808–1813, Letters of Administration, 1808–1813, Surrogate Court Records, 1808–1813, Columbia County Archives.

25. Legal Record Book, VBLC; Deed from Thomas Turner to MVB, Apr. 10, 1809; Indenture between Jacobus Van Deusen and MVB and William Pulver, Oct. 9, 1809, VBL; William Raymond, *Biographical Sketches of Distinguished Men of Columbia County* (Albany: Weed, Parsons, 1851).

26. *Jackson, ex. dem. Starr and Wife, v. Richmond,* 4 *Johnson's Reports,* 483 (1809).

27. *Jackson, ex. dem. Cantine and Others, v. Stills, (George Clark, tenant); Jackson. ex dem. Cantine and Others, v. Stiles (Buel, tenant), Jackson, ex dem. Van Gorden, v. Stiles, (Hollenbeck, tenant),* ibid., 493–497 (1809); Mark, *Agrarian Conflicts,* 23–24, 27, 30–31, 92, 115. For the resolution of this issue, see *The People of the State of New-York v. George Clarke,* in Oliver L. Barbour, *Reports of Cases in Law and Equity in the State of New-York* (New York: Banks & Bros., 1870), 10: 120–156 (1850), hereafter cited as *Barbour.*

28. *Tobey v. Barber,* 5 *Johnson's Reports,* 68–73 (1809).

29. *Jackson, ex. dem Van Dusen and Others, v. Van Dusen,* 5 *Johnson's Reports,* 145–160 (1809); Peter Van Schaack to MVB, Oct. 28, 1806, VBLC.

30. Francis Stebbins to MVB, Oct. 20, MVB (for Hogeboom) to Williams, Nov. 11, J. Rutsen Van Rensselaer (for Williams) to MVB (for Hogeboom), Nov. 11, MVB to J. Rutsen Van Rensselaer, Nov. 12, 14, December 29, 1809, VBLC; *Bee,* Jan. 9, 1810.

31. *Bee,* Jan. 3, 10, 24, 1809; Roper, "Van Buren," 170–171.

32. *Bee,* Feb. 7, 1809; Lynch, *Epoch and A Man,* 78. The extracts Van Buren used are in the VBLC.

33. *Bee,* Feb. 14, 1809.

34. Henry Dearborn to Daniel D. Tompkins, Daniel D. Tompkins Papers, NYSL; *American Citizen,* Jan. 25, Feb. 1, 9, 19, Mar. 15, 1809; *Public Advertiser,* Jan. 30, Mar. 2, 3, 6, 21, 25, July 11, Sept. 24, 1809; Tompkins to Clinton, Feb. 3, 1809, Clinton Papers, CU; *Bee,* Feb. 14, Apr. 11, 18, 25, May 2, June 5, 13, 1809; Jefferson to Tompkins, Feb. 24, 1809, Jefferson Papers.

35. *Bee,* Jan. 23, Apr. 24, 1810. Starting in May 1810, the partnership of Van Buren and Miller began advertising in local newspapers.

36. Legal Record Book, VBLC; Columbia County Common Rule Book, Court of Common Pleas, 1810; Surrogate Order Book, D, VBL; Common Rule Books (Albany), Box 31, Book 82, 83; Docket of Judgements (Albany), Box 3, Vol. 4, Box 4, Vol. 5; Docket of Judgements (New York City), Box 1.

37. *Van Alen and Another v. Vanderpool and Others,* 6 *Johnson's Reports,* 69–73 (1810).

38. Horowitz, *Transformation of American Law,* 160–252; Peter Charles Hoffer, *The Law's Conscience: Equitable Constitutionalism in America* (Chapel Hill: Univ. of North Carolina Press, 1990), 81–122.

39. *Colt and Colt v. M'Mechen,* 6 *Johnson's Reports,* 160–168 (1810).

40. *Van Slyck v. Hogeboom,* ibid., 271 (1810).

41. *Denton and Others v. John Noyes,* ibid., 296–318 (1810).

42. *Jackson, ex. dem. Van Alen and Others, v. Vosburgh,* 7 *Johnson's Reports,* 186–188 (1810).

43. *Wendover and Hinton v. Hogeboom and Others,* ibid., 308–310 (1810).

44. *Nichols v. Ingersoll,* ibid., 145–156 (1810).

45. *Bee,* Apr. 14, June 15, 1810; Chancery Minutes, Dec. 15, 1809–July 1, 1811, Box 2, Vol. 2, 832, 840, NYSA.

46. *Laws of the State of New York, Revised and Passed at the Thirty-Sixth Session,* chap. 95, 486–494; Hoffer, *The Law's Conscience,* 1–46.

47. Carter and Stone, *Proceedings and Debates,* 17; Gordon, *Gazetteer,* 281–282; Chester, *Legal and Judicial History,* 329–331; George Dangerfield, *Chancellor Robert R. Livingston of New York, 1746–1813* (New York: Harcourt, Brace, 1960), 185, 277, 445, 495.

48. Chancery Register, 1806–1817, 137, NYSA; Dockets of Judgements (Albany), Box 3, Vol. 4, Box 4, Vol. 5; Dockets of Judgements (New York City), Box 1.

49. Roger Skinner to MVB, Nov. 15, 1809, VBLC; *Bee,* July 6, 1810; *VBA,* 144–145.

50. *Bee,* Sept. 28, 1810; *Catskill Recorder,* Sept. 19, 1810.

51. Matthew Davis to William P. Van Ness, Jan. 2, Feb. 13, 1810, Van Ness Papers, NYHS; *American Citizen,* Jan. 17, Mar. 1, 1810; *New York Columbian,* Jan. 19, Feb. 15, 1810; Clinton to Henry Remsen, Feb. 4, 24, Mar. 21, 1810, Clinton Papers, CU; *Evening Post,* Feb. 6, 1810; Charles Holt to Jefferson, Oct. 25, 1810, Jefferson Papers.

52. *Bee,* Mar. 20, Apr. 3, 17, 24, 1810; MVB to Clinton, Apr. 19, 28, 1810, Clinton Papers, CU; Williams to James Van Der Poel, Van Schaack Papers, NYSL; Cole, *Van Buren,* 26.

53. Robert R. Livingston to Edward Livingston, Mar. 10, 1810, Livingston Family Papers; Williams to Foote, Mar. 23, 1810, Foote Papers; *Poughkeepsie Journal,* Apr. 4, 1810; *Bee,* Apr. 3, 17, 24, July 6, 13, 1810; *Northern Whig,* May 4, 1810; *Evening Post,* May 9, 1810; *Albany Register,* June 19, 1810; MVB to James I. Van Alen, June 28, 1810, VBLC.

54. Davis to William P. Van Ness, Jan. 27, 29, Feb. 1, 5, John P. Van Ness to William P. Van Ness, Feb. 16, 21, 1811, Van Ness Papers, NYSL; *Albany Balance,* Feb. 5, Mar. 18, 1811; *Bee,* Feb. 8, 22, Mar. 1, 15, Apr. 26, May 10, 31, June 14, 1811; Robert Macomb to Tompkins, Mar. 4, 24, 1811, Tompkins Papers; Clinton to Remsen, Mar. 16, 22, 1811, Clinton Papers, NYPL; Clinton to Edgar, Apr. 2, 1811, William Edgar Papers, NYPL; MVB to Clinton, Apr. 20, 1811, Clinton Papers, CU; *Columbian,* May 15, 1811.

55. William P. Van Ness to MVB, Feb. 21, 1807, Jan. 18, 1810, VBLC; Van Buren to William P. Van Ness, Jan. 3, 13, Dec. 4, 1810, VBL.

56. *Bee,* Mar. 22, 29, Apr. 5, 12, Dec. 20, 1808, Jan. 2, 1810; MVB to William P. Van Ness, Dec. 12, 22, 1809, Jan. 3, 1810, VBL; William P. Van Ness to MVB, Dec. 23, 27, 1810, VBLC.

57. Cornelius Miller to Stephen Miller [Jan. 1811], VBLC; Dockets of Judgements (Albany), Box 5, Vol. 6, Box 6, Vol. 7.

58. *Maigley v. Hauer,* 7 *Johnson's Reports,* 341–343 (1810); *VBA,* 107.

59. *Reed v. Pruyn and Staats, Johnson's Reports,* 426–430 (1811);

60. MVB to Peter Van Schaack, Mar. 22, 1810, VBL.

61. Minutes of the Council of Errors, vol. 1, 340, 342, 344, 345–346; *Frier and Cooper v. Jackson. ex dem. Van Allen and Van Allen,* 8 *Johnson's Reports,* 495–506 (1811).

62. Ibid., 507–520.

63. *Ex Parte John Van Ness Yates,* 4 *Johnson's Reports,* 317–376 (1809).

64. Ibid.; *John Van Ness Yates v. John Lancing, Jr.,* 5 *Johnson's Reports,* 282–299 (1810).

65. *John Van Ness Yates, Plaintiff in Error, v. The People of the State of New-York,*

Defendants in Error, 6 *Johnson's Reports*, 337–523 (1810).

66. *John Van Ness v. John Lancing, Jr.*, Brief for Argument in Court of Errors, Feb. term, 1811, VBLC; *John V. N. Yates, Plaintiff in Error, v. John Lancing, Jr., Defendant in Error*, 9 *Johnson's Reports*, 395–397 (1812).

67. Ibid., 396–398.

68. Ibid., 397–442.

69. *Vosburgh v. Rogers*, 8 *Johnson's Reports*, 91–96 (1811); *Strong v. Tompkins and Another*, ibid., 98–101 (1811); Hall, *Magic Mirror*, 46–47, 125–126.

5: REPUBLICANISM AND PROPERTY LAW

1. *VBA*, 22.

2. MVB to Manor Committee, Jan. 25, 1811, VBL; Cole, *Van Buren*, 28.

3. MVB to Manor Committee, Jan. 25, 1811, VBL. See also, *Bee*, Apr. 19, 1811, *Northern Whig*, Apr. 26, 1811, and *VBA*, 23–24.

4. MVB to Manor Committee, Jan. 25, 1811, VBL; *VBA*, 24.

5. *Northern Whig*, Apr. 26, 1811; Emmet to Van Buren, Nov. 20, 12, VBL; *VBA*, 24.

6. Ibid., 25.

7. *Bee*, Mar. 29, Apr. 19, 1811; Lynch, *An Epoch and a Man*, 80–81; *VBA*, 25–26; Ellis, *Landlords and Farmers*, 152–154.

8. MVB to Manor Committee, Apr. 25, 1811, VBL; *Northern Whig*, Apr. 26, 1811; *VBA*, 25.

9. *Northern Whig*, May 10, 1811.

10. "Notes on the Livingston Grant," VBLC.

11. Ibid.

12. Ibid.

13. Ibid.

14. *Bee*, June 28, July 12, 1811.

15. Docket of Judgements (Albany), Box 3, Vol. 4, Box 4, Vol. 5; Common Rule Books, Box 31, Book 83; *Adams v. Supervisors of Columbia County*, 8 *Johnson's Reports*, 324–327 (1811); *Pugsley v. Van Alen*, ibid., 352 (1811).

16. *Bee*, Aug. 16, 1811.

17. *Northern Whig*, Aug. 16, 1811.

18. MVB to Van Rensselaer, Aug. 19, 1811, VBLC.

19. Stebbins to Miller, Aug. 20, MVB to Stebbins, Aug. 29, 1811, VBLC; *Northern Whig*, Aug. 23, Sept. 6, 1811; *VBA*, 26.

20. *Northern Whig*, Aug. 23, Sept. 6, 1811; *VBA*, 26.

21. Van Rennselaer to MVB, Aug. 24, 1811, VBLC; *VBA*, 26; Lynch, *An Epoch and a Man*, 81.

22. Appointment of Guardians, 1811; Books of Orders, 1811; Letters of Administration, 1811; *Catskill Recorder*, Apr. 10, 11, 17, 24, May 1, 1811; *Bee*, Apr. 20, 26, May 10, 23, 31, June 3, 7, 28, July 12, Aug. 16, Oct. 22, 29, Nov. 19, 1811; Columbia County Deeds. Apr. 12, 1811, BK, D.33; Enos T. Throop to MVB, Sept. 22, 1811, VBLC; Shepard, *Van Buren*, 30–31.

23. *Jackson, ex dem. Bain and Van Slyck, v. Pulver and Another*, 8 *Johnson's Reports*, 370–374 (1811).

24. William Johnson to MVB, Sept. 1, 1811, VBL; *VBA*, 26–27.

25. *Bee,* Dec. 3, 17, 31, 1811, June 16, 23, 1812; *Northern Whig,* Dec. 23, 30, 1811; *VBA,* 27.

26. *Bee,* June 16, 1812; Emmet to Van Buren, Nov. 20, 1812, VBL.

27. Van Buren to John Suydam, Nov. 25, 1811, VBLC; *Bee,* Dec. 17, 1811; *VBA,* 27.

28. *Northern Whig,* Dec. 23, 30, 1811; *Bee,* Dec. 17, 31, 1811; Richard Riker to MVB, Feb. 17, 1812, VBLC.

29. See for example, *Van Renssalaer v. Johnson,* 2 Barbour, 643–672 (1848); *Pike v. Butler,* 4 Barbour, 650–659 (1848); *Kidd and Others v. Dennison and Others,* 6 Barbour, 2–19 (1849); *Acker v. Ledyard,* 8 Barbour, 514–518 (1850); *Van Renssalaer v. Synder,* 9 Barbour, 302–309 (1850); *Hill and Ballou v. Draper,* 10 Barbour, 454–483 (1851); *DuBois v. Kelly,* ibid., 496–511 (1851); *Carter and Carter v. Hammett and Balch,* 12 Barbour, 253–262 (1851); *Livingston v. Tanner,* ibid., 481–487 (1852).

30. Shepard, *Van Buren,* 34–36; Alexander, *American Talleyrand,* 77; Cole, *Van Buren,* 28–30.

31. Horowitz, *The Transformation of American Law,* 33–47; Curry and Goodheart, *American Chameleon: Individualism in Trans-National Context,* 66–120.

32. Figures derived from Dockets of Judgements (Albany), Box 3, Vol. 4, Box 4, Vol. 5; Dockets of Judgements (New York City), Box 1; Common Rule Books (Albany), Box 31, Book 82, 83, Box 32, Book 84.

33. Shepard, *Van Buren,* 33; Joline, *Autograph Hunter,* 51–62; Niven, *Van Buren,* 20.

34. *VBA,* 28.

35. Deed from Thomas Turner to MVB, Jan. 13, 1812, VBL; *Bee,* Jan. 14, 1812; *VBA,* 28; Docket of Judgements (Albany), Box 4, Vol. 5; *Jackson, ex dem. Rensselaer et al., v. Thomas Hogeboom and John Hogeboom,* 9 *Johnson's Reports,* 83 (1812).

36. Clinton to Pierre Van Cortlandt, Jan. 31, Apr. 7, 1812, Clinton Papers, NYPL; Davis to William P. Van Ness, Jan. 29, Feb. 5, Feb. 16, Peter Van Ness to William P. Van Ness, Feb. 21, 1812, Van Ness Papers, NYHS; Beal Lewis to Tompkins, Feb. 9, William Laughlin to Tompkins, Mar. 31, Macomb to Tompkins, Apr. 4, Elam Tilden to Tompkins, Apr. 6, 1812, Tompkins Papers; *Albany Register,* Feb. 28, Apr. 3, 1812; *Columbian,* Feb. 28, Mar. 18, Apr. 10, 1812; *Evening Post,* Mar. 31, 1812; Hammond, *Political Parties,* 1: 304–307.

37. Clinton to Van Cortlandt, Jan. 21, 1812, Clinton Papers, NYPL; *Columbian,* Feb. 26, Mar. 28, Apr. 28, 1812; Henry Dearborn to Jefferson, Mar. 10, 1812, Jefferson Papers; *Albany Register,* Apr. 3, 17, 1812; Spencer to John Armstrong, Apr. 9, 1812, Rokeby Collection, NYHS; *Bee,* Apr. 14, 28, May 12, 1812.

38. *Bee,* Mar. 3, 1812.

39. *VBA,* 29; *Bee,* Mar. 3, 14, 1812; *Poughkeepsie Republican Herald,* Apr. 1, 1812; *Catskill Recorder,* Apr. 15, 1812; *Newburgh Orange County Republican,* Apr. 21, 1812; *VBA,* 29; Niven, *Van Buren,* 27–30.

40. William P. Van Ness to MVB, Mar. 13, 1812, VBLC; MVB to William P. Van Ness, Mar. 23, 1812, VBL.

41. *Albany Register,* Mar. 24, Apr. 3, 1812; *Bee,* Mar. 27, Apr. 7, 14, 21, 1812; *Northern Whig,* Apr. 6, 20, 1812.

42. *Poughkeepsie Republican Herald,* Apr. 15, 29, 1812; *Northern Whig,* Apr. 20, 21, 28, 1812.

43. *Bee,* Apr. 7, 21, 28, 1812; Jacob Van Ness to MVB, Apr. 12, George Broom to MVB, Apr. 17, 1812, VBLC; *Catskill Recorder,* Apr. 15, 22, 1812; Williams to Foote, Apr. 21, 1812, Foote Papers; *Columbian,* Apr. 22, 1812.

44. *Catskill Recorder,* Apr. 22, 1812; *Bee,* Apr. 28, May 5, 12, 26, 1812; *Poughkeepsie Republican Herald,* Apr. 29, 1812; *Columbian,* May 6, 1812; *Northern Whig,* May 11, 1812; *Orange County Patriot,* May 12, 1812; Niven, *Van Buren,* 31–32.

45. *VBA,* 33.

6: DISTRIBUTIVE JUSTICE AND LEGAL INSTRUMENTALISM

1. *Bee,* June 2, 9, 10, 16, 30, July 7, 14, 21, Sept. 1, 1812; Robert Macomb to Tompkins, June 25, 1812, Tompkins Papers; *Public Advertiser,* July 8, Sept. 19, 24, 20, 1812; *Evening Post,* Sept. 3, 1812; Irwin, *Tompkins,* 145–161; Cole, *Van Buren,* 33.

2. Hudson Court of Common Pleas, Sept. 1812; Legal Record Book, VBLC; Chancery Register, 1806–1817, 137, 142, 154, 155, 156, 157; Dockets of Judgements (Albany), Box 6, Vol. 6.

3. *Denton et al. v. Livingston,* 9 *Johnson's Reports,* 96–100 (1812).

4. *Knickerbacker v. Killmore,* ibid., 106–107 (1812).

5. *Jackson, ex dem Hall et al., v. Burr,* ibid., 104–106 (1812).

6. *Freeman v. Adams,* ibid., 115–117 (1812).

7. *Public Advertiser,* May 2, 1812; Tompkins to Albert Gallatin, May 10, 1812, Gallatin Papers; *Bee,* May 12, 23, June 2, 16, 1812; *Laws of the State of New York for 1812,* 6: chap. 80, 418–424.

8. *Columbian,* April 10, May 21, June 1, 3, 12, Sept. 7, 12, 21, 1812; *Evening Post,* May 22, Sept. 3, 9, 12, 1812; Maturin Livingston to Madison, May 30, 1812, Madison Papers; Macomb to Tompkins, May 1812, Tompkins Papers; Elbridge Gerry to James Monroe, Aug. 24, 1812, James Monroe Papers, LC; Rufus King to Christopher Gore, Sept. 19, 1812, Rufus King Papers, NYHS; Hammond, *Political History,* 1: 315–317; Ernst, *King,* 318–319; Steven E. Siry, "The Sectional Politics of 'Practical Republicanism': De Witt Clinton's Presidential Bid, 1810–1812," *JER* 4(winter 1985): 441–462.

9. *VBA,* 37; Cole, *Van Buren,* 33.

10. *VBA,* 38.

11. Figures derived from *Johnson's Reports,* 1807–1812, and J. A. Hansen, *A List of the Attornies and Counsellors of the Supreme Court of the State of New-York, Together with the Places of Their Residence; and the Names of their Respective Agents* (Albany: J. B. Van Steenbergh, 1821).

12. *VBA,* 38.

13. Smith T. Van Buren, "Notes on Van Buren's Early Political Career, 1812–1815," 185[?], herafter cited as "Notes, 1812–1815," VBLC; Richard Riker to MVB, July 21, 1812, VBLC.

14. *VBA,* 38–43; "Notes, 1812–1815," VBLC; Martin Van Buren, Jr., "Reminiscences about Van Buren's Appointment to the Office of Attorney General," 185[?], VBLC. The discrepancy arises from Van Buren's accounts: in the *Autobiography,* 38–39, he mentions "a friend," whom editor Fitzgerald suggested was Riker; in the "Notes, 1812–1815," Van Buren indicated that he sent Gilbert.

15. *VBA,* 96; Thomas P. Robinson, "The Life of Thomas Addis Emmet" (Ph.D. diss., New York Univ., 1955), 224–260.

16. *VBA,* 39.

17. *Doe, ex dem. Clinton et al., v. Phelps,* 9 *Johnson's Reports,* 169–171 (1812); Clinton to MVB, Sept. 4, 1812, VBL.

18. William Kiteltas to Madison, Sept. 2, 1812, Madison Papers; *Bee,* Sept. 8, 15, 1812; *Columbian,* Sept. 19, 1812; *Northern Whig,* Sept. 28, 1812; Donald R. Hickey, *The War of 1812: A Forgotten Conflict* (Urbana: Univ. of Illinois Press, 1989), 80–84.

19. *Bee,* Apr. 28, July 14, 21, Nov. 10, 1812; Court of Common Pleas, 1812; *Benjamin Birdsall, Jr. v. Robert L. Livingston,* Sept. 22, 1812, VBLC.

20. *Jackson, ex dem. Livingston and Wilsey, v. Wilsey et al.,* 9 *Johnson's Reports,* 267–269 (1812).

21. *Jackson, ex dem. Van Beuren et al., v. Vosburgh,* ibid., 270–277 (1812).

22. *Columbian,* Sept. 12, 19, Oct. 19, 1812; *Public Advertiser,* Sept. 24, 30, Oct. 19, 29, 1812; *Bee,* Sept. 29, Nov. 3, 1812; *Evening Post,* Oct. 20, 1812; *Niles Weekly Register* 3 (Oct. 31, 1812): 131–132; *VBA,* 41–43; Hammond, *Political Parties,* 1: 321; Cole, *Van Buren,* 34. In Clinton's diary (NYHS), he noted meeting "M. Van Beuren" on October 27, 1812.

23. Jenkins, *Governors,* 374; *VBA,* 37–38.

24. MVB to Clinton, Nov. 14, 1812, Clinton Papers; Hammond, *Political Parties,* 1: 321–322; *Journal of the Senate of the State of New-York at their Thirty-Sixth Session, Begun and held at the City of Albany, the Third Day of November, 1812* (Albany: Solomon Southwick, 1813), 25–26, hereafter cited as *JSNY.*

25. Shepard, *Van Buren,* 58–59; Alexander, *Political History,* 1: 207–208; Niven, *Van Buren,* 32–33.

26. Robert Tillotson to Gallatin, Nov. 9, Lewis to Gallatin, Nov. 12, 1812, Gallatin Papers; *Columbian,* Nov. 11, 12, 25, 1812; *Albany Gazette,* Nov. 12, 1812; *Public Advertiser,* Nov. 12, 13, 17, 1812; Armstrong to Spencer, Dec. 22, 1812, Rokeby Collection; *New York National Advocate,* Jan. 8, 15, 1813; *JSNY,* 36th sess., 15–21; "Notes of Martin Van Buren on the Republican Presidential Nomination in 1812," [1853], VBLC; Niven, *Van Buren,* 37.

27. *Bee,* Nov. 10, 24, 1812; MVB to [?], [1812], On the Postponement of the trial of *The People v. Van Tessel and Williams,* VBLC; MVB & Cornelius Miller to John P. Van Ness, Nov. 5, 1812, VBL.

28. *Bee,* Nov. 24, 1812, Jan. 19, 1813; Jacob Radcliffe to MVB, Nov. 26, 1812; Emmet to MVB, Nov. 20, 1812, VBL; *Columbian,* Jan. 15, Feb. 11, 13, 1813.

29. See for example, *JSNY,* 36th sess., 77–81, and Van Ness and Woodworth, *Laws of the State of New-York;* composite based on Van Buren's activities in *JSNY,* 36th sess.

30. Clinton to Remsen, Nov. 11, 1812, Clinton Papers, NYPL; Henry Wheaton to Levi Wheaton, Nov. 28, 1812, Henry Wheaton Papers, Pierrepont Morgan Library; *Columbian,* Jan. 6, 9, 16, 18, 1813; *National Advocate,* Jan. 8, 13, 15, 1813; Notes of Agreement, Jan. 15, 1813, William L. Marcy Papers, LC; Holt to MVB, Jan. 20, 1813, VBLC; John Taylor to Pierre Van Cortlandt, Jan. 21, 1813, Pierre Van Cortlandt Papers, NYPL; Hammond, *Political Parties,* 1: 358.

31. *Evening Post,* Feb. 3, 1813; Ernst, *King,* 320; *VBA,* 45; "Notes, 1812–1815," VBLC; King to Gore, Feb. 14, 1813, King Papers; *VBA,* 45–46.

32. *National Advocate,* Jan. 28, Feb. 3, 8, 1813; *Columbian,* Jan. 29, Feb. 3, 5, 8, 1813; Holt to MVB, Feb. 3, 1813, VBLC; *Albany Argus,* Feb. 5, 1813; "Notes, 1812–1815," VBLC; Hammond, *Political Parties,* 1: 354–355; Lynch, *An Epoch and a Man,* 118; Niven, *Van Buren,* 38–39; *VBA,* 46–47.

33. *Evening Post,* Jan. 15, 1813; *Northern Whig,* Jan. 19, 18, 23, 1813; *Bee,* Jan. 19, Mar. 2, 1813; John Taylor to Van Courtlandt, Jan. 21, 1813, Van Courtlandt Papers,

NYPL; *Columbian,* Feb. 3, 5, 1813; *VBA,* 48; Cole, *Van Buren,* 36–37.

34. Hogenboom to MVB, Feb. 22, 1813, VBL; *JSNY,* 36th sess., 168, 171–174, 183–186, 192, 193, 199, 239, 248, 263–264, 266, 274–275, 280, 282, 318–319, 322; *Bee,* Mar. 2, 16, 1813; *Albany Argus,* Apr. 20, 1813; Hammond, *Political Parties,* 1: 351.

35. "Notes for a Speech against the Incorporation of the Catskill Bank," Mar. [24], 1813, VBLC.

36. Ibid.

37. John Jay Knox, *A History of Banking in the United States* (New York: Bradford Rhodes, 1900), 413–414; Bray Hammond, *Banks and Politics in America From the Revolution to the Civil War* (Princeton: Princeton Univ. Press, 1957), 329–332.

38. *JSNY,* 36th sess., 110, 111, 124, 128, 194, 218, 219, 232, 239, 248, 249, 263–264, 266, 365, 381; Riker to MVB, Feb. 15, 1813, VBLC; *Bee,* Mar. 2, 1813; *Albany Argus,* Mar. 3, 4, 1813; *VBA,* 44.

39. *JSNY,* 36th sess., 191.

40. "Report of a Committee of the Senate to whom were Referred Certain Resolutions, with the Recitals, Adopted by the Assembly, March 2, 1813, On the Creation and Support of a Navy," VBLC; *JSNY,* 36th sess., 241–242, 344.

41. Minutes of the Court of Errors, 340, 342; *John W. Barry and Samuel Harbeck, Survivors of Caspanus Hewson, Plaintiffs in Error, v. Ephraim Mandell, Assignee of Peter P. Dox, Esq., Sheriff of Albany, Defendant in Error,* 10 *Johnson's Report,* 563–564, 573 (1813).

42. Ibid., 566.

43. Ibid., 566–572.

44. Ibid., 576–586; Shepard, *Van Buren,* 25–25; Roper, "Van Buren," 179.

45. *Barry v. Mandell,* 10 *Johnson's Reports,* 576–579.

46. Ibid., 579.

47. Ibid., 579–582.

48. Ibid., 582–583.

49. Ibid., 584.

50. Ibid., 585–586

51. Ibid., 587.

52. Lynch, *An Epoch and a Man,* 126; *VBA,* 212; *JSNY,* 36th sess., 307; *Register of Debates,* 18th Cong., 2nd sess., 1825–1825, 1: 74.

53. "Address to the Electors of New York, drafted by Martin Van Buren and Adopted at a Meeting of Republican Members of the Legislature, in the Senate Chamber, on the 9th day of March 1813," VBL; *Albany Argus,* Mar. 23, 26, 1813; Cole, *Van Buren,* 38–40.

54. *VBA,* 47–49; *Columbian,* Mar. 23, 26, Apr. 14, 20, June 13, 1813; *Bee,* Mar. 2, 23, May 4, 1813; William P. Van Ness to MVB, Apr. 1, John Taylor to MVB, Apr. 25, 1813, VBLC; *Northern Whig,* Apr. 20, 1813; MVB to Throop, Apr. 20, 1813, VBL; *Evening Post,* Apr. 21, 1813. Few copies of the *Bee* or the *Northern Whig* for 1813 have survived; a full account of Van Buren's campaigning is not possible to ascertain.

55. *Bee,* Mar. 16, 1813; Docket Book of Judgements (Albany), Box 5, Vol. 6; Chancery Register, 1805 1817, 171, 194; MVB to George Tibbits, Mar. 29, MVB to Theodore V. W. Graham, July 18, 1813, VBL.

56. *Jones v. Gardner,* 10 *Johnson's Reports,* 266–269 (1813); *Jackson, ex dem. Livingston, v. Baker,* ibid., 270–271 (1813); *Jackson, ex dem Livingston, v. Kisselbrack,* ibid., 336–338 (1813); *Jackson, ex dem. Livingston and Others, v. Sclover,* ibid., 368 (1813); *Mat-*

ter of Esther Gardenier v. Spikeman, ibid., 368 (1813).

57. MVB and Peter Van Schaack to Jacob Radcliffe, David B. Ogden and Theron Rudd, May 26, 1814, VBL; *Jackson, ex dem. Van Alen and Van Alen, v. Ambler*, 14 *Johnson's Reports*, 96–107 (1817).

58. Docket of Judgements (New York City), Vol. 1.

59. *Gunn v. Cantine, Gent., One of the Attorneys, & etc.*, 10 *Johnson's Reports*, 387–388 (1813).

60. *The President, Directors, and Company of the Farmers' Turnpike Road v. Coventry*, ibid., 389–393 (1813).

61. James C. Curtis, *The Fox At Bay: Martin Van Buren and the Presidency, 1837–1844* (Lexington: Univ. of Kentucky Press, 1970), 6–85; Major L. Wilson, *The Presidency of Martin Van Buren* (Lawrence: Univ. Press of Kansas), 24–146.

62. *Richmond v. Dayton*, 10 *Johnson's Reports*, 393–396 (1823).

63. MVB to Nicholas Fish, Oct. 30, 1813, MVB to Archibald McIntyre, Dec. 23, 1813, VBL; Docket of Judgements (Albany), Box 4, Vol. 5.

64. MVB to John W. Taylor, Mar. 11, 1814, VBL.

65. *Niles Weekly Register* 5 (Nov. 27, 1813): 218; MVB, Special Judge Advocate, Feb. 18, 1814, MVB to Armstrong, Feb. 23, 1814, VBL; William B. Aycock and Seymour W. Wurfel, *Military Law Under the Uniform Code of Military Justice* (Westport, Conn.: Greenwood Press, 1952), 3–27; C. Edward Skeen, *John Armstrong, Jr., 1758–1843: A Biography* (Syracuse: Syracuse Univ. Press, 1981), 147–168; Hickey, *War of 1812*, 84, 106–107.

66. MVB to Alexander J. Dallas, Jan. 5, MVB to Armstrong, Jan. 6, 1814, VBLC. Dallas provided Van Buren with his own notes concerning the kind of evidence he needed to elicit from witnesses. See also, Alexander J. Dallas [?], *The United States of America Against Brigadier General William Hull, of the Army of the United States, by Order of the Secretary of War* (N.p.: [1813]) for Van Buren's notations, and Van Buren's notes on "Points of Evidence" Against General Hull, VBLC.

67. *Jackson, ex dem. Van Rensselaer, v. Collins*, 11 *Johnson's Reports*, 1–5 (1814).

68. *Raymond v. Squire*, ibid., 47–50 (1814).

69. *JSNY at their Thirty-Seventh Session, Begun and Held at the City of Albany, the Twenty-Third Day of January, 1814* (Albany: H. C. Southwick for S. Southwick, 1814), 4–6; Irwin, *Tompkins*, 167–178; John K. Mahon, *The War of 1812* (Tallahassee: Rose Printing, 1972), 107–228.

70. *Bee*, Jan. 25, 1814; MVB to John W. Taylor, Feb. 6, 1814, VBL.

71. James G. Forbes, *Report of the Trial of Brig. Genl. W. Hull; Commanding the North-Western Army of the United States. By a Court-Martial Held at Albany on Monday, January 3, 1814 and Succeeding Days* (New York: Eastburn, Kirk, 1814), appendix 1–18; Ernest A. Cruikshank, *Documents Relating to the Invasion of Canada and the Surrender of Detroit, 1812* (Ottawa: Government Printing Bureau, 1912); Lewis Mayers, *The American Legal System* (New York: Harper and Bros., 1955), 501–513.

72. Skeen, *Armstrong*, 155; Cole, *Van Buren*, 41.

73. Van Buren's "Notes on Charges Against Hull," VBLC.

74. Ibid.

75. Forbes, *Trial of Hull*, 14–154; *Albany Argus*, Mar. 22, 1814; John Taylor to John W. Taylor, Mar. 23, 1814, John Taylor Papers, NYHS.

76. Forbes, *Trial of Hull*, appendix 11: 19–102.

77. Ibid., 115–116.

78. The reconstruction of Van Buren's summation and reply to Hull is based on the outline he prepared in "Notes for Summing Up the Evidence," Mar. 20, 1814, VBLC.

79. *Bee,* Mar. 26, 28, Apr. 23, 25, May 10, 1814; *National Advocate,* May 7, 1814; *Evening Post,* May 8, 1814; William Hull, *Defense of Brigadier General William Hull Delivered before the general court-martial, of which Major General Dearborn was president, at Albany, March, 1814. With an Address to the Citizens of the United States* (Boston: Wells & Lilly, 1814).

80. MVB to John W. Taylor, Feb. 6, Mar. 11, 1814, VBL; *Northern Whig,* March 30, 1814; MVB to Armstrong, Mar. 31, 1814, VBL; *Niles Weekly Register* 6 (July 23, 1814): 345–347.

7: BECOMING A REPUBLICAN STATE ATTORNEY GENERAL

1. *JSNY,* 37th sess., 50, 99, 137, 178, 181, 182, 191, 202–203, 213, 262; John Taylor to John W. Taylor, Jan. 25, 1814, Taylor Papers; MVB to John W. Taylor, Mar. 11, 1814, VBL; Hammond, *Political Parties,* 1: 374–375; Cole, *Van Buren,* 54.

2. Edward Sparhawk, *Report of the Trial before Judges Thompson and Betts, in the Circuit Court of the U.S. for the Southern District of New York* (New York: Elam Bliss, 1827), 3–8.

3. Ibid., 9–15; Kenneth Wiggins, *John Jacob Astor: Business Man* (Cambridge: Harvard Univ. Press, 1931), 2: 876–882.

4. *JSNY,* 37th sess., 124, 222–223.

5. Ibid., 11–14, 49, 57, 81, 106, 108, 110, 146, 152, 163, 188–190, 208, 216, 218, 253, 256; MVB to Burr, July 23, 1814, VBL; *VBA,* 400.

6. Minutes of the Court of Errors, 406, 407, 408; *John B. Graves, Plaintiff in Error, v. John B. Dash, Defendant in Error,* 11 *Johnson's Reports,* 17–24 (1814); *William Ogden and John R. Murray, Plaintiffs in Error, v. The New-York Firemen Insurance Company, Defendants in Error,* ibid., 25–31 (1814); *Isaac Clason, Plaintiff in Error, v. Gilbert Shotwell, Defendant in Error,* ibid., 31–68 (1814).

7. *Ambrose Spencer, Plaintiff in Error, v. Solomon Southwick, Defendant in Error,* 11 *Johnson's Reports,* 573–595 (1814); Hammond, *Political Parties,* 1: 375.

8. *Spencer v. Southwick,* 10 *Johnson's Reports,* 259–262 (1813).

9. *Spencer v. Southwick,* 11 *Johnson's Reports,* 587–589.

10. Ibid., 589–593.

11. Ibid., 595; *Evening Post,* Apr. 2, 1814.

12. Alfred H. Kelly, "Constitutional Liberty and the Law of Libel: A Historian's Review," *AHR* 74 (December 1968): 432; Donald M. Roper, "James Kent and the Emergence of New York's Libel Law," *AJLH* 17 (July 1973): 223–231; Roper, "Van Buren," 180–181.

13. *VBA,* 44, 57; MVB to John W. Taylor, Mar. 11, 1814, VBL; Charles W. Elliott, *Winfield Scott: The Soldier and the Man* (New York: Macmillan, 1937), 142–144; Scott to Van Buren, Oct. 22, 1814, Oct. 28, 1861, VBLC.

14. MVB to John W. Taylor, Feb. 6, 1814, VBL; *Bee,* Mar. 8, 1814; Hammond, *Political Parties,* 1: 365–367.

15. *Bee,* Jan. 25, Mar. 8, 1814; MVB to Taylor, Feb. 6, 14, 1814, 11, 1814, VBL; Resolutions, War Meeting, Albany, Apr. 14, 1814, VBLC; *Columbian,* Apr. 20, 1814;

James M. Banner, *To the Hartford Convention: The Federalists and the Origins of Party Politics in Massachusetts, 1789–1815* (New York: Alfred A. Knopf, 1970), 294–322; Donald R. Hickey, "Federalist Party Unity and the War of 1812," *JAS* 12 (April 1978): 23–39; Lawrence D. Cress, "'Cool and Serious Reflection': Federalist Attitudes toward the War of 1812," *JER* 7 (summer 1987): 123–145; *VBA,* 49–50.

16. *Columbian,* Apr. 22, May 7, 1814; *Northern Whig,* May 10, June 28, 1814; *Bee,* May 10, June 14, 1814; *Evening Post,* Apr. 30, May 7, 1814; Hammond, *Political Parties,* 1: 378; Robert W. July, *The Essential New Yorker: Gulian Crommelin Verplanck* (Durham: Duke Univ. Press, 1951), 32–38.

17. *Bee,* Mar. 1, 1814; Chancery Minutes, Box 3, Vol. 24, 442, 445–446. Although surviving issues of the *Bee* between April 30 and July 1 are scattered, enough remain to hint at Van Buren's practice.

18. *Samuel Haight v. Mary Van Bergen,* Chancery Minutes, Box 3, Vol. 24, 17; *Lydia Allen v. Howard Allen,* ibid., 40; *Thomas B. Cook and Appolos Cook v. Ard Reynolds, Mark Spencer and John Brush,* ibid., 44–45; *Mary Van Bergen v. Samuel Haight,* ibid., 73; *George Kisselbrack v. Henry Livingston,* ibid., 277–278.

19. *Jenkins and Others v. Waldron,* 11 *Johnson's Reports,* 114–121 (1814).

20. Ibid., 118–121.

21. A. G. Hammond to MVB, Dec. 24, 1824, VBLC; *VBA,* 64–65; Edwin Olsen, "The Slave Code in Colonial New York," *Journal of Negro History* 29 (April 1944): 147–165; Joyce D. Goodfriend, "Burghers and Blacks: The Evolution of a Slave Society at New Amsterdam," *NYH* 59 (April 1978): 125–144; Cole, *Van Buren,* 70–71; Shane White, *Somewhat More Independent: The End of Slavery in New York City, 1770–1810* (Athens: Univ. of Georgia Press, 1991), 16–17.

22. Peter Van Schaack and MVB to Jacob Radcliffe, David B. Ogden, and Theron Rudd, May 26, 1814, VBL.

23. Notes of Agreement between George Caines and MVB for a loan and sale of a lot in the Whiteborough Patent, Franklin, Delaware County, June 23, 1814; Bond to MVB given by George Caines in fulfillment of their agreement of June 23, 1814, July 8, 1814; Conditional Assignment of the [Law] Library of George Caines to secure payment of money and interest under the above agreement, with a host of books in the library, July 8, 1814, VBLC.

24. Holland, *Van Buren,* 33–34, 56–63. This conclusion is based on Van Buren's subsequent practice.

25. The Schedule and Inventory of Books, etc. is attached to the Conditional Assignment, July 8, 1814, VBLC; Lynch, *An Epoch and a Man,* 200–201.

26. *Jackson, ex dem A. J. Staats, v. I. and A. Staats,* 11 *Johnson's Reports,* 337–351 (1814).

27. *Bee,* Sept. 6, 13, 27, 1814; John W. Taylor to MVB, Oct. 6, 1814, VBLC; Benson Lossing, *The Pictorial Field-Book of the War of 1812; or Illustrations by Pen and Pencil, of the History, Biography, Scenery, Relics and Traditions of the Last War for American Independence* (New York: Harpers and Bros., 1864), 816–853.

28. *Bee,* July 12, 1814.

29. *JSNY at their Thirty-Eighth Session, Begun and Held at the City of Albany, the Twenty-Sixth Day of September, 1814* (Albany: H. C. Southwick, 1814), 4–6; 18–19; *Evening Post,* Sept. 30, 1814; *VBA,* 53–54.

30. *JSNY,* 38th sess., 8, 9, 11–14, 15, 17, 18, 21, 22, 23, 24, 55, 58, 61; Niven, *Van Buren,* 45.

31. *Bee,* Oct. 11, 1814; MVB to John W. Taylor, Oct. 19, 31, Notes on Classification Bill, Oct. 24, 1814, VBLC; *Albany Argus,* Oct. 25, 1814; *Evening Post,* Oct. 26,
1814; *JSNY,* 38th sess., 4, 21, 22, 26, 28, 30, 33–36, 37–39, 42, 51–52, 55, 59–60, 63,
66, 72; *VBA,* 55–56; Holland, *Van Buren,* 108–109; Alfred Street, *The Council of Revision of the State of New York* (Albany: William Gould, 1859), 440–447; Cole, *Van Buren,*
43–44.

32. *VBA,* 57; Taylor to MVB, Oct. 21, MVB to John W. Taylor, Oct. 31, 1814,
VBL; Scott to MVB, Oct. 22, 1814, VBLC; Holland, *Van Buren,* 90–106.

33. *Northern Whig,* Nov. 1, 1814; *Utica Patriot,* Nov. 5, 8, 15, 1814; *Albany
Gazette,* Nov. 14, 1814; Hammond, *Political Parties,* 1: 380; Cole, *Van Buren,* 44.

34. *Utica Patriot,* Nov. 22, 25, 1814; *Northern Whig,* Nov. 15, 22, 1814; Henry
Herbert Van Dyck to MVB, Mar. 18, 1856, VBLC; Horton, *Kent,* 237–242; David
Raack, "To Preserve the Best Fruits: The Legal Thought of Chancellor James Kent,"
AJLH 33 (October 1989): 320–366; Bernard Schwartz, *Main Currents in American Le-
gal Thought* (Durham, N.C.: Carolina Academic Press, 1993), 142–151.

35. *Albany Argus,* Nov. 11, 25, 1814; *Northern Whig,* Nov. 15, 22, 29, 1814; MVB
to Taylor, Dec. 2, 1814, VBL; *Bee,* Nov. 15, Dec. 6, 1814; *Albany Gazette,* Nov. 28,
1814; Samuel Young to MVB, Dec. 1, 1814, VBLC; *VBA,* 60.

36. Introductory Address to the Chancellor, Nov. 22, 1814, VBLC; *VBA,* 60, 62.

37. *Albany Argus,* Nov. 29, 1814.

38. *Albany Gazette,* Dec. 1, 1814; *VBA,* 58.

39. Young to MVB, Dec. 1, 1814, VBLC; *Albany Argus,* Dec. 9, 14, 1814.

40. *Albany Gazette,* Dec. 6, 1814; *Albany Argus,* Dec. 9, 1814, Cole, *Van Buren,* 58.

41. *VBA,* 61; Kent to MVB, Apr. 15, 1826, VBLC.

42. *Northern Whig,* Dec. 27, 1814; *Albany Argus,* Dec. 27, 28, 1814.

43. *Whitbeck v. Van Ness,* 11 *Johnson's Reports,* 495–499 (1814).

44. *Henry Livingston, by his next friend, Mary Livingston, v. Haywood,* ibid.,
429–431 (1814).

45. *Watts v. Coffin,* ibid., 495–499 (1814); Roper, "Van Buren," 177–178.

46. MVB to Abraham Van Dyck and John L. Bronk, Nov. 21, MVB to Abraham
Van Dyck, Nov. 28, 1814, Micah Sterling to MVB, Feb. 25, 1815, MVB to Taylor,
Dec. 25, 1814, VBL.

47. Parker to MVB, Dec. 14, 1814, VBL, Niven, *Van Buren,* 46–47.

48. MVB to Monroe, Jan. 22, 1815, VBL.

49. *Northern Whig,* Dec. 27, 1814; MVB to William Crawford, Dec. 30, 1815,
Jan. 3, 1816, *The United States of America v. Brigadier General James Wilkinson,* Records
of the Proceedings at Utica & Troy, New York, Martin Van Buren Special Judge Advocate, January 3–16, 1815, VBL; MVB to Taylor, Jan. 22, MVB to James A. Alexander,
Apr. 20, James A. Alexander to MVB, Apr. 20, 1815, VBL; *Utica Patriot,* Jan. 10, 1815;
James R. Jacobs, *Tarnished Warrior: Major-General James Wilkinson* (New York: Macmillan, 1938) 309; Skeen, *Armstrong,* 205–206.

50. MVB to William P. Van Ness, Jan. 10, 1815, VBL; *Jackson, ex. dem. Gouch, v.
Wood,* 12 *Johnson's Reports,* 73–77 (1815).

51. *Evening Post,* Jan. 7, Feb. 20, 1815; *National Advocate,* Jan. 14, 22, 1815;
Columbian, Feb. 1, 1815; *Northern Whig,* Feb. 14, 20, Mar. 14, 1815; *JSNY,* 38th sess.,
329; Scott to MVB, Mar. 16, 1815, VBLC; Cole, *Van Buren,* 45–46.

52. Hubbard to MVB, Sept. 4, 1814, Sanford to MVB, Dec. 28, 1814, Notes on
Van Buren's Political Career, VBL; *VBA,* 66–71; James Emott to King, Feb. 19, 1815,

King's Correspondence, 5: 472–473; *Bee,* Feb. 21, 1815; Hammond, *Political Parties,* 1: 392; Niven, *Van Buren,* 48–49.

53. Spencer to Armstrong, Jan. 17, 1815, Rokeby Collection; Shepard, *Van Buren,* 63; Alexander, *A Political History,* 1: 232–239; Lynch, *An Epoch and a Man,* 140–144; Irwin, *Tompkins,* 197–198.

8: REPUBLICANISM AND STATE ATTORNEY GENERAL: PHASE ONE

1. *Revised Laws of the State of New-York,* 1: chap. 48, 156.

2. Ibid., chap. 44 (R.L.) 140–141; chap. 92, 153; chap. 70, 187; chap. 96 (R.L.), 225; chap. 125, 240; chap. 96, 245–247; chap. 242, 260–266; chap. 1 (R.L.), 272–279; chap. 46, 292–303; chap. 13 (R.L.), 385; chap. 48, 416–418; ibid., 2: chap. 35, 125–133.

3. Ibid., chap. 45 (R.L.), 193; chap. 46 (R.L.), 335–337; chap. 49, 413–415; chap 12 (R.L.), 479–484.

4. Ibid., chap 43, 156; chap 1 (R.L.), 209–212; chap. 41, 213–219; chap. 12, 216; chap. 48, 216; chap. 94, 217; chap. 64, 292–393; chap. 19 (R.L.), 379–382; chap. 48, 418–424; chap. 40 (R.L.), 434–436.

5. Ibid., chap. 11 (R.L.), 528; 2: chap. 78 (R.L.), 21.

6. The letters Van Buren received may be found in Attorney General's Office, Correspondence and Legal Documentation Relating to Land Sales, 1815–1819, NYSA. See also Dockets of Judgements (Albany), Box 6, Vol. 7; Attorney General's Case Registers, Boxes 1 and 2, NYSA.

7. Attorney General's Correspondence, 1815; Charles Tappan to MVB, Apr. 15, Aaron Kenkle to MVB, Apr. 25, MVB to McIntrye, May 4, Jonathan Bunse to MVB, Sept. 2, Jonas Earll to MVB, Nov. 2, Joseph Kirkland to MVB, Nov. 6, Appolos Cooper to MVB, Nov. 8, 1815, VBL.

8. *The People of the State of New-York v. Artemis Aldrich,* 1816, *The People of the State of New-York v. Robert Archibold,* 1816, Supreme Court Judgement Rolls, Box 256.

9. "Benjamin F. Butler," *The United States Magazine and Democratic Review* 11 (January 1839): 33–48; William Lyon Mackenzie, *The Lives and Opinions of Benjamin Franklin Butler, United States District of New York; and Jesse Hoyt, Counsellor at Law, formerly Collector of Customs for the Port of New York* (Boston: Cook, 1845), 13–21; Butler to MVB, Sept. 14, Oct. 11, 13, 1815, MVB to Butler, Oct. 24, 1815, Butler to Harriet Allen, Nov. 25, 1816, May 4, 1817, Apr. 5, 1818, VBL.

10. *JSNY,* 38th sess., 96, 163–164, 169, 174, 175, 178, 222, 251, 251, 276, 322, 324–325, 335, 336, 348, 382–383; McIntrye to MVB, Feb. 22, 1815, VBL.

11. Ibid., 219, 233–234, 270–272, 276–278, 288, 370–378, 391, 403, 407, 412, 415, 416. See also, Edgar J. McManus, *A History of Negro Slavery in New York* (Syracuse: Syracuse Univ. Press, 1966), 177–179.

12. *Evening Post,* Feb. 20, 1815; *Bee,* Apr. 18, May 9, 23, 1815; *Northern Whig,* Apr. 18, 25, May 16, 15, 1815; *Columbian,* Apr. 19, June 17, 1815; *National Advocate,* June 17, 1815.

13. MVB to McIntyre, May 14, 1815, VBL; Niven, *Van Buren,* 43.

14. *The People v. Johnson,* 12 *Johnson's Reports,* 292–293 (1815); *The People v. Rose,* ibid., 339 (1815).

15. *The People, ex relatione Wilson, v. The Board of Supervisors of Albany,* ibid., 414–416 (1815).

16. *Sumner v. Buel,* ibid., 475–483 (1815).

17. Ibid., 477–483; Horton, *Kent,* 139–196.

18. MVB to Butler, Oct. 24, 1815,VBL; Chancery Register, Box 3,Vol. 25, 222, 223, 228, 232, 233, 236, 246, 249; Friedman, *History of American Law,* 179–186; Norma Basch, *In the Eyes of the Law: Women, Marriage, and Property in Nineteenth-Century New York* (Ithaca: Cornell Univ. Press, 1982), 15–112.

19. *VBA,* 122; Ronald E. Shaw, *Erie Water West: A History of the Erie Canal, 1792–1864* (Lexington: Univ. of Kentucky Press, 1966), 22–55; Hammond, *Political Parties,* 1: 411–412.

20. Robert V. Remini, "New York and the Presidential Election of 1816," *NYH* 31 (July 1950): 308–324; Joseph G. Rayback, "A Myth Reexamined: Martin Van Buren's Role in the Presidential Election of 1816," *Proceedings of the American Philosophic Society* 124 (April 1980): 106–118; Cole, *Van Buren,* 47–48.

21. *Albany Argus,* Jan. 9, 1816; *Utica Patriot,* Jan. 16, Mar. 12, 1816; *Northern Whig,* Jan. 23, 1816; *Bee,* Jan. 23, Mar. 12, 1816; *Evening Post,* Jan. 26, Feb. 1, Mar. 7, 1816; Spencer to Armstrong, Jan. 26, Mar. 7, Apr. 2, 1816, Rokeby Collection; Clinton to Elliot, Apr. 4, 1816, Clinton Papers, CU; Tactitus [DeWitt Clinton], *Canal Policy of the State of New-York: Delineated in a Letter to Robert Troup, Esquire* (New York: E. E. Hosford, 1822); Hammond, *Political Parties,* 1: 425–431; Irwin, *Tompkins,* 203.

22. Dockets of Judgements (Albany), Box 6, Vol 7; Supreme Court Minutes, Vol. 5, January Term 1816 to August Term, 1816, 71, NYSA; *The People v. Herrick,* 13 *Johnson's Reports,* 82–84 (1816); *The People v. The Judges, Etc. of the General Sessions of the Peace of the County of Genesse,* ibid., 85 (1816); *The People v. Holbrook,* ibid., 90–94 (1816). Figures derived from Docket of Judgements (Albany), Box 6. Vol. 7.

23. *Bennet v. Jenkins and Others, Executors of Jenkins,* 13 *Johnson's Reports,* 50–51 (1816); *Haywood v. Sheldon,* ibid., 88–90 (1816).

24. Attorney General's Correspondence, Jan. 1816; Butler to Van Buren, Jan. 9, MVB to Butler, Jan. 10, Minott Mitchel to MVB, Jan. 16, MVB to Samuel Birsdall, Jan. 19, Samuel McCrea to MVB, Jan. 25, 1816, VBL.

25. Chancery Minutes, Box 3, Vol. 25, 429–430, 530–531.

26. *Jackson, ex dem. Brockholst Livingston, and Others, Plaintiff in Error v. Ann Delancy and Abraham Russell, Defendants in Error,* 13 *Johnson's Reports,* 539–541 (1816).

27. Ibid., 543–560.

28. *David Gelston and Peter A. Schenck, Plaintiffs in Error, v. Gould Hoyt, Defendant in Error,* ibid., 561–590 (1816).

29. *Albany Argus,* Feb. 2, 6, 1816; *Northern Whig,* Feb. 6, 27, 13, 20, 27, 1816; *Albany Register,* Feb. 6, 13, 1816; *National Advocate,* Feb. 6, 9, 11, 13, 19, 1816; *Utica Patriot,* Feb. 9, 13, 1816; *Evening Post,* Feb. 22, Mar. 7, 1816; Hammond, *Political Parties,* 1: 412–418; *VBA,* 73.

30. *Albany Argus,* Feb. 13, 14, 20, 21, 1816; *Bee,* Mar. 5, 1816.

31. *JSNY,* 38th sess., 13, 15, 19, 25, 31, 48, 66, 79, 92–94, 97, 105, 111, 130–131, 185, 216, 224, 229, 236, 238, 253, 299, 319, 306–307.

32. Ibid., 49, 124, 222–223, 256; 295–302, 389, 403.

33. *Utica Patriot,* Mar. 5, Apr. 23, 30, 1816; *National Advocate,* Apr. 18, 1816; *Evening Post,* Apr. 19, 26, 1816; James Geddes to Clinton, Apr. 24, 1816, Clinton Papers, CU; *Niles Weekly Register* 10 (Apr. 13, 1816): 100–102, 10 (May 18, 1816):

198–199; David Hosack, *Memoir of De Witt Clinton: With an Appendix Containing Numerous Documents Illustrative of the Principle Events of His Life* (New York: J. Seymour, 1829), 406–418; *VBA*, 84; Shaw, *Erie Water West*, 54; Niven, *Van Buren*, 56.

34. *Albany Argus*, Feb. 21, Mar. 19, 1816; *Bee*, Mar. 12, 19, 1816; *Northern Whig*, Mar. 19, 1816; Stafford *Gazetteer*, 40–42.

35. *Albany Register*, Feb. 20, 23, 1816; *Evening Post*, Mar. 7, 16, Apr. 20, 1816; *Northern Whig*, Mar. 12, 26, 1816; *Utica Patriot*, Apr. 30, 1816.

36. MVB to Miller, Mar. 29, 1816, VBLC; *Albany Argus*, Apr. 26, 1816; *Catskill Recorder*, Apr. 30, 1816; *Bee*, Apr. 30, 1816.

37. Tillotson to MVB, May 4, Smith Thompson to MVB, May 5, 1816, VBLC; *Northern Whig*, May 7, 1816; *Evening Post*, May 7, 1816; *Bee*, May 14, 1816; *Albany Argus*, June 7, 1816; *Columbian*, June 15, 1816.

38. *Albany Argus*, July 26, 1816, June 3, 1817; Niven, *Van Buren*, 49.

39. MVB to Butler, June 18, Butler to Mrs. Martha Coffin, May 19, Butler to MVB, June 19, July 31, "Note," July 31, Butler to Harriet Allen, Aug. 12, 1816, VBL; Joel Munsell, *The Annals of Albany* (Albany: Joel Munsell, 1853–1859), 6: 123.

40. Butler to Harriet Allen, Nov. 5, 26, 1816, Jan. 10, 25, 1817, VBL.

41. Docket of Judgements (Albany), Box 6, Vol. 7; Common Rule Book, Box 32, Book 85; Chancery Register, 265, 282, 295, 300, 303, 304, 306, 314; Supreme Court Minutes, Vol. 5, 1042; *Pain v. Parker*, 13 *Johnson's Reports*, 329–330 (1816).

42. *Northern Whig*, Sept. 17, 1816; *Evening Post*, Sept. 20, 1816.

43. *Jackson, ex dem. Livingston and Others, v. Hallenbeck*, 13 *Johnson's Reports*, 499–502 (1816); *Jackson, ex dem. Valkenburgh, v. Van Buren*, ibid., 525–529 (1816).

44. *Northern Whig*, June 18, Sept. 3, 1816; *Albany Argus*, July 19, 23, Aug. 13, 23, Sept. 20, Nov. 5, 6, 1816; Clinton to Henry Post, July 28, Aug. 14, 1816, in "De Witt Clinton as a Politician," ed. by John Bigelow, *Harper's New Monthly Magazine* 50 (February 1875): 411–412; *Evening Post*, Sept. 9, 19, Nov. 9, 1816; *Northern Whig*, Nov. 19, 1816; *VBA*, 73–79.

45. *Northern Whig*, Nov. 5, 26, 1816; *JSNY at their Fortieth Session, Begun and held at the City of Albany, the Fifth Day of November, 1816* (Albany: Jesse Buel, 1816), 4–5; Hammond, *Political Parties*, 1: 431–432.

46. *Northern Whig*, Oct. 5, 12, 15, Nov. 26, 1816; *Utica Patriot*, Nov. 16, 1816; MVB to Utica Insurance Company, Dec. 23, 1816, VBL.

47. Butler to Harriet Allen, Aug. 18, Sept. 24, Nov. 18, Dec. 12, 1816, VBL.

48. William Fraser to MVB, Nov. 9, MVB to Nathan Williams, Nov. 18, Casper Claw, Jr. to MVB, Nov. 20, MVB to John W. Taylor, Dec. 16, MVB to Francis Silvester, Dec. 15, MVB to McIntrye, Dec. 24, 1816, VBL; Chancery Minutes, 118, 135, 159, 197, 213, 225–226, Box 3, Vol. 26.

49. *Jackson, ex. dem. Van Alen and Van Alen, v. Ambler*, 14 *Johnson's Reports*, 96–111 (1817).

50. Butler to Harriet Allen, Jan. 25, 1817, VBL; *Columbian*, Jan. 29, 1817.

51. *The Attorney-General v. The Utica Insurance Company*, William Johnson, ed. *Reports of Cases Adjudged in the Court of Chancery of New-York, Containing the Cases from March, 1814 to [July 1823] Inclusive* (New York: Banks & Bros., 1883), 2: 371–372 (1817), hereafter cited as *Johnson's Chancery Reports*.

52. Ibid., 372–374.

53. Ibid., 374–391; Charles L. Todd and Robert Sonkin, *Alexander Bryan Johnson: Philosophic Banker* (Syracuse: Syracuse Univ. Press, 1977), 95–96; Roper, "Van Buren," 184.

54. MVB to Porter, Feb 5, 1817, VBL; Porter to MVB, Feb. 10, 13, Betts to MVB, Feb. 24, Robert Swartwout to MVB, Feb. 26, John Irving to MVB, Mar. 7, 17, Throop to Van Buren, Mar. 15, MVB to Worth, Apr. 27, 1817, [misdated as 1818], VBLC; Clinton to John Pintard, Feb. 24, 1817, Clinton Papers, NYPL; *Evening Post,* Feb. 27, Mar. 4, 6, 10, 28, 31; *Albany Register,* Mar. 26, 30, 31, 1817; Spencer to Armstrong, Mar. 26, 1817, Rokeby Collection; *Albany Argus,* Mar. 28, 1817; Hammond, *Political Parties,* 1: 432–438; *VBA,* 71, 79–83; Cole, *Van Buren,* 50.

55. *Moses Lyon and Edward Brockway, Appellants, v. Benjamin Tallmadge, John Tallmadge, David Wadham, David Thompson, Garret Smith, Aaron Smith, Junius Smith, William S. Tallmadge, Jonathan Richmond, and Solomon Dewey, Respondents,* 14 *Johnson's Reports,* 501–526 (1817); *Abraham Franklin, and Others, Appellants, v. Walter F. Osgood, and Others, Respondents, Walter F. Osgood, and Others, Appellants, v. Abraham Franklin, and Others, Respondents,* ibid., 527–569 (1817); Minutes of the Court of Errors, 2: 31, 42, 43, 44, 46–47; Hammond, *Political Parties,* 1: 441–442.

56. *The Executors of Isaac Clason, Plaintiffs in Error, v. John H. Bailey and Arnoldus Voorhees, Defendants in Error; The same v. Denton and Smith; The same v. Merrit and Merrit,* 14 *Johnson's Reports,* 485–492 (1817).

57. Notes on Erie Canal, Apr. 15, 1817, VBLC; *Albany Gazette,* Apr. 16, 1817; *VBA,* 84; Nathan Miller, *The Enterprise of a Free People: Aspects of Economic Development in New York during the Canal Period, 1792–1828* (Ithaca: Cornell Univ. Press, 1962), 45; Niven, *Van Buren,* 63–64.

58. *Columbian,* Apr. 22, 25, 29, 29, May 2, 1817; Charles Graham to William P. Van Ness, Apr. 23, 1817, Van Ness Papers, NYHS; *National Advocate,* Apr. 26, 1817; *Albany Gazette,* Apr. 30, 1817.

59. *Albany Argus,* Apr. 25, 29, May 13, June 10, 1817; *Evening Post,* Apr. 26, May 3, 1817.

60. Butler to Harriet Allen, Sept. 24, 1816, June 13, 1817, VBL; Docket of Judgements (Albany), Box 7., Vol. 8.

61. *Kidzie v. Sackrider and Others,* 14 *Johnson's Reports,* 195–198 (1817).

62. Horowitz, *Transformation of American Law,* 44; Hall, *Magic Mirror,* 115–116, 119.

63. Butler to Harriet Allen, June 3, 13, July 9, 1817, VBL; *Albany Argus,* June 3, 10, 13, 17, 27, July 2, 1817.

64. MVB to Peter Van Schaack, May 31, MVB to Peter Hoes, May 31, Butler to Harriet Allen, June 3, Indenture for Land to MVB, Aug. 1, 1817, Deed for Land to MVB, Sept. 23, 1817, VBL.

65. Attorney General's Correspondence, 1817; Chancery Minutes, 2, 19, Box 3, Vol. 27; David Rodgers to MVB, June 23, McIntrye to MVB, July 22, Aug. 5, MVB to Stephen Decatur, July 30, John King to MVB, Aug. 1, *The People v. Harley Strong,* Aug., *The People v. Asa L. Clark,* Aug., *Madison County v. The People,* Aug., Edmund C. Genet to MVB, Sept. 1, MVB to Abraham Van Vechten, Sept. 5, 1817, VBL.

66. *Albany Argus,* July 4, 1817; *VBA,* 89.

67. *Hart v. Ten Eyck and Others,* 2 *Johnson's Chancery Reports,* 62–64 (1816).

68. Ibid., 64–72.

69. Henry to MVB, Dec. 5, 1815, Butler to Harriet Allen, Aug. 20, 1817, VBL; *Hart v. Ten Eyck,* 2 *Johnson's Chancery Reports,* 513–518 (1817).

70. Docket of Judgments (Albany), Box 7, Vol. 8; *The People v. Anderson,* 14 *Johnson's Reports,* 294–302 (1817).

71. Chancery Register, 332; *Moody v. A. and H. Payne,* 2 *Johnson's Chancery Re-*

ports, 548–550 (1817); *McIntrye and Others v. Mancius and Brown, 3 Johnson's Chancery Reports,* 45–48 (1817).

72. Butler to Harriet Allen, Oct. 7, 17, 1817,VBL.

73. Docket of Judgements, Box 7,Vol. 8; *Jackson, ex dem. Wynkoop, v. Myers,* 14 *Johnson's Reports,* 354–357 (1817); *Caswell v. the Black River Cotton and Manufacturing Company,* ibid., 453–458 (1817).

74. *Denning and Others v. Smith and Others, 3 Johnson's Chancery Reports,* 332–346 (1818); *A. Van Bergen v. H. Van Bergen,* ibid., 282–289 (1818).

75. *Jackson, ex dem. Woodruff and Others, v. Gilchrist, 15 Johnson's Reports,* 89–90 (1818); Ruth L. Higgins, *Expansion in New York, With Especial Reference to the Eighteenth Century* (Columbus: Ohio State Univ. Press, 1931), 27, 28.

76. *Jackson, ex dem. Woodruff and Others, v. Gilchrist, 15 Johnson's Reports,* 90–91.

77. Ibid., 92–93, 102–108.

78. Ibid., 93–96.

79. Ibid., 96–102.

80. Ibid., 108–119.

81. *Albany Argus,* Jan. 30, 1818; *National Advocate,* Feb. 2, 1818; *Albany Argus,* Feb. 3, 17, 18, 27, 1818; Hammond, *Political Parties,* 1: 457–460; James Tallmadge to Clinton, Feb. 11, 1818, Clinton Papers, CU; Niven, *Van Buren,* 67–68.

82. *JSNY Begun and Held at their Forty-First Session, the Twenty-Seventh of January, 1818* (Albany: Jesse Buel, 1818), 43, 56, 58, 106, 112, 115, 126, 130, 132, 135, 138, 139, 141, 153, 155, 157–159, 168, 175–176, 180–181, 187, 195–196,, 205, 210–212, 217, 221–222, 229, 235–236, 217, 219, 235–236, 251, 253–255; 261, 303–309, 350–354; *Albany Argus,* Jan. 27, Feb. 27, Mar. 31, 1818; Butler to Harriet Butler, Feb. 18, 1818,VBL; *Utica Patriot,* Mar. 3, 1818; *National Advocate,* Mar. 6, 1818; *Albany Argus,* Mar. 10, 17, 24, 27, 31, Apr. 3, 24, 1818; *Albany Gazette,* Apr. 9, 1818; *National Advocate,* Mar. 25, 1818; David Bacon to MVB, April 2, 1818,VBL.

83. Docket of Judgements (Albany), Box 8,Vol. 9; Attorney General's Correspondence, 1818; *JSNY,* 41st sess., 138–139, 181–182; *Albany Argus,* Jan. 6, 27, 1818; *National Advocate,* Mar. 6, Apr. 23, 1818; *Albany Gazette,* Apr. 9, 1818; *Evening Post,* Apr. 11, 1818.

84. *National Advocate,* Feb. 2, 20, 21, Apr. 9, 27, 1818; *Albany Argus,* Feb. 17, 30, Mar. 3, 10, 24, 27, Apr. 14, 21, 28, 1818; Kingston *Ulster Plebeian,* Apr. 18, 1818; *Albany Gazette,* Apr. 24, 1818; MVB to Worth, Apr. 27, 1818,VBLC; Hammond, *Political History,* 1: 460–471; *VBA,* 85–86.

85. *Ulster Plebeian,* Apr. 18, 1818; *National Advocate,* Apr. 27, May 9, 1818; *Utica Patriot,* May 5, 12, 1818.

9: REPUBLICANISM AND STATE ATTORNEY GENERAL: PHASE TWO

1. Hammond, *Political Parties,* 1: 507; Attorney General Papers, 1818, Box 3; Chancery Minutes, Box 4,Vol. 28; MVB, Complainant v. Utica Insurance Company, May 1818, MVB to Nathan Williams, June 10, June 29, Thomas Hubbard to MVB, June 6, 1818, VBL; *The People v. Benjamin Seelye,* Supreme Court Judgements, Box 311; Docket to Judgements (Albany), Box 8,Vol. 3; *Jackson, ex dem. Van Alen, v. Casper I. Ham, 15 Johnson's Reports,* 261–263 (1818).

2. *The People v. The Utica Insurance Company,* May 16, 1818, VBLC.

3. See for example, *Albany Argus,* Aug. 14, 1818.

4. *The People of the State of New-York, ex relatione The Attorney-General, v. The Utica Insurance Company,* 15 *Johnson's Reports,* 358–367 (1818).

5. Ibid., 368–374.

6. Ibid., 374–375.

7. Ibid., 375–377.

8. Ibid., 378–396.

9. Roper, "Van Buren," 185–187; Edwin M. Dodd, *American Business Corporations Until 1860, with Special Reference to Massachusetts* (Cambridge: Harvard Univ. Press, 1954), 59; Harry L. Watson, *Liberty and Power: The Politics of Jacksonian America* (New York: Farrar, Straus and Giroux, 1990), 132–171.

10. *Lancing v. McPherson and Others,* 3 *Johnson's Chancery Reports,* 424–426 (1818).

11. *Albany Argus,* Sept. 8, 25, 1818; MVB to Worth, Nov. 26, Thompson to MVB, Nov. 28, 1818, VBLC.

12. *Albany Argus,* Oct. 13, 16, 1818; Evander Morse to MVB, Sept. 2, Samuel B. Beach to MVB, Sept. 8, Joseph Klein to MVB, Sept. 8, McIntrye to MVB, Sept. 16, Alexander Babee to MVB, Sept. 19, William Garrett to MVB, Sept. 21, Lewis Person to MVB, Sept. 21, Edgar Morse to MVB, Sept. 28, Joseph Clark to MVB, Oct. 1, 1818, Attorney General's Correspondence, Box 3.

13. Docket of Judgements (Albany), Box 8, Vol. 9; *Jackson, ex dem. William J. Livingston, v. Barringer,* 15 *Johnson's Reports,* 471–474 (1818).

14. *Decker v. Robert S. Livingston and Others,* ibid., 479–483 (1818).

15. *Commissioners of Highways of the Town of Kinderhook v. Claw and Another,* ibid., 537–539 (1818).

16. *Albany Argus,* Oct. 23, Nov. 17, 1818; Thompson to MVB, Nov. 3, Sanford to MVB, Nov. 4, MVB to Worth, Nov. 26, 28, 1818, VBL; *VBA,* 90.

17. *Troup v. Sherwood and Wood,* 3 *Johnson's Chancery Reports,* 558–566 (1818).

18. *P. and H. Ham v. Schuyler and Others,* 4 *Johnson's Chancery Reports,* 1–2 (1819).

19. Ibid., 2.

20. Ibid., 2.

21. Ibid., 3.

22. Ibid., 3.

23. Ibid., 3–8.

24. *VBA,* 26; Fox, *Decline of Aristocracy,* 120–148.

25. Thompson to MVB, Nov. 28, Dec. 8, 25, 1818, VBLC.

26. *Albany Argus,* Jan. 8, 15, Feb. 2, 12, 1819; *National Advocate,* Jan. 8, 15, 1819; *JSNY at their Forty-Second Session, Begun and Held at the City of Albany, the Fifty Day of January, 1819* (Albany: J. Buel, 1819), 4–41; Hammond, *Political Parties,* 1: 478–480; Niven, *Van Buren,* 68–69.

27. Docket of Judgements (Albany), Box 8, Vol. 9; *The People v. the Supervisors of the County of Ulster,* 16 *Johnson's Reports,* 59–61 (1819).

28. *Henry Livingston v. Ten Broeck,* ibid., 14–20 (1819).

29. Ibid., 17–28.

30. *Walter T. Livingston v. Potts,* ibid., 28–29 (1819).

31. Roper, "Van Buren," 178.

32. Moses Cantine to MVB, Feb. 11, 1819, VBLC; *JSNY,* 42nd sess., 57, 60, 64–65.

33. John A. King to Rufus King, Jan. 14, Rufus King to Charles King, Feb. 11, 1819, *King's Correspondence,* 6: 192–193, 213; *National Advocate,* Jan. 15, 26, Feb. 6, 1819; *Albany Argus,* Feb. 5, 12, 19, 1819; *Evening Post,* Feb. 5, 1819; Thompson to MVB, Jan. 23, 1819, VBLC; Hammond, *Political Parties,* 1: 485.

34. *Albany Argus,* Feb. 1, 5, 9, 1819; *National Advocate,* Feb. 5, 1919; *Utica Patriot,* Feb. 9, 1819.

35. *Nathaniel L. Griswold and George Griswold, Plaintiffs in Error, v. Joshua Waddington, who is impleaded with Henry Waddington, Defendant in Error,* 16 *Johnson's Reports,* 438 (1819).

36. Ibid., 439–441.

37. Ibid., 441–443.

38. Ibid., 443–508.

39. Ibid., 508–509; Bray Hammond, "The North's Empty Purse, 1861–1862," *AHR* 67 (October 1961): 1–18.

40. *James Jackson, ex dem. Brockholst Livingston and Others, Plaintiff in Error, v. James Robins, Defendant in Error,* 16 *Johnson's Reports,* 537–592 (1819).

41. *Albany Argus,* Feb. 9, 1819.

42. MVB to Butler, Feb. 11, Moses Cantine to Van Buren, Feb. 11, 1819, VBLC; John Van Buren to MVB, July 31, 1842, VBL; Niven, *Van Buren,* 72, 495.

43. Moses Cantine to Christiana Cantine, May 23, 1819, Cantine Family Papers, CU.

44. Butler to Harriet Allen, Oct. 3, 1817, Feb. 28, Apr. 3, 1818, VBL; Butler to William Allen, Feb. 19, 1819, Butler Papers, NYSL; Mackenzie, *Life and Opinions,* 13–21; Arthur Ekirch, Jr., "Benjamin F. Butler of New York: A Personal Portrait," *NYH* 58 (January 1977): 47–68.

45. *Albany Argus,* Jan. 12, Mar. 9, 23, 1819.

46. *Orange County Patriot,* Mar. 2, 9, 16, Apr. 17, 1819; *Evening Post,* Mar. 5, 11, 16, Apr. 14, 1819; *Albany Argus,* Apr. 23, 1819; Thomas B. Crowell, *Report of the Trial of the Murders of Richard Jennings* (Newburgh: Benjamin Lewis, 1819).

47. *JSNY,* 42nd sess., 45–47, 48, 50–51, 66–70, 89, 119, 123, 133, 134, 135, 140, 143, 154, 169, 176, 183, 199–200, 201–202, 204, 218, 244, 250, 275; Hammond, *Political Parties,* 1: 489; *VBA,* 92–94; Niven, *Van Buren,* 72–73.

48. *National Advocate,* Jan. 12, 1819; Nathaniel Tallmadge to Clinton, Jan. 17, 1819, Clinton Papers, CU; *Columbian,* Mar. 11, 1819; *Albany Argus,* Mar. 12, 30, Apr. 9, 1819; Cole, *Van Buren,* MVB to Worth, Apr. 22, 1819, VBLC.

49. John C. Spencer to Albert Tracy, Jan. 24, 1819, Albert Tracy Papers, NYSL; *Utica Patriot,* Feb. 23, 1819; *National Advocate,* Mar. 29, Apr. 9, 1819; *VBA,* 91; *Albany Argus,* Mar. 30, 1819.

50. *Evening Post,* Mar. 5, 16, 30, Apr. 2, 1819; *National Advocate,* Apr. 1, 1819; *Columbian,* July 10, 1819; Hammond, *Political Parties,* 1: 497–500; *VBA,* 91.

51. John A. King to Rufus King, Jan. 8, 14, Feb. 3, Charles King to Rufus King, Feb. 8, 1819, *King's Correspondence,* 6: 102, 192–193, 201, 208–209; New York *American,* Mar. 3, 10, 1819; John Duer to MVB, Mar. 27, 1819, VBLC; William Coleman to Morris Miller, 20 June, 1819, Miscellaneous Papers, NYHS; Gulian Verplanck to John Quincy Adams, Dec. 22, 1819, Adams Family Papers, MHS; Clinton to John Pintard, Jan. 20, 1820, Clinton Papers, NYHS; Shaw Livermore, *The Twilight of Federalism,*

1815–1830 (Princeton: Princeton Univ. Press, 1962), 62–79.

52. *Albany Argus,* Mar. 2, 9, 16, 26, 30, Apr. 20, 23, June 4, 1819; *New York American,* Mar. 10, Apr. 17, 1819; *Albany Register,* Apr. 9, 1819; *National Advocate,* Apr. 10, 17, May 1, 1819; *Bee,* Apr. 27, 1819; *Northern Whig,* May 4, 1819.

53. *Jackson, ex. dem. Troup and Others, v. Blodget,* 16 *Johnson's Reports,* 172–179 (1819).

54. *Niles Weekly Register* 18 (June 26, 1819): 292.

55. *Albany Argus,* June 15, 1819; Daniel Rodgers, *New York City Recorder, For the Year 1819, Containing Reports of the Most Interesting Trials and Decisions which Have Arisen in the Various Jurisdictions, For the Trial of Jury Cases, in the Hall, During that Year, Particularly in the Court of Session* (New York City: Clayton & Kingland, 1819), 4: 80–87.

56. Thompson to MVB, Feb. 8, Cantine to MVB, Feb. 11, 1819, VBLC; *Bee,* July 13, 1819; *VBA,* 93.

57. Ibid., 94; *Bee,* July 13, 1819; *Evening Post,* July 17, 1819; *Columbian,* July 20, 1819; *Albany Argus,* July 13, 16, 1819; Hammond, *Political Parties,* 1: 507.

58. *VBA,* 93; Noah to MVB, July 13, Betts to MVB, July 23, 1819, VBLC; *Albany Argus,* July 13, 16, 20, 27, Aug. 6, 1819; William W. Van Ness to Solomon Van Rennselaer, July 14, 1819; Bonney, *Legacy,* 1: 337; Henry Meigs to Josiah Meigs, Aug. 22, 1819, Henry Meigs Papers, NYHS; *Columbian,* Aug. 7, 24, 1819; *Albany Register,* Dec. 24, 1819; Niven, *Van Buren,* 76.

59. Hoyt to MVB, July 17, 1819, VBL.

60. Figures derived from Docket of Judgements (Albany), Box 5, Vol. 6, Box 6, Vol. 7, Box 7, Vol 8, Box 8, Vol. 9, and Attorney General's Correspondence, Box 1–3.

10: REPUBLICANISM IN A NEW ERA

1. Samuel H. Rezneck, "The Depression of 1819–1822: A Social History," *AHR* 39 (October 1933): 28–47; Walter Buckingham Smith and Arthur H. Cole, *Fluctuations in American Business, 1790–1860* (Cambridge: Harvard Univ. Press, 1935), 12–33; Murray N. Rothbard, *The Panic of 1819: Reactions and Policies* (New York: Columbia Univ. Press, 1962), 1–23; J. Van Fenstermaker, *The Development of American Commercial Banking: 1782–1837* (Kent: Kent State Univ. Press, 1965), 21–54; Charles G. Sellers, *The Market Revolution: Jacksonian America, 1815–1849* (New York: Oxford Univ. Press, 1991), 122–124, 137–139.

2. *Albany Argus,* June 18, 22, 25, 29, July 13, Sept. 4, 1819; *Evening Post,* July 2, 9, 1819; *Niles Weekly Register* 19 (July 3, 1819): 331.

3. MVB to Francis Bloodgood, Aug. 10, MVB to Burr, Sept. 21, Samuel Hawkins to Oakley, Oct. 8, Horace Bolden to Oakley, Oct. 16, Ephraim Boxer and William Bowen to Oakley, Oct. 20, Lawrence Van Buren, Account with MVB, Nov. 5, MVB to Henry, Dec. 5, MVB to Williams, Dec. 26, 1819, MVB to Gerrit Y. Lancing, Jan. 11, 1820, VBL; *Bregnaw v. Claw,* 4 *Johnson's Chancery Reports,* 117 (1819), *Keisselbrack v. Livingston,* ibid., 144–149 (1819).

4. Chancery Minutes, Box 3, Vol. 25, 530–531; Box 3, Vol. 26, 36–37.

5. *Robert Troup v. William Wood and Samuel Sherwood,* 4 *Johnson's Chancery Reports,* 228–262 (1820).

6. New York *American,* May 12, June 9, 1819; *National Advocate,* May 12, Dec.

17, 1819; *Albany Argus*, May 28, June 22, Aug. 3, 31, Oct. 8, 12, Dec. 7, 1819.

7. William to Rufus King, May 10, 1819, *King's Correspondence*, 6: 22; *VBA*, 95–99, 100–101; MVB to James Tallmadge, Jr., Dec. 3, 1819, VBL; MVB, *Considerations in Favour of the Appointment of Rufus King, to the Senate of the United States. Submitted to the Republican Members of the Legislature of the State of New-York* (Albany: J. Buel, 1819); *Albany Argus*, Feb. 23, 24, 25, 29, 1820; Hammond, *Political Parties*, 1: 500–502, 525–526; MVB, *Speech of the Hon. M. Van Buren of the State, on the Act to Carry into Effect, the Act of 13th April, 1819, For the Settlement of the Late Governor's Accounts* (Albany: J. Buel, 1820); Shepard, *Van Buren*, 68–71; Alexander, *Political History*, 1: 275–276; Ivor Spencer, *The Victor and the Spoils: A Life of William L. Marcy* (Providence: Brown Univ. Press, 1959), 28–30; Irwin, *Tompkins*, 229–234, 252–254; Niven, *Van Buren*, 76–78; Cole, *Van Buren*, 57–62.

8. *National Advocate*, Apr. 2, 1819; Jan. 15, 25, Feb. 10, 16, 20, 23, 1820; *Albany Argus*, Nov. 30, Dec. 28, 1819, Jan. 7, 21, 25, 1820; *Utica Patriot*, Dec. 21, 1819; *Albany Register*, Dec. 24, 31, 1819; *Albany Register*, Dec. 28, 1819, Feb. 1, 1820; Noah to MVB, Dec. 19, MVB to Noah, Dec. 17, 1819, Henry F. Jones to MVB, Jan. 19, MVB to Jones, Jan. 21, 1820, MVB, "Notes on the Missouri Question, 1819–1820," MVB, "Notes on meetings in Albany and New York on the Missouri question, 1819–1820," [185?], VBLC; *Albany Argus*, Jan. 7, 11, 14, 1820; *New York American*, Jan. 12, 1820; *VBA*, 138–139; Holland, *Van Buren*, 144–147; Hammond, *Political Parties*, 1: 517; Glover Moore, *The Missouri Controversy, 1819–1821* (Lexington: Univ. of Kentucky Press, 1953), 175–189; Richard H. Brown, "The Missouri Crisis, Slavery and the Politics of Jacksonianism," *SAQ* 65 (winter 1966): 55–72; Cole, *Van Buren*, 59–61.

9. MVB to Worth, June 1, 1820, VBLC; Joline, *Autograph Hunter*, 88–89; Shepard, *Van Buren*, 34; *VBA*, 400.

10. *The Executors of Robert T. Livingston v. James Livingston*, 4 *Johnson's Chancery Reports*, 287–293 (1820); *The Executors of Robert T. Livingston v. Henry Livingston*, ibid., 294–299 (1820).

11. *Evening Post*, Mar. 2, 1818; *National Advocate*, May 24, 1819; Jan. 24, Feb. 24, 1820; *Albany Argus*, Jan. 21, Feb. 22, 1820; *Columbian*, Feb. 18, 1820; MVB to King, Apr. 13, 1820, *King's Correspondence*, 6: 331–322; MVB to Rufus King, June 14, 1821, VBL; Charles Haines, *An Appeal to the People of the State of New-York on the Expediency of Abolishing the Council of Appointment* (New York: E. Conrad, 1819); Hammond, *Political History*, 1: 521; Williamson, *American Suffrage*, 195–207.

12. MVB to Rufus King, Mar. Feb. 26, Mar. 12, Rufus King to John A. King, Mar. 4, 5, 18, *King's Correspondence*, 6: 283–285, 285, 288–290, 304; *Albany Argus*, Mar. 11, 17, 24, 28, Apr. 4, 11, 1820; Rufus King to MVB, Mar. 25, 27, MVB to Henry Meigs, Apr. 4, 1820, VBLC; MVB to Rufus King, Apr. 13, 29, 1820, VBL; *Evening Post*, Apr. 20, 1820; Haines to Clinton, Apr. 24, 1820, Clinton Papers, CU; *Northern Whig*, May 2, 1820.

13. Talcott to MVB, Apr. 15, MVB to James Hamilton, Apr. 17, Thompson to MVB, May 9, MVB to Worth, June 1, 1820, VBLC; MVB to Rufus King, Apr. 29, 1820, VBL; *Albany Argus*, Apr. 11, June 2, 1820; John Taylor to John W. Taylor, May 3, 1820, Taylor Papers; *New York American*, May 6, 22, 1820; *Columbian*, May 1, 3, 8, 9, June 2, 1820; Haines to Clinton, May 24, 1820, Clinton Papers, CU; *National Advocate*, June 2, 1820; Niven, *Van Buren*, 80–84.

14. *VBA*, 113, 401; Shepard, *Van Buren*, 31–36; Robert V. Remini, "The Albany Regency," *NYH* 39 (October 1958): 341–355; Niven, *Van Buren*, 65, 109.

15. MVB to Abraham Van Buren, May 31, MVB to Worth, June 1, 1820, VBLC; MVB to Jesse Hoyt, June 2, July 1, 1820, Mackenzie, *Van Buren,* 184; MVB to Gerrit Yates Lancing, June 12, 1820, VBL.

16. *John K. Beekman, Appellant, v. Josiah Frost, Eli Goddard, Philo Goddard, and Jesse Kellogg, Respondents,* 18 *Johnson's Reports,* 544–549 (1820).

17. Ibid., 549–556.

18. Ibid., 557–576.

19. *VBA,* 399–400; Butler to Hoyt, Feb. 7, 1820, Mackenzie, *Life and Opinion,* 26–27; Worth to MVB, Feb. 17, 1820, MVB to Worth, June 1, 1820, VBLC; Butler to Harriet A. Butler, Mar. 16, 1820, VBL; Lynch, *An Epoch and a Man,* 200; Niven, *Van Buren,* 82–83.

20. Butler to Hoyt, July 19, 1820, Mackenzie, *Life and Opinion,* 32; Butler to Harriet A. Butler, June 21, 25, 1820, VBL; *Albany Argus,* June 23, 1820; Mackenzie, *Van Buren,* 165; Howell and Tenney, *Bi-Centennial History,* 135.

21. MVB to Henry, July 7, 1820, VBL; *Elmendorf and Beekman v. Gerrit Y. Lancing, Jr., and Others,* 4 *Johnson's Chancery Reports,* 562–566 (1820); *Steere and Others v. Steere and Others,* 5 *Johnson's Chancery Reports,* 7–20 (1820).

22. Howell and Tenney, *Bi-Centennial History,* 137; MVB to Henry Van Der Lyn, May 30, MVB to Rufus King, Nov. 29, 1820, VBL; Cornelius P. Van Ness to MVB, July 25, MVB to Worth, Aug. 27, 1820, VBLC; Butler to Hoyt, June 24, July 19, 20, Aug. 9, 17, Oct. 12, Nov. 7, 1820, Mackenzie, *Van Buren,* 164–167; MVB to Lancing, Sept. 12, 1820, VBL.

23. Docket of Judgements (Albany), Box 9, Vol. 11; Common Rule Books (Albany), Box 2, Book 5; *Fleming v. Slocum,* 18 *Johnson's Reports,* 403–405 (1820).

24. Thompson to MVB, Apr. 9, May 9, 1820, VBLC; Ekirch, "Butler," 52–53.

25. Isaac O. Leake to MVB, May 28, MVB and Peter J. Hoes to Buel, July 17, Van Buren to Hoes, Aug. 5, 1820, VBLC; *Albany Argus,* June 20, 1820, MVD to John A. King [June 1820], VBL; Niven, *Van Buren,* 82.

26. Thompson to MVB, Feb. 8, Dec. 5, 1819, VBL; *Albany New-York Statesman,* July 23, 1820; *VBA,* 104; *Albany Argus,* July 7, 11, Aug. 15, Sept. 19, 1820; Edward Livingston to MVB, Sept. 6, 1820, VBLC.

27. Charles Haines to Clinton, May 24, 1820, Clinton Papers, CU; *National Advocate,* June 2, July 7, 28, Aug. 19, 24, Sept. 1, 14, Oct. 7, Dec. 21, 1820; *VBA,* 112; *Albany Argus,* June 2, 9, 23, July 14, 1820.

28. Clinton to Solomon Van Rensselaer, Mar. 27, 1820 [misdated], in Bonney, *Legacy,* 1: 352; *Columbian,* May 27, 1820; *Albany Argus,* July 7, 12, 25, 28, Aug. 4, Sept. 12, 19, Oct. 13, 24, 1820; Butler to Hoyt, Aug. 1, 1820, Mackenzie, *Van Buren,* 166.

29. *New-York Statesman,* Oct. 13, 1820; *Albany Argus,* Oct. 17, 1820.

30. Hamilton to MVB, Oct. 18, 19, 23, Dec. 3, 1820, MVB to Hamilton, Nov. 2, 1820, VBLC; *Columbian,* Nov. 9, 1820.

31. *Albany Argus,* Nov. 9, 10, 14, 17, 28, Dec. 8, 12, 1820; *New York American,* Nov. 13, 16, 1820; *Columbian,* Nov. 14, Dec. 19, 1820; MVB to Rufus King, Nov. 19, 1820, VBL; Clinton to Henry Post, Nov. 19, 25, 1820, Bigelow, "Clinton," *Harper's,* 413, 414; John A. King to Rufus King, Nov. 20, 1820, *King's Correspondence,* 6: 355; *Utica Patriot,* Nov. 28, 1820; *New-York Statesman,* Dec. 8, 19, 1820; Hammond, *Political Parties,* 1: 542–545.

32. *Columbian,* Nov. 23, 24, 25, Dec. 7, 1820; *New-York Statesman,* Dec. 5, 8, 1820; *Albany Argus,* Nov. 28, Dec. 1, 8, 12, 26, 29, 1820; Meigs to MVB, Nov. 26,

1820,VBLC; *Evening Post,* Feb. 16, 1821; *National Advocate,* Mar. 1, 12, 17, 20, 1821.

33. MVB to King, Jan. 14, 1821,VBL; Hammond, *Political Parties,* 1: 544; Cole, *Van Buren,* 66–67.

34. Clinton to Post, Nov. 30, Dec. 20, 1820, Bigelow, "Clinton," *Harper's,* 414–415; MVB to King, Jan. 21, 1821, *King's Correspondence,* 6: 375–377; Thompson to MVB, Dec. 18, Jan. 30, 1820,VBLC; *Evening Post,* Jan. 22, 1821; *National Advocate,* Jan. 23, Feb. 2, 1821; *Albany Gazette,* Jan. 26, 1821; *Albany Argus,* Jan. 26, Mar. 27, Apr. 3, 1821.

35. *New-York Statesman,* Dec. 8, 1820, Jan. 23, 26, Feb. 6, 9, 13, 1821; *Albany Argus,* Jan. 5, Feb 6, 7, 1821; Solomon Nadler, "The Green Bag: James Monroe and the Fall of De Witt Clinton," *NYHSQ* 59 (July 1975): 203–225.

36. John A. King to Rufus King, Feb. 2, MVB to Thompson, *King's Correspondence,* 6: 382–384; *Evening Post,* Feb. 5, 9, 1821; *National Advocate,* Feb. 9, 1821; Rufus King to Van Buren, Feb. 19, 1821,VBLC; Cole, *Van Buren,* 63–64.

37. *Bank of America v. John Woodworth,* 18 *Johnson's Reports,* 315–326 (1820); *John Woodworth, Plaintiff in Error, v. The President, Directors, and Company of the Bank of America, Defendants in Error,* 19 *Johnson's Reports,* 391–392 (1821).

38. Ibid., 393–425.

39. *New-York Statesman,* Apr. 13, 1821; Hammond, *Political Parties,* 1: 547–549.

40. *Higginbotham v. Burnet and others,* 5 *Johnson's Chancery Reports,* 184–188 (1821); *Westcott and others v. Cady and others,* ibid., 334–350 (1821).

41. Butler to Hoyt, Jan. 18, Feb. 20, 1821, Mackenzie, *Van Buren,* 167; *Albany Argus,* Feb. 13, May 11, 23, 25, 29, June 1, 1821; Haines to Solomon Van Rensselaer, Feb. 27, 1821, in Bonney, *Legacy,* 1: 364; *Evening Post,* May 7, 1821; *Columbian,* May 29, 1821.

42. *Mills v. Martin,* 19 *Johnson's Reports,* 7–10 (1821).

43. Ibid., 11–13.

44. Ibid., 13–38; *Martin v. Mott* (Wheaton), 19 (1827).

45. *Whallon v. Kaufman,* 19 *Johnson's Reports,* 97–112 (1821).

46. *Manahan v. Gibbons and Others,* ibid., 108–109 (1821).

47. Ibid., 109–112.

48. MVB to John E. Wool, May 21, MVB to Elisha Foot, June 16, 1821,VBL; *Albany Argus,* May 25, June 12, 19, July 23, 1821; *Evening Post,* July 9, 1821; *VBA,* 105–106; Cole, *Van Buren,* 68.

49. *Proceedings and Debates,* 27–34; Hammond, *Political Parties,* 2: 2–6; *VBA,* 106.

50. *Proceedings and Debates,* 42–48; 70–76, 120, 133–141, 147–148, 158, 162, 177–178.

51. MVB to John A. King, Oct. 28, 1821, *King's Correspondence,* 6: 422; Hammond, *Political Parties,* 2: 1–85; Fox, *Decline of Aristocracy,* 229–270.

52. *Proceedings and Debates,* 178–195, 199, 202, 274–283, 377, 409–411; Cole, *Van Buren,* 70–71.

53. *Proceedings and Debates,* 215–222; Hammond, *Political Parties,* 2: 22–40.

54. *Proceedings and Debates,* 255–265, 270.

55. *VBA,* 112; *Proceedings and Debates,* 271–277.

56. Ibid., 356–368, 376–377; Holland, *Van Buren,* 177–180; Cole, *Van Buren,* 72–73.

57. *VBA,* 106; Niven, *Van Buren,* 96–97.

58. *Proceedings and Debates,* 159–162, 296–300; Hammond, *Political Parties,* 2: 65–73.

59. *Proceedings and Debates,* 296–302, 307–309, 319, 331–332, 593.

60. Samuel Beardsley to Ela Collins, Sept. 20, Ulshoeffer to MVB, Sept. 21, 1821, VBLC; Rufus King to John A. King, Oct. 2, 1821, *King's Correspondence,* 6: 407; Cole, *Van Buren,* 74.

61. *Proceedings and Debates,* 329–344; Cole, *Van Buren,* 75.

62. *VBA,* 107–108; *New York American,* Oct. 16, 21, 1821; *Albany Argus,* Oct. 16, 23, 1821; *National Advocate,* Oct. 16, 27, Nov. 3, 1821; *Ulster Plebeian,* Oct. 24, 1821.

63. *Proceedings and Debates,* 344–356, 382–398, 596–624, 666.

64. Ibid., 500–505, 518–519; Lincoln, *Constitutional History,* 1; 679–680.

65. *Proceedings and Debates,* 505–506, 517–520.

66. Ibid., 516–517, 520–525.

67. Ibid., 527–536; Hammond, *Political Parties,* 2: 59–60.

68. *Proceedings and Debates,* 592, 596, 602–624, 647, 664.

69. Ibid., 413–416, 466–478, 525, 559–563, 576–583, 660; *VBA,* 107–108; *Albany Argus,* Dec. 15, 1822; MVB to John V. N. Yates, Dec. 26, 1821, VBL.

70. *National Advocate,* Sept. 17, 1821; Ulshoeffer to MVB, Sept. 21, 1821, VBLC; Peter A. Jay to John Jay, Oct. 10, 1822, *The Correspondence and Public Papers of John Jay,* ed. by Henry P. Johnston (1890–1893; reprint, New York: Da Capo Press, 1971), 453; Rufus King to Charles A. King, Oct. 15, MVB to Rufus King, Oct. 28, 1821, *King's Correspondence,* 6: 416–417, 422; Hammond, *Political Parties,* 2: 76–77; *VBA,* 112; Niven, *Van Buren,* 93–101; Cole, *Van Buren,* 66, 78–79; Sellers, *Market Revolution,* 112–113.

11: THE DUAL CAREER ENDS

1. MVB, "Statement of Demands in the hands of Benjamin Butler, Esq., by MVB, Nov. 21, 1821," VBLC.

2. Ibid.; MVB to Lancing, Nov. 12, 1821, VBL.

3. MVB, Notes on Rules of Order, Dec. 1821, VBL; *Annals of the Congress of the United States, 1789–1824,* 42 vols. (Washington, D.C.: Gales and Seaton, 1821–1824), 17th Cong., 1st Sess. (1821–1823), 1–2, 9, 67, 130, 141, 154, 393, hereafter cited as *Annals of Congress; National Intelligencer,* Feb. 5, 1822.

4. James C. Curtis, *The Fox at Bay,* 12–19; Robert V. Remini, *Martin Van Buren and the Making of the Democratic Party* (New York: W. W. Norton, 1970), 12–42; Cole, *Van Buren,* 104.

5. *Annals of Congress,* 17th Cong., 1st Sess. (1821–1823), 115, 126, 131–135, 146–149, 168–174, 182–183, 194–195.

6. MVB, Outline of a speech on Maison Rouge, Feb. 12, 1822, VBLC; *VBA,* 128, 129.

7. *Annals of Congress,* 17th Cong., 1st Sess. (1821–1823), 198, 201–204; MVB to Butler, Feb. 12, 1822, VBLC; *VBA,* 129.

8. Hammond, *Political Parties,* 1: 518–520.

9. Ibid.; Jeff Roedel, "Stoking the Doctrinal Furnaces: Judicial Review and the Council of Revision," *NYH* 69 (July 1988), 264.

10. *National Advocate,* Jan. 15, 31, Apr. 17, 1820; *Albany Argus,* Feb 1, 8, 11, 22, Apr. 7, 11, 17, 1820; *Evening Post,* Apr. 17, 1820; Rufus King to John A. King, Feb. 16, Rufus King to John A. and Charles King, Feb. 20, 23, Charles King to Rufus King,

Apr. 1, Rufus King to Charles King, Apr. 5, 1820, *King's Correspondence,* 6: 310–315; *VBA,* 110; Hammond, *Political Parties,* 1: 519–520.

11. MVB's brief and papers for the defendants, [Jan. 1822], VBLC; *Van Ness v. Hamilton and Others,* 19 *Johnson's Reports,* 349–366.

12. Ibid., 366, 375.

13. Roper, "Van Buren," 180–181.

14. *VBA,* 113; MVB to Sedgwick, Jan. 9, MVB to Root, Jan. 10, MVB to Williams, Mar. 3, 1822, VBL; Duer to MVB, Feb. 7, Ulshoeffer to MVB, Feb. 17. Mar. 11, MVB to Worth, Feb. 18, Mar. 16, 1822, VBLC; *Albany Argus,* Dec. 10, 1822; Niven, *Van Buren,* 122–123.

15. MVB to Root, Jan. 16, Dudley to MVB, Jan. 18, Skinner to MVB, Feb. 15, William Duer to MVB, Feb. 17, Sutherland to MVB, Mar. 3, Cantine to MVB, Dec. 2, MVB to Yates, Dec. 10, 1822, VBLC; Hammond, *Political Parties,* 2: 106–119; Folts, *Duely & Constantly Kept,* 5, 28.

16. Niven, *Van Buren,* 120–137; Cole, *Van Buren,* 117–133.

17. Butler to Hoyt, Jan. 18, Feb. 20, 1822, Mackenzie, *Van Buren,* 167; Butler to Harriet Butler, Mar. 17, 1817, MVB to Butler, Feb. 16, 1824, Jan 13, Mar. 15, 1828, VBL; MVB to Butler, Nov. 17, 1828, VBLC; William D. Driscoll, "Benjamin Butler: Lawyer and Politician" (Ph.D. diss., New York Univ., 1965), 48–172.

18. *Albany Argus,* Mar. 14, 1824; Docket of Judgements (Albany), Box 10, Vol. 11, Vol. 12; Butler to Harriet Butler, [n.d., 1823?], VBL.

19. MVB to Ten Eyck, May 14, MVB to Arent Van Der Poel, June 26, July 8, Oct. 24, MVB to Hoes, Nov. 2, 1822, VBL.

20. Docket of Judgements (Albany), Box 9, Vol. 10, Box 10, Vol. 11, Box 12, Vol. 13; Common Rule Books (Albany), Box 33, Book 87, Box 34, Book 88; Docket of Judgements (Utica), 1823–1828.

21. *VBA,* 114; *Jonathan J. Coddington, and Joseph Coddington, who were impleaded in the Court below with John F. Randolph, and Josiah Savage, Appellants, v. Thomas Bay, Respondent,* 20 *Johnson's Reports,* 637–639 (1822).

22. Ibid., 639–658.

23. Ray A. Brown, *The Law of Personal Property* (Chicago: Callaghan, 1955), 234–236; Horowitz, *Transformation of American Law,* 244–252; Tony A. Freyer, *Forums of Order: The Federal Courts and Business in American History* (Greenwich: JAI Press, 1979), 41–98; R. Kent Newmyer, *Supreme Court Justice Joseph Story: Statesman of the Old Republic* (Chapel Hill: Univ. of North Carolina Press, 1985), 334–341.

24. *Annals of Congress,* 18th Cong., 2nd sess. (1823–1824), 65–73, 170–204, 291, 313, 327, 336, 355–362, 366–374, 381–399, 417–418, 514–523, 575, 576, 582–590, 618–620, 766; *Register of Debates in Congress* (Washington, D.C.: Gales and Seaton), 18th Cong., 2nd sess. (1824–1825), 1: 587–578, 619–620, 2: 409–423, 459–460, 517–518, 556–518, 556–570, 668–671; *Register of Debates in Congress,* 19th Cong., 2nd sess. (1826–1827), 3: 30–34, 81–83, 226–227, 279, 386–287, 409–423, 688; *Register of Debates in Congress,* 20th Cong., 1st sess. (1827–1828), 4: 68–69, 93–95, 278–303, 328–341; *VBA,* 149–243, 401. See for example Niven, *Van Buren,* 156–214; Cole, *Van Buren,* 142–181.

25. Niven, *Van Buren,* 103–155; Cole, *Van Buren,* 112–141.

26. Van Buren to Butler, Dec. 25, 1826, Van Buren to Ritchie, Jan. 13, 1827, VBL; *VBA,* 123, 448, 513, 514; Remini, *Van Buren and the Making of the Democratic Party,* 93–198; Richard Hofstader, *Toward a Political System: The Rise of Legitimate Opposition*

in the United States, 1780–1840 (Berkeley: Univ. of California Press, 1970), 212–221; Niven, *Van Buren,* 150–214; Cole, *Van Buren,* 142–215.

27. Rufus King, memoranda, Apr. 7, 1823, *King's Correspondence,* 6: 521–522; MVB to Rufus King, May 9, MVB to Thompson, June 4, 1823, VBL; *VBA,* 140–141; Gerald T. Dunne, "Smith Thompson" in *Justices of the Supreme Court, 1789–1969: Their Lives and Major Opinion,* eds. Leon Friedman and Fred L. Israel (New York: R. R. Bowker, 1969), 475–509; Niven, *Van Buren,* 133–136; Cole, *Van Buren,* 117–120.

28. MVB to Rufus King, Oct. 7, 1823, VBL.

29. *Charles Wilkes and the President, Directors, and Company of the Bank of New-York, Plaintiffs in error, v. Edward Lion, ex dem. Medcef Eden and John Wood, Otherwise called John Wood, Junior, assignee of Medcef Eden, Esek Cowen, Reports of Cases Argued and Determined in the Supreme Court; and in the Court for the Trial of Impeachments and the Correction of Errors, of the State of New York* (New York: Banks & Bros., 1873), 2: 333–336 (1823), hereafter cited as *Cowen;* Herbert S. Parmet and Marie B. Hecht, *Aaron Burr: Portrait of an Ambitious Man* (New York: Macmillan, 1967), 334; Milton Lomask, *Aaron Burr: The Conspiracy and Years of Exile, 1805–1836* (New York: Farrar, Straus, Giroux, 1982), 384.

30. *James Anderson, Plaintiff in Error, v. James Jackson, ex dem., Medcef Eden, Defendant in Error,* 16 *Johnson's Reports,* 382–437 (1819); *Wilkes v. Lyon,* 2 *Cowen,* 336–337.

31. *Lyon, ex dem. Eden et al. v. Wilkes et al,* 1 *Cowen,* 591–592; James Parton, *The Life and Times of Aaron Burr* (New York: Mason Bros., 1858), 608–610; Lomask, *Burr,* 385.

32. *Wilkes v. Lion,* 2 *Cowen* 340–400.

33. *Nicholas I. Roosevelt, Appellant, v. Dale & Wife, Executors of Robert Fulton, Respondents,* 2 *Cowen,* 129–139 (1823); Cynthia Owen Phillip, *Robert Fulton: A Biography* (New York: Franklin Watts, 1985), 308, 310.

34. *Sarah Wilson and Others, Appellants, v. Robert Troup and others, Respondents,* 2 *Cowen,* 195–207 (1823).

35. Ibid., 207–8, 215–221, 222–242.

36. Timothy Walker, *Introduction to American Law* (Philadelphia: P. H. Nicklin & T. Johnson, 1837), 301–308, 602; Friedman, *American Law,* 216–218; Horowitz, *Transformation of American Law,* 265–266.

37. MVB to Hoyt, Jan. 31, 1824, Mackenzie, *Van Buren,* 190; Hoes to MVB, Jan. 31, MVB to Worth, Feb. 22, MVB to Hoes, Nov. 24, 1824, VBLC; MVB to Buel, Jan. 31, MVB to Butler, Feb. 4, Mar. 20, 1824, MVB to Burr, Jan. 14, 1825, VBL.

38. Strong to Butler, Feb. 21, 1825, MVB to Hoes, May 8, 1825, Aug. 8, 1826, Nov. 18, 1826, Jan. 12, 1827, MVB to Butler, Jan. 19, Mar. 22, 1826, Butler to MVB, Apr. 24, 1826, Kent to MVB, Apr. 15, 1826, MVB, Account of Payments, Lawrence Van Buren's and MVB's sheep concerns, promissory noted of Lawrence Van Buren to MVB, Aug. 28, 1826–Sept. 27, 1831; MVB to Van Dyck, Sept. 8, 1826, Mar. 4, 1827, Nov. 10, 23, 1827, Pleasonton to MVB, Feb. 4, 28, 1827, MVB to Hoyt, June 6, 1827, MVB to McCarthy, July 25, 1827, MVB to Charles Butler, Aug 23, 1827, VBL; MVB to Cambreleng, Oct. 22, 1827, VBLC.

39. Ira K. Morris, *Morris' Memorial History of Staten Island* (Staten Island: West New Brighton, 1900), 2: 99–111.

40. *John Inglis, Demandant v. The Trustees of the Sailor's Snug Harbour in the City of New York,* 3 (Peters) 99–111 (1830).

41. Robinson, "Emmet," 405–406; *VBA,* 172–176; Daniel Webster to Ezekiel Webster, Mar. 15, 1829, *The Papers of Daniel Webster,* ed. by Charles M. Wiltse and

Harold Moser (Hanover: Univ. Press of New England, 1976), 2: 407.

42. Porter, *Astor,* 2: 876–883; Alfred S. Konefsky and Andrew J. King, *The Papers of Daniel Webster, Legal Papers: The Boston Practice* (Hanover: Univ. Press of New England, 1983), 2: 95–97.

43. Ibid.

44. *Kelley v. Jackson, ex dem. Theodorious Fowler et al.,* 2 *Paine* 440 No. 7659 (1827) and 14 *Federal Cases* 244 (1827).

45. Sparhawk, *Report of the Trial,* 3–18.

46. Ibid., 18–57; Konefsky and King, *Webster's Legal Papers,* 2: 11–115.

47. Sparhawk, *Report of the Trial,* 57–66.

48. *Niles Register,* 34 (June 7, 1828): 235; Webster to MVB, Sept. 27, 1828, *The Papers of Webster,* 2: 365–366; Konefsky and King, *Webster's Legal Papers,* 2: 111–115; *James Carver, Plaintiff in Error, vs. James Jackson, on the Demise of John Jacob Astor, Theodosius Fowler, Cadwallader D. Colden, Cornelius J. Boget, Henry Gage Morris, Maria Morris, Thomas Hinks and John Hinks, Defendants in Error,* 4 *Peters* 1 (1829); *Ex Parte Nathaniel Crane and Samuel Kelly; in the Matter of James Jackson, Ex Dem. of John Jacob Astor and Others, v. Nathaniel Crane and James Jackson, Ex Dem. of John Jacob Astor and Others v. Samuel Crane,* 5 *Peters* 190 (1831).

49. *Stephen Waring, Plaintiff in Error, v. James Jackson, ex dem. Medcep Eden and Another, Defendant in Error,* 1 *Peters,* 569 (1828); *Varick and Bacon, Plaintiffs in Error, and Jackson, ex dem. Eden and Wood, Defendants in Error, John L. Wendell, Reports of Cases Argued and Determined in the Supreme Court; and in the Court for the Trial of Impeachments and the Corrections of Errors, in the State of New York* (New York: Banks & Bros., 1874), 2: 166–167 (1828), hereafter cited as *Wendell.*

50. Varick to MVB, July 19, 1826, MVB to Worth, Mar. 15, 1828, MVB to Richard Peters, June 4, 1828, VBL.

51. *Varick and Bacon v. Eden and Wood,* 2 *Wendell,* 171–201, 205.

52. *VBA,* 220–221; MVB to Cambreleng, Nov. 7, 1828, VBLC; Cole, *Van Buren,* 175–176.

53. *VBA,* 33; Holland, *Van Buren,* 69–75; Shepard, *Van Buren,* 30–36; Joline, *Autograph Hunter,* 91.

12: MARTIN VAN BUREN'S LEGAL AND POLITICAL WORLD

1. Remini, *Martin Van Buren and the Making of the Democratic Party,* 196–197; Michael Wallace, "Changing Concepts of Party in the United States: New York, 1815–1828," *AHR* 74 (December 1968): 453–491; Sellers, *Market Revolution,* 293–300; Donald B. Cole, *The Presidency of Andrew Jackson* (Lawrence: Univ. Press of Kansas, 1993), 15–21.

2. Holland, *Van Buren,* 59–75; Butler, *Martin Van Buren,* 7–16; Shepard, *Van Buren,* 32; Roper, "Van Buren," 170–189.

3. *VBA,* 21; Roper, Van Buren," 176–177.

4. *VBA,* 11–12, 34.

5. Cole, *Van Buren,* 22–25.

6. Information derived from various editions of *Johnson's Reports* and Supreme Court Judgement Rolls.

7. Information derived from Statement of Van Alen and Van Buren's business

from commencement of firm until March 19, 1805, Memorandum of Debts Due US and Debts Due, Mar. 19, 1805, Legal Record Book and a Statement of Van Buren's Notes, [Dec. 24, 1808], Skinner to MVB, Nov. 15, 1809, Butler to Van Buren, Sept. 14, Oct. 11, 13, 1815, Jan. 6, May 29, June 19, July 31, 1816, MVB Statement of Demands in the hands of Benjamin Butler, Esq, by MVB, Nov. 21, 1821, VBL; Docket of Judgements (Albany, New York City, Utica), 1805–1828; Minutes of the Supreme Court, 1805–1819; Supreme Court of Judicature Judgement Rolls, 1805–1828; Common Rule Books, 1805–1828; Court of Chancery Minutes, 1805–1821; Minutes of the Court of Errors, 1811–1819; and various editions of *Johnson's Reports, Johnson's Chancery Reports, Cowen,* and *Wendell.*

8. Information derived from ibid.

9. See for example, Robert E. Shalhope, "Toward a Republican Thesis: The Emergence of an Understanding of Republicanism in American Historiography," *William and Mary Quarterly,* 3rd ser., 29 (January 1972): 49–80; Robert E. Shalhope, "Republicanism and Early American Historiography," *William and Mary Quarterly,* 3rd ser., 39 (April 1982): 334–356; Isaac Kramnick, "Republican Revisionism Revisted," *AHR* 87 (June 1982): 629–664; Major Wilson, "Republicanism and the Idea of Party in the Jacksonian Period," *JER* (winter 1988): 419–442; Rodgers, "Republicanism," 11–38; Gary J. Kornblith, "The Artisanal Response to Capitalist Transformation," *JER* (fall 1990): 324; Paul A. Gilje, "The Rise of Capitalism in the Early Republic," *JER* (summer 1996): 159–181.

10. MVB, *Inquiry,* 165, 224, 226, 230–231; Gerald S. Henig, "The Jacksonian Attitude toward Abolitionism," *Tennessee Historical Quarterly* 28 (spring 1969): 42–56; John M. McFaul, "Expediency vs. Morality: Jacksonian Politics and Slavery," *JAH* 62 (June 1975): 24–39; Niven, *Van Buren,* 87–120; Cole, *Van Buren,* 427–432; Wilson, *Presidency of Van Buren,* 191–211; Lawrence F. Kohl, *The Politics of Individualism: Parties and Character in the Jacksonian Era* (New York: Oxford Univ. Press, 1989), 21–144. See also, Joyce O. Appelby, *Capitalism and a New Social Order: The Republican Vision of the 1790s* (New York: New York Univ. Press, 1984); Daniel Feller, "Politics and Society: Toward a Jacksonian Synthesis," *JER* 10 (summer 1990): 135–141; Alexander Saxton, *The Rise and Fall of the White Republic: Class Politics and Mass Culture in Nineteenth Century America* (London: Verso, 1990), 23–160; Isaac Kramnick, *Republicanism and Bourgeois Radicalism in Late Eighteenth Century England and America* (Ithaca: Cornell Univ. Press, 1990); Major L. Wilson, "The 'Country' Versus the 'Court': A Republican Consensus and Party Debate in the Bank War," *JER* (winter 1995): 619–647.

11. MVB, *Inquiry,* 181.

12. Alexis de Tocqueville, *Democracy in America* (New York: Alfred A. Knopf, 1961), 1: 285–286; Cole, *Van Buren,* 22–24.

Bibliography

GOVERNMENT DOCUMENTS, PUBLISHED AND UNPUBLISHED

Annals of the Congress of the United States, 1789–1824. 42 vols. Washington, D.C., 1821–1824.

Butler, Benjamin F., John Duer, and John C. Spencer. *New York Commissioners to Revise the Statute Law of the State of New-York.* 3 vols. Albany: Packard and Van Bethuysen, 1829.

Map of the Division of the Kinderhook Patent Granted in 1686. New York State Library.

New York State Legislature. *Laws of the State of New-York Passed at the Sessions of the Legislature Held in the Years 1785, 1786, 1787 and 1788, inclusive, Being the Eighth, Ninth, Tenth and Eleventh Sessions.* Albany: Weed, Parsons, 1885.

———. *Laws of the State of New-York Passed at the Sessions of the Legislature Held in the Years 1789, 1790, 1791, 1792, 1793, 1794, 1795 and 1796, inclusive, Being the Twelfth, Thirteenth, Fourteenth, Fifteenth, Sixteenth, Seventeenth, Eighteenth, and Nineteenth Sessions.* Albany: Weed, Parsons, 1887.

———. *Laws of the State of New-York Passed at the Session of the Legislature Held in the Year 1801, Being the Twenty-Fourth Session, Including the Acts Commonly Called Revised Acts of that Session.* Albany: Weed, Parsons, 1887.

———. *Laws of the State of New-York, Containing All the Acts Passed at the Twenty-Eighth and Twenty-Ninth Session of the Legislature, 1804–1805 and 1806.* Albany: Websters and Skinner, 1809.

———. *Laws of the State of New-York, Containing all the Acts of the Thirtieth and the Public Acts of the Thirty-First and Thirty-Second Session of the Legislature, 1810, 1811, 1812.* Albany: Websters and Skinner, 1812.

———. *Laws of the State of New York. Revised and Passed at the Thirty-Sixth Session of the Legislature.* 2 vols. Albany: Solomon Southwick, 1813.

New York State Senate. *Journal of the Senate of the State of New-York at Their Thirty-Fifth Session, Begun and held at the City of Albany, the twenty-eighth day of January, 1812.* Albany: S. Southwick, 1812.

————. *Journal of the Senate of the State of New-York at their Thirty-Sixth Session, Begun and held at the City of Albany, the Third Day of November, 1812*. Albany: S. Southwick, 1813.

————. *Journal of the Senate of the State of New-York at their Thirty-Seventh Session, Begun and held at the City of Albany, the Twenty-Fifth Day of January, 1814*. Albany: H. C. Southwick for S. Southwick, 1814.

————. *Journal of the Senate of the State of New-York at their Thirty-Eighth Session, Begun and held at the City of Albany, the Twenty-Sixth Day of September, 1814*. Albany: H. C. Southwick for S. Southwick, 1814.

————. *Journal of the Senate of the State of New-York at their Thirty-Ninth Session, Begun and held at the City of Albany, the Thirtieth Day of January, 1816*. Albany: J. Buel, 1816.

————. *Journal of the Senate of the State of New-York, at their Fortieth Session, Begun and held at the City of Albany, the Fifth Day of November, 1816*. Albany: J. Buel, 1817.

————. *Journal of the Senate of the State of New-York, Begun and held at their Forty-First Session, the Twenty-Seventh Day of January, 1818*. Albany: J. Buel, 1818.

————. *Journal of the Senate of the State of New-York, Begun and held at their Forty-Second Session, the Fifty Day of January, 1819*. Albany: J. Buel, 1819.

Register of Debates. Washington, D.C.: Gales and Seaton, 1824–1825.

Register of Debates. Washington, D.C., Gales and Seaton, 1826–1827.

Register of Debates. Washington, D.C., Gales and Seaton, 1827–1828.

U.S. Bureau of the Census. *Heads of Families at the First Census of the United States Taken in the Year 1790, New York*. Washington, D.C., 1908.

Van Ness, William P., and John Woodworth. *Laws of the State of New-York, Revised and Passed at the Thirty-Sixth Session of the Legislature, with Marginal Notes and References, Published by the Revisors, William P. Van Ness and John Woodworth, Esq.* 2 vols. Albany: H. C. Southwick, 1813.

COURT DOCUMENTS, PUBLISHED AND UNPUBLISHED

Anthon, John, ed. *The Laws of Nisi Prius, Being Reports of the Cases Determined at Nisi Prius in the Supreme Court of the State of New-York*. New York: Banks & Bros., 1858.

Barbour, Oliver L., ed. *Reports of Cases in Law and Equity in the State of New-York*. 67 vols. New York: Banks & Bros., 1870.

Caines, George, ed. *New-York Term Reports of Cases Argued and Determined in the Supreme Court of That State*. 3 vols. New York: G. S. Diossy, 1883.

Coleman, William, ed. *Cases of Practice, Adjudged in the Supreme Court of New-York*. Albany: Banks & Bros., 1883.

Coleman, William, and George Caines, eds. *Reports of Cases of Practice Determined in the Supreme Court of Judicature of the State of New-York; from April Term, 1794, to November Term, 1805, Both Inclusive. To Which is Prefixed all the Rules and Orders of the Court to the Year 1808*. New York: Banks & Bros., 1883.

Columbia County Common Rule Book, Court of Common Pleas, 1804–1810. Hudson Court House Archives.

Columbia County Deed Book. Hudson Court House Archives.

Cowen, Esek, ed. *Reports of Cases Argued and Determined in the Supreme Court; and in the Court for the Trial of Impeachment and the Correction of Errors of the State of*

New-York. 9 vols. New York: Banks & Bros., 1873.

Crowell, Thomas B. *Report of the Trial of the Murders of Richard Jennings.* Newburgh: Benjamin Lewis, 1819.

Daly, Charles P. *History of the Court of Common Pleas for the City and County of New York.* New York: Smith's Common Pleas Reports, 1855.

Docket for Clerk of Circuit Court. Hudson Court House Archives.

Hamlin, Paul M., and Charles E. Baker, eds. *Supreme Court of Judicature of the Province of New York 1691–1704.* 3 vols. New York: New York Historical Society, 1952.

Johnson, William, ed. *Cases Argued and Determined in the Supreme Court of Judicature and in the Court for the Trial of Impeachments and Corrections of Errors, of the State of New-York.* 20 vols. New York: Banks & Bros., 1883.

————. ed. *Reports of Cases Adjudged in the Court of Chancery of New-York, Containing the Cases from March, 1814 to [July 1823] Inclusive.* 7 vols. New York: Banks & Bros., 1883.

Lockwood, Ralph, ed. *An Analytic and Practical Synopsis of all the Cases Argued and Reversed in Law and Equity in the Court for the Correction of Errors of the State of New York from 1799 to 1847, with all the names of cases and a Table of Titles.* New York: Banks, Gould, 1848.

New York State. Attorney General Case Register, vols. 3–5, 1815–1819. New York State Archives, Albany, New York.

————. Attorney General's Office. Correspondence and Legal Documentation Relating to Land Sales, 1815–1819. New York State Archives, Albany, New York.

————. Court for the Trial of Impeachments and the Correction of Errors. Minutes, 1788–1815. Microfilm. New York Public Library.

————. Court for the Trial of Impeachments and the Correction of Errors, vol. 1. Minutes, 1816–1819. New York State Archives, Albany, New York.

————. Court of Chancery. Index By Complainant to Chancellor's Enrolled Decrees, 1808–1828. New York State Archives, Albany, New York.

————. Court of Chancery. Minutes, Boxes 2–7, 1804–1829. New York State Archives, Albany, New York.

————. Court of Chancery. Registers, 4 vols., 1804–1823. New York State Archives, Albany, New York.

————. Supreme Court of Judicature. Common Rule Books (Albany), Boxes 31–34, 1805–1828. New York State Archives, Albany, New York.

————. Supreme Court of Judicature. Docket of Judgements (Albany), 1797–1828. New York State Archives, Albany, New York.

————. Supreme Court of Judicature. Docket of Judgements (Utica), 1807–1828. New York State Archives, Albany, New York.

————. Supreme Court of Judicature. Judgement Rolls (Albany), Boxes 103–312, 1806–1828. New York State Archives, Albany, New York.

————. Supreme Court of Judicature. Minutes, vols. 2–5, 1803–1828. New York State Archives, Albany, New York.

————. Supreme Court of Judicature. Oaths of Office of Attorneys, Solicitors, and Counsellors, vol. 1, 1796–1847. New York State Archives, Albany, New York.

————. Supreme Court of Judicature. Transcripts of Docket of Judgements (New York City), 1809–1828. New York State Archives, Albany, New York.

Peters, Richard, ed. *Reports of Cases Argued and Adjudged in the Supreme Court of the United States.* 16 vols. Philadelphia: John Grigg, 1890.

Rodgers, Daniel, ed. *The New-York City-Hall Recorder for the Year 1819, Containing Reports of the Most Interesting Trials and Decisions which have arisen in the Various Courts of Judicature, for the Trial of Jury Causes, in the Hall, During that Year, Particularly in the Court of Sessions, with Notes and Remarks, Critical and Explanatory.* New York: Clayton & Kingland, 1819.

Wendell, John L., ed. *Reports of Cases Argued and Determined in the Supreme Court of Judicature and in the Court For the Trial of Impeachments and the Correction of Errors of the State of New-York.* 26 vols. New York: Banks & Bros., 1874.

Wheaton, Henry, ed. *Reports of Cases Argued and Adjudged in the Supreme Court of the United States.* 12 vols. New York: R. Donaldson, 1827.

Wheeler, Jacob D., ed. *Reports of Criminal Law Cases with Notes and References; Containing, also, A View of the Current Laws of the United States.* New York: Gould and Banks, 1825.

NEWSPAPERS

Albany Advertiser, 1815–1817.

Albany Argus, 1813–1824.

Albany Balance, 1809–1811.

Albany Gazette, 1808–1820.

Albany New-York Statesman, 1820.

Albany Register, 1807–1820.

Catskill Recorder, 1809–1812.

Hudson Balance, 1801–1808.

Hudson Bee, 1802–1820.

Hudson Gazette, 1792–1803.

Hudson Northern Whig, 1809–1820.

Hudson Weekly Gazette, 1785–1792.

Kingston Plebeian, 1818.

Kingston Ulster Plebeian, 1818.

Newburgh Orange County Republican, 1812, 1819.

New York American, 1819–1822.

New York American Citizen, 1807–1810.

New York Columbian, 1813–1819.

New York Evening Post, 1810–1822.

New York Morning Chronicle, 1804.

New York National Advocate, 1813–1821.

New York Public Advertiser, 1807–1812.

New York Republican Watch Tower, 1804–1808.

Niles Weekly Register, 1813–1821.

Poughkeepsie Journal, 1804, 1810.

Poughkeepsie Political Barometer, 1807–1811.

Poughkeepsie Republican Herald, 1811–1812.

Utica Patriot, 1814–1820.

Washington (D.C.) National Intelligencer, 1821–1822.

MANUSCRIPT COLLECTIONS

Adams Family Papers. Massachusetts Historical Society, Boston.
Butler, Benjamin F. Papers. New York State Library, Albany, N.Y.
Cantine Family Papers. Butler Library, Columbia Univ., New York, N.Y.
Clinton, De Witt. "Diary." New York Historical Society, New York, N.Y.
Clinton, De Witt. Papers. Butler Library, Columbia Univ., New York, N.Y.
Clinton, De Witt. Papers. New York Public Library, New York, N.Y.
Clinton, De Witt. Papers. New York Historical Society, New York, N.Y.
Edgar, William. Papers. New York Public Library, New York, N.Y.
Foote, Ebenezer. Papers. New York State Library, Albany, N.Y.
Gallatin, Albert. Papers. New York State Library, New York, N.Y.
Jefferson, Thomas. Papers. Library of Congress, Washington, D.C.
Livingston Family Papers. New York Historical Society, New York, N.Y.
Madison, James. Papers. Library of Congress, Washington, D.C.
Marcy, William L. Papers. Library of Congress, Washington, D.C.
Meigs, Henry A. Papers. New York Historical Society, New York, N.Y.
Monroe, James. Papers. Library of Congress, Washington, D.C.
Rokeby Collection. New York Historical Society, New York, N.Y.
Taylor, John W. Papers. New York Historical Society, New York, N.Y.
Tompkins, Daniel D. Papers. New York State Library, Albany, N.Y.
Tracy, Albert. Papers. New York State Library, Albany, N.Y.
Van Buren, Martin. Papers. Library of Congress, Washington, D.C.
————. The Papers of Martin Van Buren. Chadwyck-Healy Microfilms.
Van Cortlandt, Pierre Papers. New York Public Library, New York, N.Y.
Van Ness, William Peter. Papers. New York Historical Society, New York, N.Y.
————. Papers. New York Public Library, New York, N.Y.
Van Schaack, Henry. Papers. New York Public Library, New York, N.Y.
Wheaton, Henry. Papers. J. Pierrepoint Morgan Library, New York, N.Y.

PUBLISHED PUBLIC DOCUMENTS, DIRECTORIES, AND GAZETTEERS

Cruikshank, Ernest, ed. *Documents Relating to the Invasion of Canada and the Surrender of Detroit, 1812.* Ottawa: Government Printing Bureau, 1912.
Forbes, James G. *Report of the Trial of Brig. Genl. W. Hull; Commanding the North-Western Army of the United States. By a Court-Martial Held at Albany on Monday, January 3, 1814 and Succeeding Days.* New York: Eastburn, Kirk, 1814.
Gordon, Thomas F. *Gazetteer of the State of New York.* Philadelphia: T. K. and P. G. Collins, 1836.
Hull, William. *Defense of Brigadier General William Hull Delivered before the general court-martial, of which Major General Dearborn was president, at Albany, March 1814. With an Address to the Citizens of the United States.* Boston: Wells and Lilly, 1814.
Hutchins, Stephen C. *Introduction to Civil List and Constitutional History of the Colony and State of New York.* Albany: Weed, Parsons, 1879.
Sparhawk, Edward V. *Report of the Trial before Judges Thompson and Betts, in the Circuit Court of the U.S. for The Southern District of New York.* New York: Elam Bliss, 1827.

Stafford, Horatio Gates. *A Gazetteer of the State of New York.* Albany: H. C. Southwick, 1813.

CONTEMPORARY WORKS AND PUBLISHED DIARIES, LETTERS, AND MEMOIRS

Adams, John Quincy. *Memoirs of John Quincy Adams: Comprising Part of His Diary from 1795 to 1848.* Edited by Charles Francis Adams. Philadelphia: J. B. Lippincott, 1875–1877.

Beardsley, Levi. *Reminiscences, Personal and Other Incidents; Early Settlement of Otsego County; Notices and Anecdotes of Public Men; Judicial, Legal and Legislative Matters; Field Sports; Dissertations and Discussions.* New York: Vinten, 1852.

"Benjamin F. Butler." *The United States Magazine and Democratic Review* 11 (January 1839): 33–48.

Bigelow, John. "De Witt Clinton as a Politician." *Harper's New Magazine* 50 (1874–1875): 409–417, 556–571.

Bonney, Catherina Van Rensselaer. *A Legacy of Historical Gleanings.* 2 vols. Albany: J. Munsell, 1875.

Butler, William A. *Martin Van Buren: Lawyer, Statesman and Man.* New York: D. Appleton, 1862.

Carter, Nathaniel H., William L. Stone, and Marcus T. C. Gould. *Reports of the Proceedings and Debates of the Convention of 1821, Assembled for the Purpose of Amending the Constitution of the State of New-York; Containing All the Official Documents, Relating to the Subject, and Other Valuable Material.* Albany: E. and E. Hosford, 1821.

[Dallas, Alexander J]. *The United States of America Against Brigadier General William Hull, of the Army of the United States, by Order of the Secretary of War.* N.p., n.d.

Daly, Charles P. *Historical Sketch of the Judicial Tribunals of New York from 1623 to 1846.* New York: John A. Amerman, 1855.

———. *The Nature, Extent and History of the Jurisdiction of Surrogate's Courts of the State of New York, Opinion of the Hon. Charles P. Daly.* New York: John A. Gray, 1863.

Edwards, Charles. *Pleasantries about Courts and Lawyers of the State of New York.* New York: Richardson, 1867.

Ellis, Franklin. *History of Columbia County, New York, with Illustrations and Biographical Sketches of some of Its Prominent Men.* Philadelphia: Everts and Ensign, 1878.

Fowler, Robert L. *History of the Law of Real Property in New York: An Essay Introductory to the Study of the New York Revised Statutes.* New York: Baker, Voorhis, 1895.

Haines, Charles. *An Appeal to the People of the State of New-York on the Expediency of Abolishing the Council of Appointment.* New York: E. Conrad, 1819.

Hammond, Jabez D. *History of Political Parties in the State of New York, From the Ratification of the Federal Constitution to December, 1840.* 2 vols. Albany: C. Van Benthuysen, 1842.

Hansen, J. A. *A List of the Attornies and Counsellors of the Supreme Court of the State of New-York, Together with the Place of Their Residence; and the Names of their Respective Agents.* Albany: J. B. Van Steenbergh, 1821.

Holland, William M. *The Life and Political Opinions of Martin Van Buren, Vice President of the United States.* Hartford: Belknap & Hamersley, 1835.

Hosack, David. *Memoir of De Witt Clinton: With an Appendix Containing Numerous Documents Illustrative of the Principle Events of His Life.* New York: J. Seymour, 1829.

Howell, George R., and Jonathan Tenney. *Bi-Centennial History of Albany. History of the County of Albany, N.Y., From 1609 to 1886.* New York: W. W. Munsell, 1886.

Jay, John. *The Correspondence and Public Letters of John Jay.* Edited by Henry P. Johnston. Reprint, New York: Da Capo Press, 1971.

Jenkins, John S. *The Lives of the Governors of New York.* Auburn: Derby and Miller, 1852.

Kent, James. *Memoirs and Letters of James Kent, L.L.D.* Edited by William Kent. Boston: Little, Brown, 1898.

King, Rufus. *The Life and Correspondence of Rufus King.* Edited by Charles R. King. 6 vols. New York: G. P. Putnam's Sons, 1894–1900.

Lossing, Benson. *The Pictorial Field-Book of the War of 1812; Or Illustrations by Pen and Pencil, of the History, Biography, Scenery, Relics and Traditions of the Last War for American Independence.* New York: Harpers and Bros., 1869.

Mackenzie, William L. *The Life and Times of Martin Van Buren: The Correspondence of his Friends, Family and Pupils; Together with Brief Notices, Sketches, and Anecdotes.* Boston: Cooke, 1846.

———. *The Lives and Opinions of Benjamin Franklin Butler, United States District Attorney for the Southern District of New York; and Jesse Hoyt, Counsellor at Law, formerly Collector for the Port of New York.* Boston: Cooke, 1845.

Miller, Payton. *A Group of Lawyers of Columbia County, New York.* Hudson: De Vinne Press, 1904.

Miller, Stephen B. *Historical Sketches of Hudson, Embracing the Settlement of the City, City Government, Business Enterprises, Churches, Press, Schools, Libraries.* Hudson: Bryan and Webb, 1862.

Munsell, Joel. *The Annals of Albany.* 10 vols. Albany: Joel Munsell, 1859.

O'Callaghan, Edward B. *Documentary History of the State of New-York.* 2 vols. Albany: Weed, Parsons, 1848.

———. *History of the New Netherlands; Or, New-York Under the Dutch.* 2 vols. Albany: Weed, Parsons, 1853.

Parton, James. *The Life and Times of Aaron Burr.* New York: Mason Bros., 1858.

Pearson, Jonathan. *Early Records of the City of Albany and Colony of Rensselaerwyck, 1656–1675; Translated from the Original Dutch with Notes.* Albany: Joel Munsell, 1869.

Raymond, William. *Biographical Sketches of Distinguished Men of Columbia County.* Albany: Weed, Parsons, 1851.

Spencer, Thomas. *The New Vade Macum: Or Young Clerk's Magazine.* Lansingburgh: Silvester Tiffany, 1794.

Street, Alfred. *The Council of Revision of the State of New York.* Albany: William Gould, 1859.

Tactitus [De Witt Clinton]. *Canal Policy of the State of New-York: Delineated in a Letter to Robert Troup, Esquire.* New York: E. E. Hosford, 1822.

Van Buren, Martin. "The Autobiography of Martin Van Buren." *Annual Report of the American Historical Association for the Year 1918.* Edited by John C. Fitzpatrick. Washington, D.C.: Government Printing Office, 1920.

———. *Considerations in Favour of the Appointment of Rufus King, to the Senate of the United States. Submitted to the Republican Members of the Legislature of the State of*

New-York. Albany: J. Buel, 1819.

————. *Inquiry into the Origins and Course of Political Parties in the United States.* New York: Hurd & Houghton, 1867.

————. *Speech of the Hon. M. Van Buren of the Senate, on the Act to Carry into Effect, the Act of 13th April, 1819, For the Settlement of the Late Governor's Accounts.* Albany: J. Buel, 1820.

Van Schaack, Henry C. *The Life of Peter Van Schaack, LLD. Embracing Selections from his Correspondence and Other Writings, During the American Revolution, and His Exile in England.* New York: D. Appleton, 1842.

Walker, Timothy. *Introduction to American Law.* Philadelphia: P. H. Nicklin and T. Johnson, 1837.

Webster, Charles R. *The Clerk's Magazine.* Albany: N.p., 1800.

Wyche, William. *Treatise on the Practice of the Supreme Court of the State of New-York in Civil Actions.* New York: T. and J. Swords, 1794.

BIOGRAPHIES, MONOGRAPHS, AND SYNTHETIC BOOKS

Alexander, De Alva S. *A Political History of the State of New York.* 4 vols. Port Washington: Ira J. Friedman, 1969.

Alexander, Holmes. *The American Talleyrand: The Career and Contemporaries of Martin Van Buren, Eighth President.* New York: Harper and Bros., 1935.

Appleby, Joyce O. *Capitalism and a New Social Order: The Republican Vision of the 1790s.* New York: New York Univ. Press, 1984.

Armour, David A. *The Merchants of Albany, 1686–1760.* New York: Garland, 1986.

Aycock, William B., and Seymour W. Wurfel. *Military Law Under the Uniform Code of Military Justice.* Westport. Conn.: Greenwood Press, 1972.

Balmer, Randall H. *A Perfect Babel: Dutch Religion and English Culture in the Middle Colonies.* New York: Oxford Univ. Press, 1989.

Bancroft, George. *Martin Van Buren to the End of His Public Career.* New York: Harper and Bros., 1889.

Banner, James M. *To the Hartford Convention: The Federalists and the Origins of Party Politics in Massachusetts, 1789–1815.* New York: Alfred A. Knopf, 1970.

Basch, Norma. *In the Eyes of the Law: Women, Marriage, and Property in Nineteenth-Century New York.* Ithaca: Cornell Univ. Press, 1982.

Bergan, Francis. *The History of the New York Court of Appeals, 1847–1932.* New York: Columbia Univ. Press, 1985.

Black, Henry C. *Black's Law Dictionary.* St Paul: West Publishing, 1990.

Bloomfield, Maxwell. *American Lawyers in a Changing Society, 1776–1876.* Cambridge: Harvard Univ. Press, 1976.

Bond, Beverley W. *The Quit-Rent System in the American Colonies.* New Haven: Yale Univ. Press, 1919.

Bonomi, Patricia U. *A Factious People: Politics and Society in Colonial New York.* New York: Columbia Univ. Press, 1967.

Brown, Elizabeth G. *British Statutes in American Law.* Ann Arbor: Univ. of Michigan Press, 1964.

Brown, Ray A. *The Law of Personal Property.* Chicago: Callaghan, 1955.

Burke, Thomas E., Jr. *Mohawk Frontier: The Dutch Community of Schenectady, New York,*

1661–1710. Ithaca: Cornell Univ. Press, 1991.

Butler, Harriet A., ed. *A Retrospective of Forty Years.* New York: Charles Scribner's Sons, 1911.

Calhoun, Daniel H. *Professional Lives in America: Structure and Aspirations, 1750–1850.* Cambridge: Harvard Univ. Press, 1965.

Chandler, Alfred N. *Land Title Origins: A Tale of Force and Fraud.* New York: Robert Schalkenbach Foundation, 1945.

Chester, Alden, ed. *Legal and Judicial History of New York.* 3 vols. New York: National Americana Society, 1911.

Chroust, Anton-H. *The Rise of the Legal Profession in America.* Norman: Univ. of Oklahoma Press, 1965.

Cohen, David S. *The Dutch-American Farm.* New York: New York Univ. Press, 1992.

Cole, Donald B. *Martin Van Buren and The American Political System.* Princeton: Princeton Univ. Press, 1984.

———. *The Presidency of Andrew Jackson.* Lawrence: Univ. Press of Kansas, 1993.

Collier, Edward A. *A History of Old Kinderhook.* New York: G. P. Putnam's Sons, 1914.

Condon, Thomas J. *New York Beginnings: The Commercial Origins of New Netherlands.* New York: New York Univ. Press, 1968.

Cook, Charles M. *The American Codification Movement: A Study of Antebellum Legal Reform.* Westport, Conn.: Greenwood Press, 1981.

Countryman, Edward. *A People in Revolution: The American Revolution and Political Society in New York, 1760–1790.* Baltimore: Johns Hopkins Univ. Press, 1981.

Crowley, J. E. *This Sheba, Self: The Conceptualization of Economic Life in Eighteenth Century America.* Baltimore: John Hopkins Univ. Press, 1974.

Cunningham, Nobel. *The Jeffersonian Republicans: The Formation of Party Organization.* Chapel Hill: Univ. of North Carolina Press, 1957.

Curry, Richard O., and Lawrence B. Goodheart. *American Chameleon: Individualism in Trans-National Context.* Kent: Kent State Univ. Press, 1991.

Curtis, James C. *The Fox at Bay: Martin Van Buren and the Presidency, 1837–1841.* Lexington: Univ. of Kentucky Press, 1970.

Dangerfield, George. *Chancellor Robert R. Livingston of New York, 1746–1813.* New York: Harcourt, Brace, 1960.

De Pauw, Linda G. *The Eleventh Pillar: New York State and the Federal Constitution.* Ithaca: Cornell Univ. Press, 1986.

De Tocqueville, Alexis. *Democracy in America.* New York: Alfred A. Knopf, 1961.

Dodd, Edwin M. *American Business Corporations Until 1860 with Special Reference to Massachusetts.* Cambridge: Harvard Univ. Press, 1954.

Dunne, Gerald T. *Justice Joseph Story and the Rise of the Supreme Court.* New York: Simon and Schuster, 1970.

———. "Smith Thompson." In *Justices of the Supreme Court, 1789–1969: Their Lives and Major Opinions.* 4 vols. Edited by Leon Friedman and Fred Israel, 1: 475–509. New York: R. R. Bowker, 1969.

Elliott, Charles W. *Winfield Scott: The Soldier and the Man.* New York: Macmillan, 1937.

Ellis, David M. *Landlords and Farmers in the Hudson-Mohawk Region, 1790–1850.* Ithaca: Cornell Univ. Press, 1946.

Elting, Irving. *Dutch Village Communities on the Hudson River.* Baltimore: Johns Hopkins Univ. Press, 1886.

Ernst, Robert A. *Rufus King: American Federalist.* Chapel Hill: Univ. of North Carolina Press, 1968.

Fenstermaker, J. Van. *The Development of American Commercial Banking, 1782–1837.* Kent: Kent State Univ. Press, 1965.

Fischer, David H. *The Revolution of American Conservatism: The Federalist Party in the Era of Jeffersonian Democracy.* New York: Harper and Row, 1965.

Folts, James D. *"Duely & Constantly Kept": A History of the New York Supreme Court, 1691–1847 and An Inventory of Its Records (Albany, Utica, and Geneva Offices, 1797–1847.* Albany: N.p., 1991.

Fox, Dixon R. *The Decline of Aristocracy in the Politics of New York, 1801–1840.* New York: Columbia Univ. Press, 1919.

———. *Yankees and Yorkers.* New York: New York Univ. Press, 1940.

Freyer, Allan Tony. *Forums of Order: The Federal Courts and Business in American History.* Greenwich, Conn.: JAI Press, 1979.

Friedenberg, Daniel M. *Life, Liberty, and the Pursuit of Land.* Buffalo: Prometheus Books, 1992.

Friedman, Lawrence M. *A History of American Law.* New York: Simon and Schuster, 1973.

Gerlach, Don R. *Philip Schuyler and the American Revolution in New York, 1733–1777.* Lincoln: Univ. of Nebraska Press, 1964.

Goodfriend, Joyce D. *Before the Melting Pot: Society and Culture in Colonial New York City, 1664–1730.* Princeton: Princeton Univ. Press, 1991.

Hackett, David G. *The Rude Hand of Innovation: Religion and Social Order in Albany, New York, 1652–1836.* New York: Oxford Univ. Press, 1991.

Hall, Kermit L. *The Magic Mirror: Law in American History.* New York: Oxford Univ. Press, 1989.

Hamlin, Paul M. *Legal Education in Colonial New York.* 1939. Reprint, New York: De Capo Press, 1970.

Hammond, Bray. *Banks and Politics in America From the Revolution to the Civil War.* Princeton: Princeton Univ. Press, 1957.

Hanyan, Craig R. *De Witt Clinton: Years of Molding, 1769–1807.* New York: Garling, 1988.

Harris, Marshall D. *Origin of the Land Tenure System in the United States.* Ames: Iowa State Univ. Press, 1953.

Hartog, Hendrik. *Public Property and Private Power: The Corporation of the City of New York in American Law, 1730–1870.* Chapel Hill: Univ. of North Carolina Press, 1983.

Hedrick, Ulysses P. *A History of Agriculture in the State of New York.* Albany: New York State Agricultural Society, 1933.

Hickey, Donald R. *The War of 1812: A Forgotten Conflict.* Urbana: Univ. of Illinois Press, 1989.

Higgins, Ruth. *Expansion in New York With Especial References to the Eighteenth Century.* Columbus: Ohio State Univ. Press, 1931.

Hofstader, Richard. *Toward a Political System: The Rise of Legitimate Opposition in the United State, 1780–1840.* Berkeley: Univ. of California Press, 1970.

Hoffer, Peter C. *Law and People in Colonial America.* Baltimore: Johns Hopkins Univ. Press, 1992.

———. *The Law's Conscience: Equitable Constitutionalism in America.* Chapel Hill: Univ. of North Carolina Press, 1990.

Holloway, Laura C. *The Ladies of the White House, Or in the Homes of the Presidents.* Philadelphia: Bradley, 1881.

Horowitz, Milton J. *The Transformation of American Law, 1780–1860*. Cambridge: Harvard Univ. Press, 1977.

Horton, John T. *James Kent: A Study in Conservatism, 1763–1847*. 1939. Reprint, New York: De Capo Press, 1969.

Hurst, James W. *The Growth of American Law: The Law Makers*. Boston: Little, Brown, 1950.

———. *Law and Social Process in United States History*. Ann Arbor: Univ. of Michigan Press, 1960.

Irwin, Ray W. *Daniel D. Tompkins: Governor of New York and Vice President of the United States*. New York: New York Historical Society, 1968.

Jacobs, James R. *Tarnished Warrior: Major-General James Wilkerson*. New York: Macmillan, 1938.

Joline, Adrian H. *The Autograph Hunter and Other Papers*. Chicago: Alderbrink Press, 1907.

July, Robert W. *The Essential New Yorker: Gulian Crommelin Verplanck*. Durham: Duke Univ. Press, 1951.

Kammen, Michael M. *Colonial New York: A History*. New York: Charles Scribner's Sons, 1975.

Kass, Alvin. *Politics in New York State, 1800–1830*. Syracuse: Syracuse Univ. Press, 1965.

Kenney, Alice B. *Stubborn for Liberty: The Dutch in New York*. Syracuse: Syracuse Univ. Press, 1975.

Kierner, Cynthia A. *Traders and Gentlefolk: The Livingstons of New York, 1675–1790*. Ithaca: Cornell Univ. Press, 1992.

Kim, Sung Bok. *Landlord and Tenant in Colonial New York: Manorial Society, 1664–1775*. Chapel Hill: The Univ. of North Carolina Press, 1978.

Knox, John J. *A History of Banking in the United States*. New York: Bradford Rhodes, 1900.

Kohl, Lawrence F. *The Politics of Individualism: Parties and the American Character in the Jacksonian Era*. New York: Oxford Univ. Press, 1989.

Konefsky, Alfred S., and Andrew J. King. *The Papers of Daniel Webster, Legal Papers: The Boston Practice*. Series 2. Hanover: Univ. Press of New England, 1983.

Kramnick, Isaac. *Republicanism and Bourgeois Radicalism in Late Eighteenth-Century England and America*. Ithaca: Cornell Univ. Press, 1990.

Leder, Lawrence H. *Robert Livingston, 1654–1728, and the Politics of Colonial New York*. Chapel Hill: Univ. of North Carolina Press, 1961.

Lincoln, Charles Z. *The Constitutional History of New York From the Beginning of the Colonial Period to the Year, 1906, Showing the Origin, Development, and Judicial Construction of the Constitution*. 5 vols. Rochester: Lawyers Co-Operative Publishing, 1906.

Livermore, Shaw. *The Twilight of Federalism, 1815–1830*. Princeton: Princeton Univ. Press, 1962.

Lomask, Milton. *Aaron Burr: The Conspiracy and Years of Exile, 1805–1836*. New York: Farrar, Straus and Giroux, 1982.

———. *Aaron Burr: The Years from Princeton to Vice President*. New York: Farrar, Straus and Giroux, 1979.

Lynch, Denis T. *An Epoch and a Man: Martin Van Buren and His Times*. New York: Horace Liveright, 1929.

Mahon, John K. *The War of 1812*. Tallahassee: Rose Printing, 1972.

Mark, Irving. *Agrarian Conflicts in Colonial New York*. New York: Columbia Univ. Press, 1940.

Markle, Julius, and Richard Sloane. *Legal Research and Law Library Management*. New York: Law Journals Seminars-Press, 1982.

Mayers, Lewis. *The American Legal System*. New York: Harper and Bros., 1955.

McBain, Howard. *De Witt Clinton and the Origins of the Spoils System in New York*. New York: Columbia Univ. Press, 1907.

McCusker, John J., and Russell R. Menard. *The Economy of British America, 1607–1789*. Chapel Hill: Univ. of North Carolina Press, 1985.

McManus, Edgar J. *A History of Negro Slavery in New York*. Syracuse: Syracuse Univ. Press, 1966.

Meyers, Marvin. *The Jacksonian Persuasion: Politics and Belief*. Palo Alto: Stanford Univ. Press, 1957.

Miller, Nathan. *The Enterprise of a Free People: Aspects of Economic Development in New York during the Canal Period, 1792–1828*. Ithaca: Cornell Univ. Press, 1962.

Moore, Glover. *The Missouri Controversy, 1819–1821*. Lexington: Univ. of Kentucky Press, 1953.

Morris, Ira K. *Morris' Memorial History of Staten Island*. 2 vols. West New Brighton, N.Y.: Memorial Publishing, 1900.

Newmyer, R. Kent. *Supreme Court Justice Joseph Story: Statesman of the Old Republic*. Chapel Hill: Univ. of North Carolina Press, 1985.

Niven, John. *Martin Van Buren: The Romantic Age of American Politics*. New York: Oxford Univ. Press, 1983.

Parmet, Herbert S., and Marie B. Hecht. *Aaron Burr: Portrait of an Ambitious Man*. New York: Macmillan, 1967.

Peckham, Harriet C. *History of Cornelius Maessem Van Buren, who Came from Holland to the New Netherlands in 1634, and his descendants, including the Genealogy of the family of Bloomingdale, who are descended from Maas. a son of Cornelius Maessem*. New York: Tobias W. Wright, 1913.

Phillip, Cynthia Owen. *Robert Fulton: A Biography*. New York: Franklin Watts, 1985.

Price, Edward T. *Dividing the Land: Early American Beginnings of Our Private Property Mosaic*. Chicago: Univ. of Chicago Press, 1995.

Ranlet, Philip. *The New York Loyalists*. Knoxville: Univ. of Tennessee Press, 1986.

Remini, Robert V. *The Election of Andrew Jackson*. Philadelphia: J. B. Lippincott, 1963.

———. *Henry Clay: Statesman for the Union*. New York: W. W. Norton, 1991.

———. *Martin Van Buren and the Making of the Democratic Party*. New York: W. W. Norton, 1970.

Rink, Oliver A. *Holland on the Hudson: An Economic and Social History of Dutch New York*. Ithaca: Cornell Univ. Press, 1968.

Rothbard, Murray. *The Panic of 1819: Reactions and Policies*. New York: Columbia Univ. Press, 1962.

Saxton, Alexander. *The Rise and Fall of the White Republic: Class Politics and Mass Culture in Nineteenth-Century America*. London: Vargo, 1990.

Schachner, Nathan. *Aaron Burr: A Biography*. New York: Frederick A. Stokes, 1937.

Schwartz, Bernard. *Main Currents in American Legal Thought*. Durham: Carolina Academic Press, 1993.

Scott, Henry W. *The Courts of the State of New York: Their History, Development and Jurisdiction*. New York: Wilson Publishing, 1909.

Sellers, Charles G. *The Market Revolution: Jacksonian America, 1815–1846.* New York: Oxford Univ. Press, 1991.

Shain Barry A. *The Myth of American Individualism: The Protestant Origins of American Political Thought.* Princeton: Princeton Univ. Press, 1994.

Shalhope, Robert E. *The Roots of Democracy: American Thought and Culture, 1760–1800.* Boston: Twayne Publishers, 1990.

Shaw, Ronald E. *Erie Water West: A History of the Erie Canal: 1792–1864.* Lexington: Univ. of Kentucky Press, 1966.

Shepard, Edward M. *Martin Van Buren.* Boston: Houghton Mifflin, 1888.

Skeen, Edward C. *John Armstrong, Jr., 1758–1843.* Syracuse: Syracuse Univ. Press, 1981.

Smith, Walter B., and Arthur H. Cole. *Fluctuations in American Business, 1790–1860.* Cambridge: Harvard Univ. Press, 1935.

Spaulding, E. Wilder. *His Excellency George Clinton: Critic of the Constitution.* New York: Macmillian, 1938.

Spencer, Ivor D. *The Victors and the Spoils: A Life of William L. Marcy.* Providence, R.I.: Brown Univ. Press, 1959.

Todd, Charles L., and Robert Sonkin. *Alexander Bryan Johnson: Philosophical Banker.* Syracuse: Syracuse Univ. Press, 1977.

Watson, Harry L. *Liberty and Power: The Politics of Jacksonian America.* New York: Farrar, Straus and Giroux, 1990.

White, Shane. *Somewhat More Independent: The End of Slavery in New York City.* Athens: Univ. of Georgia Press, 1991.

Wiggins, Kenneth. *John Jacob Astor: Business Man.* 2 vols. Cambridge: Harvard Univ. Press, 1931.

Wilentz, Sean. *Chants Democratic: New York City and the Rise of the American Working Class.* New York: Oxford Univ. Press, 1984.

Williamson, Chilton. *American Suffrage, from Property to Democracy, 1760–1860.* Princeton: Princeton Univ. Press, 1960.

Wilson, Major L. *The Presidency of Martin Van Buren.* Lawrence: Univ. Press of Kansas, 1984.

Wiltse, Charles M., and Harold Moser. *The Papers of Daniel Webster.* Hanover, N.H.: Univ. Press of New England, 1976.

Wurfel, Seymour W. *Military Law Under the Uniform Code of Militiary Justice.* Westport, Conn.: Greenwood Press, 1952.

Young, Alfred F. *The Democratic Republicans of New York: Their Origins: 1763–1797.* Chapel Hill: Univ. of North Carolina Press, 1967.

ARTICLES

Bloomfield, Maxwell. "Lawyers and Public Criticism: Challenge and Response in Nineteenth-Century America." *American Journal of Legal History* 15 (October 1971): 269–277.

Brown, Richard H. "The Missouri Crisis, Slavery and the Politics of Jacksonianism." *The South Atlantic Quarterly* 65 (winter 1966): 55–72.

Bruegel, Martin. "Unrest: Manorial Society and the Market in the Hudson Valley, 1780–1850." *The Journal of American History* 82 (March 1996): 1393–1424.

Cohen, David S. "How Dutch Were the Dutch of New Netherlands?" *New York History* 62 (January 1981): 43–60.

Collin, Charles A. "Statutory Revision in New York." *Albany Law Journal* 49 (January 1894): 72–76.

Conkling, Frank J. "Martin Van Buren, With a Sketch of the Van Buren Family in America." *New York Genealogical and Biographical Record* 28 (July and October 1897): 121–125, 207–211.

Cress, Lawrence D. "'Cool and Serious Reflection': Federalist Attitudes Toward The War of 1812." *The Journal of the Early Republic* 7 (summer 1987): 123–145.

Currency, Edwin C. "The Lawyer and the American Revolution." *American Journal of Legal History* 8 (April 1964): 125–132.

Ekirch, Arthur A., Jr. "Benjamin F. Butler of New York: A Personal Portrait." *New York History* 58 (January 1977): 47–62.

Ellis, David M. "The Yankee Invasion of New York, 1783–1850." *New York History* 32 (January 1951): 1–17.

Feller, Daniel. "Politics and Society: Toward a Jacksonian Synthesis." *The Journal of the Early Republic* 10 (summer 1990): 135–161.

Gilje, Paul A. "The Rise of Capitalism in the Early Republic." *The Journal of the Early Republic* 16 (summer 1996): 159–181.

Goodfriend, Joyce D. "Burghers and Blacks: The Evolution of a Slave Society at New Amsterdam." *New York History* 59 (April 1978): 125–144.

Hammond, Bray. "The North's Empty Purse, 1861–1862." *American Historical Review* 67 (October 1961): 1–18.

Hanyan, Craig R. "De Witt Clinton and Partisanship: The Development of Clintonianism from 1811 to 1820." *New-York Historical Society Quarterly* 56 (April 1972): 109–131.

Harrington, Virginia D. "New York and the Embargo of 1807." *Proceedings of the New York State Historical Association* 25 (January 1926): 143–151.

Henig, Gerald S. "The Jacksonian Attitude toward Abolitionism." *Tennessee Historical Quarterly* 28 (spring 1969): 42–56.

Hickey, Donald R. "Federalist Party Unity and the War of 1812." *The Journal of American Studies* 12 (April 1978): 23–39.

Howe, Mark De Wolfe. "The Process of Outlawry in New York: A Study of the Selective Reception of English Law." *Cornell Law Quarterly* 23 (June 1938): 559–573.

Hurst, James W. "The Law in United States History." *Proceedings of the American Philosophic Society* 106 (1960): 518–526.

Irwin, Ray W. "Governor Daniel D. Tompkins and the Embargo, 1807–1809." *New York History* 22 (July 1941): 309–320.

Johnson, Herbert A. "Civil Procedure in John Jay's New York." *American Journal of Legal History* 9 (January 1967): 69–70.

———. "English Statutes in Colonial New York." *New York History* 58 (July 1977): 277–296.

Kelly, Alfred H. "Constitutional Liberty and the Law of Libel: A Historian's View." *American Historical Review* 74 (December 1968): 429–452.

Kempin, Frederick G., Jr. "Precedent and Stare Decisis: The Critical Years, 1800–1850." *American Journal of Legal History* 3 (January 1959): 28–54.

Kenney, Alice P. "The Albany Dutch: Loyalists and Patriots." *New York History* 59 (October 1961): 331–350.

———. "Dutch Patricians in Colonial History." *New York History* 49 (July 1968): 383–407.

———. "Private Worlds in the Middle Colonies: An Introduction to Human Tradition in American History." *New York History* 51 (January 1970): 3–31.

Kierner, Cynthia A. "Landlord and Tenant in Revolutionary New York: The Case of Livingston Manor." *New York History* 70 (April 1989): 133–152.

King, Andrew. "The Law of Slander in Early Antebellum America." *American Journal of Legal History* 35 (January 1991): 1–43.

Kirkpatrick, John T. "The Revised Statutes of New York." *Law Library Journal* 19 (October 1926): 72–79.

Klein, Milton M. "Democracy and Politics in Colonial New York." *New York History* 40 (July 1959): 221–246.

———. "From Community to Status: The Development of the Legal Profession in Colonial New York." *New York History* 60 (April 1979): 133–157.

———. "New York Lawyers and the Coming of the Revolution." *New York History* 55 (October 1974): 383–407.

———. "Prelude to Revolution in New York: Jury Trials and Judicial Tenure." *William and Mary Quarterly*, 3rd ser., 17 (October 1960): 439–462.

———. "The Rise of the New York Bar: The Legal Career of William Livingston." *William and Mary Quarterly*, 3rd ser., 15 (July 1958): 334–358.

Kornblith, Gary J. "The Artisanal Response to Capitalist Transformation." *The Journal of the Early Republic* 10 (fall 1990): 315–321.

Kramnick, Isaac. "Republican Revisionism Revisited." *American Historical Review* 87 (June 1982): 629–664.

Main, Jackson T. "Government by the People: The American Revolution and the Democratization of the Legislatures." *William and Mary Quarterly*, 3rd ser., 23 (July 1966): 391–407.

McFaul, John M. "Expediency vs. Morality: Jacksonian Politics and Slavery" *The Journal of American History* 62 (June 1975): 24–39.

Merwick, Donna. "Becoming English: Anglo-Dutch Conflict in the 1670s in Albany, New York." *New York History* 61 (October 1981): 389–414.

———. "Being Dutch: An Interpretation of Why Jacob Leisler Died." *New York History* 70 (October 1989): 373–404.

———. "Dutch Townsmen and Land Use: A Spatial Perspective on Seventeenth-Century Albany, New York." *William and Mary Quarterly*, 3rd ser., 37 (January 1980): 53–78.

Mintz, Max. "The Political Ideas of Martin Van Buren." *New York History* 30 (October 1949): 422–448.

Moore, John H. "One Hundred Fifty Years of Official Law Reporting and the Courts in New York." *Syracuse Law Review* 6 (spring 1955): 273–306.

Nadler, Solomon. "The Green Bag: James Monroe and the Fall of De Witt Clinton." *New-York Historical Society Quarterly* 59 (July 1975): 203–225.

Nelson, William E. "Emerging Notions of Modern Criminal Law in the Revolutionary Era: An Historical Perspective." *New York University Law Review* 42 (1967): 450–482.

Nissenson, S. G. "The Development of a Land Registration System in New York." *Proceedings of the New York State Historical Association* 37 (January 1939): 16–42.

Olsen, Edwin. "The Slave Code in Colonial New York." *Journal of Negro History* 29 (April 1944): 147–165.

Raack, David W. "To Preserve the Best Fruits: The Legal Thought of Chancellor James Kent." *American Journal of Legal History* 33 (October 1989): 320–366.

Rayback, Joseph G. "Martin Van Buren: His Place in the History of New York and the United States." *New York History* 64 (April 1983): 122–135.

———. "A Myth Reexamined: Martin Van Buren's Role in the Presidential Election of 1816." *Proceedings of the American Philosophic Society* 124 (April 1980): 106–118.

Remini, Robert V. "The Albany Regency." *New York History* 39 (October 1958): 341–355.

———. "New York and the Presidential Election of 1816." *New York History* 31 (July 1950): 308–324.

Rezneck, Samuel H. "The Depression of 1819–1822: A Social History." *American Historical Review* 39 (October 1933): 28–47.

Rink, Oliver A. "The People of New Netherlands: Notes on Non-English Immigration to New York in the Seventeenth-Century." *New York History* 62 (January 1981): 5–60.

Rodgers, Daniel T. "Republicanism: The Career of a Concept." *The Journal of American History* 79 (June 1992): 11–38.

Roedel, Jeff. "Stoking the Doctrinal Furnaces: Judicial Review and the Council of Revision." *New York History* 69 (July 1988): 261–283.

Roper, Donald M. "James Kent and the Emergence of New York's Libel Law." *American Journal of Legal History* 17 (July 1973): 223–231.

———. "Martin Van Buren as Tocqueville's Lawyer: The Jurisprudence of Politics." *The Journal of the Early Republic* 2 (summer 1982): 169–189.

Ross, Steven J. "The Transformation of Republican Ideology." *The Journal of the Early Republic* 10 (fall 1990): 324–330.

Setaro, Franklyn. "The Surrogate's Court of New York: Its Historical Antecedents." *New York Law Forum* 2 (July 1956): 283–304.

Shalhope, Robert E. "Republicanism and Early American Historiography." *William and Mary Quarterly,* 3rd ser., 39 (April 1982): 334–356.

———. "Toward a Republican Synthesis: The Emergence of an Understanding of Republicanism in American Historiography." *William and Mary Quarterly,* 3rd ser., 29 (January 1972): 49–80.

Shammas, Carole. "English Inheritance Law and Its Transfer to the Colonies." *American Journal of Legal History* 31 (April 1987): 145–163.

Sherwood, Jeannette. "The Military Tract." *Proceedings of the New York State Historical Association* 24 (January 1926): 169–179.

Siry, Steven E. "The Sectional Politics of 'Practical Republicanism': De Witt Clinton's Presidential Bid, 1810–1812." *The Journal of the Early Republic* 4 (winter 1985): 441–462.

Spencer, Charles W. "The Land System of Colonial New York." *Proceedings of the New York State Historical Association* 16 (1917): 150–164.

Strum, Harvey. "Property Qualification and Voting Behavior in New York, 1807–1816." *The Journal of the Early Republic* 1 (winter 1981): 347–371.

Surrency, Erwin C. "The Lawyer and the Revolution." *American Journal of Legal History* 8 (April 1964): 125–132.

Van Laer, Arnold J. F. "Some Early Dutch Manuscripts." *Proceedings of the New York State Historical Association* 20 (October 1922): 221–233.

Varga, Nicholas. "Election Procedures and Practices in Colonial New York." *New York History* 46 (July 1960): 249–277.

Vosburgh, Royden W. "Surrogate Courts and Records in the Colony and State of New York." *Proceedings of the New York State Historical Association* 20 (January 1922): 105–110.

Wallace, Michael. "Changing Concepts of Party in the United States: New York, 1815–1828." *American Historical Review* 74 (December 1968): 453–491.

Weintraub, Harold. "Mandamus and Certiorari in New York from the Revolution to 1800: A Chapter in Legal History." *Fordham Law Review* 32 (May 1964): 681–748.

Wilson, Major L. "The 'Country' Versus the 'Court': A Republican Consensus and Party Debate in the Bank War." *The Journal of the Early Republic* (winter 1995): 619–647.

———. "Republicanism and the Idea of Party in the Jacksonian Period." *The Journal of the Early Republic* (winter 1988): 419–442.

UNPUBLISHED DISSERTATIONS

Driscoll, William D. "Benjamin F. Butler: Lawyer and Regency Politician." Ph. D. diss., Fordham Univ., 1965.

Robinson, Thomas P. "The Life of Thomas Addis Emmet." Ph.D. diss., New York Univ., 1955.

Index

3 5282 00428 1781